POLITICAL IDEAS OF ENLIGHTENMENT WOMEN

Political Ideas of Enlightenment Women

Virtue and Citizenship

Edited by

LISA CURTIS-WENDLANDT
Monash University, Australia

PAUL GIBBARD
The University of Western Australia

and

KAREN GREEN
Monash University, Australia

Routledge
Taylor & Francis Group
LONDON AND NEW YORK

First published 2013 by Ashgate Publishing

Published 2016 by Routledge
2 Park Square, Milton Park, Abingdon, Oxon OX14 4RN
711 Third Avenue, New York, NY 10017, USA

Routledge is an imprint of the Taylor & Francis Group, an informa business

British Library Cataloguing in Publication Data
A catalogue record for this book is available from the British Library

The Library of Congress has cataloged the printed edition as follows:
Political ideas of Enlightenment women: virtue and citizenship / edited by Lisa Curtis-Wendlandt, Paul Gibbard and Karen Green.
pages cm
Includes bibliographical references and index.
ISBN 978-1-4724-0953-9 (hardcover: alk. paper)

1. Women—Europe—History—18th century. 2. Women intellectuals—Europe—History—18th century. 3. Europe—Intellectual life—18th century. 4. Enlightenment 5. Political science—Philosophy—History—18th century. 6. Women and literature—Europe—History—18th century. I. Curtis-Wendlandt, Lisa, author, editor of compilation. II. Gibbard, Paul Richard, author, editor of compilation. III. Green, Karen, 1951–, author, editor of compilation.
HQ1587.P64 2013
305.409409'033—dc23

2013013166

ISBN 9781472409539 (hbk)

Contents

Notes on the Contributors *vii*
Acknowledgements *xi*

Introduction 1

PART I WOMEN'S POLITICAL IDEAS IN CONTINENTAL EUROPE

1 Emilie Du Châtelet's Views on the Pillars of French Society: King, Church, and Family 17
Judith P. Zinsser

2 Royalist and Radical: Octavie Belot on Rousseau and the Social Order 33
Paul Gibbard

3 Performing Citizenship: Marie-Madeleine Jodin Enacting Diderot's and Rousseau's Dramatic and Ethical Theories 49
Felicia Gordon

4 Etta Palm d'Aelders and Louise Keralio-Robert: Feminist Controversy during the French Revolution 63
Calogero Alberto Petix and Karen Green

5 Marie-Armande Gacon-Dufour: A Radical Intellectual at the Turn of the Nineteenth Century 79
Erica J. Mannucci

6 Legality and Morality in the Political Thought of Elise Reimarus and Immanuel Kant 91
Lisa Curtis-Wendlandt

7 Italian Women Intellectuals and Their Cultural Networks: The Making of a European 'Life of the Mind' 109
Marianna D'Ezio

8 Women's Intellectual Agency in the History of Eighteenth- and Nineteenth-Century French Salons 123
Steven Kale

PART II WOMEN'S POLITICAL IDEAS IN THE BRITISH ISLES

9 The Right to Resist: Women's Citizenship in Catharine Trotter Cockburn's *The Revolution of Sweden* 141
Elizabeth M.K.A. Sund

10 Catharine Macaulay and Laetitia Barbauld: Two Eighteenth-Century 'Republicans' 157
Karen Green

11 'The Manly Virtues': Macaulay's Influence, Wollstonecraft's Legacy 173
Mary Caputi

12 Between Enlightenment, Feminism, and Abolitionism: Mary Wollstonecraft's Thoughts on Women and Slavery 189
Jeanette Ehrmann

13 'Doing an Acceptable Service to my Country': Political Thought in Charlotte Brooke's *Reliques of Irish Poetry* 203
Lesa Ní Mhunghaile

Bibliography *217*
Index *243*

Notes on the Contributors

Mary Caputi is a Professor of Political Theory at California State University, Long Beach, where she has taught since 1995, researching in postcolonial scholarship, cultural studies, contemporary political thought, and psychoanalysis. She recently published *Feminism and Power: The Need for Critical Theory* (Lexington, 2013), and with Vincent Del Casino, Jr. co-edited *Derrida and the Future of the Liberal Arts* (Continuum, 2013). Earlier publications include *A Kinder, Gentler America* (University of Minnesota Press, 2005) and *Voluptuous Yearnings* (Rowman and Littlefield, 1994).

Lisa Curtis-Wendlandt is an Adjunct Research Fellow in the School of Philosophical, Historical, and International Studies at Monash University, where she worked on the ARC-funded research project 'A History of Women's Political Thought in Europe, 1700–1800' between 2009 and 2011. She holds a PhD in History from Monash University, as well as an MA in Philosophy and English Philology from the Technical University and the Free University of Berlin, Germany. Her publications have been in feminist philosophy and Ancient Greek philosophy, as well as in the history of missions.

Marianna D'Ezio completed a PhD in English Literature at the University of Rome Sapienza. A resident in Italy, she has taught English at three universities (Cassino, Perugia, and Rome) and Italian at the University of California Rome Study Center. She has researched eighteenth-century literature and travel writing (especially of women writers) and produced many conference papers and articles, for example, on eighteenth-century women's travels in Italy. She wrote *Hester Lynch Thrale Piozzi: A Taste for Eccentricity* (Cambridge Scholars, 2010) and a grammar book of English for Italian speakers (*Grammatica Inglese*, Mondadori, 2010), and she edited the collection *Literary and Cultural Intersections during the Long Eighteenth Century* (Cambridge Scholars, 2008).

Jeanette Ehrmann is a PhD candidate in Political Science at Goethe University Frankfurt and a fellow of the Franco-German doctorate program 'Normes et constructions sociales' at Université Paris I Panthéon-Sorbonne. Her thesis deals with the Haitian Revolution as an event and critique of European modernity.

Paul Gibbard wrote his doctorate on anarchism in late nineteenth-century French and English literature at the University of Oxford, where he subsequently worked as a post-doctoral researcher and editor of the *Œuvres complètes de Voltaire* (*Complete Works of Voltaire*) at the Voltaire Foundation. He has also taken part in 'The Baudin Legacy' research project at the University of Adelaide, and conducted research on eighteenth-century women's political thought and Octavie Belot while a Postdoctoral Research Fellow in Philosophy at Monash University. He is currently Assistant Professor of French at the University of Western Australia.

Felicia Gordon, Senior Research Associate (formerly Principal Lecturer in Philosophy and European Literature) at Anglia Ruskin University, is a Senior Member of Wolfson College, Cambridge and has published in women's history and early French feminism. She is the author of *The Integral Feminist: Madeleine Pelletier, 1874–1939* (Polity Press, 1990), *Early French Feminisms, 1830–1940* with Máire Cross (Edward Elgar, 1996), *Marie-Madeleine Jodin, 1741–1790* with P.N. Furbank (Ashgate, 2001). With Gina Luria Walker she edited *Rational Passions: Women and Scholarship in Britain, 1702–1870* (Broadview Press, 2008). She has recently published a biography of France's first woman psychiatrist: *Constance Pascal (1877–1937): Authority, Femininity and Feminism in French Psychiatry* (The Institute of Germanic and Romance Studies, University of London, 2013).

Karen Green is Associate Professor in the School of Philosophical, Historical, and International Studies at Monash University. She is the author, with Jacqueline Broad, of *A History of Women's Political Thought in Europe, 1400–1700* (Cambridge University Press, 2009) and editor with her of *Virtue, Liberty, and Toleration: Political Ideas of European Women, 1400–1800* (Springer, 2007). With Constant Mews and Janice Pinder she translated Christine de Pizan's *Book of Peace* (Penn State Press, 2008) and edited with Constant Mews *Virtue Ethics for Women 1250–1500* (Springer, 2011). Her *A History of Women's Political Thought in Europe, 1700–1800* should appear in 2014.

Steven Kale is a Professor of History at Washington State University. He is the author of *French Salons: High Society and Political Sociability from the Old Regime to the Revolution of 1848* (Johns Hopkins University Press, 2004) and has published numerous articles on women and the public sphere in eighteenth- and nineteenth-century France. He is currently working on a series of essays exploring the relationship between nineteenth-century French intellectual history and transnational encounters.

Erica Joy Mannucci, Professor of Modern History (Sixteenth to Eighteenth Centuries) at University of Milano–Bicocca, researches European intellectual history and eighteenth-century French history. She is Italian correspondent for *Dix-huitième siècle* (review of the Société française d'étude du XVIIIe siècle) and has served on the Executive Committee of the International Society for Eighteenth-Century Studies (ISECS). Her books include: *Il patriota e il vaudeville: Teatro, pubblico e potere nella Parigi della Rivoluzione* (Vivarium, 1998); *L'età della ragione* (first Italian edition of Paine's *The Age of Reason*, Part I; Ibis, 2000); *La rivoluzione francese* (Carocci, 2002); and *La cena di Pitagora: Storia del vegetarianismo dall'antica Grecia a Internet* (Carocci, 2008). On Sylvain Maréchal she has published *Finalmente il popolo pensa: Sylvain Maréchal nell'immagine della Rivoluzione francese* (Guida, 2012).

Lesa Ní Mhunghaile studied in Ireland and Germany, and lectures at Mary Immaculate College, University of Limerick. Her PhD thesis, on the Protestant antiquarian Joseph Cooper Walker and his *Historical Memoirs of the Irish Bards* (1789), earned her an Oireachtas na Gaelige literary prize. She has published in Irish and English on Protestant antiquarians' interactions with Gaelic scribes, with 'An Eighteenth-Century Gaelic Scribe's Private Library' (*Proceedings of the Royal Irish Academy*, 2010), and is Irish language editor of the journal *Eighteenth-Century Ireland / Iris an dá chultúr*. Recent interests are Gaelic scribal culture of the Oriel district, eighteenth-century German travel literature on Ireland, and Irish language in nineteenth-century Ontario. She has made an annotated edition of Charlotte Brooke's *Reliques of Irish Poetry* of 1789 (Irish Manuscripts Commission, 2009).

Calogero Alberto Petix graduated in 2005 in public relations at the University of Catania, Italy, with a dissertation on constitutionalism and the political pamphlets of Sismondi. He completed his doctorate in the Political Thought and Institutions in Mediterranean Societies Program (University of Catania) in 2009, with a thesis on Condorcet and democracy. In 2010 he completed a master's degree in contemporary history, focusing on justice reform during the French Revolution. His other interests in French political thought include the unpublished correspondence of Condorcet, pursued in a project financed by Université Paris VIII. He has published on Condorcet's writings concerning public opinion and international relations. He is currently editing the unpublished correspondence between Condorcet and Brissot. Since 2011 he has been an officer of the Italian Ministry of Instruction, University and Research.

Elizabeth M.K.A. Sund was awarded her PhD on Catharine Cockburn's moral philosophy in the School of Philosophical, Historical, and International Studies at Monash University, in 2013.

Judith P. Zinsser is professor of history emerita at Miami University (Ohio). She wrote *Emilie Du Châtelet: Daring Genius of the Enlightenment* (2006) and edited or co-edited collections of articles on Du Châtelet and on women in early modern science. With Isabelle Bour she translated a selection of Du Châtelet's writings for the series The Other Voice of Early Modern Europe (Chicago, 2009), and is co-author of the two-volume *A History of Their Own: Women in Europe from Prehistory to the Present* (Oxford University Press, 2000).

Acknowledgements

We gratefully acknowledge support from the Australian Research Council, who provided a generous Discovery Project grant. Without it the research on which this collection is based would not have been possible. In particular, this grant allowed us to host the international conference, Women's Political Thought in Europe, 1700–1800, held at the Monash University Prato Centre in Italy during August 2010, where early versions of many of the papers that make up the collection were first presented. Many conference participants whose papers do not appear in this collection made significant contributions to the research project, and we appreciate their participation and support.

We would like in particular to acknowledge the painstaking editorial work of Alan Crosier, without whose meticulous attention to every accent, comma, and bibliographical detail we would not have been able to produce a collection of this standard. Alan's many editorial interventions have improved the style and readability of most of the contributions, and his tireless work freed the editors from a great deal of burdensome and finicky elements in the editorial process. He should, perhaps, be acknowledged as a fourth editor, and we are immensely grateful for his work.

Our sincere thanks also go to the participants of our monthly eighteenth-century research group at Monash University – in particular to Jacqueline Broad, David Garrioch, Wallace Kirsop, and Elizabeth Sund. Their insights and comments on our various papers and presentations played a vital role in the genesis of ideas that underlie this collection.

Introduction

The history of political philosophy, as it is currently taught, is dominated by texts authored by men. This is as true for the period of the Enlightenment as it is for earlier centuries. It is as true of the 'new intellectual history' as it is of the old.[1] The old intellectual history tended to study the works of great men independently of social context. During the second half of the twentieth century the traditional study of 'great thinkers' was overtaken by the history of social movements and economic transformations, which minimized the influence of ideas and had the advantage of encouraging research into women and other marginalized groups. While this research was initially inspired by the rise of sociology and Marxism, by the 1970s the adequacy of traditional analyses of power, and of the epistemological bases of knowledge in general, was being challenged by post-structuralism and post-modernism. However, this development did nothing to reinstate the study of individual texts or thinkers. If anything, the claimed 'death of the author' reinforced the tendency to overlook the ideas of individual early modern and Enlightenment women. The complex and interconnected emergence of social history, post-modernism, and women's history resulted in research on women as social actors and in the study of general features of gendered discourse; but it did little to encourage the examination of the texts of individual women as interlocutors in the development of ideas.[2] As a consequence, apart from the history of feminism, women's history has tended to ignore women's contribution to the history of ideas in general.

Depicting itself as more sensitive to social movements than the old intellectual history, the new intellectual history has turned back to the study of individual texts. At the same time, it has begun to explore works beyond those penned by the canonical thinkers, including marginalized, popular, erotic, and ephemeral texts, and to read both standard and marginal works through the social context of their production, in order to better understand the development of ideas and their impact on events.[3] Yet despite this turn to marginal texts, the influence of works authored by women continues to be neglected.[4] Scholarly editions reflect these omissions.

---

1 For an account of the 'new intellectual history' see for example J. Israel, *Enlightenment Contested: Philosophy, Modernity, and the Emancipation of Man 1670–1752* (Oxford, 2006); and *Democratic Enlightenment: Philosophy, Revolution, and Human Rights 1750–1790* (Oxford, 2011).

2 H.L. Smith, 'Women Intellectuals and Intellectual History: Their Paradigmatic Separation', *Women's History Review*, 16:3 (2007): p. 357.

3 R. Darnton, *The Literary Underground of the Old Regime* (Cambridge, MA, 1982); L. Hunt, *The Family Romance of the French Revolution* (Berkeley and Los Angeles, 1992).

4 H.L. Smith, 'Women's History as Intellectual History: A Perspective on the *Journal of Women's History*', *Journal of Women's History*, 20:1 (2008): pp. 26–32.

The prestigious Cambridge Texts in the History of Political Thought series currently includes 110 titles. Four are by women, only two of whom published in the eighteenth century: Mary Astell and Mary Wollstonecraft.[5] If one searches the websites of major presses such as Cambridge and Oxford for 'eighteenth-century philosophy', the result is even more disheartening: no texts by women are listed. This is not because they entirely neglect eighteenth-century women, but rather because, when published, women are categorized as contributing to women's writing, general literature, or the history of romanticism, but not to political philosophy or philosophy more broadly. At the time of writing this introduction, even Pickering & Chatto, which pioneered serious scholarly editions of women's texts with its publication of the *Works of Mary Wollstonecraft* in 1989, does not list this as a contribution under Philosophy and Religion.[6]

This omission threatens to distort our understanding of intellectual developments during the seventeenth and eighteenth centuries that underpin modernity. Although the entitlement of women authors to write was still often contested, women became significant contributors to popular literature during the period. They played a central role in the rise of the novel, and published, often anonymously, in the popular moral weeklies. It can be argued that because they were in general less highly educated than men of the same class, the texts they read, and the issues they engaged with, were the most widely discussed and disseminated. Women writers were among the 'popular' authors who served as important mediators between elite male theorists and the general literate public. At the same time, since they wrote from a female perspective, they also challenged those theorists, exposing their gender bias and extending their principles to incorporate women. Intellectual history that is genuinely committed to exploring the way in which the interaction between text and context leads to social change is in danger of reproducing the failings of the old intellectual history if it ignores women's significant contributions to political discourse.

In this collection we make a small step toward the retrieval of an alternative, female-authored intellectual history concentrating on women's contributions to political theory and practice. During the eighteenth century as an increasing number of women went into print, they used a number of different genres in order to engage in philosophical and political debates. As well as political tracts, we find histories, plays, essays, poems, journalism, translations, household manuals, and novels among the genres exploited by women for political ends. Many of the women whose ideas are discussed in the following chapters have been almost entirely forgotten and have only become the focus of scholarly research in the last couple of decades. This is particularly true of Octavie Belot, Elise Reimarus, Marie-Armande

---

[5] M. Astell, *Political Writings*, ed. P. Springborg (Cambridge, 1996); M. Wollstonecraft, *Wollstonecraft: A Vindication of the Rights of Men and a Vindication of the Rights of Woman and Hints*, ed. Sylvana Tomaselli (Cambridge, 1995).

[6] M. Wollstonecraft, *The Works of Mary Wollstonecraft*, ed. J. Todd and M. Butler (7 vols, London, 1989).

Gacon-Dufour, Catharine Trotter Cockburn, and Charlotte Brooke. Others such as Emilie Du Châtelet, Marie Jodin, Catharine Macaulay, Anna Laetitia Barbauld, Etta Palm d'Aelders, Louise Keralio-Robert, Germaine de Staël, and Elisabetta Caminer Turra are somewhat better known. In this collection we offer a distinctive focus on the political ideas expressed in their works and on the ways in which they responded to each other, as well as to male political thinkers of the period such as Harrington, Mandeville, Locke, Montesquieu, Rousseau, Diderot, Burke, and Kant. While Mary Wollstonecraft is exceptional in having attracted significant levels of scholarship since the 1970s, this collection deepens our understanding of the relationship of her political philosophy to that of Catharine Macaulay, and throws new light on her use of the analogy between marriage and slavery.

Given the paucity, before the end of the twentieth century, of serious scholarship on pre-twentieth-century women as political theorists, it is little wonder that feminist interpreters of the history of European political philosophy have been led to declare that the political subject is male and grounded on what has been aptly called a 'false universal'.[7] The male-authored texts that make up the history of political thought take the citizen to be a man; and if they discuss women at all, they assign them a subsidiary position. According to Aristotle and those influenced by him, woman's reason is not authoritative.[8] Women lack prudence and are therefore naturally subject to man.[9] While Thomas Hobbes is exceptional in not grounding women's political subjection in nature, many later men, Jean-Jacques Rousseau in particular, followed Aristotle and argued that women's subjection was natural, hence appropriate and inevitable.[10]

---

[7] H.L. Smith, *All Men and Both Sexes: Gender, Politics, and the False Universal in England, 1640–1832* (University Park, PA, 2002).

[8] M.L. Homiak, 'Feminism and Aristotle's Rational Ideal', in *A Mind of One's Own*, ed. L.M. Antony and C.E. Witt (Boulder, San Francisco, and Oxford, 1993), pp. 1–18.

[9] For the influence of this way of interpreting Aristotle during the Medieval and Early Modern periods see J. Broad and K. Green, *A History of Women's Political Thought in Europe, 1400–1700* (Cambridge, 2009); K. Green, 'On Translating Christine de Pizan as a Philosopher', in K. Green and C.J. Mews (eds), *Healing the Body Politic: The Political Thought of Christine de Pizan* (Turnhout, 2005), pp. 117–37; Green, '*Phronesis* Feminized: Prudence from Christine de Pizan to Elizabeth I', in J. Broad and K. Green (eds), *Virtue, Liberty, and Toleration: Political Ideas of European Women 1400–1800* (Dordrecht, 2007), pp. 23–38.

[10] For discussion of Hobbes and Rousseau on women see C. Pateman, *The Disorder of Women* (Cambridge, 1989); Pateman, '"God Hath Ordained to Man a Helper": Hobbes, Patriarchy and Conjugal Right', in C. Pateman and M.L. Shanley (eds), *Feminist Interpretations and Political Theory* (University Park, PA, 1991), pp. 53–73; T. Brennan and C. Pateman, '"Mere Auxiliaries to the Commonwealth": Women and the Origins of Liberalism', *Political Studies*, 27:2 (1979): pp. 183–200; J. Wright, 'Going against the Grain: Hobbes's Case for Original Maternal Domination', *Journal of Women's History*, 14:1 (2002): pp. 123–48, and the essays in N. Hirschmann and J. Wright (eds), *Feminist Interpretations of Thomas Hobbes* (University Park, PA, 2012).

In the 1970s women began to question the way their sex had been characterized in mainstream political theory. Susan Moller Okin's *Women in Western Political Thought* of 1979 provided an early influential overview, and since then numerous books and articles have appeared that offer feminist critiques and interpretations of the 'standard' male political theorists.[11] But this reactive and critical attitude has its limitations, since it reinforces the perception that there have historically been no female contributors to political philosophy. In fact, more women have written on political themes than is usually appreciated – although it may be that, in order to appreciate women's contribution to political debates, one has to broaden the genres that are taken into account.[12] Nevertheless, as the contributions to this collection demonstrate, by the eighteenth century women were publishing on a wide variety of political issues – such as the relationship between morality and politics (and between marriage and the state), the structure of a republican constitution, and the acceptability of inequality.

Since the 1990s a new trend has emerged which seeks to revise rather than merely criticize the philosophical canon, and with it the canon of political theory.[13] For although they have been neglected, a significant number of historical women did produce philosophical and political works – particularly over the course of the

---

[11] S.M. Okin, *Women in Western Political Thought* (Princeton, 1979); C. Pateman and M. Lyndon Shanley (eds), *Feminist Interpretations of Political Theory* (University Park, 1991); C. Pateman, *The Sexual Contract* (Cambridge, 1988); C. Pateman, *The Disorder of Women* (Cambridge, 1989); G. Lloyd (ed.), *Feminism and History of Philosophy* (Oxford, 2002). See also other volumes in Penn State's *Feminist Interpretations* series.

[12] The point was made with regard to history by D. Looser, *British Women Writers and the Writing of History* (Baltimore, 2000), and with regard to philosophy by C. Villanueva Gardner, *Rediscovering Women Philosophers: Philosophical Genre and the Boundaries of Philosophy* (Boulder, 2000).

[13] K. Green, *The Woman of Reason: Feminism, Humanism, and Political Thought* (New York, 1995); E. O'Neill, 'Disappearing Ink: Early Modern Women Philosophers and their Fate in History', in *Philosophy in a Feminist Voice: Critiques and Reconstructions*, ed. J.A. Kourany (Princeton, 1998), pp. 17–62; E. O'Neill, 'Women Philosophers and the History of Philosophy', *Australian Journal of French Studies*, 40:3 (2003): pp. 257–74; E. O'Neill, 'Early Modern Women Philosophers and the History of Philosophy', *Hypatia*, 20:3 (2005): pp. 185–97; E. O'Neill, 'Justifying the Inclusion of Women in Our Histories of Philosophy', in *The Blackwell Guide to Feminist Philosophy*, ed. L. Alcoff and E. Kittay (Oxford, 2007), pp. 17–42; Broad and Green, *A History of Women's Political Thought in Europe, 1400–1700*; J. Broad, *Women Philosophers of the Seventeenth Century* (Cambridge, 2002); P.A. Weiss, *Canon Fodder* (University Park, PA, 2009); K. Offen, 'Women's Memory, Women's History, Women's Political Action: The French Revolution in Retrospect, 1789–1889–1989', *Journal of Women's History*, 1:3 (1990): pp. 211–30; K. Offen, 'Republishing French Feminist Texts', *History of European Ideas*, 17:2–3 (1993): pp. 319–23; H.L. Smith (ed.), *Women Writers and the Early Modern British Political Tradition* (Cambridge, 1998); B.A. Carroll and H.L. Smith (eds), *Women's Political and Social Thought: An Anthology* (Indiana, 2000); H.L. Smith, M. Suzuki, and S. Wiseman (eds), *Women's Political Writings, 1610–1725* (4 vols, London, 2007).

eighteenth century, as educational opportunities enabled increasing numbers of women to write for publication.[14] The present collection makes a further contribution to this project of retrieval. We hope it will ultimately reinforce appreciation of the impact women's texts have had on the development of our political and social institutions. When women write, it cannot plausibly be claimed that the political subject is exclusively male. The women whose works are discussed in these chapters broke new ground both in their conceptualisations of marriage and in their perspectives on questions of morality, justice, and political organization.

In the three centuries before the eighteenth, a small but significant cohort of women produced political texts of various kinds. Some of these texts – like the *Book of the Body Politic* by Christine de Pizan or the 'Farewell of the Soul of the King' by Marie le Jars de Gournay – described the virtues of princes and set out principles of good government.[15] Others defended the female sex against the Aristotelian misrepresentation of women's capacities, argued for their equal or greater virtue compared to men's, or promoted women's education and criticized their subjection in marriage. Already in 1405, Christine de Pizan addressed herself to the 'citoyennes' whose good was incorporated into the good of the people.[16] By the early 1600s, Venetian women were criticizing marriage as slavery, and demanding 'rights for women'.[17] From the second half of the seventeenth century, women in France and Italy increasingly participated in the intellectual life of the nation by hosting and attending salons, and (particularly in France) through the production of novels, essays, and moral maxims.[18] The novels of Madeleine de Scudéry, Mme de Lafayette, Mme d'Aulnoy and others were widely read and translated, providing new vehicles for the discussion of political and social themes. The few women granted a systematic education tended to receive it from their learned fathers, like the classical scholar Anne Dacier. But the trend for

---

14 C. Hesse, *The Other Enlightenment: How French Women Became Modern* (Princeton, 2001).

15 For an overview of this period see Broad and Green, *A History of Women's Political Thought in Europe, 1400–1700*; C. de Pizan, *The Book of the Body Politic*, trans. Kate Langdon Forhan (Cambridge, 1994); M. le Jars de Gournay, 'Adieu de l'âme du Roy de France et de Navarre Henry le Grand, à la Royne, avec la Defence des Peres Jesuistes', in *Œuvres Complètes*, ed. Jean-Claude Arnould et al. (Paris, 2002).

16 C. de Pizan, *Le Livre des trois vertus*, ed. C. Cannon Willard and E. Hicks (Paris, 1989), p. 9; C. de Pizan, *The Treasure of the City of Ladies*, trans. S. Lawson (Harmondsworth, 1985), p. 32.

17 M. Fonte, *Il Merito delle donne*, ed. A. Chemello (Venice, 1988); Moderata Fonte, *The Worth of Women*, ed. and trans. V. Cox (Chicago, 1997).

18 P. Findlen, W.W. Roworth, and C.M. Sama (eds), *Italy's Eighteenth Century: Gender and Culture in the Age of the Grand Tour* (Stanford, 2009); S.D. Kale, *French Salons: High Society and Political Sociability from the Old Regime to the Revolution of 1848* (Baltimore and London, 2004); F.E. Beasley, *Salons, History, and the Creation of Seventeenth-Century France: Mastering Memory* (Aldershot, 2006); J. DeJean, *Tender Geographies: The Politics of Female Authorship under the Late Ancien Régime* (New York, 1991).

philosophical and political works to be published in the vernacular allowed more and more aristocratic or middle-class women to educate themselves. Scudéry's novels promoted an ideal of cultured feminine participation in conversation, which required considerable erudition – so that by the beginning of the eighteenth century, many Europeans appreciated women of wit, so long as they tempered their learning with a sufficient measure of modesty.

Although early modern women opposed the Aristotelian claim that women's capacity to exercise the intellectual and moral virtues is defective, they tended to work within a broadly Aristotelian political paradigm, in which the good of the body politic and the virtues of the people were intertwined. In this regard they were not different from their male contemporaries.[19] Women disagreed with men over women's capacity for virtue and to a certain extent over what was required of women to be virtuous; but they agreed that political harmony depended on the exercise of appropriate virtues by the sovereign and the people. Thomas Hobbes was among the first political theorists to move away from this emphasis on virtue, adopting a new 'scientific' approach to political theory and attempting to show that political subjection is a matter of rational self-interest. His political works developed an original response to the defenders of the Parliament in the English Civil War and were directed against those who claimed a right to overthrow their monarch when he infringed their liberties. Although Hobbes accepted that government is grounded in an implicit contract, he argued that this was a covenant of a very special kind, and one that was necessary in order for all other contracts, and for justice in general, to be effective. Since a sovereign is necessary for there to be a just regime, rebellion would result in the reinstatement of a state of nature (which is a state of war); and it could rarely be rational, given the rational preferability of peace as a means for pursuing one's self-interest.[20]

Contrary to Hobbes, John Locke argued that the natural law, which can be understood through the use of reason, is operative in the state of nature. A civil state is necessary in order to uphold the principles of justice and liberty, which are implied by the law of nature; and since the purpose of the state is to guarantee the effectiveness of such principles of justice, a people has the right to overthrow a sovereign whose government does not conform to the principles of the natural law.[21] Locke's political philosophy was particularly influential in the British Isles, as emerges in the works of the women discussed in the second part of this collection. He was also read on the Continent; but his immediate influence on the French, German, and Italian women whose political philosophies are discussed here is not as evident as his influence on the writings of British women.

---

19 A. MacIntyre, *After Virtue* (London, 1981).

20 T. Hobbes, *Leviathan: Or the Matter, Forme, and Power of a Common-Wealth Ecclesiasticall and Civill*, ed. I. Shapiro (New Haven and London, 2010). For a very readable overview of the development of Hobbes's ideas on liberty see Q. Skinner, *Hobbes and Republican Liberty* (Cambridge, 2008).

21 J. Locke, *Two Treatises of Government*, ed. P. Laslett (Cambridge, 1997).

At the beginning of the eighteenth century, following the path opened up by Hobbes, Bernard Mandeville published *The Fable of the Bees*: a further provocative attack on the idea that the public good requires private virtue. This early examination of the causes of material prosperity argued that the economic vibrancy of a great and populous nation depended on the pride, avarice, profligacy, and other vices of its people. Part of his work was translated by Gabrielle Emilie le Tonnelier de Breteuil, marquise Du Châtelet, whose political outlook is introduced in the first chapter in this volume. Voltaire's lover and collaborator until her untimely death (resulting from a pregnancy at the age of forty-two, late for those times), she is more famous for her translation of Isaac Newton's *Principia* and her contributions to science than for her political ideas. Judith Zinsser's 'King, Church and Family: Emilie Du Châtelet's Views on the Pillars of French Society' outlines her response to Mandeville and discusses the feminist attitudes evinced in the introduction to her translation. Zinsser also discusses her two-volume critique of the Bible and essay on happiness, as well as her original synthesis of Leibnizian metaphysics and Newtonian mechanics in the *Institutions de physique*. Although Du Châtelet never wrote a clear description of her political beliefs, like many *philosophes* of the period she was convinced that humans have an innate disposition to be moral, but paradoxically agreed with Mandeville's claim that public good is served by private vice. As a mathematician and metaphysician she embraced Leibniz's rules of reasoning, including the concept of the Creator's 'sufficient reason' for all that transpired in the universe, whether it be the orbiting of the planets or the existence of evil. All of these philosophical activities and ideas combined into a basically conservative view of the actual world in which she functioned as a woman, aristocrat, and intellectual. Despite her forceful aversion to prejudice and superstition, Du Châtelet consented (very much like Voltaire) to the fundamental tenets of French political culture, which made king, church, and family the pillars of French political life.

Like Du Châtelet, and in opposition to Hobbes and Mandeville, Jean-Jacques Rousseau accepted that the natural disposition of human beings was to be virtuous but argued that this had been corrupted by the development of society. He nevertheless furthered the social-contract tradition by building on the work of Hobbes and Locke, and by embellishing his version of the theory with an account of women's sexual difference from men and the consequent domestic destiny of the female sex. The result was an influential strand of sexist republicanism, which dominated the nineteenth century. Rousseau credited the growth of luxury and inequality to the baneful social influence of women, whose stimulation of men's pride and vanity he thought responsible for the increase in private property and social distinction. Consequently, in order to combat such tendencies, the virtuous republican woman would dedicate herself to home and family, guaranteeing her husband's commitment to republican virtue and equality. One of the earliest critiques of Rousseau's account of the origins of inequality was written by a woman, Octavie Belot. In 1756 she published *Réflexions d'une provinciale sur le discours de Monsieur Rousseau, citoyen de Genève, touchant l'origine de l'inégalité des conditions parmi les hommes* [*Reflections of a Provincial Woman on the Discourse of Monsieur Rousseau, touching the origin of the social inequality among men*], which represents her response to Rousseau's *Discourse on Inequality* (1755).[22] Belot's defence of aristocratic society is introduced by Paul Gibbard in 'Royalist and Radical: Octavie Belot on Rousseau and the Social Order'. Despite her sex, Belot only lightly touches on Rousseau's views with regard to women and focuses her critique on his claim that people can only achieve virtue in simple egalitarian societies. She argues that social inequalities originate in natural inequalities. In subsequent publications, she endorsed the contemporary law that prevented the aristocracy from pursuing commercial enterprises in France, defending the virtues and morality of honour of the French nobility. While she also later recognized that inherited privilege is in some sense philosophically unjustifiable, she argued that it would be dangerous to dismantle it. Gibbard's chapter is the first extended discussion of her political philosophy to be published and also explores the correspondence between her and the English bluestocking Elizabeth Montagu.

A more radical response to Rousseau's confinement of women to the private sphere was penned by Marie de Jodin, who prefaced her *Vues législatives pour les femmes* [*Opinions on legislation for women*] (1789–1790) with the declaration 'Et nous aussi, nous sommes citoyennes.' Felicia Gordon's chapter, 'Performing Citizenship: Marie-Madeleine Jodin Enacting Diderot's and Rousseau's Dramatic and Ethical Theories', examines Jodin's career as actress, *philosophe*, and proto-legislator, analysing her rhetoric in its connection with the drama theories of Diderot and Rousseau, as well as with debates on citizenship for women, and republicanism. It argues that Jodin should be read as a contributor to the Radical Enlightenment, in Jonathan Israel's sense, and details the significant interaction between Jodin and her mentor Denis Diderot, suggesting that Diderot's support for Jodin derived from his radical secular morality. Jodin's experiences as a young woman, accused of prostitution and imprisoned for it, as well as her colourful life as an actress who had to battle for her rights, led her to argue that society needed to be reformed so that women no longer resorted to prostitution, the existence of which debased all women. In her *Vues législatives*, she cleverly used Rousseau's rhetoric against him, transforming his defence of men's liberty, and women's moral influence, into an argument for the public participation of women in a new legislature, in which women's status as citizens and their influence over public morals would be fully recognized. With her advocacy of the reform of prostitutes and proposals for the elimination of prostitution, aimed at eradicating the association between sexual promiscuity and women's ability to operate in the public sphere, Jodin anticipates later feminist critiques of prostitution and the sexualization of women. She recognizes that women's full inclusion in the status of citizen is tied up with their ceasing to be sexually objectified for male use.

Another woman opponent of Rousseau's exclusion of women from citizenship was Etta Palm d'Aelders, who explicitly argued for laws that treat men and

---

22 J.-J. Rousseau, *On the Inequality among Mankind* (Minneapolis, 2007).

women equally. Her political views are outlined by Calogero Alberto Petix and Karen Green in their chapter, 'Etta Palm d'Aelders and Louise Keralio-Robert: Feminist Controversy during the French Revolution', which also discusses her dispute with Louise Keralio-Robert. D'Aelders was a vocal participant in the *Cercle social*, one of the political clubs that sprang up during the first years of the Revolution. Her right to become a member of one of the other fraternal associations was questioned by Keralio-Robert, editor from 1789 of one of the many new revolutionary journals of the time. The dispute between these women over what liberty and citizenship imply for the female sex throws light on the contested notion of women's citizenship, and the notion of feminine virtue, as it was understood during this period of political and intellectual ferment. In this chapter it is argued that their dispute should be read as grounded in disagreement over what republican citizenship implies with regard to female virtue and the sexual double standard.

One woman whose writing might seem to conform to the stereotype set up by Rousseau, however, is Marie-Armande Gacon-Dufour, whose works include housekeeping manuals for rural women. In her contribution, 'Marie-Armande Gacon-Dufour, a Radical Intellectual at the Turn of the Nineteenth Century', Erica Mannucci argues that, contrary to her standard interpretation as a mainstream novelist whose moderate feminism is limited to calls for a mostly practical education, Gacon-Dufour was in fact a free-thinking radical. Mannucci demonstrates that Gacon-Dufour's historical works mount a thorough critique of the French monarchy and of the censorship, intolerance, and religious persecution that she argues were its inevitable offshoots. This chapter explores her association with, and response to, contemporary atheists who were her friends, such as Jérôme Lalande and the anti-feminist Sylvain Maréchal. Even Gacon-Dufour's works on housekeeping celebrated women's practical rationality and continued the tradition of the *Encyclopédie*, seen from the point of view of its program of reclaiming forms of local, empirical knowledge. They had the radical purpose of educating the ordinary people, and affirming the importance of practical knowledge for the women, workers, and peasants who had been emancipated by the Revolution. In this way, in the face of the conservative pressures developing during the Napoleonic era, Gacon-Dufour worked to preserve the advances won in 1789.

The next contribution to the collection introduces us to the little-known German republican Elise Reimarus who, although she wrote clearly political texts concerned with the limits of freedom and the relationship between legality and morality, did not explicitly challenge women's traditional domestic role.[23] Lisa Curtis-Wendlandt's contribution, 'Legality and Morality in the Political Thought of Elise Reimarus and Immanuel Kant', compares the account of the relationship between legal and moral justice in her political writings with those of her famous contemporary Immanuel Kant (1724–1804). Arguing against a remedial reading of either thinker's account of the state, this chapter traces striking similarities in

---

[23] See L. Curtis-Wendlandt, 'Staging Virtue: Women, Death, and Liberty in Elise Reimarus's *Cato*', *Journal of the History of Ideas*, 74:1 (2013): [in press].

Reimarus and Kant's insistence on the conceptual independence of legality from questions of moral teleology. In contrast to Reimarus's elaborate discussion of this point in her political works, Curtis-Wendlandt notes her relative silence on the woman question. While Reimarus defended women's status as moral citizens, her views about the desirability of their legal citizenship remain opaque. Compared to the more overt 'feminism' of a Mary Wollstonecraft, for example, this silence in Reimarus's texts drives home the important realization that women's self-conceptions as political subjects differed vastly across Europe, and that their writing was by no means always focused on women's lack of political rights.

In the English-speaking world Mary Wollstonecraft is often taken to be the originator of liberal feminism, an assessment subjected to review in essays in the second part of this collection. Her critique of Rousseau in *A Vindication of the Rights of Woman* is well known, and she is perhaps the most widely studied female political thinker of the eighteenth century. It is arguable that her high profile should at least partly be put down to the influence of her works in other parts of Europe – an influence far greater than that of any of her English precursors. In 'Italian Women Intellectuals and their Cultural Networks: The Making of a European "Life of the Mind"', Marianna D'Ezio takes up the reception of Wollstonecraft's work in Italy and explores the complex relationship between Italian salon sociability and the more political aspirations inherent in Wollstonecraft's *Vindication of the Rights of Woman*. It examines the influence of Wollstonecraft's work, which circulated in Italy in the French language soon after its publication, on Rosa Califronia's possibly pseudonymous *Breve difesa dei diritti delle donne* [*Short Defence of the Rights of Women*] of 1794. D'Ezio demonstrates that Wollstonecraft's *Vindication* quickly established itself as an authoritative call for women's rights beyond the confines of Great Britain. Nevertheless many Italian women, such as Califronia, remained torn between the new call for political rights in Wollstonecraft's work and the more modest aspirations of the *salonnières* and bluestockings, who accepted a limited, mediating social role for women that remained within the confines of traditional constraints of modesty and female virtue.

In Italy and France during the seventeenth and eighteenth century, a small elite of educated women oversaw and participated in the literary salons, some of which facilitated the discussion of radical new ideas. Twentieth-century theorists have represented their activities as important for the rise of democratic ideas, and have attributed to the salonists a considerable political influence.[24] More recently, both the extent of women's political influence and the democratic tendencies expressed in the salons have been questioned by Antoine Lilti.[25] This debate is taken up

---

[24] D. Goodman, 'Enlightenment Salons: The Convergence of Female and Philosophic Ambitions', *Eighteenth-Century Studies*, 22:3 (1989): pp. 329–50; D. Goodman, *The Republic of Letters: A Cultural History of the French Enlightenment* (Ithaca, NY, 1994); D. Gordon, *Citizens Without Sovereignty: Equality and Sociability in French Thought, 1670–1789* (Princeton, 1994); and J. DeJean, *Ancients against Moderns: Cultural Wars and the Making of the Fin de Siècle* (Chicago and London, 1997).

[25] A. Lilti, *Le Monde des salons: Sociabilité et mondanité à Paris au XVIIIe siècle* (Paris, 2005).

by Steven Kale in Chapter 8, 'Women's Intellectual Agency in the History of Eighteenth- and Nineteenth-Century French Salons', in which he argues that whatever the reality of their political influence (a question difficult to resolve), women salonists at the beginning of the nineteenth century certainly represented themselves as mediators between political factions threatening to tear France apart during the Bourbon Restoration. He demonstrates that women such as Blanche-Joséphine Le Bascle d'Argenteuil (duchesse de Maillé), Delphine de Girardin, and Anne Louise Germaine de Staël-Holstein saw the salon as playing an important role in the new regime by offering an alternative space to the parliament, which was riven with bitter disputes, and an alternative atmosphere where consensus and reconciliation were possible. *Salonnières* worked to moderate hostility, teach civility, inspire heroism, and generally draw out the best part of human nature; not to elicit positive characteristics in individuals, but to cultivate an aristocracy capable of governing. Like Madeleine de Scudéry, they continued to believe in women's role as advocates for peace and virtue. The sociability of the past was reconstrued by these women as a path to political reconciliation – even though they were at the same time members of a reactionary generation, fearful of electoral democracy and worried about the politically and socially destructive consequences of conflict within a small ruling elite.

In Great Britain, the influence of Locke and Hobbes on women's political thought was more immediate and direct than on the continent. The first chapter of the second section of this collection, 'The Right to Resist: Women's Citizenship in Catharine Trotter Cockburn's *Revolution of Sweden*' by Elizabeth Sund, analyses the political philosophy evident in the last play written by Catharine Trotter, who after her marriage became Catharine Cockburn. In 1702, Trotter had published a defence of Locke's *Essay Concerning Human Understanding*, supporting it against the charge that its empiricist epistemology cannot ground an adequate account of moral truth.[26] Her play, while it contains no direct reference to Locke, defends the kind of right to resist an unjust sovereign for which he had argued in his *Two Treatises of Government*, and extends the doctrine of the right to resist to the case of marriage. Although Cockburn does not go so far as to discuss political representation for women, she has clear ideas of women's duties as virtuous citizens, and offers a forward-looking representation of ideal marriage as a friendship between equals, who gain and deserve each other's respect. Her play pits women's duty as wives against their duty as citizens, concluding in favour of the second whenever they conflict.

Locke figures prominently also in the writings of the British historian Catharine Macaulay, the subject of Karen Green's contribution, 'Catharine Macaulay and

---

[26] C.T. Cockburn, *A Defence of the Essay of Human Understanding Written by Mr Locke. Wherein its Principles with reference to Morality, Reveal'd Religion, and the Immortality of the Soul, are Consider'd and Justify'd: In Answer to Some Remarks on that Essay* (London, 1702); John Locke, *An Essay Concerning Human Understanding*, ed. P. H. Nidditch (Oxford, 1975).

Laetitia Barbauld: Two Eighteenth-Century "Republicans"'. Political theory in the eighteenth century tended to focus on the nature of the social contract and questions of the origin of political authority and the proper constitution for a just state; but the older Aristotelian idea that virtue is important for political progress remained influential. Montesquieu, whose *Spirit of the Laws* appeared in 1748, developed the theory that different political constitutions rested on different expectations concerning the people. A democratic or republican state demanded equality and the virtue of frugality; aristocratic or oligarchic government accepted some inequality and called for the virtue of moderation; monarchy required nobles motivated by honour; and finally, despotic governments relied on fear and a populace that is timid and ignorant.[27] Women writing in the eighteenth century continued to explore the connection between the flourishing of society and the virtues and other characteristics of the people.

Macaulay's history of England, which ultimately covered the period from the accession of James I to the Glorious Revolution, offered an influential Lockean reading of the Civil War, citing his *Two Treatises* to justify the execution of Charles I.[28] Green's chapter examines some of Macaulay's shorter political pamphlets, particularly those directed at Edmund Burke, comparing her republicanism with that of her near contemporary Anna Laetitia Barbauld. Both writers promoted liberty, equality, and 'frugal' republican virtues, celebrating first the Corsican republic and later the French Revolution, in direct opposition to the conservatism of Burke.

In *Letters on Education* (1790), her next to last publication, Macaulay discussed at length how education could have a role in forming virtuous citizens committed to upholding justice, and a constitution that protected human rights. She also argued that girls and boys should be educated together and study the same demanding curriculum and that their virtues should not be thought to differ. Her book was favourably reviewed by Wollstonecraft, whose feminist ideas it helped to form. In Chapter 11, '"The Manly Virtues": Macaulay's Influence, Wollstonecraft's Legacy', Mary Caputi argues that nevertheless, Wollstonecraft's generally accepted status as the originator of later feminist attitudes is not unjustified, since gender was at the heart of her concerns, while it was peripheral to Macaulay's.

In the next chapter, 'Between Enlightenment Feminism and Abolitionism: Mary Wollstonecraft's Thoughts on Women and Slavery', Jeanette Ehrmann approaches Wollstonecraft's writing from the perspective of race relations. She re-examines the problematic analogy between marriage and slavery, to counter Eurocentric conceptions of universalism and to draw out the complexity of Enlightenment political ideas. She places Wollstonecraft's thought in the broader context of feminist and abolitionist discourses of her time, providing a tableau of the multifaceted gender-race relations observed in the transatlantic slave trade and in Caribbean slavery. Judith Drake's 'Essay in defence of the female sex'

---

27 C.L. de Secondat baron de Montesquieu, *The Spirit of the Laws*, trans. A.M. Cohler et al. (Cambridge, 1989), pp. 42–59.

28 C. Macaulay, *The history of England from the accession of James 1. to that of the Brunswick line* (8 vols, London, 1763–1783), vol. 4, pp. 430–31.

of 1696 had already developed the analogy, and writers like Hannah More and Olympe de Gouges also published against black slavery. But Ehrmann focuses on the *Vindication*'s even closer association of the two issues, and argues that it masks real situational differences between black slave women and women of the white bourgeoisie – who to an extent were accomplices in and beneficiaries of slavery and European colonialism. Inadvertently, Wollstonecraft's critique of European gender stereotypes conceals a new false universalism, and risks trivializing the oppression of black women in slavery.

The last chapter in the collection focuses on women in the life of the nation and the formation of Irish national consciousness and identity. With '"Doing an Acceptable Service to my Country": Political Thought in Charlotte Brooke's *Reliques of Irish Poetry*', Lesa Ní Mhunghaile introduces us to Charlotte Brooke's contributions to such development. She shows that Brooke saw herself as a mediator between Ireland and England, and that her *Reliques of Irish Poetry* was aimed at improving relations between the Irish, the Anglo-Irish, and the English. Brooke likened Ireland and Britain to sisters, Ireland being the elder and by implication having cultural supremacy, emphasizing the enrichment that a mixture of Gaelic blood and English blood could produce, as in the case of the Anglo-Irish. With her metaphor she aspired to encourage a closer and more respectful connection between the two antagonistic regions of the British Isles.

At the end of the seventeenth century Margaret Cavendish made a succinct declaration concerning women's paradoxical status as excluded citizens: 'If we be not citizens of the Commonwealth, I know no reason we should be Subjects of the Commonwealth.'[29] As the eighteenth century drew to a close, women's full and equal citizenship still remained elusive. Yet, as is clear from the contributions presented here, women could now at least *imagine* themselves as citizens.[30] They entered into the vibrant eighteenth-century debates about the nature of just government, the virtues of citizens, and the prospects for political progress. Whether like the radical Jodin they explicitly conceived of women playing a legislative role, or merely claimed a right to intervene as commentators, mediators, and conciliators in the political process, they represented themselves as part of the polity. By the dawn of the nineteenth century the earlier defence of women's equal virtue had become a claim for equal rights. The fruit of these imaginings would take until the twentieth century to mature. But it is important to acknowledge that, already in the eighteenth century, the political subject comes in two sexes. Here we present a study of serious women thinkers, whose eloquence and power of argument commends them as full members in any balanced polity; and equally, it demonstrates that their texts can no longer be excluded when the history of political philosophy is taught.

---

[29] M. Cavendish, *Sociable Letters*, ed. J. Fitzmaurice (Peterborough, Ontario, 2004), p. 61; discussed in H.L. Smith, 'Margaret Cavendish and the False Universal', in Broad and Green (eds), *Virtue, Liberty, and Toleration* (Dordrecht, 2007), pp. 95–110.

[30] A.K. Smart, *Citoyennes: Women and the Idea of Citizenship in Eighteenth-Century France* (Newark, 2011).

PART I
Women's Political Ideas in Continental Europe

Chapter 1
Emilie Du Châtelet's Views on the Pillars of French Society: King, Church, and Family

Judith P. Zinsser

Introduction

France's rules of censorship in the eighteenth century were simple. The royal *garde des sceaux* [Keeper of the Seals] instructed his agents to seek out and confiscate any writings that challenged the pillars of state: the king, the Church, and the family. 'Family' meant not only the implicit patriarchy of the family unit (the king was, in fact, often portrayed as the father of his subjects) but also the whole hierarchy of families with the *haute noblesse* at its highest level, the barbarous 'rabble' scrambling to serve their betters at its base. The *philosophe* Gabrielle Emilie le Tonnelier de Breteuil, Marquise Du Châtelet (1706–1749), as the daughter of the Baron de Breteuil and the wife of a nobleman descended from one of the first families of Lorraine, stood close to the top of this social edifice.[1] Yet everything she wrote that related to the three protected institutions would have been condemned by the royal censors, then seized and burned in the Place des Grèves – the usual fate for publications deemed injurious to the French polity.

Du Châtelet did not shy away from controversy. She claimed victory in her debates with the eminent physicists of France and England over the correct formula for mechanical force, and her exchange of pamphlets with the perpetual secretary of the French Royal Academy of Sciences settled her reputation as a member of the 'Republic of Letters'. However, she would not have described herself as a rebel, nor the political comments scattered through her works as potentially revolutionary. Unlike many other women discussed in this collection, Du Châtelet never formulated a distinct, coherent theory of politics, nor did she belong to the forerunners of those who made a systematic investigation of the political significance of sexual difference.[2] Du Châtelet accepted the patriarchal restrictions of her day: that many of her choices required her husband's permission; that she

1 'Du Châtelet' is with a capital 'D', indicating that 'Du' is an integral part of the name, not as in other cases an indication of association with a particular place, as in the 'Duc de Richelieu'.

2 See 'Introduction', in C. Pateman and M.L. Shanley (eds), *Feminist Interpretations of Political Theory* (University Park, PA, 1991), pp. 1–10.

could not travel to England without him. She accepted societal constraints: that, as a woman, she 'was excluded from every sort of glory' open to men, as generals, government ministers, and ambassadors. She chafed, however, at 'the full weight of prejudice' that excluded women 'so universally from the sciences', and believed that through study she (and by implication other women in similar circumstances) could overcome the disability of their sex. Study, she argued in her *Discours sur le bonheur* [*Discourse on Happiness*], could bring fame to a woman as surely as other avenues brought fame to men.[3] Like other European women of the eighteenth and nineteenth centuries, she protested at the state of women's education. Seemingly born only to deceive, women were allowed no other way to use their intelligence. In an early draft of her translator's preface to *The Fable of the Bees* (1714; the work of Bernard Mandeville, a Dutch Huguenot émigré living in England), she asserted that if she were king, she would establish a 'collège' for women. In the final version, using the language of the new natural philosophy, she imagined an 'experiment in physics' which 'would allow women to share in all the rights of humanity, and most of all those of the mind'.[4] Her remedy in her own lifetime was to educate herself. She became her own successful scientific experiment.[5]

With the constraints and restrictions of womanhood came duties and responsibilities. Practically, like other women of her rank, Du Châtelet played an active role in the political and economic life of the new family that she and her husband created by marrying in 1725. While he was away at the numerous wars of the mid-eighteenth century, she ran their estates – centred in Champagne, but with outlying holdings in Normandy and across the border in Flanders. It was she who made decisions in the lengthy litigation involved with inheritance of his Flemish lands and routinely supervised the household as it moved between Paris, Versailles, Brussels, and her husband's chateau, Cirey. Du Châtelet herself came from a family with close ties to King Louis XIV and his queen. The titular head of the Breteuil

3 Du Châtelet, *Discours sur le bonheur*, in *Selected Philosophical and Scientific Writings*, ed. J.P. Zinsser, trans. I. Bour and J.P. Zinsser (Chicago, 2009), p. 357. Where possible, translated passages come from this collection (called *Selections* hereafter), perhaps slightly adapted. In other instances, the French text is referenced in the footnotes and the translations are my own.

4 Du Châtelet, 'Translator's Preface' to B.[de] Mandeville, *The Fable of the Bees*, in *Selections*, pp. 48–9. See also Du Châtelet, *Discours*, in *Selections*, p. 357. See, on the various drafts of her 'Preface' and for an extended discussion of her translation, J.P. Zinsser, 'Entrepreneur of the "Republic of Letters": Emilie de Breteuil, marquise Du Châtelet, and Bernard Mandeville's *Fable of the Bees*', *French Historical Studies*, 25:4 (2002): pp. 595–624.

5 No systematic study of Du Châtelet's reading has been done, though scholars have made educated guesses. See for example A. Brown and U. Kölving, 'A la recherche des livres d'Emilie Du Châtelet', in U. Kölving and O. Courcelle (eds), *Emilie Du Châtelet: Eclairages et documents nouveaux* (Ferney-Voltaire, 2008), pp. 111–20. For details of her life see J.P. Zinsser, *Emilie Du Châtelet: Daring Genius of the Enlightenment* (New York, 2006), and on her education, pp. 26–31. For the background specific to particular writings see the introductions to each selection in Du Châtelet, *Selections*.

family became a government minister to Louis XV, and remained an advisor in the queen's household. Other cousins served as ambassadors and army officers. These connections – and the support of her relative by marriage Louis François Armand Du Plessis, Duc de Richelieu, one of Louis XV's closest friends – gave her clear access to the intricate political world of favour and patronage. She played these connections astutely and persistently. She won advancement for her husband and protection for her lover and companion Voltaire, and secured appropriate futures for her son and daughter. Her son, Florent Louis, as heir to such an illustrious and noble family, served in the royal army; and later, long after his mother's death, as an ambassador and finally as an advisor to Louis XVI. Her daughter, Gabrielle Pauline was married into the Neapolitan papal nobility and rose to be principal lady-in-waiting to the Queen of Naples. Though as a woman Du Châtelet was in theory marginal to the political, economic, and religious institutions of her male-governed society, she enjoyed its privileges and benefits and never doubted her right to comment on its foibles or to discern and describe its natural laws, however much they might challenge the accepted 'trinity' of king, Church, and family.

What then were Du Châtelet's ideas about government, in its relation to the economy and society as a whole? What was her political philosophy? To answer these questions, to place her within the history of political theory, it is necessary to examine four of her writings. First, she worked from 1734 to 1736 on her free translation of *The Fable of the Bees*; when she finished this project, there was her 'Translator's Preface' and twelve added chapters which gave her version, not of the verse *Fable* itself, but of the ancillary material Mandeville had included: his 'Enquiry into the Origin of Moral Virtue' and eleven of the 'Remarks' he wrote to explain and expand upon phrases in the poem to his English audience. Second, in 1740 Du Châtelet published her *Institutions de physique* [*Foundations of Physics*], a study of metaphysics, philosophy, mathematics, and mechanics: her original synthesis of works by René Descartes, Gottfried Wilhelm von Leibniz, and Isaac Newton. Of significance to an understanding of her views on politics is a chapter entitled 'De la liberté' ['Of Free Will'], planned for the *Institutions* but never included.[6] Third is her two-volume *Examens de la Bible* [*Examinations of the Bible*], which she had begun with Voltaire at Cirey and completed in the early 1740s. Fourth among the works relevant to Du Châtelet's place in the history of political theory is her *Discours sur le bonheur* (1747–1748), again a revision and expansion of an earlier project.

6 The closest English translation to give Du Châtelet's intended meaning of 'liberté' is 'free will'. Today, 'volonté' is considered to be the French equivalent. There is some controversy about this essay. Voltaire scholars dismiss it as a version of the chapter of the same name that ultimately became part of his *Traité de métaphysique*. Du Châtelet scholars disagree. During 1734–1738 Du Châtelet and Voltaire argued over these issues, and passed their writings back and forth: so specific attribution is difficult. See Zinsser, *Emilie Du Châtelet*, pp. 137, 319n65, 144–5, 320nn78–9. Quotations come from the version published in I.O. Wade, *Studies on Voltaire, with some Unpublished Papers of Mme Du Châtelet* (Princeton, 1947).

Of these writings related to her ideas on king, Church, and family, only the chapter in the *Institutions* on the nature of God circulated freely in a published text. The others, because of their unorthodox views, she allowed to be read only in manuscript. They were part of an extensive traffic in clandestine texts in the first half of the eighteenth century: books and pamphlets copied and recopied, passed from hand to hand, to evade confiscation or condemnation by the royal censors and their agents.[7] Like many of her intellectual contemporaries in early Enlightenment France, Du Châtelet adhered to the letter if not the spirit of laws against free expression. In her search for what she distinguished as 'truth', she perceived herself as outside and above the royal restrictions, just as the same quest justified her daring disregard of societal constraints imposed on her sex.

Uniting these apparently disparate texts in philosophy, science, and metaphysics was a very characteristic eighteenth-century assumption of their interconnectedness, even if they are in our time established as separate disciplines and ways of thinking. For Du Châtelet, as for Pierre-Louis Moreau de Maupertuis and her other *philosophe* mentors, 'several truths of Physics, Metaphysics and Geometry are obviously interconnected.'[8] Geometry, in the broad sense of mathematics, was the key to all underlying certainty: the one true 'science' as that term is understood today. She often used such mathematical allusions and comparisons to explain and to stamp with authority her more weighty philosophical statements. For example, searching for a way to describe the nature of God's power to choose, she used the geometrical example of a circle to explain his relationship to the creation of matter. The essences of things are fixed and cannot depend on the will of their Creator, just as 'the essence of a circle consists of a line of which all the points are equally distant from another point that one calls the centre.' One cannot conceive of any other possible figure with those essential qualities.[9] Though she never tried to reduce politics to mathematics, she relied on reasoning of the same style when puzzling through her observations of human behaviour and presented her conclusions with the same kind of certainty. As she explains in the first two chapters of the *Institutions*, and by implication in the rest of her writings, Du Châtelet had a clear image of a regulated universe – a cosmos governed by mathematically precise natural laws. These same kinds of laws, she believed, existed for the earthly social world of king, Church, and family.

---

7 These writings survived in archives in France, Belgium, and Russia. The *Discours sur le bonheur* has been published a number of times since Du Châtelet's death and exists in an outdated scholarly edition. A version of the Mandeville is mentioned in note 4, above. Du Châtelet made two editions of the *Institutions de physique*, in 1740 and 1742. The essay on 'liberté' was probably intended for this work along with other chapters on grammar, optics, and hearing, but it was never included, in either the first or the second edition. Her two-volume exegesis of the Bible exists in three manuscript copies, and it has recently been edited: E. Du Châtelet, *Examens de la Bible*, ed. B.E. Schwarzbach (Paris, 2009).

8 Du Châtelet, *Institutions de physique*, in *Selections*, p. 124.

9 Du Châtelet, *Institutions de physique* (Paris, 1740), p. 67.

Royal Government and Kings

In eighteenth-century France the king notionally embodied all the power of government. But this had little to do with the practical reality of French politics, with its many overlapping, antiquated authorities derived from manorialism and feudalism, centuries of local customs, dynastic conquests, and royal decrees – all augmented by the newer layers of ministerial and judicial bureaucracy. Such a complexity of powers was manifest in Du Châtelet's own experience. The litigation concerning her husband's Flanders inheritance drew her into a legal morass involving lawyers, philologists, the gathering of testimony from witnesses, and submission of numerous briefs and notarial records. The eventual negotiated settlement took years to achieve and forced her unwilling sojourn in Brussels from 1739 to 1742. More than once she had to attend the queen, Marie Leszczyńska, over long weeks at Versailles or Fontainebleau; she was no stranger to the antechambers of government ministers, nor to holding counsel with friends close to King Louis XV, such as the Duc de Richelieu. Patronage from these personal relationships brought Du Châtelet many successes, as it did for other aristocratic women of the *haute noblesse*. Between 1744 and 1747 she manoeuvred to have Voltaire elected to the Académie française (an appointment long overdue, and delayed by the queen's distaste for his apparent lack of respect toward the Church), arranged her daughter's marriage on better terms than she could have without patronage, and finessed her husband's military rank so that he became one of the eleven lieutenants-general commanding the king's armies.

Given these experiences, it is not surprising that Du Châtelet paints a sceptical picture of legislators and their governing devices, in her rendering of Mandeville's *Fable*. While she omitted his Protestant criticism of the clergy, she accurately conveyed his contemptuous image of how politics worked. His society originated when 'legislators' manipulated men's nature, using pride to make even the most selfish aspire to be good. Further, they 'had found the means to have the vices of its different members serve the happiness of society'.[10] In this way, Mandeville introduced the central thesis of his *Fable*: that the most prosperous nation was the one with the greatest vices, for one man's vice supported vast numbers of the poor. But Du Châtelet made an uneasy alliance with Mandeville. She agreed that 'the wisdom of a government consists in tolerating the abuses that save [society] from a greater evil.'[11] Even the vices of humble sailors contributed to the commerce

---

[10] B. [de] Mandeville, 'Preface de l'autheur' to *The Fable of the Bees*, trans. Du Châtelet, in Wade, *Studies*, p. 139. Here and in subsequent notes, though Mandeville is cited as the author, the phrasing and sentiments are usually those of Du Châtelet: her own interpretations or additions, not literal translation. On Du Chatelet's manipulation of the text see J.P. Zinsser, 'Entrepreneur'. On its relationship to Voltaire's positive view of a commercial society see F. Gottman, 'Du Châtelet, Voltaire, and the Transformation of Mandeville's Fable', *History of European Ideas*, 38:2 (2012): pp. 218–32; I am grateful to Karen Green for this second reference.

[11] Mandeville, *Fable*, in Wade, *Studies*, Chapter 9, p. 178.

of the nation. She grafted into her translation the observation that these men, instead of saving their wages when they came on shore, spent them in the brothels clustered near the docks. In this way their money returned to the economy, and they were forced to return to work on their ships.[12] Such tolerance, however, and the vice that was 'inseparable from the grandeur and the power of a state', did not mean for her that the 'particularly vicious who troubled the order of the society must not be rigorously punished'.[13] For her then, society was not as self-regulating as Mandeville had supposed. Du Châtelet was firm regarding the application of law; clearly a social conservative where those of lesser rank were involved, she expected them to be subject to conscientiously enforced laws.

When she came to consider the institution of monarchy, Du Châtelet offered both positive and negative comments on the uses of royal power. She faithfully translates as 'the fountain of honour' Mandeville's characterization of the king of this corrupted, prosperous state; she continues, drawing on her personal experience of the courtier's world, 'that he can give to whom he pleases certain marks of distinction,' and these are 'the source of the respect that one has for him, whether he merits them or not'. She also accepts Mandeville's assumption that a king will have 'good qualities' founded on 'the consideration that society requires that each have for the others'.[14] From her observations, however, society could turn quickly on its king, at one minute admiring Louis XV as 'bien aimé' [well loved], and at the next mocking him for his public adulteries. In her *Discours sur le bonheur* she offered a realistic picture of the man she had observed at court, and of the ideal to which she imagined he and all kings should aspire. He was prone to boredom because his tastes were so 'easily blunted by satiation'. This made it

> impossible for him to be happy, unless Heaven has given him a soul magnanimous enough to be susceptible to the pleasure of his position, that is to say, the pleasure of making a great number of men happy. Then this position becomes the first above all for the happiness it brings, as it is by its power.[15]

In her *Examens de la Bible*, Du Châtelet writes harshly about kings who not only ignored 'the pleasure' of their subjects but also abused their exercise of royal power. The *Examens* was composed during two periods. She and Voltaire had begun the project in the late 1730s, when together they were pondering the major questions of metaphysics and morality. Early in the 1740s after she had completed revisions for the second edition of her *Institutions*, Du Châtelet returned to their notes and created her extensive commentary. In their quest for answers, she and Voltaire had read widely in philosophy and theological commentaries – such as the works of Plato, Pierre Bayle, John Locke, and Alexander Pope – and particularly

---

[12] Ibid., p. 180.

[13] Mandeville, 'Preface de l'autheur' to *Fable*, p. 140.

[14] Mandeville, *Fable*, Chapter 4, pp. 155, 166.

[15] Du Châtelet, *Discours*, in *Selections*, pp. 259–60.

in multi-volume studies by the Augustinian monk Dom Calmet.[16] From these notes and from additional sources she created her two-volume critical study of the Old and New Testaments. Most striking is Du Châtelet's condemnation of kings and their wars. Even though the Bible indicates that Joshua, Saul, David, and Solomon acted on orders from God, Du Châtelet cannot excuse their cruelties and the horrors of their conquests. She writes at length on the book of Joshua: one chapter after another telling of the slaughter of men, women, and children. She calls it 'the most revolting' of all such accounts: 'butchery' and 'barbarity'.[17] What is worse by her lights, these kings break laws, and like Solomon they gain their thrones through murder and even fratricide.[18]

God and the Institutional Church

It is no wonder that Du Châtelet's *Examens* exists only in manuscript. Not only was she disrespectful of the institution of monarchy: her comments about the Old and New Testaments are clearly heretical, standing against the Catholic Church doctrine of the divine authority of Holy Scripture and the clergy's exclusive right to interpret and explain its meaning. For Du Châtelet the God of the Old Testament is even worse than the kings to whom he issues precepts. A cruel deity who acts on a whim, he makes promises then breaks them, punishes out of all proportion to the crimes committed, and abandons those he supposedly had favoured, killing them 'bit by bit'. The story of Adam and Eve, the tree of knowledge and the serpent – Du Châtelet describes them as 'a ridiculous old maid's tale'. She cannot conceal her outrage at a God 'who acted towards man as a strange king who wanted to test the obedience of his subjects on ridiculous things, and who punished them afterwards well beyond their crimes'. His actions, as described in the Book of Genesis, are 'the work of an entirely deranged mind'.[19] His miracles are no better. They are 'of two kinds: pointless or cruel'. She lists 'the scourges of Egypt':

[16] Dom Augustin Calmet (1672–1757) published numerous versions of his commentary. Voltaire's library at the time of his death included many of these volumes and also a number of the seventeenth- and early eighteenth-century attacks on the authenticity of the Old and New Testaments. For her commentary on the Gospels, Du Châtelet translated Thomas Woolston's *Six Discourses on the Miracles* (proving Jesus's miracles to be fraudulent, including the resurrection). In many instances, she took what Dom Calmet discussed in his commentaries, but drew different conclusions. See, on clandestine and radical texts of her era, J.I. Israel, *Radical Enlightenment: Philosophy and the Making of Modernity 1650–1750* (New York, 2001), especially pp. 684–703. B.E. Schwarzbach has made an extensive study of the possible correlation between Voltaire's and Du Châtelet's religious views. Voltaire's most serious works on this subject were written long after his companion's death, and Schwarzbach has found no direct and very few indirect references to the *Examens*. See his numerous articles on this subject and particularly the introduction to his critical edition of the *Examens* (see note 7, above).

[17] Du Châtelet, *Examens*, Josué 8:3–29; 10:22–6; Genèse, *passim*.

[18] Ibid., 1 Rois, 2 Rois, 3 Rois, *passim*.

[19] Ibid., p. 211, Exode 33:18.

> Waters that changed into blood to poison an entire people, frogs, locusts, flies sent to lay them waste, contagious illnesses that attack some animals, ulcers which eat into men, storms, hail, darkness over an entire kingdom, children in their cradles killed by an angel.[20]

Finally, and perhaps most reprehensibly, this God shows irrational and senseless disregard for his own laws of nature. He enables Joshua to stop the sun, a 'pointless miracle'. She adds: 'One is also a little puzzled to explain this order that Joshua gives to the sun, since it was proved that what turns is the earth, not the sun. Apparently the H. Spirit did not know the true system of the world.'[21] Similarly, she ridicules the story of Jonah, 'for assuredly there is nothing so difficult, as to save this adventure from absurdity':

> A man fully dressed thrown into the sea without being drowned, who finds in the nick of time a fish that had the courtesy to eat him, and this, so honourably as not to hurt him; who swallows him without suffocating him; who keeps him alive in his stomach all shod and clothed for 3 days and 3 nights.[22]

These are 'fables', as ridiculous as the stories of Jesus's miracles and even his resurrection, all of which she mocks in her commentary on the Gospels of the New Testament.[23] There was no place for such a God in her ordered universe. Not only could she not countenance such an outrageously cruel and tyrannical being, but she also could not accept a God who intervened at will and broke the very laws of nature he had ordained for his universe. If such an arbitrary God existed, there could be no certain knowledge, and no science in its new modern sense.

Like Western theologians both before and after her time, Du Châtelet dismissed this Old Testament figure and constructed her own image of the deity. Using the writings of Descartes, Leibniz, and Christian Wolff (Leibniz's follower) in her *Institutions de physique*, she presents a perfect God suited to a cosmos governed by rational, natural laws. With no reference to faith – and ignoring inconsistencies, implausibilities, and what she considered to be the gibberish of the Bible – she *reasoned* her God's existence, and his nature and attributes. The first chapter of the *Institutions* sets out her epistemology – the means by which we can know anything with certainty. Two rules ensured this ability to recognize and 'know' the truth: Descartes's principle of non-contradiction (nothing can be at the same time both true and untrue); and Leibniz's principle of 'raison suffisante' [sufficient reason] (for everything that exists or occurs, there must be a reason for it that excludes any alternative dispensation). To her, this second principle was incontrovertible: 'All men follow it naturally; because no one decides for one thing rather than another, without a sufficient reason which makes him see that this thing is preferable to

20 Ibid., p. 216.

21 Ibid., pp. 218, 219; 'H. Spirit' represents her abbreviation for the Holy Spirit.

22 Ibid., p. 224.

23 Ibid., pp. 223–4.

the other.'[24] She could therefore logically argue that the world she saw with her senses had been created by a perfect, all-powerful being – who was separate from this universe, and whose choices were without contradictions and based on sufficient reason. Du Châtelet's God, as described in Chapter II of the *Institutions*, was a God 'free' to choose any one possible 'succession of things' to make actual, and who rationally chose to create one succession of things and not another 'because it pleased him the most'. This explained the perfection of his creations. Like Leibniz, Du Châtelet viewed the actual world as the best of all those that the Creator could have chosen, from the infinite range that he had contemplated. Thus, her God was the first to follow the rule of sufficient reason.[25]

These conclusions about the nature of the divine were the result of a long period of reading, discussion, consultation, and thinking. Near the beginning of this intellectual enterprise, in October of 1734, Du Châtelet had written to Maupertuis that she was reading Locke, 'for I am looking for the basis of things'.[26] Her views of kings, and the role of God in the universe, gave her part of the answers; but much more remained to be pondered and put to paper. For example, all Christian philosophers and theologians who wrestled with such a metaphysical endeavour inevitably had to deal with two paradoxes that had a direct impact on the religious and political institutions evolving in their societies. In the first, the existence of evil was for the *philosophe* a self-evident fact; but it had to be accounted for somehow, given that reality was created by a being of perfect goodness. Similarly self-evident were other attributes of God: his omnipotence and omniscience. How then to explain the second paradox: the simultaneous existence of such a God and man's *liberté*, or free will? Without free will, men would be nothing more than passive agents of God's will and not responsible for any actions whether good or bad. In Du Châtelet's France, the whole panoply of Catholic dogma, rituals, and clergy was intended to deal with these two apparent contradictions and the moral problems they posed.

Although Du Châtelet outwardly accepted these forms and rituals of the institutional Church – for example, the priest at Cirey regularly said mass in the chapel of the chateau, and she observed the appropriate period of confinement after the birth of her children – she did not look to the Catholic Church for answers. In her commentary on Genesis in the *Examens*, she rejects the whole concept of the 'original sin' and ridicules the role of the unassuming snake and God's punishments. She points out that there was only apocryphal mention of the rebellion of the fallen angel who became Satan, the source of evil in Christianity.[27] By implication, the need for man's redemption and the war between forces of good and evil had been fabricated. Both existed only as interpreted and mediated by

---

24 Du Châtelet, *Institutions*, in *Selections*, Chapter 1, p. 128.

25 Ibid., Chapter 2, pp. 143–4.

26 Du Châtelet to Maupertuis, Nos 24, 23, Oct 1734, *Lettres de la marquise du Châtelet*, ed. T. Besterman (Geneva, 1958), vol. 1, p. 52.

27 In the Epistle of St. Jude; Du Châtelet, *Examens*, in *Selections*, Genèse, p. 209.

churches and priests. Elsewhere, Du Châtelet explicitly rejected the basic rituals and dogma of Catholicism. In her *Discours* devoted to happiness, she light-heartedly dismisses repentance as 'one of the most useless and most disagreeable [feelings] that our soul can experience'. She tells her readers that 'one of the great secrets [of happiness] is to know how to guard against it.' She accepts that one should make 'amends' but sees no point in 'looking back, and one must always brush from one's mind the memory of one's errors'.[28] In one sentence she eliminates the need for confession, the sacrament of penance, and any fear of the consequences of sin.

Instead, Du Châtelet offered her own explanation of the Creator's relationship to evil and her own resolution of the contradictions accompanying man's free will. Though evil might be viewed as an 'imperfection', it must of necessity, as she explained in Chapter 2 of the *Institutions*, have its 'raison suffisante'. Evil existed within the broader context of existence, which only God in his omniscience could know and bring into harmony. She compared our impressions to those of the human eye, which 'could not see the least parts of an object without losing sight of the whole; we would see a few points very distinctly if our eyes were microscopes, but in so doing we would lose the whole'.[29] For Du Châtelet such insights seemed incontrovertible. This use of reason and of analogy from experience, as she told her son in the Preface to the *Institutions*, could turn even 'la Métaphysique' into a 'science'. In her metaphysics, she could thus arrive at a theorem as certain as any in geometry: 'So this world is the best of the possible worlds, the one where the greatest variety exists with the greatest order, and where the largest number of effects is produced by the simplest laws.'[30]

As Du Châtelet's knowledge of physics increased – with her reading in all of the major seventeenth- and early eighteenth-century texts in natural philosophy, including Newton and his English commentators – the question of man's free will in this 'best of the possible worlds' became complicated. This was not just because of her accepting the supreme attributes of the deity (omnipotence, omniscience) but also because of her understanding of the laws of motion, about which she and her contemporaries reflected and argued. Du Châtelet followed Descartes and Leibniz: there is a fixed sum of force in the universe, and therefore also of motion in the sense of action and reaction. As creator, God was the first mover. All force in nature derived from this first motion and was observable in its endless natural consequences: in the manner of 'perpetual motion' machines hypothesized by inventors familiar with Newton's mechanics. This ordinance of the amount of force and motion, however, created another serious challenge to man's free will. As Du Châtelet explained, an 'invariable quantity of movement in the universe denies man this faculty of self-movement.'[31] Further complicating the issue were the effects on man's choices and actions of a natural law governing the precise detail

---

[28] Du Châtelet, *Discours*, in *Selections*, pp. 355, 356.

[29] Du Châtelet, *Institutions*, in *Selections*, Chapter 2, p. 145.

[30] Ibid., p. 144.

[31] Du Châtelet, 'De la liberté', in Wade, *Studies*, p. 92.

of all motion. Even if man were not hemmed in by a fixed quantity of motion, is he not, she queried, also subject to the same laws as other matter? What of gravity and attraction? Once again, as a being composed of particles he loses his free will – his ability to do this and not that. Most importantly for any system of morality, he loses his ability to choose and to act independently according to his reason.

In a chapter originally intended for the *Institutions*, the essay 'De la liberté', Du Châtelet indicates how she resolved this metaphysical and now scientific paradox. This, in combination with other thoughts drawn from her additions to Mandeville's writings and a few comments from the *Examens*, completes what she might have called a 'science of good and evil'.[32] The piece on *liberté*, in her original sequence of chapters planned for the *Institutions*, would have followed one on motion that underlines the dual nature of the incongruity she had uncovered. In this prospective chapter Du Châtelet began by giving her meaning of *liberté*: 'the power to think a thing, or not to think it, to move or not to move, in conformity with the choice of one's own mind'.[33] She then made the whole congruent, by a rhetorical sleight of hand that owed more to acceptance of an omnipotent God than to her radical proclivities. Free will is the gift of God, and therefore not subject to nature's constraints. To those who might question the reasons for this gift she replies: to deny it to man is also to deny to God his absolute power and his free will. He has given 'his creatures a small portion of free will, in the same way he gave them a small portion of intelligence'. However, Du Châtelet continues, this *liberté* is not unlimited. If it were, then man would be assimilated too closely to God. Instead, in accord with her acceptance of a hierarchical society, she explains that each of us enjoys 'a share appropriate to the rank that we hold in nature'.[34]

La Morale and the Family

Having equated order in society with order in nature, Du Châtelet awarded more *liberté* to some and less to others. This logical progression took her from the realm of metaphysics to that of ethics – of *la morale*, as it was called in French. Given this *liberté*, in whatever way it is circumscribed, how are we to deal with those who choose to take their pleasure at the expense of others? In fact it was in search of an answer to this question that Du Châtelet had embarked on her translation of Mandeville's *Fable*, which she introduced to her readers as 'the best book of ethics ever written; that is to say, the one that most leads men to the true source of the feelings to which they abandon themselves almost without examining them'.[35] Such feelings Mandeville identified as 'appetites': lust, pride, and selfishness being the most powerful. He had explained the origin of society, and its subsequent order

---

32 Du Châtelet, *Examens*, in *Selections*, Genèse, p. 208.

33 Du Châtelet, 'De la liberté', in Wade, *Studies*, p. 93.

34 Ibid., pp. 107–8.

35 Du Châtelet, 'Translator's Preface', in *Selections*, p. 50.

and prosperity, by the manipulation and interrelationships of these feelings. By her careful translation, and the additions she made to his text, Du Châtelet gave readers her own explanation for the origins and workings of a civilized, moral society.

Unlike Mandeville, Du Châtelet identified *l'amour* (the context suggests this was her synonym for 'lust') as the feeling that occasioned 'the beginning of all society', for man like all animals had 'an invincible inclination for the propagation of his species'. She imagined the man and woman, one child, and then another: 'these mutual needs will have given birth to society.'[36] This was a society of families, heterosexual couples with offspring, gathered together for self-preservation. Following this explanation, she added her own description of the internal forces governing the behaviour of human beings. Although she had complimented Locke in her Translator's Preface, in this chapter she disagreed with one of his principal philosophical assertions: his denial of innate ideas. In contrast to the English natural philosopher, Du Châtelet maintained that all men shared the feeling of 'bienveillance', or benevolence towards their fellows, which 'the creator placed in us, and of which we involuntarily sense [the] effects, like hunger and thirst'. It was so strong that it set man apart from the other animals.[37] This 'natural benevolence' was linked to her insistence on a second innate idea: 'a universal law for all men that god engraved on their heart'. Ironically, despite her condemnation of the Scriptures, this law commonly known as the Golden Rule came from the Bible: 'do not do to others what you would not have done to you.'[38]

However, the initial problem remained. What of individuals who ignored the guidance of these innate ideas? Mandeville easily incorporated such men into his society, where 'man's frailties ... can be useful to his own happiness and that of others.'[39] This was his central thesis: that vice was good for the nation, and in fact was sometimes needed to make virtue possible, as with the accepted promiscuity of prostitutes which protects the chastity of other women.[40] Du Châtelet added her own analogy. The vice-ridden were like 'poisons' in chemistry: 'they are fatal, but art has known how to draw salutary remedies from them.'[41] She also accepted Mandeville's general definition of vice and virtue: that 'men are in agreement in naming all action prejudicial to a society *vice*', and '*virtue* all those [actions] that the ambition to be just [makes] happen'. But she added an important qualification: this was 'true only up to a certain point'.[42] Where Mandeville was content with paradox and ambiguity, Du Châtelet wanted simple fact and certainty. She believed that these definitions might not be the same in all societies: they could vary according to climate and geography. She offered a comparison to the

36 Mandeville, *Fable*, in Wade, *Studies*, Chapter 1, pp. 142–3.

37 Ibid., pp. 145, 150.

38 Ibid., p. 145.

39 Ibid., p. 152.

40 Ibid., Chapter 9, p. 181.

41 Ibid., Chapter 11, p. 185.

42 Ibid., Chapter 1, p. 144; Chapter 8, p. 173n4.

rules of card games: 'That which is a fault in *piquet* is not one in *renversi*[;] also that which is vice in Paris is virtue in Constantinople.'[43] So too with the customs of different cultures: they also could vary from society to society. This did not mean, however, that all had equal moral authority. Just as she assumed the universality of the Golden Rule, so she advocated the universal applicability of the principle of sufficient reason. She explained in her *Institutions* that one custom 'may be judged better than another; that is to say, when it has more reason on its side'.[44]

Even so, Du Châtelet had to assume that some passions and what Mandeville called 'personal interest' had the power to carry one away from the exercise of sufficient reason; so she postulated learned values that effectively dealt with such lapses. Although there would be laws and punishments to deal with the worst offenders, such as 'thieves, assassins, and poisoners', she believed with Mandeville that 'amour propre', pride, honour, and 'la honte' – the fear of dishonour, shame, ridicule, and disdain – could be even more powerful regulators of human behaviour.[45] Flattery too – as another quality by which Mandeville claimed men are manipulated – could explain the simplest adherence to what she described in her *Discours* on happiness as 'la bienséance' [social propriety]: conventional truths taught from childhood, which also acted as a check on men's and women's ill-considered 'appetites'. For Du Châtelet, 'exact conformity to the proprieties' was a virtue, and 'no one can in good faith claim not to be aware of them.' However, like customs and laws, these proprieties were not the same for everyone. In her *Discours* she explained: 'they vary according to rank in society, age, and circumstances.'[46]

In all her writings Du Châtelet indicated that she had a clear sense of her place in this ordered social world. At the core of her system of ethics was her understanding of the proper hierarchy of her society. Individuals functioned as part of a family. Families took their place in this hierarchy according to their rank, or état, as it would be identified in eighteenth-century French. Although she faithfully replicated Mandeville's sarcastic image of the well-born – 'des grands', as she calls them – with their ability to mask their self-interested behaviour, in other sections, and in her own *Discours* on happiness, she ignores these negative comments and presents a flattering picture of such privileged families. In her political philosophy it is they, not the king and his Church, who are the true pillars of French society, the models of moral and ethical behaviour. She intended her *Discours* as a guide for

> those who are called people of quality; that is to say, for those who are born with a fortune already made, more or less distinguished, more or less opulent, but such that they can maintain their station without being ashamed, and they are perhaps not the easiest to make happy.[47]

---

43 Ibid., p. 145. This assumption of links between culture, climate, and geography was common in her day. She might have first read of it in Montaigne.

44 Du Châtelet, *Institutions*, in *Selections*, Chapter 1, p. 132.

45 Du Châtelet, *Discours*, in *Selections*, p. 353; Mandeville, *Fable*, in Wade, *Studies*, Chapter 4, pp. 162–3.

46 Du Châtelet, *Discours*, in *Selections*, p. 353.

47 Ibid., pp. 350–51.

Following Mandeville, who ascribes 'manners and good-breeding' to these 'people of quality', she accepts his assumption that 'le savoir-vivre' and 'la politesse' are the outward means of hiding 'the most violent desires', but continues on a less cynical note. She believes that 'however ridiculous it is, *la politesse* enables us to live together in a more agreeable fashion than would be possible in the crude simplicity of nature.'[48]

Mandeville claimed that any man, even a savage, could learn these forms ('the proprieties'), and so make his behaviour acceptable to the best families. Although Du Châtelet faithfully presented Mandeville's example of such a transformation, she did not agree with its assumption of social mobility. For her, *bienséance* carried more than just the literal sense of 'the proprieties'. Unlike *politesse* and étiquette, which are taught to little boys and girls by their families, *bienséance* in its fullest sense, like the speed and lines of the thoroughbred horse, was the result of breeding. From these families of the highest état or station come those men of her *Discours* whose ambition it is 'to make their talents useful to their country and to serve their fellow citizens'. These are the individuals who seek 'the esteem of honourable men' rather than simple flattery, and who attain glory in war, diplomacy, and government.[49] For Du Châtelet her sex also represented an état – one just as defining as her social rank.

Though her sex kept her from any explicit political role beyond that dictated by her duties to family, she never doubted the privileges and the innate moral qualities of her birth. Like the men of the *haute noblesse*, she had no need to stifle all her passions in order to be virtuous. As she explains in the *Discours*, 'one must have passions to be happy, but they must be made to serve our happiness.'[50] For people of her rank, this is a simple task. True to her penchant for mathematical certainty in matters of morality, she laid down an 'axiom that lies in the depths of the hearts of all men'. It is the 'reproaches of his conscience', 'the scorn that he feels he deserves and that he experiences', that is 'a kind of torture' for a man. To be despised is to feel despair. 'So', she concludes, 'one must never be immoral if one does not want to be unhappy.' To her, a happy life is by definition a moral, virtuous life. The women and men of her état therefore monitor themselves:

> One is an exacting judge of oneself, and the more one can bear witness to oneself that one has fulfilled one's duties, done all the good that one could do, that in short, one is virtuous, the more one tastes this interior satisfaction that one can call the health of the soul.[51]

Mandeville had imagined a society of individuals whose everyday actions, however venal and selfish, contributed to the advance of the nation. In theory, in this commercially advantaged nation any individual – however immoral, and

[48] Du Châtelet, *Fable*, in Wade, *Studies*, Chapter 4, pp. 164–6.

[49] Du Châtelet, *Discours*, in *Selections*, p. 354.

[50] Ibid., p. 357.

[51] Du Châtelet, *Discours*, in *Selections*, p. 354.

regardless of birth or family connection – could rise and prosper. Du Châtelet, in contrast, remained committed to a society based on distance and deference. Like the order of the planetary universe, the best families had their natural place and function; those of lesser birth, theirs. She, like the others of her rank, acted from well-considered reasonable choices. Their happiness was by definition a moral state.[52] In Du Châtelet's society, those of lesser birth could marvel at those placed so far above them – the individuals nurtured and protected by their privileged families who could ignore the external authorities of king and Church, and who required no such entities to regulate their behaviour and punish their transgressions. Instead, they lived by their own internal sense of *la morale*. Even she, a female, could formulate moral sentiments and assert that she had found the most reasonable, and therefore the best, laws of ethical behaviour: laws as certain as those governing other aspects of her universe.

Inadvertently, Du Châtelet espoused a political philosophy that challenged all three pillars of the French state. Her critical view of kings and her heretical comments on the Bible are obviously antagonistic. However, even when she was positive in her portrayal of the power and significance of family to the French state, her internalization of rules of *la morale* by select members of a society posed a threat more dangerous to France's institutions than Mandeville's parable to show vice's beneficial effects. Her 'axioms' on the moral power of one's own conscience, cleansed of their aristocratic taint, would be repeated in the radical political philosophies of the future. Du Châtelet assumed her clandestine writings would be read only by the 'gens qui pensent': thinking people. In this she assumed membership of another hierarchy – one based on intellectual attainments, not of the formally educated, but of those Locke characterized in his *Essay Concerning Human Understanding* as able to use their reason to evaluate, categorize, and analyse the information gained through the senses. In this she belongs with other *philosophes*, such as d'Holbach, Helvétius, and Jean-Jacques Rousseau: each of whom formulated his own moral system, and all of whom challenged the system enshrined in the traditional dictates of France's king, Church, and family privilege. Du Châtelet had created her own paradox: a noblewoman espousing a doctrine that could be the justification for destroying the very pillars on which her society was based. In a real sense, among her heirs are not just the feminists of the twenty-first century, but all those inspired with similar rational certainty about the universality of their moral sentiments – sentiments that not only conferred elite status but also confirmed it. Intellect rather than birth became the measure. Sadly, intellectual prowess has proved no more trustworthy as a support for ethical systems than the flawed moralities produced, in previous centuries, by other measures.

---

[52] Although Du Châtelet makes no direct reference in any of her writings to her reading in Cicero and Horace, or to Voltaire's and other contemporaries' interest in the Stoics (such as that of Bernard le Bovier de Fontenelle, a leading *philosophe* of early Enlightenment Paris), these could easily have been factors in her equation of elite happiness with exemplary morality.

Chapter 2
Royalist and Radical: Octavie Belot on Rousseau and the Social Order

Paul Gibbard

Introduction

In the 1750s Octavie Belot published two treatises on political subjects, the first a polemic against Rousseau's *Discourse on Inequality* (1755), the second a contribution to the debate then unfolding about the proper role of the nobility in French society. At this time political works by women writers were considered oddities in France: the novel, the memoir, and the private letter were deemed more suitable forms of female expression. Any woman writer who sought to publish a work on a scientific, philosophical, or political topic faced a major obstacle – as Jean Bloch points out, inadequately educated women had little hope of having their work acknowledged when they were competing with highly educated men in these areas.[1] A small number of women, including Emilie Du Châtelet (1706–1749) and Elisabeth Ferrand (1700–1752), were able to make contributions to scientific knowledge. In the philosophical and political spheres, women's contributions tended to fall into a limited range of categories: they produced pamphlets on education, on the equality of the sexes, or on correct behaviour in society. Direct engagement with the ideas of the male philosophers outside these areas was rarer: Marie Huber (1695–1753) did so on theological questions, and Du Châtelet's writings in such domains, such as her *Discourse on Happiness*, were in the main published posthumously. It was only toward the end of the century, on the 'eve of the Revolution' as Bloch puts it, that women's writing became 'more political and we find them writing petitions, pamphlets and articles.'[2] Only then were women writers – such as Olympe de Gouges (1748–1793), Marie Jodin (1741–1790), Louise-Félicité de Keralio (1758–1821), and Sophie de Grouchy (1764–1822) – able to disseminate political ideas more broadly. Belot therefore occupies a highly unusual position, as one of the few published female political commentators of the mid-century. In what follows I analyse Belot's arguments in her treatises on Rousseau and on the role of the nobility, and trace the ways in which she both

1 J. Bloch, 'The Eighteenth Century: Women Writing, Women Learning', in S. Stephens (ed.) *A History of Women's Writing in France* (Cambridge, 2000), p. 84.

2 Ibid., p. 98.

defends the status quo and yet, in seeming contradiction, proposes changes to the class structure. I relate the ideas she expresses in the treatises to the political observations she makes in later writings – in the prefaces to her translations of English-language works, and in her private letters of the 1770s, 1780s, and 1790s – which reveal her increasing disillusionment with political processes.

When in 1756 she published her first treatise, *Reflections of a Provincial Woman on the Discourse of Monsieur Rousseau, Citizen of Geneva, Touching on the Origin of the Inequality of Conditions among Men,*[3] Belot was little known in French literary circles. Born Octavie Guichard in Paris in 1719, she was the daughter of a bourgeois father and a mother who belonged to the Burgundian branch of a noble family of Flanders.[4] At the age of 19 she had married the Parisian lawyer Charles-Edme Belot: a widower, and her senior by a considerable number of years. He was plagued by financial difficulties, and one of the recurrent themes of Octavie's life was established at this time: her long struggle with penury. Their union produced a son, who would follow his father's example and make a career in the law.[5] Octavie's marriage to Charles-Edme Belot was not a happy one, according to later comments in her correspondence. It was only after his death that she would achieve a certain prominence through her literary work and become acquainted or correspond with leading intellectual figures including Voltaire, David Hume, Helvétius, the Comte de Buffon, and Benjamin Franklin.

Reflections of a Provincial Woman on the Discourse of Monsieur Rousseau (1756)

Belot's *Reflections* take the form of a detailed reply to Rousseau's *Discourse on Inequality*, which had been published in 1755. This discourse was a sort of continuation of the argument he had made five years earlier in *Discourse on the Sciences and the Arts*, in which he had held that the development of the sciences and arts had been accompanied by an increase in moral corruption. Rousseau also linked the sciences and arts to social inequality, arguing in a letter to a critic that

---

3 O. Belot, *Réflexions d'une provinciale sur le discours de Monsieur Rousseau, citoyen de Genève, touchant l'origine de l'inégalité des conditions parmi les hommes* (London, 1756).

4 For details about Belot's life see M.-L. Girou Swiderski, 'Une chambre à soi: Le thème du logement dans la correspondance de Mme Belot', in Servanne Woodward (ed.), *Altered Narratives: Female Eighteenth-Century French Authors Reinterpreted* (London, Ontario, 1997), pp. 15–31; and 'Lettres de Mme de Meinières à Mme de Lénoncourt (1770–1774)', in E.C. Goldsmith and C.H. Winn (eds), *Lettres de femmes: Textes inédits et oubliés du XVIe au XVIIIe siècle* (Paris, 2005), pp. 379–420. I am very grateful to Mme Girou Swiderski for sending me transcripts of Belot's correspondence with the Marquise de Lénoncourt and François-Antoine Devaux.

5 See Voltaire's letter to Belot of 9 September 1772, in which he thanks her for sending him a copy of a legal *mémoire* written by her son: Voltaire, *Correspondence and Related Documents*, ed. T. Besterman (52 vols, Oxford, 1968–1977), D17905.

wealth arises from inequality, and from wealth come luxury and idleness – 'and from luxury come the fine arts, and from idleness, the sciences'.[6] Rousseau took the opportunity to expand on these ideas when the Academy of Dijon offered a prize for an essay on the question: 'What is the origin of inequality among men, and whether it is authorized by the law of nature.'

To find the cause of inequality in society, Rousseau felt it necessary to examine both the process by which society had developed and the nature of man prior to the existence of society. He wished to show that both Hobbes and Locke had been wrong about natural man: Hobbes arguing that men's equality in a state of nature would keep them at war with one another, and Locke that a superior power must be instituted not so much for the maintenance of peace as for the protection of property. Rousseau sought to show that man in the state of nature had no interest in violence or property, and that these were things that developed as society formed: Hobbes and Locke had got things the wrong way round.[7] In the second part of the discourse Rousseau describes the changes accompanying man's progression from the state of nature to living in society, and how this gave rise to all the world's evils.

Although his *Discourse on Inequality* was read across Europe, Rousseau complained that very few people properly understood it. Critical reviews appeared in the literary journals, and long attempts at refutation were published. Rousseau was seen to be taking aim at a wide range of targets: progress, science, the arts, the monarchy, the nation, the Church, God, and even humanity itself. Priests, scientists, and moral philosophers joined in opposition to his claim that man in a state of nature had lacked moral sense and the faculty of reason.[8] A Jesuit priest, Louis-Bertrand Castel, in his book *Moral Man Opposed to the Physical Man of Monsieur Rousseau* (1756), argued that 'man is, according to the Scriptures, the Gospel, and the Catechism, according to experience itself, an entirely moral and supernatural being,' and furthermore, as man is made in God's image, he cannot not simply have 'the physical and corporeal being of an animal'.[9] The naturalist Charles Bonnet suggested that Rousseau was wrong to distinguish two types of man: natural man and social man. 'Everything that derives immediately from the faculties of man', Bonnet argued, 'must be the result of his nature.... If the state of society derives from man's faculties, then it is *natural* to man.' Voltaire dressed his rejection of Rousseau's argument in humour, declaring that while Rousseau painted an attractive picture of the state of nature, he himself was too old to go back to 'walking on all fours'.[10]

---

6 J.-J. Rousseau, *Œuvres complètes*, ed. B. Gagnebin and M. Raymond (5 vols, Paris, 1961–1995), vol. 3, p. 50. The translations from the French in this chapter are my own.

7 On this point see R. Wokler, *Rousseau* (Oxford, 1995), pp. 36–7.

8 On the reception of Rousseau's *Discourse on Inequality* see G.R. Havens, 'Eighteenth-Century Critics of Rousseau's Second *Discourse*', in J. Macary (ed.), *Essays on the Age of Enlightenment* (Geneva, 1977), pp. 143–54; and R. Trousson, *Jean-Jacques Rousseau jugé par ses contemporains* (Paris, 2000), Chapter 2.

9 L.-B. Castel, *L'Homme moral opposé à l'homme physique de M. R***: Lettres philosophiques où l'on réfute le déisme du jour* (Toulouse, 1756), p. 44.

10 Voltaire to Rousseau, 30 August 1755, in Voltaire, *Correspondence*, D6451.

In her own response, Belot immediately sets herself apart from other critics of the *Discourse on Inequality*. The very title of her book, *Reflections of a Provincial Woman on the Discourse of Monsieur Rousseau*, draws attention to her sex, and in the first lines she declares:

> I am perhaps going to embitter M. Rousseau still more against the consequences of perfected reason. He will view with indignation the audacity of a woman who dares to think and even to write. However, if I do not exaggerate my rights and my capacities, it seems to me that, as I am a part of humanity, I am permitted to raise my weak voice up to the philosopher who addresses his words to humanity.[11]

She differs from other commentators not just in this respect, but also through her social position. In her penniless state, she explains, she is 'persecuted by fortune', a 'victim of prejudice', 'disgraced by nature', and 'quite unhappy with society'. She has therefore reached a sort of neutral state from which she can equably judge Rousseau's arguments as to 'which is preferable, between the pure state of nature and civil life'.[12] She explains her method:

> Although I refrain from proudly entering the lists with M. Rousseau, I dare to resist his eloquence, to propose my objections, to follow his steps, and halt them sometimes to dispute the ground, like an Iroquois woman unfamiliar with literary reputations, or like a female citizen of the civilized world, who defends as a good patriot the laws, morals, and privileges of her country.[13]

Belot seems to be responding directly to words Rousseau had addressed to the 'kind and virtuous female citizens' of Geneva in the 'Dedication' to his *Discourse on Inequality*. He had spoken of 'that precious half of the Republic that creates the happiness of the other half, and whose gentleness and wisdom maintain peace and good morals' – but had restricted women's influence on the state to their actions in the domestic sphere.[14] Belot implies that the role of a 'good female citizen' may extend beyond this limited realm – and out into the male world of letters. In what follows, Belot traces Rousseau's argument, at times point by point, and seeks to show first that Rousseau's state of nature could never have in fact existed, and second that, even if it had, such a state of nature is on balance inferior to life in civil society.

The title of Belot's work and her opening comments raise a number of questions. Belot declares herself to be a provincial, but it is not clear how accurate this claim is. Although her mother's family had links with Burgundy, Belot herself was born in Paris and seems to have spent most of her life there. The 'provincial' label may derive from a sort of modesty – as a way for Belot to seek the reader's indulgence and to emphasize the marginal position from which she launches her

11 Belot, *Réflexions*, pp. 1–2.
12 Belot, *Réflexions*, p. 2.
13 Belot, *Réflexions*, pp. 3–4.
14 Rousseau, *Œuvres complètes*, vol. 3, pp. 119–20.

polemic against Rousseau. Equally, her publisher may have felt there was some novelty in a response to Rousseau authored not just by a woman, but by a provincial woman, and he may have included these two elements in the title to arouse interest. Certainly the sex of the book's author drew comment from reviewers:

> We think that this provincial woman has the best manners in Paris, that her reflections are those of an intelligent woman who writes just as well as she reasons, and that they would do honour to the most highly educated man. She battles Monsieur Rousseau's opinions with all the grace of her sex, and all the robustness of ours.[15]

Elie Fréron commented on the situation with irony in the *Année littéraire*, suggesting that Rousseau's declaration of war on humanity had caused even women to enlist in its defence:

> Women are picking up their pens to avenge the human race, which has been degraded and defiled by the philosopher of Geneva. I am not making this up: the in-octavo brochure I announce here ... is genuinely the work of a woman.[16]

And Fréron went on to observe that Belot's writing style, which he judged distinctively feminine, was one of the virtues of the book: 'The author combats her opponent with as much strength as courtesy, and her arguments, which are always accompanied by words of praise, are all the more persuasive in the mouth of a woman.'[17] When Belot's *Reflections* were later brought to Voltaire's attention, he wrote to Belot:

> I would have been enchanted by your works even if you had been a man. But judge of my sentiments when I learn that you are of the sex that has civilized our own, and without which we would be mere savages as Jean-Jacques wishes us to be.[18]

In the first section of her argument, Belot takes issue with the state of nature that Rousseau describes. According to Rousseau's theory, individuals lived alone in the wild, which supplied all their physical needs; they were healthy and had few passions, no sense of family, no concern with the acquisition of knowledge, and very little natural inequality. He saw man as a type of animal driven by two instincts: toward self-preservation, and toward pity or compassion for other creatures. But man was distinguished from other animals by two particular qualities: being a 'free agent' (that is, able to act according to choice rather than simply by instinct), and having the ability to perfect himself, for which Rousseau coined the term 'perfectibility'.

---

15 *Mercure de France* (June 1756), p. 119.

16 *Année littéraire* (1756), vol. 3, pp. 73–4.

17 Ibid., p. 82.

18 Voltaire to Belot, 26 March 1759, in Voltaire, *Correspondence*, D8213.

Belot finds this approach flawed from the beginning. Rousseau removes man's 'supernatural gifts', memory, reason, understanding, will, and so on, in order to return man to a state of nature; but, Belot argues, as long as man has these gifts, he will never reside in a state of nature. They must in some sense be essential to man, she suggests; otherwise, animals would have developed them over time. To put it simply, the creature Rousseau is describing in a state of nature cannot be thought of as man. Seeking to refute Rousseau's picture of man in nature possessing only a very low order of ideas, Belot invokes Locke's theory of knowledge from *An Essay Concerning Human Understanding* (1690). Rousseau had himself discussed Locke in the *Discourse*, but with reference to the *Two Treatises on Government*. Belot argues that while both men and animals share ideas based on sensation, or the perception of exterior objects, man has 'another source of ideas which animals do not – what Locke calls reflection, or interior sense, that is the perception of the operation of our soul on the ideas it receives from our senses'.[19] As long as man is granted this capacity for reflection, then he is able to develop complex ideas, which will quickly take him out of the state of nature.

Belot swiftly dismisses another of Rousseau's arguments. She says she does not clearly understand the metaphysical distinction he introduces by which man differs from the animals in his quality of being a 'free agent'. While Rousseau meant simply that man unlike animals has the capacity to choose whether or not to obey the commands of instinct, Belot argues that if man has this quality then he has the ability to choose and compare – which is another way of saying he possesses the capacity to reason. She also sees Rousseau's idea of perfectibility as being at odds with man remaining in a state of nature. If man has perfectibility, she argues, why would it have remained in abeyance for a long period; would it not have lifted man out of the state of nature in the earliest times? Belot is particularly horrified by Rousseau's characterization of man in a state of nature as an anti-social creature. She instead appeals to experience, and suggests that love is a powerful force for drawing people together, establishing familial bonds, and for inducing people to perceive the mutual benefits of society.

Having established that man could never have dwelt in Rousseau's state of nature, Belot then goes on to argue that, even if that had once been the way of things, it was in no way superior to life in civilized society. She believes that Rousseau is self-serving in his argument – he deliberately avoids giving a realistic picture of the hardships endured by natural man while neglecting to mention any of the benefits that accrue from living in civilized society.

Unlike many commentators, who concerned themselves only with addressing Rousseau's theory of man in the state of nature, Belot also addressed the second part of Rousseau's discourse, which dealt with the entrenchment of inequality in society. Rousseau had suggested that society arose out of a trick played on the poor by the wealthy, who sought to protect their own property by proposing universal submission to a supreme authority that would protect all people alike. It was at

---

[19] Belot, *Réflexions*, p. 17.

this point that natural inequalities of abilities and talents, which had enabled some to get ahead of others, were enshrined as political inequality. Belot does not agree that the wealthy perpetrate a 'trick' on the poor; rather she considers that natural inequalities in the area of individual talents or characteristics must lead to the creation of political inequality, in the following manner:

> If humanity separated into different groupings, it is likely that the man who was the shrewdest, the most intelligent, the strongest, the most compassionate – in short, of the greatest help – inspired confidence in others, and took them, so to speak, under his protection. If humanity separated into different herds, the strongest, the wildest, the most courageous and most violent man inspired fear in all, and put them in the position of having either to unite against him or to side with him. From this moment you have nascent inequality marking out different classes of men. Here you have tribute obtained or demanded; here you have the monarch and his subjects, or the despot and his slaves.[20]

This line of argument allows Belot to arrive at a conclusion that encapsulates the political slant of her book as a whole: if natural inequality was the 'initial cause' of political inequality, it is 'no longer the cause of daily political inequality'.[21] This is a conservative argument, favouring the maintenance of the status quo, as it asserts that current social inequality is not attributable to current actions. In any case, she suggests, social or political inequality is not necessarily a bad thing:

> Moral inequality is not degrading in itself ...; for either it is founded on merit, and is therefore just, or it results from some abuse of power, and therefore offers no affront to one's self-respect or philosophical pride.[22]

While Belot agrees with Rousseau that political power is often founded on arbitrary inequality in power and property rather than inequality of merit, she nevertheless affirms:

> Power built on such a base is legitimate: all that follows from it is good, for if the human race had not entrusted power to anybody, the same vices that cause some to abuse authority would cause them to abuse their freedom.[23]

She offers one further reason for respecting an authority that is based on natural inequality:

> Political inequality, so deadly to humanity according to Monsieur Rousseau, retains a benefit that he does not perceive, in at least conserving the appearance of natural inequality. I shall explain: those who hold power at present solely

20 Ibid., pp. 49–50.
21 Ibid., p. 50.
22 Ibid., p. 85.
23 Ibid., p. 87.

> through the right of birth, reputation, or wealth contract with society the undertaking to conduct themselves in their place as if they occupied this as a result of their greater merit.[24]

Belot supports this logic by arguing that laws, along with public opinion and prejudices, act to constrain rulers, and to orient them toward virtue. Her defence of the existing order does not neglect the sensibilities of those who lack money or power: she urges them to accept their lot with stoical endurance, in recognition of the fact that the stability of society is more important than equality among its members.

These criticisms of Rousseau perhaps amount not so much to a point-by-point refutation of the *Discourse on Inequality* as a general dismissal of it. Once Belot states that Rousseau is wrong to argue that man in a state of nature does not possess reason, her other arguments more or less follow. Nevertheless, several contemporary reviewers agreed that hers was the most coherent and best-written of the published responses; and in addition to the praise offered by the *Année littéraire* and the *Mercure de France*, the *Journal des savants* called Belot's work 'agreeable, ingenious, and often well thought-out', while the *Bibliothèque des sciences et des beaux-arts* stated that 'this provincial woman is one of the most successful adversaries that M. Rousseau has encountered'. Belot's attack on Rousseau won her admirers across a spectrum of positions: her defence of the political status quo pleased conservative readers, while her rejection of Rousseau's notion of primitive man appealed to the philosophers, who had been shocked when the Genevan, whom they had considered to be one of their own, rejected the notion that growth in property, luxury, and the arts and sciences were conducive to progress toward enlightenment.

Observations on the Nobility and the Third Estate (1758)

Two years after the *Reflections*, Belot returned to some of the same arguments in a different context when she published her *Observations on the Nobility and the Third Estate* (1758).[25] It was a treatise on a topical question of the day – a question concerning the role of the nobility of French society, and more particularly whether the nobility should engage in trade. The debate had waxed and waned for decades. Voltaire for example, in the *Philosophical Letters* (1734), had urged the French aristocracy to follow the example of the younger sons of British peers who conducted commercial ventures; but Montesquieu argued against this in *Of the Spirit of Laws* (1748) on the grounds that it would destroy the nobility without benefiting trade.[26] The debate intensified in 1756, when the Abbé Coyer produced

---

24 Ibid., p. 93.

25 O. Belot, *Observations sur la noblesse et le tiers-état* ('Amsterdam' [Rouen], 1758).

26 See W. Doyle, *Aristocracy and its Enemies in the Age of Revolution* (Oxford, 2009), p. 50.

a book in response to the posthumous publication of the views of the Marquis de Lassay, who had held that the true role of the nobility lay in their military calling. Coyer's riposte, *The Commercial Nobility*, was scathing: he attacked the idle and penniless ranks of the French nobility, and suggested that the law preventing their entry to the world of business should be abolished. This was the only measure, he held, that offered hope for the preservation of the nobility. After Coyer, many more writers joined the debate.[27] Among these was the Chevalier d'Arcq, whose book *The Military Nobility* (1756) reiterated the argument that the true calling of the nobility lay in the military sphere and highlighted the nefarious connection between commerce and republicanism.[28]

When Belot entered into the controversy with her *Observations on the Nobility and the Third Estate* in 1758, she was not a complete outsider to what was occurring. In 1757, the year after the publication of her *Reflections*, Belot's husband had died and she had begun a liaison with the Chevalier d'Arcq. It became common knowledge in literary circles, and Thiriot commented in a letter to Voltaire of 1759:

> For several years she has been living with M. le Chevalier d'Arcq who has instilled in her a taste for studying and writing, and it appears that the pupil has surpassed her teacher.[29]

This association seems to have continued until 1764, when the *Mémoires secrets* reported that she 'broke with the Chevalier d'Arcq, with whom she was living'.[30] Of aristocratic origins, Philippe-Auguste de Sainte-Foix, the Chevalier d'Arcq, was a cavalry captain who had left the military and entered the literary milieu, writing fiction, history, and philosophy.[31] He was described by the *Mémoires secrets* as a 'man strongly criticized for his morals', and like Belot was continually short of money.[32]

---

27 For a list of the pamphlets published see H. Lévy-Bruhl, 'La noblesse de France et le commerce à la fin de l'ancien régime', *Revue de l'histoire moderne*, 8:8 (1933): pp. 221–2.

28 See S. Maza, 'Luxury, Morality, and Social Change: Why there was no Middle-Class Consciousness in Pre-Revolutionary France', in G. Kates (ed.), *The French Revolution*, 2nd edn (London, 2008), p. 117; and J.M. Smith, *Nobility Reimagined: The Patriotic Nation in Eighteenth-Century France* (Ithaca, NY, 2005), pp. 135–7.

29 Thiriot to Voltaire, 23 February 1759, in Voltaire, *Correspondence*, D8137.

30 *Mémoires secrets pour servir à l'histoire de la République des Lettres en France depuis 1762 jusqu'à nos jours* (London, 1783–1789), vol. 2 , p. 63, entry of 26 May 1764.

31 See J.-P. Brancourt, 'Un théoricien de la société au XVIIIe siècle: Le chevalier d'Arcq', *Revue historique*, 250 (1973): pp. 337–62; and F.E. Sutcliffe, 'The Abbé Coyer and the Chevalier d'Arcq', *Bulletin of the John Rylands University Library of Manchester*, 65:1 (1982): pp. 235–45.

32 *Mémoires secrets*, vol. 2, pp. 298–9, entry of 10 December 1765; d'Arcq's financial difficulties are revealed in his private papers, Bibliothèque nationale de France, Manuscrits Français, 33001–33002, according to P.B. Cheney, *Revolutionary Commerce: Globalization and the French Monarchy* (Cambridge, MA, 2010), p. 253n14.

The attitude Belot expresses toward existing social hierarchies in her *Observations* is broadly consistent with that adopted by the Chevalier d'Arcq and with the general argument she herself had made in her *Reflections*. She is of the view that it is necessary to conserve the nobility in its current form in order to ensure France's military security. Within this overarching framework, however, Belot offers a number of original and radical contributions to the debate.

She opens the work by drawing attention to the claims of the common people, which she believes have been overlooked by both Coyer and d'Arcq:

> Does not this most numerous, and perhaps most useful, portion of the kingdom ... have a right to attract the recognition and attention of the others?[33]

She exposes flaws in the arguments of both Coyer and d'Arcq. Coyer, she says, errs in advocating that nobles should enter into commerce, as this would risk eroding the social divisions, and removing the middle ground between the artisans and the nobility. Equally, d'Arcq is at fault for suggesting that only the nobility is capable of heroism: this sort of argument may offend the great majority of the French. But one of the main problems with the controversy over the role of the nobility, she suggests, is that by its very existence it risks stirring up resentment among the commoners:

> It is ... obvious that *The Commercial Nobility* and *The Military Nobility* and all the satellites of these two works have served only to awaken the self-regard of the common people, which until now has been sleeping enfolded by wealth or labour, and to bring to their attention the supposed distance that exists between a commoner and a gentleman, and to make this interval more humiliating.[34]

Belot then considers recasting the debate in the language Rousseau had used in his *Discourse on Inequality*, and suggests that if one does so, doubts may arise about the right of the nobility to enjoy their position:

> Perhaps, if it were a question of discussing natural inequality, or moral inequality, the nobility would appear out of place; perhaps if one wished to form a new society, or create a good government, it would be better not to admit these hereditary distinctions. Certain striking actions, certain useful qualities, certain brilliant virtues lay at their origin, but can one deny that often the sign remains when the thing no longer exists?[35]

A 'legislator-philosopher' who wished to devise a society of the future, she says, would undoubtedly discard hereditary distinctions; and she then sets about describing in detail her vision of this possible new society. Belot considers the most important elements in any society to be the means of subsistence, freedom, security, and the pleasures of society, in that order; or more simply: wheat, good laws,

33 Belot, *Observations*, pp. 2–3.

34 Ibid., pp. 20–21.

35 Ibid., p. 30.

courage, and morals. She structures her society accordingly. The wisest men would be given the task of leading the nation and devising laws. The most able men would then be given the task of cultivating the nation's agricultural produce; the next most able group would form the military, and the group after that the artisans. The particular form of government is not important, she suggests; it could as easily be a democracy as a monarchy. This leads to the radical suggestion that no boundaries should prevent individuals with suitable talents from moving between classes:

> Once this government had been established, whether it be democratic, aristocratic, or monarchical, and the class divisions made according to the talents and virtues of each person, equitably employed, it appears simple to allow nature and the laws to follow their own course, filling out each class with subjects who are suitable to it, without regard to the class in which they are born.[36]

The society envisioned here by Belot embodies one of the principles she had set out in her *Reflections*: natural inequalities of talent shape the initial structure of society. But then she diverges from her earlier assertion that those who find themselves without money or power should bear their lot with stoical endurance. Instead, she suggests, those who have particular talents should face no constraints in moving between social classes.

Having formulated this radical proposal, Belot then seeks to soften its impact by declaring that her vision of society is simply a harmless piece of invention. She restates her support for the French monarchy, and in an elaborate metaphor comparing its structure to that of a palace, argues that it would be dangerous to make any alterations to it, as these might cause it, like the palace, to come tumbling down.

The most original elements in Belot's *Observations* are not to be found in her arguments over which side should be taken in the debate over the nobility – that is, whether it is Coyer or d'Arcq who is substantially correct. In fact, she opts simply to endorse d'Arcq's conclusion: 'France is a monarchy,' she states; 'its dominant cast of mind must be a military one.' And as the nobility have successfully borne this military obligation in the past, it is they, she says, who must continue to do so in the future, rather than be distracted by commercial ventures. What is more interesting than the side she comes down on in the debate is the apparent influence of Rousseau's *Discourse on Inequality* on her work, which seems to have impelled her to consider the question of how naturally unequal talents affect the shape of society. Her conclusion is a bold one: in any rational future society, she suggests, the rise of talent must not be impeded by boundaries of class. For this, her second and final treatise on political philosophy, Belot drew praise from the *Mercure de France*, which if 'undecided about the principles of Madame ***' nevertheless applauded her 'courageous zeal', and the 'liveliness and precision of her style'.[37] The *Journal encyclopédique* was less favourable, arguing that her arguments were not as convincing as those of the Chevalier d'Arcq.[38]

---

36 Ibid., pp. 40–41.

37 *Mercure de France* (September 1758), p. 117.

38 *Journal encyclopédique* 8:1 (November 1758), pp. 123–9.

Later Years: Prefaces and Correspondence

It is not entirely clear why Belot gave up writing political treatises after the *Observations*. She may have decided that she stood a better chance of making money by publishing translations from the English. Friedrich Grimm, in the *Correspondance littéraire*, described her change of career in these somewhat fanciful terms:

> Madame Belot is the widow of a lawyer, who at his death left her with no means apart from a pension of 60 *livres* a year. In order to avoid any expenses, she lived on milk, sold her pension and used the 1,200 *livres* that she got for it to learn English, with the aim acquiring a means of supporting herself, through translating.[39]

In any case, over the seven years from 1759 to 1765 Belot published five works of translation based on English originals. Her first was a *Miscellany of English Literature* (1759),[40] which included verse, short fiction, and essays by writers including Samuel Johnson, Hume, and Matthew Prior. It was followed by translations of Johnson's *Rasselas* in 1760,[41] Sarah Fielding's *Ophelia* in 1763,[42] and of sections of Hume's *History of England* in 1763 and 1765.[43] Although Belot changed the mode of her literary output, she continued to express political views, making use of the opportunities that fell to her. She addressed political topics in the prefaces to her translations – perhaps an oblique way of overcoming the problems of the market-place. She maintained a prolific correspondence, and from the 1760s to the 1790s her letters reveal a close interest in the turmoil enveloping French society.

The modesty Belot had expressed at the start of the *Reflections* is a recurring motif in her prefaces. Introducing the *Miscellany*, she confesses that her translation of Matthew Prior's poem 'The Nut-Brown Maid' does not do justice to the original, and that she in fact has 'no right to rank herself in any class of belletrists'.[44] But

---

39 F.M. Grimm and D. Diderot, *Correspondance littéraire, philosophique et critique par Grimm, Diderot, Raynal, Meister, etc.*, ed. Maurice Tourneur (16 vols, Paris, 1877–1882), part 4, vol. 2, pp. 195–6.

40 O. Belot, *Mélanges de littérature angloise, traduits par Madame B**** (2 parts in 1 vol., 'La Haye' [Paris], 1759).

41 O. Belot, *Histoire de Rasselas, prince d'Abyssinie, par M. Jhonnson* [*sic*] *et traduite de l'anglois par Mme B**** ('Amsterdam' [Paris], 1760).

42 O. Belot, *Ophélie, roman traduit de l'anglois par M. B**** (2 vols, 'Amsterdam', 1763).

43 O. Belot, *Histoire de la maison de Tudor sur le trône d'Angleterre. Traduite de l'anglois* (2 vols, 'Amsterdam' [Paris], 1763); O. Belot, *Histoire de la maison de Plantagenet sur le trône d'Angleterre depuis l'invasion de Jules César jusqu'à l'avènement de Henri VI, par M. Hume. Traduite de l'anglois par madame B***** (2 vols, 'Amsterdam', 1765).

44 Belot, 'Préface', *Mélanges*, p. vi.

such modesty, which had not prevented her from launching strong criticisms of Rousseau in the *Reflections*, does not restrain her hand in the preface to the *Miscellany*. She devotes forty of its forty-eight pages to a dismissal of Hume's *The Liberty of the Press*, and especially disapproves of the contrast he draws between liberty under England's 'mixed government' and France's 'absolute monarchy':

> Monsieur Hume considers a people subject to monarchical government to be highly enslaved, and that subject to a republican government to be highly free; is this not to create too vague and exaggerated an idea of the two?[45]

For Belot, the most important thing is not the nature of a particular government, but rather the type of laws the government enforces:

> What does it matter whether it is one or several people that preside over affairs, once fundamental rules have been established to guide the administration and these are out of the grasp of arbitrary power?[46]

In a defence of the status quo in France as strong as she had mounted in *Reflections*, Belot here denies that republican government is superior to monarchy, and accuses those who disagree of a 'secret inclination towards licence'.[47] In her preface to Johnson's *Rasselas* she again reaffirms an earlier view, advocating stoical acceptance of one's lot. By 1763, her attitude toward Hume is more conciliatory; she assures readers of her translation of the *History* that Hume is an impartial historian whose only aim is to reveal the truth.

When Belot remarried in 1765, her public literary career came to an end. She devoted herself instead to helping her new husband, Jean-Baptiste-François Durey de Meinières, in his legal research. Durey de Meinières had been *président* of the second *chambre des enquêtes* in the *parlement* of Paris, aligned with those who had sometimes stood firm against the king's wishes. Having endured exile in Bourges from 1753 to 1754 (following the crisis over the denial of sacraments),[48] he retired from the *parlement* in 1758. The entry that Belot (henceforth Mme de Meinières) gained into the milieu of the Paris *parlement* undoubtedly brought a shift in her political perspective, as she began associating with figures intent on constraining royal power.

A brief survey of some of Mme de Meinières's letters from the 1770s through to the 1790s reveals her changing attitudes toward political institutions. In July

---

45 Ibid., p. xiv.

46 Ibid., p. xxix.

47 Ibid., p. xxx.

48 On this crisis see J. Rogister, *Louis XV and the Parlement de Paris (1737–1755)* (Cambridge, 1995), pp. 101–21; and on Durey de Meinières see F. Bluche, *Les Magistrats du parlement de Paris au XVIIIe siècle (1715–1771)* (Besançon, 1960), p. 293; and J. Swann, *Politics and the Parlement of Paris under Louis XV, 1754–1774* (Cambridge, 1995), pp. 145–7.

1771, after Louis XV had sought to limit the *parlement*'s power to question his decisions by their use of remonstrances, Belot wrote of her concern to her friend the Marquise de Lénoncourt. Without questioning the king's own integrity, she was anxious about what his successors might do:

> If Louis XV were immortal or if Henri IV could be reborn, I would applaud: I would be the first to sign article three of the December edict. But do their successors, and the ministers of their successors, have an equal right to the people's confidence?

She then drew a comparison between the king and the head of a family, and asked:

> I would like to know who would run the risk of marriage without fully knowing her husband, if a law permitted the husband to impose and recognize no other law than his own will within his family.... Isn't a king, a good king, the head of a family? Does he wish to transfer to posterity the unhappy power to do evil, and does he wish to expose posterity to all the risks engendered by the abuse of power? To institute this edict would entail an unending list of terrible risks for monarchs and their subjects. It goes against natural law, which is inalienable; it will introduce the reign of might, violence, strife, etc. etc.[49]

It is generally the king's ministers, rather than the king himself, who bear the brunt of her criticism. In a letter of 1774 to François-Antoine ('Panpan') Devaux she decries the ministers who abused the king's 'name and authority, and sought to give the character of laws to arbitrary wishes that were contrary to the good of his subjects, to the rights of his subjects, and to the very interests of royal authority'.[50] It is this precise problem – relating to the imposition of laws – that she had alluded to in the preface to her *Miscellany* of 1759, seemingly with no thought that such a problem could arise in France.

An increasing cynicism about political processes becomes evident in her letters to Elizabeth Montagu, the English bluestocking whom she met during the latter's visit to Paris in 1776. Montagu had stayed in Chaillot, near Mme de Meinières, and the two may have been introduced by their mutual friend the Marquise du Deffand. In March 1777, for example, at a time when Britain and France were again heading toward war, Mme de Meinières offers Montagu a gloomy reflection combining Hobbes's pessimistic view of man in the state of nature with Rousseau's criticisms of the evils of society:

> If man could remain in that chimeric state of nature, he would be in a state of war with his fellow; and yet as soon as he is in society, inequality is introduced; each person is distinguished by his rank, order, or function. The right of the strongest or the cleverest is established: the great men oppress; the little men groan; the

49 Mme de Meinières to the Marquise de Lénoncourt, 24 July 1771 (Moscow, State Historical Museum: G.V. Orlov Collection, collection 166).

50 Mme de Meinières to Devaux, 3 December 1774 (Paris, BnF: n. a. fr. 15582).

> soldier allows himself to be killed in trying to earn a living; the general gets killed in trying to win a blue or yellow ribbon ... Sovereigns believe what their courtesans and ministers tell them, and, preoccupied by the vain glow of false glory, become persuaded that an acre of ground is worth a thousand subjects.[51]

It is notable that Mme de Meinières is prepared to criticise the vanity of 'sovereigns', having been loath in the past ever to offer criticism either of Louis XV or of Louis XVI once he had acceded to the throne.

Only a small number of Belot's letters of the 1780s and 1790s have survived. The last of these is addressed to Montagu, and dates from September 1792 – by when the Legislative Assembly had suspended the monarchy, Louis XVI had been imprisoned, massacres of prisoners were occurring across Paris, and the Prussian army had entered the country. Belot points a finger at the debt, corruption, and taste for luxuries that had over many decades undermined the nation:

> The French were intoxicated by the brilliance of Louis XIV's reign, and are still crushed by the deficit of our finances, which goes back to that time. The deficit, the taste for luxury, the corruption of morals, the mentality of intrigue ... grew under the succeeding reigns.[52]

Indulgence in luxuries by some has led to deprivation among others, sparking their desire for freedom:

> Wherever oppression is felt, or feared, a furious desire for unbounded freedom flares up. It is impossible that it should not degenerate somewhere into licence, and that it should not consume victims.[53]

In the face of this turmoil, Mme de Meinières expresses her weariness with life: she is old, many of her friends are dead, and she leads a lonely and secluded life in the lodgings she has occupied for more than twenty years in Chaillot, in the grounds of the Convent of Sainte-Marie. She has no further wish to engage with the world, and in her isolation has become, she confesses, something of a 'savage'.

Belot's writings on political subjects – her treatises, prefaces, and letters – span five decades. She maintains a certain consistency across this period, defending France's absolute monarchy against republican arguments in her *Reflections*, and with special force in her preface to the *Miscellany*. It seems, however, that even as she censured Rousseau's second *Discourse*, his arguments and phrasings on the question of inequality embedded themselves in her mind. She returned to them, with wording reminiscent of Rousseau's, in her *Observations* and in her later letters. Of course, the problem of social and political inequality was no mere abstraction

---

[51] Mme de Meinières to Elizabeth Montagu, undated [March 1777] (San Marino, California, Huntington Library: Elizabeth Montagu Collection).

[52] Mme de Meinières to Elizabeth Montagu, 30 September 1792 (San Marino, California, Huntington Library: Elizabeth Montagu Collection).

[53] Ibid.

for Belot: she had come from aristocratic stock on her mother's side but struggled with poverty for most of her life. In her *Observations*, prompted either by purely theoretical concerns or by personal experience, she proposes a new model of society in which the boundaries of class count for little and are easily crossed; and even as she reaffirms her faith in monarchical rule, she suggests that her invented society could function perfectly well under democracy, aristocracy, or monarchy. Her entry into judicial circles does not seem to have led her to question in any profound way the authority of the king – but it did lead her to express doubts over the legitimacy of his ministers' actions. This reluctance to place blame on the king accords with the position she had adopted in the *Observations*, in which she had refused to identify any close link between the ruler of the state and the nature of the social order over which he presides. Even as the crises of the 1770s, 1780s, and 1790s unfolded, Belot was loath to voice any anti-monarchical sentiment in her letters. She would not have wished, either, to grant Rousseau prophetic status for his claim in the *Discourse on Inequality* that the evils inherent in a society contain the seeds of its downfall, and that despotic government must eventually be overthrown and man return to his primitive state. It is perhaps ironic that one of the final images we have of Belot from her letters of the 1790s is that of her living in the quiet grounds of the convent at Chaillot, disillusioned by the disorder and turmoil all around, cut off from society, as isolated, she says, as a 'savage'.

Chapter 3
Performing Citizenship: Marie-Madeleine Jodin Enacting Diderot's and Rousseau's Dramatic and Ethical Theories

Felicia Gordon

Marie-Madeleine Jodin (1741–1790), author of *Vues législatives pour les femmes* (1789–1790), the first signed feminist treatise by a woman, during the French Revolutionary period, had a dramatic career in every sense. A deeply troubled childhood, forcible conversion to Catholicism at the age of nine, and her rebellion against a convent education kindled in this child of a Protestant Genevan watchmaker an enduring hatred of arbitrary authority, whether religious or secular, and infused in her a firm belief in equality and the right to citizenship. At eighteen she was imprisoned by *lettre de cachet*, in the Salpêtrière prison for prostitutes, for 'libertinage'. She emerged after two years, probably through the good offices of Denis Diderot, a friend of her father, and began a successful though tempestuous career as an actress. In 1790, the last year of her life, she published her *Vues législatives*, addressed to the deputies of the Constituent Assembly, prefaced by the declaration: 'Et nous aussi, nous sommes citoyennes.'[1] This assertion – by someone doubly excluded from civic participation, as a woman and as an actress, along with the further identifier she added under her own name, 'fille d'un citoyen de Genève' – locates Jodin in the culture of the Radical Enlightenment and of republicanism, and flags her complex identification with Rousseau.[2]

---

1 M.M. Jodin, *Vues législatives pour les femmes* (Angers, 1790), p. 1. Subsequent English quotations are taken from the English translation by the authors in F. Gordon and P.N. Furbank, *Marie Madeleine Jodin, 1741–1790: Actress, Philosophe, and Feminist* (Aldershot, 2001).

2 J. Israel, *Enlightenment Contested: Philosophy, Modernity, and the Emancipation of Man 1670–1752* (Oxford, 2006); E.J. Gardener, 'The Philosophes and Women: Sensationalism and Sentiment', in E. Jacobs et al. (eds), *Women and Society in Eighteenth-Century France* (London, 1979); D. Gordon, 'Philosophy, Sociology, and Gender in the Enlightenment', in 'Forum: The Public Sphere in the Eighteenth Century', *French Historical Studies*, 17:4 (1992): pp. 882–911; S. Tomaselli, 'The Enlightenment Debate on Women', *History Workshop Journal*, 20:1 (1985): pp. 101–24. For the status of actors and actresses in France in the eighteenth century see J. McManners, *Abbés and Actresses: The Church and the Theatrical Profession in Eighteenth-Century France* (Oxford, 1986); G. Maugras,

It is germane here to consider Jonathan Israel's thesis on the Radical Enlightenment and the origins of modern republicanism. He represents it as rooted in Spinozan monism in the seventeenth century and carried through to French Enlightenment theorists such as Diderot, d'Alembert, Helvétius, and d'Holbach. The republicanism promoted by such thinkers, as well as the limited monarchy favoured by the more religiously conservative Locke, implied rejection of rule by divine right, and acceptance of some entitlement in the governed to choose their ruler.[3] In practice, it was not necessarily fully democratic, as limited franchises like Geneva, Venice, Poland, and Saxony illustrate. It did not preclude a monarchy, provided that the monarch ruled on the basis of consent, not divine authority. Rejection of the divine right of rulers did not always derive from an atheistic premise, as is clear from Locke's refutation of Filmer, but was certainly supported by atheism. As Israel argues, the Moderate Enlightenment represented in France most notably by Voltaire and Rousseau retained the idea of a divine order upon which the political order should rest; whereas *philosophes* like Diderot figure in Israel's Radical Enlightenment as prepared to question what had previously been considered immutable and divinely ordained truths. It is my contention that Jodin, by her critique of traditional gender roles (also divinely ordained, for many) – along with her insistence on human rights, and her almost certain atheism – represented an important and original strand of this radicalism. Like other materialist atheists of pre-revolutionary France she could not openly air her views on religion; when she did so by mocking a religious procession in Bordeaux in 1769 she was arrested and was fortunate not to be severely punished – like the unfortunate Chevalier de la Barre, who had been sentenced to death for defacing a crucifix in 1766. Her anti-clerical sentiments emerge clearly in her *Vues Législatives*; and even more suggestive is the fact that the text makes no reference to the Supreme Being or Providence, an almost obligatory trope for the period. Nevertheless, Jodin also took much from Rousseau, perhaps hoping to exploit his popularity.

Jodin's republicanism, modelled like Rousseau's on Geneva, was by no means egalitarian or fully democratic. The citizens of the Genevan Republic with its limited franchise, among whom were Jodin's and Rousseau's fathers, considered themselves self-governing, although by the eighteenth century this ideal was undermined by the increasingly oligarchic nature of the state.[4] Jodin herself

---

Les Comédiens hors la loi (Paris, 1887); B.G. Mittman, 'Women and the Theater Arts', in *French Women and the Age of Enlightenment*, ed. S.I. Spencer (Bloomington, 1984); L.R. Berlanstein, 'Women and Power in Eighteenth-Century France: Actresses at the Comédie Française', in C. Adams et al. (eds), *Visions and Revisions of Eighteenth-Century France* (University Park, PA, 1997).

[3] Israel, *Enlightenment Contested*, p. 43; on classical republicanism versus democratic republicanism on the Dutch model, pp. 240–41.

[4] For the shifts in Genevan republicanism and Rousseau's critique see C. Blum, *Rousseau and the Republic of Virtue: The Language of Politics in the French Revolution* (Ithaca, NY, 1986); H. Rosenblatt, *Rousseau and Geneva: From the First Discourse to the Social Contract, 1749–1762* (Cambridge, 1997).

believed that she had inherited, as the daughter of a citizen of Geneva, an honourable and superior social status, one that gave her confidence to defend her rights. As Diderot reminded her: 'You are an unfortunate child, but you are a well-born one.'[5] The characterization 'fille d'un citoyen de Genève' on the title page of her *Vues législatives pour les femmes* is an assertion of status, but also of authority – of the right to speak as a citizen. In Jodin's formulation, women would form the necessary link between *l'esprit social*, which incorporated morality ('mœurs'), and a formal code of laws.[6]

Jodin's eighty-six page treatise proposed the eradication of prostitution, the establishment of a women's legislature with jurisdiction over women's issues, and the institution of divorce. When she wrote her *Vues législatives*, Jodin had long been retired from the stage, but the document bears the marks of her profession as she flatters her audience of bourgeois legislators – by appealing to the desire she ascribes to them, to regenerate France morally in the 'new politics'.[7] To bolster her advocacy of reform, Jodin frequently invokes Rousseau, that celebrated citizen of Geneva; but there is no mention at all of Diderot: her moral, dramatic, and financial advisor and steadfast friend, with whom she remained in contact until his death in 1784. Jodin would certainly have known of Rousseau's repudiation of Diderot after the notorious quarrel between the two in 1757 and Rousseau's rejection of the *encyclopédistes* and *philosophes* generally – through her father, if not from Diderot himself. Rousseau's adherence to what Jonathan Israel terms the Moderate Enlightenment (his belief in a deity and the body-soul duality, and his rejection of Spinoza's monism) set him apart not only from the *encyclopédistes* but also from Jodin.[8] Why then is it not Diderot but Rousseau, whose religious views and sexual politics were the antithesis of hers, who is invoked so persistently in her *Vues législatives*?

The revolutionaries' identification with the persona of Rousseau, along with his language of a monolithic virtue, permeated the thinking of the revolutionary period.[9] In Robespierre's revolutionary rhetoric, the *encyclopédistes* and Diderot in particular were anathematized as atheists, decadents, sceptics, and reactionaries.[10] Though this vilification of Diderot, wholly mistaken as far as his social views were concerned (see for example the *Histoire des deux Indes* and the *Supplément au Voyage de Bougainville*), post-dates Jodin's text, she would have been aware that by 1789 stocks in Diderot and the *encyclopédistes* were at a low ebb, while those

---

5 Diderot to Jodin, August 1765, Gordon and Furbank, *Marie Madeleine Jodin*, p. 29.

6 Gordon and Furbank, *Marie Madeleine Jodin*.

7 Jodin wrote her *Vues legislatives* in response to a *cahier de doléance* calling for a series of municipal reforms including the elimination of public prostitution: Cahier du Tiers-Etat de la Ville de Paris, *Archives Parlementaires de 1787–1860*, 1st series, 5 (Paris, 1879), p. 290.

8 J. Israel, *A Revolution of the Mind* (Princeton, 2010).

9 Blum, *Rousseau and the Republic of Virtue*.

10 R. Tarin, *Diderot et la Révolution française: Controverses et polémiques autour d'un philosophe* (Paris, 2001).

in Rousseau were booming.[11] Enlisting Rousseau to argue for moral improvement in her *Vues législatives* also enabled Jodin to co-opt the model of citizenship he had designed for men and apply it to women.

Rousseau, who since his First Discourse of 1749 had inscribed himself as 'Citizen of Geneva', frequented Genevan exiles in Paris and may have known Jean Jodin, Marie Madeleine's father.[12] Jodin's self-conscious identification as 'fille d'un citoyen de Genève' not only confirms an affinity with Rousseau and republicanism, but validates that identification. One key to Jodin's text and to her life is the idea of a fractured self, arising from several sources: her repudiated childhood conversion from Protestantism to Catholicism; the traumas of her religious education (she was expelled from six convent schools for bad behaviour); her two-year prison term, by which, even if she had not been a prostitute, she was branded as one; her acting career, where she attempted in various well-publicized rows to assert her 'rights'; the fact of acting itself, in which she was tempted to become the characters she played; and finally Diderot's efforts as mentor, encouraging her to a reformed life through rebuilding her character according to his dramatic and ethical theories. Although it is clear that Jodin identifies with Rousseau in his Genevan persona, endorsing the cult of virtue, in her *Vues législatives* she draws primarily upon Diderot's ideas of human freedom, the social good, and secular morality. Diderot is absent from her treatise in name only.

It may seem counter-intuitive to identify Diderot as a source of Jodin's feminist-political theory. His essay *Sur les Femmes* (1773), written as a critique of Antoine-Léonard Thomas's *Qu'est-ce qu'une femme*?[13] paints an almost unrelievedly negative picture of female potential, based on the materialist premise that women are ruled by their uterus – and if not at the mercy of their biology, then at the mercy of men on whom they are necessarily dependent. Women function only as objects of male desire, and when their beauty fades they have no *raison d'être*: 'What then is a woman? Neglected by her husband, deserted by her children, a nonentity in society, religious devotion is her unique and last resource.'[14] This seems to echo almost exactly d'Holbach's 'Des femmes' in his *Système social* (1773), which however also ascribes women's weakness to their defective education. The tyranny of men, coupled with women's contradictory training in modesty and flirtatiousness, leaves women nothing in their old age but the consolations of religion.[15]

---

[11] G.-T. Raynal, *Histoire philosophique et politique des établissemens et du commerce des Européens dans les deux Indes* (Geneva, 1780). A large part of the work is said to have been written by Diderot and others. The sentiments and criticisms it contained prevented its publication in France; D. Diderot, *Supplément au Voyage de Bougainville* (1770–1773), ed. H. Dieckmann (Genève, 1955).

[12] Rosenblatt, *Rousseau and Geneva.*

[13] A.L. Thomas, D. Diderot, and L. d'Epinay, *Qu'est-ce qu'une femme?* ed. E. Badinter (Paris, 1989).

[14] Ibid., pp. 37–8.

[15] P.H. d'Holbach, *Système Social ou Principes Naturels de la Morale et de la Politique avec un examen de l'Influence du Gouvernement sur le mœurs* (Paris and London, 1773), p. 129.

Contrasting Diderot's materialistically reductive essay with Rousseau's youthful sketch, also entitled *Sur les Femmes* (probably 1735), we find in the latter that women's inferior position is ascribed to centuries of male despotism. Rousseau at this juncture adopts a progressive position: 'Women could have given the finest examples of greatness of mind and the love of virtue and to a greater extent than men, if our [men's] injustice had not robbed them, along with their liberty, of all the possibilities to manifest these qualities in the eyes of the world.'[16] As we know, Rousseau later changed his mind radically on the desirability of women achieving liberty, in *Emile* and in the *Lettre à d'Alembert sur les spectacles*. He became convinced that women's domestic subjection was necessary to maintain their virtue and society's, and that their latently great qualities should be hidden from the eyes of the world.

The debate as to whether women's subjection was biologically or socially based engaged not only Thomas, Diderot, and Rousseau, but also Condorcet, Mme d'Épinay, Rétif de la Bretonne, and d'Holbach, involving many contradictions and inconsistencies. For his part, though theoretically pessimistic about women's capacities (given the exigencies of their biology), Diderot was in practice a lover of women: an admirer of talented women and a bourgeois father and husband.[17] He considered Jodin a highly intelligent but emotionally wayward individual and treated her as a rational and potentially responsible human being – a mark of his sexual egalitarianism. He encouraged her intellectual as well as her moral development and did not reduce her to a mere body.[18] Diderot's practice appears, in regard to Jodin at least, superior to his theory.

Jodin first became known to twentieth-century scholars thanks to the twenty-one letters Diderot wrote to her when she was on tour in the provinces and abroad.[19] Why did Diderot take it upon himself to lecture Jodin, urging her repeatedly to curb the violence of her character, as he put it, and to control her fits of rage?[20] This show of officiousness relates to the Spinozan concept of *le bien général*: the importance of social responsibility in a godless universe, a shift from a theological to a secular morality.[21] Israel's distinction between what he terms the reformist Moderate Enlightenment and the implicitly or explicitly revolutionary Radical Enlightenment helps to clarify Diderot's involvement in Jodin's ethical, political, and thespian education.[22] For Diderot, all social action for the common good, as

---

16 J.-J. Rousseau, (1735?), 'Sur les femmes', in *Œuvres complètes*, ed. B. Gagnebin and M. Raymond (5 vols, Paris, 1961–1995) vol. 2, pp. 1254–5.

17 E. Fontenay, *Diderot ou le matérialisme enchanté* (Paris, 1981).

18 Thomas et al., *Qu'est-ce qu'une femme?*, p. 23.

19 See P.N. Furbank, *Diderot: A Critical Biography* (London, 1992); P. Vernière, 'Marie Madeleine Jodin, amie de Diderot et témoin des Lumières', *Studies on Voltaire*, 58 (1967): pp. 1765–75.

20 See for example Diderot to Jodin, August 1765 and November 1765, Gordon and Furbank, *Marie Madeleine Jodin*, pp. 32, 60.

21 Israel, *A Revolution of the Mind*, p. 831.

22 Ibid., pp. 12–22.

he understood it – whether it be befriending Jodin and her mother, writing plays of a moral bent, or arguing against superstition and in favour of reason – was part of the same secular moral imperative.[23] Jodin's trajectory (from rebellious hoyden, to prima donna actress, to *philosophe*) demonstrates the power and dissemination of Radical Enlightenment ideas beyond the confines of salon and court culture: what some have deemed 'the corrosive action of Enlightenment thought on uncultured and passionate minds'.[24] A reading of the *Vues législatives*, however, reveals that Jodin was anything but uncultured.

We have evidence that Jodin cherished a concept of human rights even from her teen years.[25] She read widely in philosophy, admired the writing of materialists like Helvétius and d'Holbach, was a fervent anti-clerical and almost certainly an atheist. While both Diderot in his *Paradoxe sur le comédien* and Rousseau in his *Lettre à d'Alembert sur les spectacles* analysed issues of sincerity, honesty and pretence, seeming and being, Jodin in her own life grappled, not always successfully, with the reality of attempting to live authentically as an actress and as a woman under the sway of arbitrary or absolute power in *ancien régime* Europe. Jodin, in short, directly experienced what Rousseau and Diderot theorized.

Diderot's correspondence with Jodin ran from 1765 when she joined a French theatrical troupe in Warsaw to 1769 when she performed in Bordeaux – the year Diderot finished his first version of *Paradoxe sur le comédien.* There are striking parallels between issues raised in the *Paradoxe* and Diderot's advice to Jodin on stagecraft and ethics in the letters. Jodin became in those four years a sounding board for Diderot's dramatic, social, and ethical theories: a not-always-cooperative Galatea to his Pygmalion. Like Galatea, she escaped from the control of her 'creator'; she was neither the passive recipient of advice nor the ideal creation Diderot may have envisaged.

As Stéphane Lojkine observes, the *Paradoxe* constitutes an inner debate for Diderot between his own theory of spontaneity and enthusiasm promulgated in his *Entretiens sur Le Fils naturel* (1757) and the actor's need for cold detachment when playing a role, the better to produce the illusion of passionate engagement.[26] This was not just a question of technique but of ethics, as Rousseau also realized. What was the moral status of the actor in this manoeuvre? How could the theatre, by being most 'false' (that is, through trading in *illusions* of the 'true and ethical'), become a form of social and moral education, as Diderot wished? How could it genuinely serve the social good? Diderot was not only engaged in dialogue with himself in the *Paradoxe*, he was debating the educative and moral role of the theatre with Rousseau, whose 1757 *Lettre à d'Alembert sur les spectacles* had constituted a watershed in his relationship with the *philosophes* of the Radical Enlightenment, epitomizing Genevan republican hostility towards the theatre and

---

23 Ibid., p. 22.

24 Vernière, 'Marie Madeleine Jodin', p. 1765; Israel, *A Revolution of the Mind*, p. 53.

25 Gordon and Furbank, *Marie Madeleine Jodin*, pp. 10–13.

26 D. Diderot, (1771), *Paradoxe sur le comédien* (Paris, 1992), pp. 13–14.

Rousseau's personal rejection of the worldly life.[27] At the core of the Rousseau–Diderot disagreement lay questions of what constituted the social good, whether the role of theatre was to educate or corrupt, whether morality was purely secular or divinely ordained, and whether human improvement was possible.

Within Rousseau's arguments against luxury and his efforts to revitalize the moral core of Genevan republicanism, his attack on the acting profession went beyond empirical descriptions of the debased morality of actors.[28] Justifying the contempt and aversion with which actors and actresses were held (in terms of historical precedent and contemporary observation), Rousseau argued that they were debased persons not contingently but necessarily. Their *état* or status as proscribed individuals (as they were under French law) was just, because not only did actors lead profligate lives, by the very fact of acting, they also pretended to be what they were not. They violated Rousseau's cult of sincerity. As intrinsically immoral persons, they mimicked moral and elevated sentiments in the roles they performed. Actresses were even more tainted than actors because their profession made them virtually 'public women' – that is to say, prostitutes (*femmes en monde, femmes publiques*). Actresses contravened what Rousseau believed was the necessary relation between the sexes, consisting of a balance of opposites:

> I wonder how a profession whose sole object is to display oneself in public and, which is worse, to display oneself for money, could be congruent with modesty and good morals.[29]

On the other hand Diderot – confronting in his *Paradoxe* and his letters to Jodin the problem of the acting profession, in relation to constructing a morally elevating theatre – attempted to construct a general model of behaviour that might reconcile the paradox of seeming and being, of pretence and authenticity. He stressed connections between the moral, the theatrical, and the civic life. Diderot said he had recognized, in Jodin's acting, a spontaneous talent: 'a soul able to alienate itself, to stir itself profoundly, to transport itself, to become this person or that'.[30] In tutoring or mentoring Jodin, however, he attempted to modify and control her sensibility: 'Concentrate on the quiet scenes; these are the most difficult.'[31] In the same letter

---

[27] J.H. Mason, 'The *Lettre à d'Alembert* and its Place in Rousseau's Thought', in M. Hobson et al. (eds), *Rousseau and the Eighteenth Century* (Oxford, 1992); Rosenblatt, *Rousseau and Geneva*.

[28] For the status of actors in France under the *ancien régime* see L.R. Berlanstein, 'Women and Power in Eighteenth-Century France: Actresses at the Comédie Française', in Christine Adams et al. (eds), *Visions and Revisions of Eighteenth-Century France* (University Park, PA, 1997); B.G. Mittman, 'Women and the Theater Arts', in *French Women and the Age of Enlightenment*, ed. Samia I. Spencer (Bloomington, 1984); M.M. Moffat, *Rousseau et la querelle du théâtre au XVIIIe siècle* (Paris, 1930).

[29] J.-J. Rousseau, (1757), *Lettre à Mr. D'Alembert sur les spectacles*, ed. M. Fuch (Geneva, 1948), p. 120.

[30] Gordon and Furbank, *Marie Madeleine Jodin*, p. 30.

[31] Ibid., p. 30.

(August 1765) following this theatrical coaching, Diderot explicitly linked stage and ethical performances in urging Jodin to help her destitute mother, then living in Paris. Diderot may not have known that the Jodin family at large had signed the *lettres de cachet* directed against Marie Madeleine and her mother. Whatever the case, Diderot emphasized throughout his correspondence with Jodin that public and private morals should be unified, though he did inject an anti-clerical aside:

> Let it not be said that on the boards as in the pulpit, the actor and the Sorbonne doctor are as eager as each other in preaching right conduct and as expert in not performing it.[32]

Contrary to Rousseau's views on *amour-propre*, Diderot thinks that we *should* wish to be thought well of by others.[33] Though he tells actors to become natural by doing without a mirror, he argues that in our social actions we should always be aware of how we are seen by others; our mirror is the social world. His advice, strictures, and admonitions to Jodin, he tells her, are tolerable because: 'I have the feeling that you care for my good opinion.' Diderot functions as Jodin's mirror of social responsibility. He believes that one should not wish to live in isolation from the opinion of others.[34]

Diderot like Rousseau recognized the debased moral behaviour of actors and actresses, as summed up in his *Paradoxe*:

> Actors are isolated, restless; they have few morals, no friends at all, and almost none of those blessed and agreeable relationships that link us to the sorrows and pleasures of another person who shares our own.[35]

The actor's profession lacks the social glue that secures our human bonds and that constitutes secular morality. In effect, Diderot's account of the morality of actors differs little from Rousseau's. The difference lies in Diderot assigning social causes to their licentious manner of living, whereas Rousseau considers them essentially prone to vice, not only in their behaviour, but by the fact of counterfeiting nature, and, for women, by displaying themselves in public when they should be exercising only private virtues.

If we consider Jodin's actual life experiences (her theatrical performances, amorous entanglements, and financial affairs, in Warsaw, Dresden, Bordeaux, or Angers) in relation to these debates, we see that Diderot tried to reform Jodin, in the sense of giving her self-control, and therefore a greater degree of freedom. He did not disapprove of her sexual relationships – actresses were expected to take wealthy lovers – but of her impulsiveness and her sometimes ungovernable temper. Diderot's repeated moral homilies did not by any means bear immediate

---

32 Ibid., Diderot to Jodin, p. 31.

33 Rousseau, *Œuvres Choisis* III, p. 219.

34 Furbank, *Diderot: A Critical Biography*, pp. 148–64.

35 Diderot, *Paradoxe*, pp. 137–8.

fruit, as a series of quarrels, scandals, lawsuits, and arrests demonstrate. These serve as illustrations, not merely of Jodin's prima donna temperament but of her visceral belief in her human rights – rights that of course in law she did not possess.

It is not easy to summarize Jodin's complex and highly coloured imbroglios – part political, part personal – with actors, managers, and lovers. In Warsaw in the autumn of 1766, she quarrelled violently with one of the actors and her manager, a confrontation sparked by a satirical pamphlet on the French troupe thought to be by Jodin, followed by an anonymous and extraordinarily vicious satirical libel on her character. She refused to act until she received a public apology, risking imprisonment for breach of contract. The king, Stanislas Poniatowski – ex-lover of Catherine the Great, whose mistress Jodin may also have been – paid her off and allowed her to take up an acting post in Dresden. There in 1768, she carried on a passionate and very public affair with the Danish envoy to Saxony, Count Werner XXV von der Schulenburg. The Saxon Minister of State, to revenge himself on Schulenburg for slights real or imagined, had Jodin summarily arrested, imprisoned, and then deported from Saxony. The following year in Bordeaux, her next acting venue, she allegedly mocked a religious procession and was again imprisoned, but released probably thanks to Schulenburg's intervention. Also in 1769 she quarrelled with her manager in Angers and was sacked, but successfully sued him for breach of contract.[36] These adventures of Jodin's have in common that they are attempts to assert her rights and to gain some form of symbolic or legal redress in the face of arbitrary power. They suggest that her *Vues législatives* were grounded in her lived experience, as much as in her immersion in the philosophy of the Radical Enlightenment.

How does Diderot's voice find echoes in Jodin's *Vues législatives*? At a first reading, her text seems highly prescriptive and even puritanical. Attacking public prostitution and wider moral decadence (for example the easy availability of pornography), Jodin calls for their suppression. Prostitutes figure in her text as vermin to be cleansed from the streets. However, rather than seeking to control their sexual promiscuity by imprisonment (a fate she herself had suffered) or even more violent methods such as branding that some reformers favoured, Jodin seeks prostitutes' transformation by allowing them to become useful, productive citizens. Women, she argues, prostitute themselves largely out of economic necessity:

> When one considers the mortifications which must accompany their vile mode of life, exposing them to such cruel insults, it is plain that only sheer destitution, or the lack of any foothold in society, could lead women to it.[37]

Jodin had become an actress out of necessity (though she grew to love the stage) as the one profession, other than prostitution, open to her after her imprisonment

[36] For detailed accounts of these adventures see Gordon and Furbank, *Marie Madeleine Jodin*, pp. 36–55, 70–99, 119–20, 130–36.

[37] Ibid., p. 189.

for *libertinage*. Her comments just quoted echo Diderot's letter to Jodin (May 1766) on actors' backgrounds:

> When one thinks of the reasons which have decided a man to become an actor, or a woman to become an actress – of the place where Providence found them and the bizarre circumstances which attracted them to the stage – one is no longer amazed that talent, good behaviour and probity are all equally rare among the acting fraternity.[38]

For Diderot, the *avilissement* of the profession results from actors' ostracized social position; if this were changed, if actors were recruited from good families and suitably educated and rewarded, they would be moral examples on and off the stage.[39] Diderot looks to social causation rather than essentialist conceptions, to transform a despised profession of 'puppets and courtesans' into a force for the common good. Similarly, Jodin's plan for the reformation of prostitutes argues that if prostitutes were to be taught useful and remunerative skills, they could earn their living honourably and become honourable persons. Her analysis of prostitution reflects Diderot's belief in human improvement, shared by all the radical *philosophes*. Women's degradation is not the result of innate weakness and depravity but of unjust laws and prejudices. For Jodin, the Rousseau-Diderot debate on the moral status of actors has direct relevance to the issue of sexual equality. All women are implicated in a general degradation of the sex through prostitution; Jodin's plan for reform goes beyond this particular social problem to envisage a change in women's status and public recognition.

Rousseau's thought is indubitably a key to the second strand of Jodin's plan, which entailed establishing a women's judiciary to oversee delinquent women, a legislative body of women to legislate on all matters pertaining to their sex, and overthrowing the indissolubility of marriage. When Jodin invokes Rousseau as an authority for her schemes of moral reform for women, with a nice sense of irony she employs Rousseau's own arguments against him for her own ends, while purporting to endorse his views. The three principal texts of Rousseau's that she quotes or paraphrases in *Vues législatives* are his *Letter to d'Alembert on the Theatre*, *Social Contract*, and *Discourse on Inequality*.

A few examples will illustrate Jodin's method. In a discussion about women's aptitude for serving the public good, she conflates two sections of Rousseau's *Letter to d'Alembert*:

> 'If you want to know men,' said the celebrated Citizen of Geneva, 'study women. In every country, in every state, in every condition, the two sexes have so strong, so natural a connection that the morals of the one always determine those of the other.'[40]

---

38 Ibid., p. 21.

39 Diderot, *Paradoxe*, p. 142.

40 Gordon and Furbank, *Marie Madeleine Jodin*, p. 184; J.-J. Rousseau, *Collected Writings*, ed. and trans. A. Bloom et al. (Lebanon, NH, 1990), vol. 10, p. 311.

Jodin's version implies that women should be granted, in her words, 'this honourable ascendancy which, making your Laws more effective, and perhaps more just, will revive in them those Virtues which are the measure of yours'. What Rousseau actually said, however was: 'Do you want to know men? Study women.... There are no good morals for women outside of a withdrawn and domestic life.'[41] This conclusion is absent from Jodin's text: understandably, since her whole thesis rests on the premise that women should be drawn into public life to legislate for women.

It is no accident that Jodin draws heavily on the *Letter to d'Alembert*, the text in which Rousseau both identifies himself as a citizen of Geneva, bent on saving the Republic from decadence (the role Jodin also allots herself in her *Vues législatives*), and flays the acting profession and women in it as intrinsically immoral. Jodin's strategic move, given her love of the theatre and her claim to self-respect as a citizen and an actress, is not to argue against Rousseau's vilification of the stage, but to co-opt his idea of women's domestic virtues in order to sanctify the public sphere:

> Women, being sedentary by habit, devote themselves entirely to the place and the duties assigned to them. As a result, they have more respect for their sovereigns, more submissiveness towards their superiors, more respect for their equals, more compassion for the unfortunate, more attachment to their relatives, more attentiveness to their children, more love for their spouse.... If moral Laws derive their force from opinion, it is on women that they will have the most sway.[42]

The feminine virtues listed above, if perhaps the historical result of domestic seclusion, should not in Jodin's view debar women from participation in public life. Like Poulain de la Barre[43] whom she quotes, differences in lived circumstance,

---

[41] The full quotation from J.-J. Jacques Rousseau, *Letter to D'Alembert and writings for the Theater* in *Collected Writings of Rousseau*, vol. 10, edited and translated by A. Bloom, C. Butterworth and C. Kelly, (Lebanon NH: University Press of New England, 2004), pp. 311–12 runs:

> Do you want to know men? Study women. This maxim is general and up to this point everybody will agree with me. But if I add that there are no good morals for women outside of a withdrawn and domestic life; if I say that the peaceful care of the family and the home are their lot, that the dignity of their Sex consists in modesty, that shame and chasteness are inseparable from decency for them, that when they seek for men's looks they are already letting themselves be corrupted by them, and that any woman who shows herself off disgraces herself, I will be immediately attacked by this philosophy of the day which is born and dies in the corner of a big City and wishes to smother the cry of nature and the unanimous voice of humankind.

[42] M.M. Jodin, 'Legislative Views for Women', in Gordon and Furbank, *Marie Madeleine Jodin*, p. 184.

[43] F. Poulain de la Barre, *De l'Egalité des deux sexes: Discours physique et moral où l'on voit l'importance de se défaire des préjugez* (Paris, 1673), p. 109. On the feminist implications of Cartesianism see M. Angeto, *Les Champions des femmes* (Quebec, 1977), pp. 58–65; S. Sturmann, 'The Deconstruction of Gender: Seventeenth-Century Feminism and Modern Equality', in S. Knott and B. Taylor (eds), *Women, Gender and Enlightenment* (Basingstoke, 2005), pp. 371–88.

which may have reinforced women's potential for virtue, do not preclude equality of minds:

> The love of country, of liberty and fame, animate our sex as much as yours, Messieurs. We are not on this earth a different species from you. *The mind has no sex any more than does virtue*; but vices of the mind and the heart belong almost exclusively to yours.[44]

Similarly in her discussion favouring the right to divorce and against the indissolubility of marriage, Jodin cites, among other sources, Rousseau's early text the *Discourse on Inequality*: 'The duty of an eternal fidelity serves only to propagate adultery; and the very laws of continence and honour necessarily contribute to increase dissoluteness, and multiply abortions.'[45] And turning Rousseau against himself in paraphrase, Jodin remarks in relation to the marriage contract: 'According to Jean-Jacques in his *Social Contract* (1762), all institutions which put the human being at odds with himself *or herself* [Jodin's addition] are worthless.'[46]

Finally, Jodin both endorses and transforms Rousseau's argument for responsible citizenship in the *Social Contract*, namely that abnegation of freedom is abnegation of moral autonomy:

> To renounce freedom is to renounce one's humanity, one's rights as a man and equally one's duties. There is no possible *quid pro quo* for one who renounces everything; indeed such renunciation is contrary to man's very nature, for if you take away all freedom of the will, you strip a man's actions of all moral significance.[47]

Rousseau did not apply this analysis to women, who, as described in *Emile* and the *Lettre à d'Alembert sur les spectacles*, possess separate sexual natures that require a separate morality and protection from engagement in the public sphere. The logic of Rousseau's position, outlined in the above quotation, is that women, who he believes must renounce their freedom, have also renounced their humanity. Jodin, by applying to women Rousseau's requirement that freedom of the will is a requisite for morality, converts Rousseau's 'man' to its inclusive, non-gendered sense, following his link between freedom and ethics.

Though basing much of her argument for women's fitness to fill a legislative and judicial role on Rousseau's idealization of the maternal ethos, Jodin overturns his structure of male authority and female subordination by abolishing men's perpetual guardianship (*tutelle*) over women, first as daughters and then as wives –

---

44 M.M. Jodin, *Legislative Views for Women*, in Gordon and Furbank, *Marie Madeleine Jodin*, p. 181.

45 J.-J. Rousseau, *On the Inequality among Mankind* (Minneapolis, 2007), p. 53.

46 Gordon and Furbank, *Marie Madeleine Jodin*, p. 194.

47 J.-J. Rousseau, *The Social Contract*, trans. Maurice Cranston (Harmondsworth, 2003), p. 55.

and by creating new civic responsibilities for women in the public sphere.[48] This is the new public sphere of her imagination, where women as public figures are no longer identified as whores, courtesans, or debased actresses (the *femmes en monde* or *filles publiques*, of common parlance) but full citizens fulfilling their responsibilities to society. The ringing lines of the opening paragraph of *Vues législatives* claim these rights in the language of Diderot, d'Holbach, and Helvétius:

> At a time when true Philosophy is beginning to enlighten all minds, when the defeat of Despotism leaves the prejudices which owed their existence to it helpless and without defence, shall the weaker sex, excluded by force from public deliberations, demand its inalienable rights in vain? Shall that essential half of Society not have any share in the legislative Code proclaimed in the name of Society as a whole? I can picture the reason and equity which animate the august Assembly of Representatives of the Nation, amazed that these questions have not been raised before and hastening to welcome them. So let us obey the general impulse which directs all ideas towards the goal of liberty regained, a liberty usurped by oppression from all of us equally.[49]

In identifying her demand for citizenship for women with the overthrow of prejudice by reason ('true Philosophy') Jodin shows herself at one with the *philosophes*. She renders Rousseau's inconsistent views on human freedom (inconsistent, that is, with human as opposed to purely male rights) consistent with justice and equity. In effect she finesses Rousseau for her own ends – but without directly criticizing him, unlike her English contemporaries Mary Wollstonecraft and Catharine Macaulay. Jodin, in the persona of an actress and mindful of her audience, the legislators of the Constituent Assembly, invokes Rousseau in an appeal to their ambition of effecting a political transformation that would ensure the moral improvement of society. In spite of her many citations of Rousseau in a positive vein, Jodin's project in her *Vues législatives*, though borrowing his discourse of republican virtue, repudiates his separation of the moral and sexual spheres. Viewed in another light, her literal implementation of Rousseau's separate spheres, by advocating women's exclusive jurisdiction over women, radicalizes even as it undermines his gender prescriptions. Her declaration 'and we too are citizens' was a direct challenge to Rousseau's exclusion of women from the 'city': that public space where one can function as a citizen, part of the body politic and subject to the same laws and law-giving powers as men. Therefore, though appearing to endorse a separate spheres ideology in her plan for a legislative body to deal exclusively with women's affairs, Jodin was in fact offering a critique of the failures and injustices inherent in male authority and proposing to dismantle this authority over women in both private and public life. If arbitrary royal power contravened human rights, then just as decisively absolute jurisdiction of men

---

48 P.D. Jimack, 'The Paradox of Sophie and Julie: Contemporary Response to Rousseau's Ideal Wife and Ideal Mother', in E. Jacobs et al. (eds), *Women and Society in Eighteenth-Century France* (London, 1979).

49 Gordon and Furbank, *Marie Madeleine Jodin*, p. 177.

over women did the same. The legislators whom she addressed, concerned to implement the rights of man, must not do so piecemeal. If they genuinely wished to inaugurate Rousseau's republic of virtue, its despotic powers over women must be abolished.

Citizen of an ideal republic not yet in existence, Jodin recognized in her disasters as well as in her successes that her experience was not hers alone. Performing the role of a public woman, she saw it as relevant to all women. Jodin confronted the issue of prostitution partly because of her own experience in la Salpêtrière, and partly because she recognized that women of all classes were contaminated by the debased view of women in public, as implicitly or explicitly prostituting themselves. Jodin saw an urgent need to reform both manners and *mœurs* as a prerequisite for women's participation in citizenship; and she insisted on a single standard for both sexes. She enlisted Rousseau as the apostle of liberty and social morality – avoiding, given the audience she was addressing in the heat of revolutionary turmoil, direct criticism of his gender prescriptions, and disguising her adherence to the radical thought of Diderot and other *philosophes*. Mirroring the secular moral preoccupations of the *philosophes*, Jodin saw the necessity of a common social purpose and participation for all citizens. To be virtuous – that is, socially responsible – women equally with men must have a public role in performing the duties of citizenship. The legacies of Rousseau and Diderot find their articulation in the distinctive and polemical voice of this daughter of the Radical Enlightenment.

Chapter 4
Etta Palm d'Aelders and Louise Keralio-Robert: Feminist Controversy during the French Revolution

Calogero Alberto Petix and Karen Green

Introduction

Sometimes historians are reluctant to study theorists who have not clearly shaped the course of events of their age. This may be one reason for the scholarly neglect of Etta Palm d'Aelders (1743–1799) who, despite Judith Vega's attempts to rectify the situation, remains a little-known contributor to the revolutionary debates over women's rights.[1] Another reason could be that she was a Dutch operating in France. Despite her adventurous life and her relevant speeches to the *Société des amis de la vérité* and the National Assembly, she plays a cameo part in accounts of the French Revolution, if she appears at all, and the content of her publications is rarely discussed in detail.[2] Yet like the somewhat better-studied

---

1 J. Vega, 'Geschiedenis als fictie: Het geromantiseerde leven van Etta Palm', *Historica*, 22:3 (1999): pp. 22–4; J. Vega, 'Etta Palm, une Hollandaise à Paris', in W. Frijhoff, R. Dekker (ed.), *Le Voyage révolutionnaire* (Hilversum, 1991), pp. 49–57; J. Vega, 'Luxury, Necessity, or the Morality of Men: The Republican Discourse of Etta Palm-Aelders', in M.F. Brive (ed.), *Les Femmes et la Révolution française* (Toulouse, 1989), vol. 1, pp. 363–70; J. Vega, 'Feminist Republicanism: Etta Palm-Aelders on Justice, Virtue and Men', *History of European Ideas*, 10:3 (1989): pp. 333–51.

2 One of the first historians to refer to Etta Palm d'Aelders is Jules Michelet, describing her as a Dutch of good heart and good spirit, the spokeswoman who preaches in favour of woman's rights: J. Michelet, *Histoire de la Révolution française* (Paris, 1869), vol. 2, p. 311. She is also discussed in Baron Marc de Villiers, *Histoire des clubs de femmes et des légions d'amazones* (Paris, 1910); and J.M.H. Mathorez, *Les Etrangers en France sous l'ancien régime: Histoire de la formation de la population française* (Paris, 1919). For more recent discussions see: B. Applewhite and D.G. Levy, *Women and Politics in the Age of the Democratic Revolution* (Ann Arbor, 1993); L. Beckstrand, *Deviant Women of the French Revolution and the Rise of Feminism* (Cranbury, NJ, 2009); C.E. Proctor, *Women, Equality, and the French Revolution* (New York, 1990); J. Abray, 'Feminism in the French Revolution', *The American Historical Review*, 80:1 (1975): pp. 43–62; R. Voet, *Feminism and Citizenship* (Thousand Oaks, 1998); J.B. Landes, *Women and the Public Sphere in the Age of the French Revolution* (Ithaca, NY, 1988). Two biographies (in Dutch) are:

Olympe de Gouges (1748–1793), Marie Jodin, and Louise-Félicité Keralio-Robert (1758–1821), she was one of those who attempted to extend the logic of human rights to women. A closer look at her works, and at the attack on her probity by Louise Keralio-Robert, reveals more clearly the female predicament in the French revolutionary agenda; and it shows the limits to the notion of female citizenship that republican women were able to develop during the early years of the Revolution.

We focus first on the life of Etta Palm d'Aelders, then on her advocacy of women's rights and her troubled relationship with Keralio-Robert, comparing and contrasting their views on the role of women (as well as the views of other enlightenment thinkers). We look particularly at the extent of their support for women's involvement in the polity, and how both developed ideas that seem to anticipate a new secular welfare system.

Biography

The woman who came to be known as Etta d'Aelders was born in April 1743 at Groningen, Netherlands, a daughter of the Protestant middle-class merchant Jacob Aelders van Nieuwenhuys and Agatha Petronella de Sitter, and lived her childhood at Stret Marsh in Groningen.[3] Her father died when she was six, but her mother was able to provide her with a very good education, including piano and ballet classes and the study of foreign languages: rare accomplishments for the daughter of a non-aristocratic family. Famous for her beauty, and already sufficiently notorious that she was not approved of by his parents, Etta eloped with Christian Ferdinand Lodewijk Palm, the son of a French attorney, on 3 September 1762. The couple soon experienced a crisis. Following the death of their only daughter, whose paternity was disputed, Lodewijk Palm left for the East Indies and disappeared from Etta's life. Now styling herself 'baroness' (baselessly claimed from her marriage to Lodewijk Palm), on 13 April 1768 Etta was befriended by Jan Munnik, a young lawyer of Groningen who was soon after appointed consul

H. Hardenberg, *Etta Palm: Een Hollandse Parisienne, 1743–1799* (Assen, 1962); and W.J. Koppius, *Etta Palm (Barones Aelders): Nederland's eerste féministe tijdens de Fransche revolutie te Parijs* (Zeist, 1929). See also: O. Blanc, *Les Libertines: Plaisir et liberté au temps des Lumières* (Paris, 1997); G. Arboit, '"Souvent femme varie": Une espionne hollandaise à Paris', *Notes historiques*, 12 (March 2008), at http://www.cf2r.org/fr/notes-historiques/souvent-femme-varie-une-espionne-hollandaise-paris.php; N. Hofmeester, *Etta Palm: Feministe van Hollandse bodem* (Amsterdam, 1978); C. Michelle, 'Etta Lubina Johanna Derista Aelders', in K.M. Wilson (ed.), *An Encyclopedia of Continental Women Writers* (New York, 1991), vol. 1.

3 Primary sources on her biography can be found in the *Regional History Center Groningen Archives*. The original Dutch orthography of her name was 'Alders'; she changed it to 'd'Aelders' when she moved in France. As for her birth, traditionally the baptisms took place about fifteen days after birth. Etta was baptized on 3 May 1743.

at Messina. The couple travelled through Europe, though there is no evidence that Etta settled with Munnik in Italy. Instead she formed a relationship with Lieutenant-General Douwe van Sirtina Grovestins, one of the former retainers of late Anne of Hannover (wife of the Stadtholder, William IV) who took her to Brussels and introduced her into the upper echelons of society.[4]

By 1773 she had left Brussels and settled in the rue Villedo near the Palais Royal in Paris – an area of ill repute, known for its courtesans.[5] A secret mission to Holland improved her finances, and in 1778 she opened her own salon in her new abode at the rue Favard, where she continued to be known as Baronesse d'Aelders.[6] Foreign policy was the main topic at the salon, which was attended by such men as Charles Alexandre de Calonne (the *contrôleur général des finances*), Louis Auguste de Breteuil (a former minister of France at The Hague, 1768–1771 and cousin of Emilie Du Châtelet), and the French foreign minister Armand Marc Montmorin Saint Hérem (1745–1792). At the beginning of the French Revolution, frequent guests of the salon were Jacobins such as Jean-Paul Marat, François Chabot, and Claude Basire.[7] Gérald Arboit has reconstructed her work as a diplomat and spy for the Dutch government, and documents her regular correspondence with van de Spiegel, Grand Pensionary of Holland.[8] She was close to the Stadtholder – and therefore against the Dutch Patriots,[9] who struggled for the removal of the Stadtholder William V of Orange and for reform of the Dutch Constitution, following what they represented as enlightened principles. The Patriots fled to France in 1787, but returned in 1795 and, with help from the French army, founded the Batavian republic. D'Aelders's promotion of the Orange cause at first sight sits uneasily with her later support for the French Revolution; but Judith Vega argues that the Patriots were in effect fighting for aristocratic privilege, so that d'Aelders's early advocacy for the Stadtholder and her later advocacy for the National Assembly are not inconsistent.[10] The shift would cost her dear, however, when in 1795 she was condemned as an enemy of the Batavian republic.

D'Aelders's first published essay sought to refute a pamphlet in which Honoré-Gabriel Riqueti (Count Mirabeau, 1749–1791) praised the Patriots for trying to reconfine the stadtholdership within its old boundaries during the so-called first

---

4 Arboit, 'Souvent femme varie'.

5 See Papiers d'Elisa Lubina Johanna, baronne d'Aelders, épouse de Chrétien Ferdinand Louis Palin [*sic*] (Archives Nationales [AN, hereafter]: AN T 364).

6 Villiers, *Histoire des clubs de femmes*, p. 22.

7 Arboit, 'Souvent femme varie'. Etta had a relationship with the youngest Basire, as documented by some letters whose content is described in Alexandre Tuetey, *Répertoire générale des sources manuscrits de l'histoire de Paris pendant la Révolution française* (Paris, 1842–1918), vol. 11, pp. 224–5. See Blanc, *Les Libertines*, pp. 222–4.

8 Arboit, 'Souvent femme varie'.

9 See S. Schama, *Patriots and Liberators: Revolution in the Netherlands, 1780–1813* (New York, 2005).

10 Vega, 'Feminist republicanism'.

Batavian Revolution (1786–1787).[11] According to d'Aelders, however, the Patriots were guided only by self-interest and were threatening the real peace and true freedom that could only be guaranteed by a stadtholder: 'Patriots have never had a reform plan; each one had a plan for his interest in the overthrow of the whole.'[12]

The genuineness of d'Aelders's advocacy for the French Revolution is attested by the fact that the last letter sent to her by van de Spiegel (on 2 September 1791) advises her to moderate her support for the people's cause. Her generous provision of French revolutionary and feminist pamphlets was no longer appreciated by her Dutch connections.[13] Arguably then, the French Revolution was a better setting than the *ancien régime* for the assertion and dissemination of her political ideas.

In 1790, when the *Cercle social* was created by Claude Fauchet and Nicolas de Bonneville, it was one of the few political associations to admit women.[14] D'Aelders soon joined, and on 30 November she intervened to support Charles-Louis Rousseau, whose speech in favour of women's political and civil existence was being rudely interrupted.[15] She urged her audience: 'You have been, till now, the companions of men enervated by the sentiments of corrupt slaves. As Frenchmen have become like Romans, imitate the virtues and the patriotism of Roman ladies.'[16] Scholars who situate d'Aelders among the republicans generally refer to these words to show the Roman republican roots of her thought; but the reference to Roman virtue is such a common trope during the period that little can be made of it.

On 30 December 1790, in front of the federative assembly of the *Cercle social*, one of the secretaries read a speech of hers in which she developed her political ideas: 'Discours sur l'injustice des lois en faveur des hommes, au dépend [sic] des femmes' [Discourse on the injustice of laws in favour of men, at women's expense], in which argues for justice and equality for both sexes.[17] The speech was approved by the Société and one thousand copies were printed. It was particularly appreciated by the women of Creil, who had formed themselves into a company of the national guard; on 8 February 1791 they made her an honorary member of their

---

[11] D'Aelders, *Réflexions sur l'ouvrage intitulé Aux Bataves sur le stadhoudérat, par le comte de Mirabeau* (Paris, 1788). The work is anonymous, but compare the original manuscript by d'Aelders in Dutch at the French National Archives: *Réflexions en hollandaise de divers questions de politique*, in Papiers d'Elisa Lubina Johanna (AN T 364); and see H.-G. de Mirabeau, *Aux Bataves sur le Stathoudérat* (Amsterdam, 1788).

[12] D'Aelders, *Réflexions sur l'ouvrage intitulé Aux Bataves sur le stadhoudérat*, p. 14.

[13] Arboit, 'Souvent femme varie'.

[14] Villiers, *Histoire des clubs de femmes*, pp. 15–16.

[15] Ibid., pp. 16–20.

[16] Ibid., pp. 19–20.

[17] P.-J.-B. Bouchez and P.C. Roux, *Histoire Parlementaire de la Révolution française* (Paris, 1834), vol. 8, p. 424. The speech is reprinted in E.P. d'Aelders, *Appel aux françoises sur la régénération des mœurs, et la nécessité de l'influence des femmes dans un gouvernement libre* (Paris, 1791), pp. 1–9.

troupe, sending her a medallion and the national cockade.[18] D'Aelders received this recognition as an important counter to the calumnies to which she claims she was subjected.[19]

On 23 March 1791, she read her 'Lettre d'une amie de la vérité, Etta Palm, née d'Aelders, Hollandoise, sur les démarches des ennemis extérieurs et intérieurs de la France' [Letter of a (female) friend of liberty, Etta Palm, née d'Aelders, on the advances of the exterior and interior enemies of France].[20] This was an appeal for unity, especially against the emigrés who d'Aelders thought were implementing a *divide et impera* policy against the Revolution; and she suggested that women step forward to champion the national cause. The speech was also an occasion to propose the *Société patriotique et de bienfaisance des Amies de la vérité*, whose meetings were recorded in the journal of the *Cercle social*, *La Bouche de fer*, edited by Nicolas de Bonneville and supervised by Claude Fauchet. This group was set up to work on several issues, such as childcare facilities, support for hospitals, protection from poverty and domestic violence, education, paid work for women, and in particular the founding of a school to take in the daughters, between the ages of six and thirteen, of indigent families.

On 19 July 1791, following the Champs de Mars demonstration of 17 June, d'Aelders was arrested and imprisoned for a few days.[21] As a result of this demonstration, the *Cercle social* was banned. Nevertheless, on 1 April 1792 d'Aelders was at the head of a delegation of women to the National Assembly, demanding admission of women to all civil and military occupations, a scheme of national education for girls, women's entry into majority at twenty, and a right to divorce.[22]

At about the same time, having lost all hope of income from van de Spiegel, she tried to profit from her changed allegiance; from 1792 she began to provide Pierre Marie Henri Tondu, called Lebrun-Tondu, with intelligence on her country for the French revolutionary government.[23] She returned to Holland sometime during 1792 or 1793, settling in The Hague; but her services and information were soon rejected.[24] In early 1795, when France invaded the Netherlands and the Batavian republic was proclaimed, d'Aelders became suspect. On 18 May 1795 an attorney of the Court of Justice, Cornelius Maanem, denounced her for machinations against the security of the Republic.[25] The Hague revolutionary committee put her under arrest in the fortress of Woerden. She was released at

18 See P. Bordeaux, *La Médaille d'honneur offerte par la Municipalité de Creil à Madame Palm Dalder, en février 1791* (Beauvais, 1908); and Villiers, *Histoire des clubs de femmes*, pp. 28, 92.

19 D'Aelders, *Appel aux françoises*, p. 16.

20 Ibid., pp. 16–31.

21 See *Réimpression de l'Ancien Moniteur* (Paris, 1858), vol. 9, p. 198.

22 Villiers, *Histoire des clubs de femmes*, pp. 36–7.

23 See Blanc, *Les Libertines*, p. 226; and Arboit, 'Souvent femme varie'.

24 Villiers, *Histoire des clubs de femmes*, p. 37.

25 Blanc, *Les Libertines*, p. 229.

the end of 1798; but she was seriously weakened by the captivity and died on 28 March 1799, apparently due to inflammation of her breasts.[26] Ultimately then, her earlier support for the Stadtholder made her an enemy to French Republicans. Yet it appears that she had not given up her feminist aspirations when she returned to Holland. An article in the Netherlands journal *Oprechte nationale courant* reports that she invited Dutch women to found clubs for women on the French model, excluding men so that women's claims could be heard.[27]

What is Implied by the Transition from the Rights of Men to the Rights of Human Beings?

Born and raised in a republic, d'Aelders claimed that republicanism was in her blood; but she was attacked by various critics, and it was to rebut these calumnies that she published her collected speeches.[28] Not least among her detractors was Louise Keralio-Robert, founding editor of the revolutionary *Journal d'état et de citoyen*.[29] Before the Revolution, Louise Keralio had defended women's intellectual equality with men and celebrated their contribution to French literature.[30] Sœur Louise – as she was to style herself during the Revolution, after she had married François Robert and had become an active member of the Cordeliers society – had opposed d'Aelders's admission to one of the fraternal clubs with which she was associated and threatened to publish a denunciation of her. While we do not have this document, we can gather something of its tendency in the response it prompted from d'Aelders.[31]

In her recent discussion of Keralio-Robert's differences with d'Aelders, Annie Geffroy claims that unlike d'Aelders, Keralio-Robert did not think of women as in

---

[26] Ibid.

[27] The anonymous speech is signed 'a friend of truth'. See C. Fauré, *Enciclopedia histórica y política de las mujeres: Europa y América* (Madrid, 2010), p. 236.

[28] D'Aelders, 'Au Lecteur', *Appel aux françoises*, p. 35.

[29] For the details of the complex evolution of this journal which became the *Mercure national* see: A. Geffroy, 'Louise de Keralio-Robert: Pionnière du républicanisme sexiste', *Annales historiques de la Révolution française*, 344 (2006): pp. 107–24; K.A. Dahl, 'At the Center of the Movement towards Enlightenment: Louise Keralio Robert and the French Revolution', PhD thesis (University of Minnesota, 1996); G. Mazel, 'Louise Kéralio et Pierre-François Robert, précurseurs de l'idée républicaine', *Bulletin de la Société de l'Histoire de Paris et de l'Ile-de-France*, 116 (1989): pp. 163–237.

[30] See L.-F. Keralio-Robert, *Collection des Meilleurs ouvrages François composés par des femmes, dédiée aux femmes françoises* (14 vols, Paris, 1786–1789). As well as many translations, her pre-revolutionary works included *Adelaide, ou mémoires de la Marquise de M***, écrits par elle-même* (Paris, 1783), and *Histoire d'Elizabeth reine d'Angleterre* (5 vols, Paris, 1786–1788).

[31] D'Aelders, 'Discours de réception prononcé à la société fraternelle par Etta Palm, née d'Aelders le 12 juin 1791, et justification sur la dénonciation de Louise Robert', in her *Appel aux françoises*, pp. 31–6.

any sense men's equals. Geffroy considers that in contrast to Keralio, d'Aelders is the thoroughly egalitarian republican woman of the period.[32] Kathleen Dahl offers a slightly different account, holding that they 'led differing factions in women's struggles to find ways to enter into the public arena and to define citizenship for themselves'.[33] We are persuaded, with Dahl, that both d'Aelders and Keralio-Robert were genuinely committed to extending the doctrine of equal rights and citizenship to women, and that in fact their views on women's citizenship are not strikingly different. Where they at least implicitly diverge is in their concept of liberty, and especially in their understanding of the proper behaviour of female republican citizens. To make this case we first outline d'Aelders's ideas as they are expressed in her speeches, and then consider the content of Keralio-Robert's attack and its origins in her political convictions.

D'Aelders on Equal Rights

D'Aelders begins her 'Discours sur l'injustice des lois en faveur des hommes' by applauding the inclusion of women in the patriotic *Société des amis de la vérité*, an organ of the *Cercle social*, and by praising the intrepid courage of the 'amazons' who have been allowed to raise a corps for the defence of the nation.[34]

Like Olympe de Gouges, who did not publish her declaration concerning the rights of women as citizens until nine months later,[35] d'Aelders takes it as obvious that the declaration of the rights of men implies the validity of the rights of women. She says:

> I shan't speak to you, gentlemen, of those iniquitous men who pretend that nothing can relieve us from our eternal subordination. Isn't this as much of an absurdity as if one had said to the French on 15 July 1789: 'Stop there your just claims, you are born for slavery; nothing can relieve you from eternal obedience to an arbitrary will'?[36]

And like Gouges, she is not averse to implying also the moral superiority of women. According to Gouges women were 'the sex superior in beauty as in courage during childbirth';[37] while d'Aelders suggests that women, while being men's moral equals, are perhaps their superiors in imagination, delicacy of sentiment, patience, and generosity of soul.[38]

---

[32] Geffroy, 'Louise de Keralio-Robert: Pionnière du républicanisme sexiste', pp. 107, 114.

[33] Dahl, 'At the Center of the Movement towards Enlightenment', p. 105.

[34] D'Aelders, *Appel aux françoises*, p. 2.

[35] Olympe de Gouges, *Declaration des droits de la femme et de la citoyenne* (1791), eds E. Gaulier and O. Fontvieille (Paris, 2007).

[36] D'Aelders, *Appel aux françoises*, pp. 5–6.

[37] Olympe de Gouges, *Ecrits politiques* (Paris, 1993), p. 206

[38] D'Aelders, *Appel aux françoises*, pp. 6–7.

D'Aelders's rhetoric could be taken to imply the full recognition of legal and social equality between the sexes as a final step in emancipation from the despotism of the *ancien régime*, initiated by the Revolution and by the Enlightenment:

> Do not then be just only by halves, gentlemen: you wished it, and immediately the walls of the proud fortresses, which were the humiliation and disgrace of the French, collapsed with a crash; in the same way destroy the ramparts of prejudice, more dangerous perhaps because they are more harmful to the general happiness. Justice should be the primary virtue of free men and justice demands that the laws are common to all beings as the air and sun; yet everywhere the laws are still in favour of men at the expense of women, because all power is in your hands. What! Will free men, an enlightened people, in an age of illumination and philosophy, consecrate that which was already an abuse of force in an age of ignorance?[39]

She returns to the same idea in addressing the National Assembly:

> You have returned to man the dignity of his being by recognizing his rights. No longer will you allow women to groan beneath an arbitrary authority; to do so would be to overturn the fundamental principles on which rests the majestic building that you have raised through your tireless work, for the happiness of the French.[40]

But when one looks closely at what D'Aelders is claiming for women, it is specifically equality within marriage and does not clearly extend to an equal right to representation. This may be taken as implied by the later deputation to the National Assembly, in which there is a claim for the right to all civil and military employments; but this is still somewhat equivocal. In her earlier address she follows many earlier eighteenth-century women in depicting the harmful effects of arranged marriage, and she calls for equal marriage based on love. Her understanding of what equality implies focuses on equal rights and duties within marriage. The issue prompting her address to the National Assembly is a matter of marriage law. Article XIII had been proposed, which would allow men to charge their wives with adultery, but would not give the same right to women.[41] D'Aelders makes an impassioned plea for the demolition of the sexual double standard in marriage, and for laws that give the husband and wife equal rights, powers, and duties. In these writings she does not go beyond the clear call for equality within marriage to an explicit appeal for women's legal and social equality in the public sphere.

Of course, one should not underestimate how radical the claim for equality in marriage was. From Diderot to Rousseau it was maintained that women's physical inferiority and the specificity of their sexual nature justified their subordinate

39 Ibid., pp. 2–3.

40 Ibid., p. 37.

41 Ibid., pp. 38–9.

status within the family.[42] Antoine-Léonard Thomas praised the *specific qualities* of women as especially sentimental and moral but had no confidence in their rationality and ability to play important roles in society.[43] All the encyclopaedists of the period (except for the Marquis of Jaucourt) promote a conservative image of women: from Desmahis[44] to Boucher d'Argis,[45] who defends the use of considering two women as a single witness in courts of law, and who considers it necessary to exclude them from the army, church, and government. Similar ideas based on difference in female qualities were advanced by doctors.[46] The authority of husbands was accompanied by the exclusion of women from autonomous public roles. However, the fact that d'Aelders argued for equality within marriage, without making an explicit claim to the equal right of women to be representatives, or even to vote for representatives, means that the conception of female citizenship that she deduced from the recognition of the rights of men was not in fact radically different from that assumed by Keralio-Robert.

D'Aelders nevertheless did map out a kind of public citizenship for women, calling in her speech to the *Société des amis de la vérité* for the setting up of women's clubs, the *Amies de la vérité*, which would take on the task of overseeing wet-nurses, public education, and the dispensing of charity, in particular to poor women giving birth.[47] The welfare programme elaborated by d'Aelders included the creation of a women's association in each section of Paris and in each department. The whole network would have responded to the central association that would be, according to d'Aelders, 'at the same time, a tie of alliance and friendship between the citizens of all sections'.[48]

The idea, however, that the duties of female republican citizenship extended to the organization of public charities run by women was not original with d'Aelders. In her journal, Keralio-Robert had foregrounded the activities of a women's group, the *Vingt-deux citoyennes de Civray*, whose secretary, Rose Pressac de la Chagnaie, had sent a letter to the journal with suggestions for the relief of orphans, the indigent, etc. She put forward a proposal: either all of the well-off should be required to take at least one such into their home, or there should be a tax that provided pensions for the poor.[49] The same group had earlier suggested setting up sewing circles to mend clothes for the indigent.[50] In an article

42 See Diderot, *Sur les Femmes*, in André Billy (ed.), *Œuvres* (Paris, 1951), p. 957; and J.-J. Rousseau, *Emile, or On Education*, trans. A. Bloom (New York, 1979).

43 Thomas et al., *Qu'est-ce qu'une femme?* p. 113.

44 J. Desmahis, 'Femme, morale', in Diderot and d'Alembert (eds), *Encyclopédie* (Paris, 1750–1765), vol. 6, p. 475.

45 Ibid., vol. 9 pp. 80ff.

46 See P. Roussel, *Système physique et moral de la femme* (Paris, 1775).

47 D'Aelders, *Appel aux françoises*, pp. 27–9.

48 Ibid., p. 45.

49 L.-F. Keralio-Robert [and various] (eds), *Mercure national ou Journal d'état et du citoyen* (Paris, 1789–1790), 1:14 (28 March 1790), pp. 898–901.

50 L.-F. Keralio-Robert, *Journal d'état et du citoyen*, 5:10 (September 1789), pp. 94–5.

on unjust imprisonment, Keralio-Robert also proposed that women should be deputed to oversee the running of prisons, to mitigate the shocking conditions that prevailed in them.[51] The thought that the duties of female citizenship extended beyond the home, and the proposals made by women at this period for their active engagement in the amelioration of society, are interesting precursors of the social welfare organizations that arose in the next century; but they are made equally by Keralio-Robert, d'Aelders, and others.

Keralio-Robert's Attack on D'Aelders

We do not possess the text of the denunciation of d'Aelders by Keralio-Robert, but the refutation that d'Aelders feels obliged to publish gives us some idea of its substance. She presented her self-justification to the fraternal society on 12 June 1791, suggesting first that the attack was prompted by envy. (By all accounts, while d'Aelders remained beautiful, Keralio-Robert, despite being fifteen years younger, was far plainer.) She goes on to defend herself, her italics suggesting that she is reusing quoted material:

> *Never, no never, have I been lacking in filial devotion. Never have I made my parents' tears flow, never did I cover with bitterness the last moments of the authors of my days, never have I abused the confidence of friendship; its treasures like its secrets have always been kept intact in my hands.*[52]

She calls on Brissot, Carra, and Pio to confirm her loyalty to France and to counter the accusation that she has had criminal dealings with the nation's enemies. By naming these men as vouching for her, she is putting pressure on Keralio-Robert's associates Carra and Pio, who had been co-editors of the *Mercure national*. As for Brissot, he had been admiringly reviewed in the journal, in particular for his work defending the blacks, and for arguing for the abolition of slavery. D'Aelders claims they will attest that she is not venal and has not become a patriot merely for the sake of commercial gain.[53]

From this self-justification it is reasonable to deduce that Keralio-Robert had attacked d'Aelders as self-serving, and as demonstrating less than adequate filial devotion and probity. Given what we know of d'Aelders's life, it was surely her personal relationships, and her position as something close to a courtesan spy, that raised the ire of Keralio-Robert and led her to object to the older woman's admission into the fraternal society. The republican Keralio-Robert had definite ideas as to what was required in a female republican citizen, which can be traced to her concept of liberty.

---

51 L.-F. Keralio-Robert et al. (eds), *Mercure national et révolutions de l'Europe, journal démocratique*, 45 (7 December 1790), pp. 1733–50.

52 D'Aelders, *Appel aux françoises*, p. 33.

53 Ibid., pp. 34–5.

In the introduction to her biography of Elizabeth I, Keralio-Robert follows Locke in distinguishing liberty from licence:

> The state of nature or state of greatest liberty is not a state of licence. There the law of nature operates, and this law teaches men that since all are equal and independent, none should harm another's freedom, life, or goods.[54]

She returns to this principle in the first issue of her journal, insisting that liberty should not be identified with licence.[55] Rather, freedom is guaranteed by a law that protects personal property and recognizes the equality of all. Following the most optimistic elements of the Enlightenment, Keralio-Robert believes in free discussion and rational argument as paths to moral knowledge and social perfection. But her understanding of what morality rationally requires of women is quite traditional. Women have a moral duty to be modest and to care for their servants and the education of their children so that ultimately all can play their part in the discursive development of a just, egalitarian, and cosmopolitan society.

For the encyclopaedist, the word *citoyen* – that is, one who possesses political rights – is not applicable to servants, women, or young children. In her article on Keralio-Robert as a sexist republican, Geffroy argues, on the basis of the conventional understanding she develops of women's role, that Keralio-Robert accepts women's status as passive citizens only.[56] But Keralio-Robert's name is not appended to the article in the *Mercure national* on which Geffroy bases this judgement, so it cannot be clearly attributed to her, unlike the many articles that she does sign.[57] There is also evidence that Keralio-Robert in fact considered fulfilment of the duties of mother and wife sufficient for women to count as active citizens.

In the second issue of the *Journal d'état et du citoyen* one finds a vigorous critique of l'Abbé Sièyes, who groups women with children as passive citizens. The author of this critique, who at this stage is probably the still unmarried Mlle de Keralio, editing the paper with the help of her father, says:

> We do not understand what the author means when he says that not all citizens can take an active part in the formation of the active part of government, and that women and children have no active influence on the polity.[58] Certainly women and children are not in employment. But is that the only way of actively influencing the polity? The discourses, the sentiments, the principles engraved on the souls of children from their first youth, whose care belongs to women, the

---

54 Keralio-Robert, *Histoire d'Elizabeth reine d'Angleterre*, vol. 1, p. vii.

55 Keralio-Robert, ed., *Journal d'état et du citoyen* 1, August 13, p. 3.

56 Geffroy, 'Louise de Keralio-Robert: Pionnière du républicanisme sexiste', p. 112.

57 The offending review is found at Keralio-Robert et al., *Mercure national ou journal d'état et du citoyen*, 2:1 (18 April 1790), pp. 26–7.

58 The translation of 'la chose publique' presents some problems. Here we have adopted the practice decided on in translating Christine de Pizan's *Livre de Paix*; see C. de Pizan, *The Book of Peace*, trans. K. Green et al. (University Park, PA, 2008).

> energy transmitted into society by her among her servants and vassals, are these matters of indifference to the fatherland? ... Oh! Let us avoid at this moment reducing any being whatever to a humiliating uselessness.[59]

This suggests that Keralio-Robert's conception of republican woman's role is that women become citizens in virtue of fulfilling their familial obligations. True, she sees the care of children as women's special duty; but she also envisages women taking part in the deliberative democracy through 'discours', ambiguously both written and spoken discussion, and as actively influencing the public sphere through their activities in the private domain. In a later article she defends the sexually mixed fraternal societies in similar terms:

> Every society of men ought by right to be a society deliberating over the nature and effects of the law; for having chosen representative government as best adapted to the extent of the French Republic, the association of men has delegated to their envoys the power of making and of instituting laws. But they could not surrender, in part or in whole, the inalienable right to examine those same laws, *proposed* rather than *made* by mere representatives; nor to censure them, nor indeed in the end to modify them or completely eradicate them – while at the same time provisionally submitting to them, and even protecting them with all the force of each individual citizen, in order to safeguard the social order, until such time as they should be changed.[60]

In this article Keralio-Robert appears to view the doctrine that the people are sovereign as implying that women as well as men retain inalienable rights.

At the same time, her other writings show a tendency to withhold full citizenship from women whose behaviour reveals them as not understanding their moral duties. In a letter sent to the journal *Le Batave* in September 1793, she offered her own original take on the controversial obligation on women to wear the cockade.[61] Rather than simply endorsing this proposal, Keralio-Robert expresses her pain at seeing 'liberty profaned' when the cockade is displayed by those committed to impropriety. That prostitutes should wear the cockade brings it into disrepute; and she suggests that encouraging them to wear it is a ploy of the enemies of the Revolution. She endorses a proposal that this symbol should be a right accorded to virtuous women, as a badge marking their status as true citizens.

It is against this moralised understanding of the requirements of citizenship that one should, we suggest, understand Keralio-Robert's opposition to d'Aelders – who she suspected was a libertine, intent on promoting quite a different concept of liberty. In this she may have been factually mistaken, though d'Aelders' early life and associates add weight to the accusation. Nevertheless, d'Aelders does not

---

[59] Keralio-Robert, *Journal d'état et du citoyen*, 2:20 (August 1789), p. 24.

[60] Keralio-Robert et al., *Mercure national et étranger ou journal politique de l'Europe*, 1:8 (23 April 1791), p. 115. For an account of the history of the mixed fraternal societies see Villiers, *Histoire des clubs de femmes*, pp. 42–52.

[61] Letter to *Le Batave*, 221, 24 September 1793; reprinted in Geffroy, 'Louise de Keralio-Robert: Pionnière du républicanisme sexiste', pp. 117–18.

herself argue explicitly for sexual libertinism, but suggests that the women of Creil raise a statue to the wife of Phocion, in order to have before their eyes a model of wisdom, modesty, simplicity, and moral and civic virtues.[62] Nevertheless, modern authors such as Olivier Blanc do place d'Aelders among the libertines. Her behaviour was certainly not the epitome of sexual propriety, and her own discourses are at least compatible with this interpretation. She begins her appeal for equality in laws with this demand:

> Be just to us, gentlemen: you whom nature created so superior in physical strength. You have reserved to yourselves the easy way of vice, whereas to us – whose being is so fragile, whose stock of hardships is enormous – to us you have left all the difficulty of virtue, as our share. And this delicate formation by Nature makes your injustice even more trenchant, since rather than fortifying it by education and by laws in our favour, you seem to treat us as formed for your pleasure – though it would be so sweet, so easy, to make us instead your allies in glory![63]

Clearly, d'Aelders is asking for an end to the sexual double standard. But is she asking that women be allowed to enjoy with men the ease of vice, or that men should be required to conform to the difficult requirements of virtue? No doubt if pressed she would say the latter, for she blames forced marriage for men's infidelities. But the passage is at least equivocal; and given d'Aelders's private life, Keralio-Robert may well have read her as condemning those prejudices by which women's sexual peccadilloes are assessed more harshly than men's. If there is something ideological rather than merely personal that divides Keralio-Robert and d'Aelders, we suggest it is the issue of what liberty implies for women. Clearly for Keralio-Robert true liberty is not licence, but government by the law of nature, which endorses traditional virtues for women; but d'Aelders has a more modern concept of liberty as freedom from external constraint, and certainly her rhetoric in favour of sexual equality is more robust than Keralio-Robert's. The real issue that divides these women is not the extent of women's freedom to participate in public politics, but rather what sort of sexual relations will be acceptable under laws written by a free people, guided by a rational moral law. Keralio-Robert's opposition to d'Aelders anticipates a problem that remains in disputes over prostitution, pornography, and sexual liberation: the paradoxical implications of liberty and equal rights when, given sexual difference, one considers what counts as acceptable sexual freedom.

Paradoxes of Female Citizenship

Pierre Guyomar became, on 29 April 1793, the only deputy of the National Convention during the Revolution to ask for perfect equality of the sexes, with

[62] D'Aelders, *Appel aux françoises*, p. 13.

[63] Ibid., p. 3.

full citizenship for women.[64] Already in 1787, and again in 1790, Condorcet had pointed out the inconsistency of denying women citizenship, arguing far more explicitly than either d'Aelders or Keralio-Robert for women's right to be elected, and to participate in the formation of the law.[65] He pointed out the anomaly that some noble women exercised, in virtue of their feudal rights, control over the election of deputies to the National Assembly, yet women were denied the natural right of voting. He proposed an extension of the property franchise, a step that would have resulted in only a few women exercising actual power, but which had the virtue of consistency.[66] Paradoxically then, it may seem that it was by a man that women's exclusion from political representation was first clearly opposed during the Revolution.

Before Condorcet's July 1790 publication, various anonymous pamphlets touching on women's representation had appeared. One has been judged so extreme that it must have been intended as a satire.[67] It presented a request and projected a decree to the National Assembly, in late 1789, which amounted to a call for the complete overthrow of all masculine privilege. The proposed decree would abolish all the privileges of the male sex in France, would give women all the same rights as men, demanded that people would cease to treat the masculine gender as more noble (even in grammar), would give women the same power and authority in marriage as men, and would allow women to wear trousers. It demands the abolition of the tradition of dressing a cowardly soldier in female clothes, and that women should be elected, on the same criteria as men, to all assemblies, including the National Assembly, and be allowed to hold municipal positions, to be magistrates, and to serve in the military. This pamphlet even suggests that the position of French Marshal be occupied alternately by a man and a woman. Last, it hints at the ordination of women, while promising not to take religious devotion too far. The author or authors of these radical demands remains anonymous, like that of an earlier and more humorous suggestion that the all-male Estates General should be replaced by a completely female one.[68]

---

64 Archives parlementaires de 1787 à 1860 (Paris), 1903, vol. DXIII, p. 599.

65 J.-A.-N. de Condorcet, 'Sur l'admission des femmes au droit de cité' ['On giving women the right of citizenship'], *Journal de la société de 1789*, 5 (3 July 1790), pp. 1–13; see also Condorcet, 'Letters from a Freeman of New Haven to a Citizen of Virginia on the Futility of Dividing the Legislative Power among Several Bodies (1787)', in I. McLean and F. Hewitt (eds.) *Condorcet: Foundations of Social Choice and Political Theory* (Aldershot, 1994), pp. 292–3.

66 Condorcet, 'On giving women the right of citizenship', p. 13.

67 'Requête des dames à l'Assemblée nationale,' (late 1789) in A. Soboul, (ed.), *Les Femmes dans la Révolution Française* (Paris: Editions d'Histoire Sociale, 1982), vol. 1; Proctor, *Women, Equality, and the French Revolution*, pp. 139–41.

68 Anonymous [M.L.P.P.D.St.L.], 'Rémonstrances plaintes et doléances des dames françoises, a l'occasion de l'assemblée des Etats-Géneraux,' (May 1789), in A. Soboul, (ed.), *Les Femmes dans la Révolution française* [1789–1794] (reprint Paris, 1982), vol. 1. Candice Proctor treats this pamphlet as serious; see *Women, Equality, and the French Revolution*, pp. 119–20.

Of identifiable women it was first Marie Jodin and then Olympe de Gouges who made explicit serious demands for women's representation.[69] Jodin's proposal for a separate female legislature did not, however, imply that women would vote for men or sit with them in the National Assembly. This was the clear and serious demand made by Gouges in her 'Declaration of the Rights of Women and the Female Citizen' dedicated by her to the queen, Marie Antoinette, nine months after d'Aelders had addressed the *Amis de la vérité*. It has seemed paradoxical that Gouges, who continued to support a monarchy, is the earliest identifiable woman to have published the demand for a right to vote and to be representatives.[70] However, a well-established tradition of writing in support of women's political aptitude had pointed to queens, such as Marie Antoinette's mother and Elizabeth I. These examples had been cited in the earlier anonymous pamphlets in support of claims for female representation. Hence it was natural for Gouges, whose aims were for reform rather than revolution, to call on the queen to support the progress of enlightenment, by using her authority to endorse its implications for women. Keralio-Robert, whose husband was among the earliest to publish in support of a republicanism free of monarchy, was far more equivocal. Between these extremes is d'Aelders. The implications of her early demands, delivered before the National Assembly, were explicitly drawn by Gouges – never by d'Aelders herself, in any of her own published works.[71]

---

69 M.M. Jodin, *Vues législatives pour les femmes* (Angers, 1790), and English translation in F. Gordon and P.N. Furbank, *Marie Madeleine Jodin, 1741–1790: Actress, Philosophe, and Feminist* (Aldershot, 2001); Gouges, *Ecrits politiques*, pp. 207–8. For an account of the earlier pamphlets see Proctor, *Women, Equality, and the French Revolution*, pp. 118–19.

70 J.W. Scott, 'A Woman who has only Paradoxes to Offer', in *Rebel Daughters*, ed. S.E. Melzer and L.W. Rabine (Oxford, 1992), pp. 102–20.

71 This chapter is the result of combining two lines of research: Calogero Alberto Petix's investigations into the life and thought of Etta Palm d'Aelders, and Karen Green's work on the life and thought of Louise-Félicité Keralio-Robert.

Chapter 5
Marie-Armande Gacon-Dufour: A Radical Intellectual at the Turn of the Nineteenth Century

Erica J. Mannucci

Marie-Armande-Jeanne Gacon, born in 1753, was a published author since just before the Revolution. Her first writings had been rather conventional. The epistolary novel *L'Homme errant fixé par la raison* (1787) told a typical story of conflict between duty and passion, with a heroine whose inspiration was Rousseau's universally admired Julie. Only between the lines did the novel reveal Gacon's support for physiocracy (as a policy and as a way of life, especially for the nobility). Her anonymous *Mémoire pour le sexe féminin contre le sexe masculin* (1787) was a reply to the Chevalier de Feucher's *Réflexions d'un jeune homme* (1786), in which she disputed what he had presented as the nefarious effects of a pretended predominant influence of women on society. Gacon's tone was so guileless that a reader must suspect irony concerning the whole subordinate condition of women: on the surface, she simply argued the utility and solace a married woman could derive in her middle and old age from education and culture.[1]

Marie-Armande married twice. From the first marriage she was known as Madame d'Humières, and from the second (to Jules-Michel Dufour de St-Pathus, *avocat* at the Paris Parliament before the Revolution, judge in the Seine court during and after the Revolution, and *avocat* at the Cour royale in Paris) as Madame Gacon-Dufour. It is with the latter name that she signed her novels and other writings in the first decade of the nineteenth century. This stage of her career seems most worthy of attention: she was then at her most productive, and most aware of her own motives and of the role she could play as a writer in civil society. In the increasingly authoritarian climate of Bonaparte's regime (the Consulate, and the Empire after 1804) and particularly of his cynical religious and cultural

---

1 M.-A. Gacon-Dufour, *L'Homme errant fixé par la raison, ou Lettres de Célidor et du marquis de Tobers, par le Comte d'Ay ... et Madame Filh. D'Hu...* (Paris, 1787); Gacon-Dufour [anonymously], *Mémoire pour le sexe féminin contre le sexe masculin* (London [Paris], n.d.), modern edition in G. Fraisse (ed.), *Opinions de femmes de la ville au lendemain de la Révolution française* (Paris, 1989), on pp. 20–46. The dispute was pursued by Feucher d'Artaize in other essays; see d'Artaize, *Réflexions d'un jeune homme* (Paris, 1786), and for example d'Artaize, *Lettre à Mme Gacon-Dufour* (Paris, 1788).

policy, Gacon was driven to rethink both *ancien régime* history and the political and human experience of the Revolution, now terminated by Napoleon. She also had to choose which side she was on.

Her work has been treated briefly by a few historians, such as Geneviève Fraisse; more recently also by Jean-Clément Martin and by June K. Burton, who focuses in *Napoleon and the Woman Question* on Gacon's writings on housekeeping. But her output has never really been put in context or shown alongside details of her actual *milieu*.[2] This is in part due, quite prosaically, to the lack of sufficient information on her life, let alone a scholarly biography; but the result is nonetheless paradoxical. She does not stand out as the bold and original thinker she actually was, but seems rather a submissive little lady: a mainstream novelist whose moderate feminism goes no further than calls for a mostly practical education.

In 1806 Gacon published the first in a series of three historical books. Although their titles are deceptive, they were not simply the stories or collected letters of queens and favourites, but could be read – though Gacon did not declare this intention – as a coherent interpretation of the political history of the French monarchy. From the age of Catherine de' Medici (and particularly since the massacre of thousands of Protestants on Saint-Bartholomew's Day, 1572) Gacon traced a long drift toward the inevitable final crisis.

Her targets were royal despotism, priestly and Jesuit influence, intolerance and religious persecution, and censorship or 'inquisition de la pensée',[3] along with the privilege, pride, and economic uselessness of nobles. Those real women of the past who became the characters of her historical narrative were political actors and power brokers. Gacon did not spend one line on their looks or on nostalgic sentimentalities. Nor was she a contributor to an afterlife for the revolutionary discourse on the 'influence of women' – corrupt courtesans presented as the ruin of the nation – though some of the women she wrote about (Madame de Maintenon, for example) remained negative figures in her estimation. Marie-Armande Gacon had herself been educated by the Sisters of the Convent of Montfort-l'Amaury, and moreover was acquainted with the court, where it seems she had served as a *lectrice*, an appointment that theoretically involved reading aloud to a member of the royal family.

At the end of the first book of Gacon's historical series, Madame de Châteauroux (Marie Anne de Mailly, duchesse de Châteauroux: one of four sisters who were among the mistresses of Louis XV) dies in 1744 while dictating a political testament with suggestions including the choice of a future mistress for the king. The duchess points out also the profound changes the country would need

---

[2] See G. Fraisse, *Muse de la Raison: Démocratie et exclusion des femmes en France* (Paris, 1995), pp. 60–68; J.-C. Martin, *La Révolte brisée: Femmes dans la Révolution française et l'Empire* (Paris, 2008), p. 209; J.K. Burton, *Napoleon and the Woman Question: Discourses of the Other Sex in French Education, Medicine, and Medical Law, 1799–1815* (Lubbock, TX, 2007), pp. 74–7.

[3] Gacon-Dufour, *Mémoires*, vol. 2, p. 40.

in order to survive as a monarchy: the king should abandon religious fanaticism and free himself from the 'cabale des prêtres', first of all repealing the Edict of Fontainebleau and welcoming back the Protestants, an act of justice that would be beneficial to the French economy. Common people should be introduced into the Church hierarchies themselves; this would turn the characteristic ambition of lower clergy to the advantage of social change. The nobility should be reformed and institutions that had been open to them alone be made accessible to all; their code of honour should be abandoned in favour of a *noblesse commerçante* such as the abbé Gabriel-François Coyer, much appreciated by Voltaire, would boldly define in 1756.[4]

The financier Joseph Paris-Duverney, as the friend who takes down Châteauroux's words, replies that the whole system cannot take even one reform, and so will continue as it is 'in France, where all the gears of the machine are linked so that the attempt to make one cog move in the opposite direction would shake it to the core'. In fact, Châteauroux is here represented as a positive figure and as consequently a political loser ('Must one die knowing for certain that good will never be effected in France?' she exclaims), because the monarchy itself was unreformable.[5]

Gacon did not indicate sources for the correspondence she published in her book, though a few matches can be found with memoirs in print at her time, such as those of Châteauroux's mentor the duc de Richelieu.[6] Similarly, Gacon did not add references to the title she gave the testament: *Copie de ce qui a été dicté à M. Duverney par Madame de Châteauroux*. Several contemporary witnesses and later historians mention the content of Châteauroux's moral testament, improvising the exact words (as was usual until the late nineteenth century), but in sufficient

---

4 Abbé Gabriel-François Coyer's *La Noblesse commerçante* (Paris, 1756) – a work that prompted Voltaire's joke, 'the abbé wants to see the Montmorencys and the Châtillons at shop-counters' – sparked off heated debate when it appeared; see P. Serna, 'The Noble', in M. Vovelle (ed.) *Enlightenment Portraits*, trans. L.G. Cochrane (Chicago, 1997), pp. 30–79. Among the most interesting participants in the debate was writer and translator Octavie Belot, *Observations sur la noblesse et le tiers-état* ('Amsterdam' [Rouen], 1758); see S. Maza, 'Luxury, Morality, and Social Change: Why there was no Middle-Class Consciousness in Pre-Revolutionary France', in G. Kates (ed.), *The French Revolution*, 2nd edn (London, 2008), pp. 113–30; and see Paul Gibbard's contribution in the present volume.

5 M.-A. Gacon-Dufour, *Correspondance inédite de Mme de Châteauroux avec le duc de Richelieu, le maréchal de Belle-Isle, MM. Duverney, de Chavigni, Mme de Flavacourt et autres, précédée d'une notice historique* (2 vols, Paris, 1806), quotations on p. 274 and p. 265, vol. 2 (all translations are mine). On political gossip on Châteauroux and other favourites see R. Darnton, *George Washington's False Teeth: An Unconventional Guide to the Eighteenth Century* (Cambridge, MA, 2003), Chapter 2.

6 L.F.A. de Richelieu, *Mémoires* (8 vols, Paris, 1793). The first work with footnotes is E. de Goncourt, *La duchesse de Châteauroux et ses sœurs, Nouvelle édition, revue et augmentée de lettres et documents inédits, tirés de la Bibliothèque nationale, de la Bibliothèque de Rouen, des Archives nationales et des collections particulières* (Paris, 1906).

agreement on the basic themes and on the concern the lady showed for the welfare of France. Gacon too, apparently, improvised the words of the testament and the conversation between Châteauroux and Duverney, probably to the point of interpolating content – on religious policy, for example. She chose those words with a conscious aim: to make her own reading of Louis XV's period very plain. She tried, however, not to be anachronistic: though her perspective was indeed post-revolutionary, she had her character speak a language of reform compatible with those earlier times. Nonetheless, in these years from 1806 to 1808 she clearly stated through her historical characters that though a reform of the *ancien régime* might have been imaginable, it would not have been feasible. Even before its golden age, the French monarchy's final collapse was already looming.[7]

Gacon had earlier felt the need to defend the revolutionary experience, when Bonaparte was showing his true colours in 1801. Her vehicle was *La Femme grenadier*, an interesting novel directly related to *La Femme abbé* which was published at the same time by her friend Sylvain Maréchal, formerly a leading member of Gracchus Babeuf's clandestine 'communist' group, the Conspiracy of Equals (1796), and one of the earliest critics of general Bonaparte.[8] Developing a political perspective that remained faithful to revolutionary republicanism – in other words, it did not condemn the Revolution itself along with the Terror – Gacon narrated the adventures of two young aristocrats, brother and sister. In Year II, the hero and heroine embrace patriotism and egalitarianism, while at the same time they must avoid the dangers of the Terror. In that novel too, Gacon's anti-clerical stance was prominent. So was her idea that the people, misguided and sent to die with the priests' false promise of immediate resurrection – as in the Vendée rebellion – should have been the object of an educational effort, persuaded by good arguments and equitable treatment to support revolutionary change. This is what the girl referred to in the title of her 1801 novel attempted to achieve, disguised as a republican soldier.[9]

---

7 It would be interesting to know if Sarah Buell Hale, in her *Woman's Record: Or, Sketches of all Distinguished Women, from the Creation to A.D. 1868* (New York, 1874), was influenced by Gacon's portrait of Madame de Châteauroux when she wrote: 'Madame de Châteauroux was one of those far-seeing women, who, with that instinctive foresight which arises from keenness of perception, had predicted the breaking out of the storm already gathering over France' (p. 258).

8 His pamphlet was published in semi-clandestine fashion in Paris in 1797, and later circulated and translated in European countries such as Italy and Poland: S. Maréchal, *Correctif à la gloire de Bonaparte: Ou lettre à ce général* (Venice, 1798). The literature on Babeuf – and his conspiracy and its individual members – is copious, though not particularly useful on Sylvain Maréchal. On studies regarding Babeuf, see M. Vovelle, 'Une troisième voie pour la lecture de la *Conspiration des égaux*?', *Annales historiques de la Révolution française*, 312:1 (1998): pp. 217–27.

9 M.-A. Gacon-Dufour, *La Femme grenadier* (Paris, 1801); see in particular pp. 165–86. The volume has an appendix by S. Maréchal: 'Revue historique de toutes les Jeannes célèbres'.

A few years later in her *Mémoires, anecdotes secrètes* (1807), Gacon reflects like other witnesses on the long-range course of French history – and praises Napoleon's regime, though for what it retained of the Revolution rather than as a form of restoration. Touching on religious freedom, one of the rights of men that was dearest to her heart, she stresses that Napoleon's policy is universal tolerance, even if he professes Catholicism. She eulogises the '*liberté des cultes*' (in fact a revolutionary principle) in what is seemingly a servile homage to the Emperor, though the outright assimilation of the Emperor to a deity is excessive enough to sound ironic. Her praise contains a veiled criticism, because Napoleon's tolerance, after the Concordat, amounts to less than total religious freedom:

> The attachment of men to their religion shows us that freedom of worship is one of the greatest benefits of humanity. The sovereign who maintains it in his states resembles the Divinity, who protects all breathing beings and considers in the same way the allegiances of the Muslim, the Calvinist, the Catholic and the Jew.[10]

Beginning in 1804, along with despotism of a new imperial variety, Bonaparte had re-established the organization and pre-eminence of the Catholic cult in France, with a particular devotion – not surprisingly – for 'saint Napoléon'. (The very existence of this 'Corsican saint', for whom Napoleon claimed to be named, was greeted with doubt within the Church; undeterred, he fixed his own birthday, 15 August, as the saint's day.) The clergy was still subservient at the time, and Bonaparte used their help in presenting his Empire as a reconstruction of the French Christian monarchy under a fourth dynasty, his own. In February of 1806 he launched a plan to restore the burial place of the French kings in the church of Saint-Denis, which had been destroyed in the late summer of 1793 following a vote of the republican Convention. He said that Saint-Denis was the monument that contained the whole history of the French Nation, and that it would become the necropolis of French *emperors* as well as French kings.[11] Combining as usual traditional elements and new controlling structures, in the *Code civil* Napoleon had restored the full legal subordination of married women – and consequently married female authors – to their husbands, along with full paternal authority over children and a diminished right to divorce.[12] The eminently political view of relations inside the family that had prevailed in the republican years from 1792 to 1794 was now treated as a cause of social disorder, though of course the so-called 'natural' relations that the law restored were no less politically expedient.

---

[10] Gacon-Dufour, *Mémoires, anecdotes secrètes*, vol. 1, p. 284.

[11] On Napoleon's religious policy see J.-O. Boudon, *Napoléon et les cultes: Les religions en Europe à l'aube du XIXe siècle, 1800–1815* (Paris, 2002).

[12] On the legal problems of female authorship see C. Hesse, 'Reading Signatures: Female Authorship and Revolutionary Law in France, 1750–1850', *Eighteenth-Century Studies*, 22:3 (Spring 1989): pp. 469–87. On the evolution of French private law in this period, M. Garaud, and R. Szramkiewicz, *La Révolution française et la famille* (Paris, 1978) is still an essential reference, though the subject has of course been treated from various perspectives since then.

In January 1807, a reviewer in the *Mercure de France* attacked Gacon's *Mémoires*, with a tone of warning and a sinister reference to an alchemical death allegory:

> I suppose that Madame Gacon-Dufour, carried away by a spirit of inquisitiveness that I do not understand, has meant to make an experiment in morals such as one sometimes makes in physics, and tried to transmute vice into virtue, like alchemists seeking to make gold with copper.... In the end only a *caput mortuum* remains; or else the vessel ... explodes in their faces, disfiguring them for the rest of their lives. I hope, for Madame Gacon-Dufour, that such a misfortune never happens to her.[13]

The reviews of this book in the few authorized newspapers and periodicals of the time – subject to direct police control and forced to pay government censors to read their copy – went well beyond condescension and suggestions that the author keep to the 'admirable' field of rural and household economy where she had successfully proved herself. They amounted to an assault.

Therefore, even as she interspersed her research on the French monarchic past with praise of Napoleon's regime, this woman writer, by stressing the subject of religious freedom, patently provoked acrimony and alarm in mainstream critics. Gacon went against the tide, and not so covertly; her opinions, not unusual in France a few years before (though rarely expressed by women authors), were dangerous now that public opinion was becoming more and more conservative.

It is evidence of the direction in which the tide was turning that, just recently, Madame de Genlis (one of the best-known women authors and former exponent of the *noblesse libérale*, an *émigrée* who had been welcomed back by Napoleon) had rejected, particularly in her *Étude du cœur humain* (1805),[14] the reconciliation between the Enlightenment and Catholicism that she had subscribed to twenty years earlier. (Before the Revolution, Jean Le Rond d'Alembert had tried to propose her admission to the Académie française in which he was himself prominent, though this was a male preserve. He was rare among *philosophes* in considering women to be equal, and sought the admission of a few women authors.) A gothic image of the Revolution – a construction of collective memory whose long evolution had started after Thermidor – along with an ambiguous return to the past, particularly the Catholic past, seemed to be the cultural order of the day. In her historical novels, Madame de Genlis herself went so far down this conservative or reactionary path as to glorify the Middle Ages and the nobles of those times; that is, models that were the negation not only of revolutionary principles, but even of more moderate Enlightenment visions of history.

---

13 Anonymous review by 'G-', '*Mémoires, anecdotes secrètes, galantes, historiques et inédites, sur mesdames de la Vallière, de Montespan, de Fontanges, de Maintenon, et autres illustres personnages du siècle de Louis XIV*, par Madame Gacon-Dufour', *Mercure de France* (January 1807), pp. 112–13.

14 S.-F. Genlis, *Étude du cœur humain, suivie des cinq premières semaines d'un journal écrit sur les Pyrénées* (Paris: Cellot, 1805).

Against this mood, Gacon maintained her anticlericalism and republicanism. She impressed herself upon critics as part of a scattered and almost silenced intellectual opposition, not least by references to the wisdom of a famous heroine of freethinkers, the courtesan Ninon de l'Enclos; or to the religious hypocrisy of a great bishop of Louis XIV's court, Jacques Bénigne Bossuet – enemy of Protestants and pride of the *Église*, who 'jouait la dévotion par état' ['played religious devotion by trade'], as Gacon wrote. This estimation was confirmed by her preference for the opposite moral model, represented by prelate François de la Mothe-Fénelon – often referred to as '*sensible* Fénelon' during the Enlightenment. To her servile reviewers, such recollections of the imagery and language of the Radical Enlightenment seemed all the worse because she was a woman, who should be murmuring her rosary and ratafia recipes at home, rather than having the effrontery to sign such political works.

The atheist astronomer Jérôme Lalande (an authoritative intellectual and member of the Institut, who in the 1770s had been among the founders of the famous Parisian Masonic lodge for *philosophe* writers and artists, called 'Les Neuf Sœurs') had incurred Napoleon's wrath and an enduring prohibition on publishing again because in 1805 he had privately printed his second supplement to the *Dictionnaire des athées.* The author of the *Dictionnaire* was his younger friend, the materialist poet and revolutionary journalist Sylvain Maréchal (mentioned earlier), who had unrepentantly maintained his opinions until his death in January 1803.

To the inventory of figures praised in Maréchal's original dictionary of 1800 – a book already attacked by Catholics and Deists alike, and destined to become an object of both controversy and secular cult during the nineteenth century – Lalande added new entries. Among these was Gacon. A friend of both men, she had in all likelihood given her consent to what for many was, in that time of recantation, a scandalous mention. This made her one of very few women discussed in the book, and perhaps the only one still living, although Lalande wrote that there were quite a few women in what he called their 'Socratic sect'.[15] Gacon had moreover provided Lalande with excerpts from the biography of Maréchal that she was preparing, to use in this publication; and Lalande duly expressed in print his hope that she would bring it to publication. This she did in the year 1807, as a preface to Maréchal's posthumous *De la Vertu.* This time she prudently maintained formal anonymity and posed as a man, so as to avoid any equivocation on the nature of her twenty-year friendship with Maréchal.[16]

Among the heroines of the radical freethinking tradition listed in the *Dictionnaire des athées* was Ninon de l'Enclos; but notably omitted was the Alexandrian philosopher Hypatia (subject of a section of John Toland's *Tetradymus* of 1720), who had fallen victim to the fanaticism of Christian clergy. For her part, Gacon reflected on Hypatia's atrocious fate as a woman who dared to love knowledge and teach philosophy, in her reply to a reviewer for the *Journal*

---

15 J. Lalande, *Notice sur Sylvain Maréchal, avec des supplémens pour le Dictionnaire des athées* (n.d., but Paris, 1805).

16 M.-A. Gacon-Dufour [anonymously], 'Notice sur Sylvain Maréchal', in S. Maréchal, *De la Vertu, suivi du Livre de tous les âges* (Paris, 1807), pp. 1–71.

de l'Empire, Abbé Charles-Marie de Féletz (also known as Abbé Dorimon; later elected to the Académie française).[17] The abbé's contempt for her style revealed the underlying problem. Not only was Gacon anti-Catholic and 'of no religion because she belongs to all'; she was herself evidence for what amounted to a social control issue: evidence that the attitude was not limited to some males, but 'infected' some women as well.[18]

Gacon challenged Dorimon's hatred for cultivated women who expressed independent ideas. After her description of the way Hypatia had been torn apart by pretended 'ministers of a God of peace', she concluded: 'My eyes are swollen with tears, my heart surges with indignation; but I will nonetheless continue to love science, detest persecution, and preach tolerance.'[19] In the very last lines of this reply she was explicit: her work on French history opposed those who *now*, even as she wrote, considered 'odious intolerance' a virtue.[20]

This short text was illuminating, as were other polemical replies Gacon had used to elucidate her own positions at various times. The best-known had been her reply in 1801 to Maréchal's personal provocation, *Projet d'une loi portant défense d'apprendre à lire aux femmes*.[21] This was the year of Napoleon's Concordat with the Pope (10 September 1801), settled in a context of Catholic revival in France and bitter reactions from anticlerical republicans. In the same year François Peyrard, another member of Maréchal and Gacon's intimate circle, published a work that we may consider linked to the other two in a sort of literary game *à trois*. This was his translation of Agrippa of Nettesheim's famous Latin essay on woman's excellence and superiority, all construed from an atheistic point of view in the Dedication ('Aux femmes') and in the translator's footnotes.[22] This post-

---

17 M.-A. Gacon-Dufour, *Réponse à M. A. ..., l'un des Rédacteurs du 'Journal de l'Empire' ... L'Abbé Félès Dorimon* (Paris, 1807), in particular on Bossuet and Fénelon, pp. 12–15. This pamphlet is at the Bibliothèque Nationale in Paris, LN-27–8120: it has now been digitized, at my request, and is accessible online.

18 C.-M. Féletz [anonymously], *'Mémoires, anecdotes secrètes, galantes, historiques et inédites, sur mesmades de la Vallière, de Montespan, de Fontanges, de Maintenon, et autres illustres personnages du siècle de Louis XIV*; par Mad. Gacon-Dufour', *Journal de l'Empire* (31 Janvier 1807), pp. 3–4.

19 Gacon-Dufour, *Réponse*, p. 5.

20 '... my latest work is a drug against persecution. I hope ... the time will come when it will be regarded as a beneficial remedy even by those who, today, consider odious intolerance a virtue,' Gacon-Dufour, *Réponse*, pp. 16–17.

21 M.-A. Gacon-Dufour [anonymously], *Contre le projet de loi de S***M***, Portant défense d'apprendre à lire aux femmes, Par une femme qui ne se pique pas d'être femme de lettres* (Paris, 1801).

22 [F. Peyrard, ed.], *De l'Excellence et de la supériorité de la femme: Ouvrage traduit du latin d'Agrippa, avec les commentaires de Roétig* (Paris, 1801). It is worth noting that Agrippa's work was dusted off in 1990 by a well-known feminist publisher – notwithstanding that the author was male – in so far, among other reasons, as it revealed 'paradoxically, its modernity; because he prefigures, *simultaneously*, in his method and the

revolutionary editor was certainly not the first so to interpret that sixteenth-century work, in which Agrippa wrote that the story of Creation was 'very credible, even more believed, but absolutely inconceivable'. The interesting point was the translator's statement that telling the (atheistic) truth about religion entailed telling the truth about *woman*: that she is not inferior but in fact 'excellent', even though the victim of men's tyranny. In Peyrard's interpretation, a feminist stance became a basic element of atheism. His part in the literary drama would be to defend an interpretation of the Radical Enlightenment as inherently feminist – and of religion as intrinsically against women.

It would be beside the point here to go into possible interpretations of Maréchal's famous anti-feminist text, in which he goes so far as to deny women the right to learn to read. We certainly could never discover a feminist side in his whole literary and journalistic production.[23] At the same time, given that he was a chronic outsider as an intellectual and in his political concerns, interpreting him as representing a nascent modern ideology of the exclusion of women from the public sphere, or a Napoleonic turn in the attitude toward the woman question, seems in many senses to miss the mark.[24] But here Maréchal's pamphlet can be seen – maintaining for the sake of argumentative clarity our conjecture about the game *à trois* – as the polar opposite of Peyrard's work, in so far as it undoubtedly implies that woman has not enough intellect and independence of judgement to grasp the atheistic truth.

What is interesting here is Gacon's public reply to Maréchal's pamphlet; or better, the way she understood the moral, intellectual, and political stakes in his provocation. Hers was not simply a sound but moderate feminist argument for the social utility of women's education, lacking the boldness to shed the 'equality in difference' ideological framework.[25]

---

mode of his argumentation, the two main and opposed currents of today's feminism', that is, basically, two ideas of the relationship between difference and equality: M.-J. Dhavernas, 'Préface' to H.C. Agrippa de Nettesheim, *Discours abrégé sur la noblesse et l'excellence du sexe féminin, de sa prééminence sur l'autre sexe et du sacrement du mariage* (Paris, 1990). The publication in 1537 was posthumous, though the work dated from 1519.

[23] On Maréchal's positions on women and his relationship with Gacon see E.J. Mannucci, 'Sylvain Maréchal, le donne, una donna', in S. Levati and M. Meriggi (eds), *Con la ragione e col cuore: Studi dedicati a Carlo Capra* (Milano, 2008), pp. 405–24. On his political positions see E.J. Mannucci, 'Conformité et hétérodoxie chez Sylvain Maréchal', in M. Biard (ed.), *Les politiques de la Terreur, 1793–1794* (Rennes, 2008), pp. 379–89; see also E.J. Mannucci, 'Opposizioni al Concordato: L'ultima fiammata dei lumi?', in A. De Francesco (ed.), *Da Brumaio ai Cento giorni: Cultura di governo e dissenso politico nell'Europa di Bonaparte* (Milan, 2007), pp. 157–76; and E.J. Mannucci, *Finalmente il popolo pensa: Sylvain Maréchal nell'immagine della Rivoluzione francese* (Naples, 2012).

[24] See Fraisse, *Muse de la Raison*; see also F. Aubert, *Sylvain Maréchal: Passion et faillite d'un égalitaire* (Pisa, 1975), and L. Hunt, *The Family Romance of the French Revolution* (Berkeley and Los Angeles, 1992), pp. 158–9.

[25] See Fraisse, *Muse de la Raison*, pp. 60–68.

It is true that she did not talk the language of rights, as did the other woman who answered Maréchal, Albertine Clément-Hémery.[26] Gacon pragmatically kept to the familiar symbolic ground of virtuous wives and prudent mothers. Her main concern, though – reaffirming more openly what she had written in 1787 in another dispute with a man – was on a different level. It was the role books could play in an individual woman's life, securing personal resources for her: an inner strength and independence of judgement that would in turn have public effects.[27] This was perhaps why the sage Hypatia was her chosen heroine, though we should not misconstrue: Gacon was no sophisticate, and no Madame de Staël. She can perhaps be seen rather as a late version of the eighteenth-century moralist, as in a sense her friend Maréchal was also.

Gacon's reply to him is a down-to-earth vindication of the Enlightenment promise of liberation from *minority* into *autonomy*. She accuses the radical eighteenth-century materialist Maréchal – 'the intrepid thinker of his century' – of being the one who forsakes those ideals (including his proclaimed egalitarianism) though all the while he invokes 'Reason' in his text:

> If women could not read, superstition [i.e. *the Catholic priests*] would still rule them and their children as well. Their fathers, returning to childhood's prejudice, would make the vaults of temples [i.e. *churches*] (which would all be still in place) ring with curses against the *philosophes* and the founders of the republic. Oh Voltaire, Voltaire! What would you say, if you saw the *projet de loi* today ...[28]

To Maréchal, who said that women almost always held quills sharpened by men, Gacon replied exposing both his true fear of the influence of born-again Catholics like Madame de Genlis and the error of his proposed remedy: 'Yes, they do, when they insist on lighting the torches of fanaticism ... becoming political schemers and discussing theology, censoring the *philosophes* and extolling their denigrators'.[29] To stop reactionary women, Maréchal was ready to refuse the intellectual contribution of the whole gender. Again in 1801, another well-known secular intellectual, playwright Marie-Joseph Chénier, attacked in his heavily satirical poem *Les Nouveaux saints* the female zealots of the Catholic revival: 'I perceive the phoenix of female wits,' he wrote, showing how easy it could be to deal unvaryingly with all women authors for the sake of polemic effect.[30]

Gacon's case shows what the revolutionary and post-revolutionary experience could mean – in the intellectual evolution of a bourgeois woman who remained

---

[26] A. Clément-Hémery [anonymously], *Les Femmes vengées de la sottise d'un philosophe du jour, ou réponse au projet de loi de M. S – M – portant défense d'apprendre à lire aux femmes, par Madame* – (Paris, 1801); modern edition in G. Fraisse (ed.), *Opinions de femmes de la ville au lendemain de la Révolution française* (Paris, 1989), pp. 81–128.

[27] Gacon-Dufour, *Mémoire pour le sexe féminin.*

[28] Gacon-Dufour, *Contre le projet*, p. 22 (the explanations in brackets of what the terms implied at the time are of course mine).

[29] Ibid., p. 30.

[30] M.-J. Chénier, *Les Nouveaux saints* (Paris, 1801).

a pragmatic, dedicated daughter of the eighteenth century, not tempted by Catholicism, romanticism, aesthetics, or pessimism. The Revolution, if it had not fulfilled them, had at least enhanced the promises of the Enlightenment. In particular it had focused the democratic inclination in Gacon's own support of physiocracy and of economic education: through her writing and her membership in agricultural societies and by means of her periodical *Bibliothèque Physico-Économique*. Compared with Gacon's first writings, her reply to Abbé Dorimon twenty years later shows evidence of a sharpened clarity of mind, suggesting that if the Revolution failed to assure women's emancipation by law, it apparently liberated the thought at least of some women.

Answering Dorimon's punchline suggesting that she keep to her 'little recipes' for jams and liquors ('if drugs it must be, I prefer her ratafia to her books'), Gacon explains her ambitious social aims: her *Recueil pratique d'économie rurale et domestique*, into its fourth edition, is a *medicinal* drug to reduce and put an end to the misery of the working people, the 'indigent and labouring class'; her *Manuel de la menagère, à la ville et à la campagne* (1805) is a drug to eradicate rural poverty, promising work for all – just as her concrete medical remedies also aim at preserving health in the countryside.

In other words, she now accords the commitment to physiocracy, dating from her youth, a more democratic meaning. Now she offers her collection of empirical knowledge in simple language directly to the peasants, and particularly country women, rather than to enlightened landowners. In her *Manuel de la menagère* she quotes Voltaire, invoking for farmers a new world without chains and persecution. This new world now exists, she adds, thanks to the Constituent Assembly: on the night of 4 August 1789, feudality and tithes were abolished. Now peasants – men and women – need only public education, from a government without any vested interest in ignorance. She quotes Nicolas-Louis François de Neufchâteau – an *homme de lettres* who before adapting to Napoleon's regime had been a prominent member of every legislative assembly of the Revolution. He had argued for a redistribution of land through sale of the *biens nationaux* in small lots accessible to the poor. The Revolution, he said, had liberated peasants and agriculture itself from servitude, but there is no full liberty without education. It is all very well to free a blind man from prison, guaranteeing for him the use of what faculties he has, Neufchâteau said; but the issue with agriculture is to give the blind man vision, to create 'the sense that is missing'.[31]

That is what Gacon wanted to do: she did not simply want to prepare brides for housekeeping (Napoleon would soon be planning state schools for girls). Rather, once again a faithful interpreter of the promise of the eighteenth century, she was continuing the spirit of the *Encyclopédie*, in so far as the monument of

---

[31] M.-A. Gacon-Dufour, *Manuel de la ménagère, à la ville et à la campagne, et de la femme de basse-cour* (Paris, 1805); Neufchâteau is cited on p. 62, Voltaire and the theme of the Revolution on pp. 71–2. Compare her *Recueil pratique d'économie rurale et domestique* (Paris, 1804), where she mentioned other revolutionary examples and made a point of still naming the months according to the revolutionary calendar.

the Enlightenment had also codified what Carlo Ginzburg calls the 'evidential knowledge', or 'local knowledge'. It was the knowledge of artisans and farmers, of wisewomen and midwives as well. *Their* cognitive paradigm was elevated as a part of philosophy, and what had been taken as 'atemporal' was brought into the historical realm; soldering high and low together.[32]

As we have seen, the significance of Gacon's acceptably *feminine* writings on housekeeping and empirical remedies is revealed by what else she does. Not just symptomatic of a moderate feminism that admits gender roles, demanding only a little more control for women within their sphere, and a little betterment for middle-class wives. Not just a way to act out and to suggest a survival strategy for women. Rather, her work expresses, as a post-revolutionary Enlightenment project, the rationalistic and *philosophique* reclamation of knowledge, *of* and *for* those political and social subjects that had briefly but in fact irreversibly emerged in the revolutionary experience: the peasants, the urban working-class, and women.

---

[32] See C. Ginzburg, *Clues, Myths, and the Historical Method*, trans. J. and A.C. Tedeschi (Baltimore, 1989).

Chapter 6
Legality and Morality in the Political Thought of Elise Reimarus and Immanuel Kant

Lisa Curtis-Wendlandt

Introduction

Elise Reimarus (1735–1805) is a scarcely known figure of German Enlightenment thought. A prolific and respected writer and intellectual in her own day, she bestowed on Enlightenment Europe and its inheritors a substantial body of original contributions in philosophy and political theory. My intention in this chapter is to reclaim Elise Reimarus as a political thinker of eighteenth-century Germany by exploring a central theme in her philosophical writings: the distinctively ambiguous relationship between the legal and moral realms, which oscillates between an emphasis on their conceptual difference and a discourse on their possible identity. Tracing close parallels between the political works of Elise Reimarus and Immanuel Kant, I will argue that they conceptualize the distinction between legal and moral justice in remarkably similar ways.

This can be seen first in their stipulation of an autonomous legal sphere that is solely concerned with securing rightful external relations, rather than with people's inner moral intentions. Second, however, Reimarus and Kant are clearly not legal positivists, since neither of them holds justice to be solely dependent on enforcement of law. As I will show, their distinction between legal and moral justice presupposes a fundamentally non-Hobbesian image of human nature, according to which mankind's 'liberty to reason' makes legal and moral agency possible in the first place. For Reimarus and Kant, the rationality of the social contract is not founded on self-interest à la Hobbes, but on the 'goodness' of external right, which consists in its capacity to secure the liberty of all, and thus to guard against the arbitrary instrumentalization of human beings *qua* persons.

Third, this normative basis of legality has led several scholars to develop a 'remedial reading' of Kant's legal theory, which derives the need for coercive legal justice from the anthropological fact of human evil. Comparing the cases of Reimarus and Kant, I will argue that both indeed regard the republican state and its legal system as facilitating duty-conformant (but not necessarily duty-informed) action, and so as maintaining the coextensivity of legal and moral right. It is equally apparent, however, that this 'facilitative effect' is indeterminate in the reverse: there is evidence to suggest that neither theorist considered moral goodness a sufficient cause of external right. I will therefore conclude, against the remedial reading, that legality retains its conceptual independence from questions of moral teleology in the political thought of both Elise Reimarus and Immanuel Kant.

Elise Reimarus as Legal and Moral Theorist

Historical accounts of German Enlightenment thought usually limit their memory of Elise Reimarus to her role as epistolary mediator in the famous 'Pantheism debate', between philosophers Moses Mendelssohn and Friedrich Heinrich Jacobi.[1] The fact that Reimarus produced a wide variety of philosophical, literary, and pedagogical texts that complement her role as a letter writer is generally overlooked. Even at the present time, detailed literary or philosophical studies of her work are virtually non-existent.[2] Born into the free city-state of Hamburg as the daughter of philosopher Hermann Samuel Reimarus, Elise Reimarus (1735–1805) never married, but from an early age achieved fame as an intellectual and a talented author. Her works included political tracts, poems, pedagogical dialogues for children, and German renditions of stage plays by Joseph Addison, Voltaire, and Madame de Graffigny. Much of this work suffered almost complete erasure from Enlightenment intellectual history, and some has appeared in print for the very first time in Almut Spalding's recent intellectual biography of Elise Reimarus.[3]

Compared to other women political theorists of her time, Reimarus's political works are clearly (and perhaps self-consciously) formulated outside the gender paradigm, and they largely abstain from commenting on the 'woman question' – a fact that may have contributed, ironically, to her neglect by feminist historians of philosophy. Her discussion of the relationship between legal and moral justice, which I explore in this chapter, is a case in point. Cast in more or less gender-neutral terms, this relationship occupies a central place in Reimarus's political thought, and will be shown to be construed in a rather 'Kantian' fashion.[4] While Kant scholarship

---

[1] This debate was triggered by the death of the famous German writer G.E. Lessing, and the controversial question of whether or not he embraced a Spinozist philosophy.

[2] Even Sieveking's 1940 paper – the only free-standing study of Elise Reimarus's thought apart from Spalding's groundbreaking biography – traces Reimarus's ideas in a rather general fashion, and mainly through her correspondence. See H. Sieveking, 'Elise Reimarus (1735–1805) in den Geistigen Kämpfen ihrer Zeit', *Zeitschrift des Vereins für Hamburgische Geschichte*, 39 (1940): pp. 86–138. See also A.M.G. Spalding, *Elise Reimarus (1735–1805): The Muse of Hamburg; a Woman of the German Enlightenment* (Würzburg, 2005).

[3] On Reimarus's plays see Spalding, *Elise Reimarus*, pp. 199–217, and L. Curtis-Wendlandt, 'Staging Virtue: Women, Death, and Liberty in Elise Reimarus's *Cato*', *Journal of the History of Ideas*, 74:1 (2013): 69–92.

[4] The similarity between Reimarus and Kant observed in this chapter does not extend to claims about Reimarus's actual reception of Kant's philosophy, or the matter of a possible reverse influence of her writings on Kant. Such questions lead into uncharted territory, and would require extensive research into the unpublished correspondence of the Reimarus family. It is known that Elise Reimarus's brother, J.A.H. Reimarus, personally corresponded with Kant, and Spalding asserts that Elise herself commented on Kant in her letters (A. Spalding, personal communication).

has paid significant attention to the legality-morality distinction in his works, the same certainly cannot be said of Reimarus's writings. Apart from Spalding's biography, which offers an invaluable first overview of some of the content of her political works, detailed studies of her political philosophy are only now beginning to appear.[5] A good starting-point for analysing Reimarus's political thought (and the morality-legality relationship in particular), is her treatise on civil law, the *Versuch einer Erläuterung und Vereinfachung der Begriffe vom natürlichen Staatsrecht* [*Attempt to Explain and Simplify the Concepts Contained in Natural Civil Law*] of 1789–1792, together with her philosophical dialogue *Freiheit* [*Freedom*] of 1791.[6] Despite the different style and tone of these works – one depicting a lively conversation in colloquial German, the other a dense technical argument structured by paragraph (§) headings – both works promote a contractarian model of politics that draws on British and Continental theories of the social contract.[7]

Interestingly, Reimarus's contractarianism in both works also relies on a careful distinction between the moral and legal domains. Her legal-political treatise *Versuch* attempts to explicate the core concepts of civil law (such as freedom, rights and obligations, different forms of government administration, and the aim and legitimacy of state power). The distinction between morality and legality is subtly introduced in the first few paragraphs, where Reimarus outlines two different notions of liberty and law. Using the spatial metaphors of 'inner' and 'outer', Reimarus proclaims that the realm of politics is concerned only with what she calls 'outer law' (i.e., 'äusseres Recht', which we might also translate as 'external right'), or the 'law of nature' ('Naturrecht').[8] This outer law is distinguished from 'the inner law (the law of conscience)', and both are said to differ 'like the outer action ... from the inner (intention) of the will'. In effect, Reimarus establishes two separate spheres or ways of speaking about law in the context of human agency: there are the outwardly lawful (or unlawful) actions of persons that define them as *legal* agents; and there are the inwardly lawful (or unlawful) intentions of the human will, which characterize persons as *moral* agents. The civil laws of a state, Reimarus affirms, should only be concerned 'with the outer [law], certainly not

---

5 See L. Curtis-Wendlandt, 'No Right to Resist? Elise Reimarus's *Freedom* as a Kantian Response to the Problem of Violent Revolt', *Hypatia*, 27:4 (2012): pp. 755–73.

6 The *Versuch* has survived as a manuscript in the Hamburg State Archive and first appeared in print in Spalding, *Elise Reimarus*, pp. 504–13. The dialogue *Freiheit* was published anonymously in response to a violent journeymen rebellion in Hamburg in 1791 and is still wrongly catalogued under the name of Johann Albert Heinrich Reimarus, Elise's brother. See J.A.H. Reimarus, *Freiheit* (Hamburg, 1791). Spalding convincingly argues that the attribution of *Freiheit* to J.A.H. Reimarus is a casually repeated error dating back to the dialogue's first listing in a bibliographical reference work of learned Germany from 1798; see Spalding, *Elise Reimarus*, pp. 280–98.

7 For a detailed discussion of Reimarus's contractarianism vis-à-vis the political theories of Hobbes, Locke, and Kant see Curtis-Wendlandt, 'No Right to Resist?'.

8 The German word 'Recht' – translated as both 'right' and 'law' in English – is well known for its ambiguity. In the context of Reimarus's *Versuch*, it appears appropriate to translate 'Recht' as 'law'.

with the inner law'.[9] In other words, civil law does not address questions of morality and conscience. Instead, it aims to secure the 'external right' of people, which is defined as the compatibility of the free, outward actions of one person with those of all other persons.[10] Civil law's concern with the external relationships between men is thus categorically distinct from questions of people's inner, moral intentionality. This stipulation of an autonomous legal sphere marks a first important similarity between Reimarus and Kant, who similarly reduces legality to outer action in his *Metaphysics of Morals* by arguing that inner motives are not relevant for the determination of rightful legal agency.[11] In *Theory and Practice* too, Kant's notion of 'external right' is tied to the idea that coercive public laws secure a state of outer liberty and justice that is categorically distinct from questions of individual happiness or other empirical states of mind. For as Kant asserts, 'no generally valid [i.e., objective] principle of legislation can be based on happiness,' since people's definitions and methods of attaining it are so 'highly conflicting and variable' that they make 'all fixed principles impossible'.[12] The conceptual autonomy of the legal sphere is emphasized by Reimarus's view on legal obligation. What makes civil law *legally* binding (so that it obliges men to live by its rules), she suggests, is not its potential moral content, but its formal enactment by a governing power that represents the general will, and to which people would rationally choose to submit.[13] This contractarian presupposition means that law enforcement is ultimately willed by the people itself. Civil law is therefore legally binding (and just) by virtue of its being enforced through a *potestas executoria*, as Kant later called it – and not by virtue of its links with morality.[14]

Non-Positivist Justice

The stipulation of an autonomous legal sphere in Reimarus and Kant does not imply that civil law is necessarily amoral. For Reimarus, civil law seems to derive from some form of natural law, as is suggested by the wording 'natural civil law' in the title of her treatise and throughout the text. While none of

9 Reimarus, *Versuch*, p. 504, §2.

10 Ibid., p. 504, §2; see also pp. 505–6, §6.

11 I. Kant, *The Metaphysics of Morals* (Cambridge and New York, 1991), at pp. 56–7. See the authoritative 'Akademie edition' (Akademie-Ausgabe, referred to hereafter as AA): I. Kant, *Gesammelte Schriften*, edited by the Königlich-Preussische Akademie der Wissenschaften zu Berlin (Berlin, 1902–), vol. 6, p. 231.

12 I. Kant, *Political Writings*, ed. H.S. Reiss (Cambridge, 1991), p. 80 [AA, vol. 8, 298]. In his *Groundwork* Kant presents reason (unconditional, objective) as almost antithetical to happiness (conditional, subjective); but he speaks also of the assurance of one's happiness as being a duty and distinguishes between 'happiness from inclination' and 'happiness from duty'. See I. Kant, *Groundwork of the Metaphysics of Morals*, ed. and trans. M.J. Gregor (Cambridge, 1998), pp. 9–10, 12. [AA, vol. 4, 395–6, 398–9].

13 See Reimarus, *Versuch*, pp. 504–5, § 2–3.

14 See Kant, *The Metaphysics of Morals*, p. 127 [AA, vol. 6, 316].

Reimarus's writings spell out an explicit theory of natural law, both *Versuch* and *Freiheit* assume the existence either of a moral law or of a law of nature.[15] The relationship between morality and legality – as important as the distinction might be in Reimarus's political thought – is thus not exclusively a matter of difference. This is demonstrated by her comments on justice in *Versuch*, which show that she is not a legal positivist, since she does not make justice dependent on the notion of law enforcement alone (as Hobbes is often taken to have done in *Leviathan*, for example).[16] For Reimarus, it makes sense to speak of justice beyond the existence of the political state and its coercive power. Resorting again to spatial metaphors, she makes this distinction: 'An action can be internally unjust and outwardly just, if it stems from an immoral disposition but does not compromise another person's outer freedom; and inversely, an action can be outwardly unjust that was believed to be just by an innocent error inside.'[17] In other words, an action may be legally just if it is in line with the principles of civil law; and it may be morally just if it is an intentional expression of the moral law or law of nature. Again, Kant's *Groundwork* sets up a similar contrast when he problematizes the relationship between actions that externally 'conform with duty', and those that are [actually] done 'from duty'. Here Kant also argues that the external consequences of a person's wilful act cannot be used to establish whether that person is motivated by a good will, and thus by 'respect for [moral] law'.[18]

Reimarus's non-positivist distinction between outer and inner justice – which closely resembles Kant's distinction of legal and moral 'right' – assumes a particular kind of human liberty. In Reimarus's words, 'one cannot suffer injustice from ... a person ... who cannot act freely.'[19] This freedom of the person is not just a mechanical liberty in the Hobbesian sense of an absence of external obstruction to action (which he attributes to animate and inanimate moving bodies alike), but an exclusive property of the human mind founded in rationality.[20] For Reimarus, the expression of what she terms outer liberty, 'in so far as it presupposes the will and thus also reason, is ... the external characteristic that distinguishes a person from a mere thing.' It therefore consists in the ability of persons to choose a particular action based on their own deliberations. In addition, Reimarus recognizes a certain 'inner

---

15 In *Freiheit*, this is implied in a discussion of man's fallible understanding of justice, which is contrasted with a notion of objective moral truth (see Reimarus, *Freiheit*, pp. 10–11). In *Versuch*, such objective moral truth (or law) is implied by Reimarus's placing of the politico-legal realm into a broader teleological framework, which considers man's moral enlightenment as the ultimate natural end of human existence (see Reimarus, *Versuch*, p. 513, § 29).

16 See T. Hobbes, *Leviathan: Or the Matter, Forme, and Power of a Common-Wealth Ecclesiasticall and Civill*, ed. I. Shapiro (New Haven and London, 2010), Chapter 15, p. 88.

17 Reimarus, *Versuch*, p. 504, §2.

18 Kant, *Groundwork*, pp. 11, 13 [AA, vol. 4, 397–8; 400]. For Kant, 'duty is the necessity of an action from respect for law': *Groundwork*, p. 13 [AA, vol. 4, 400].

19 Reimarus, *Versuch*, p. 504, §2.

20 See Hobbes, *Leviathan*, Chapter 21, pp. 127–8.

liberty', or liberty of conscience, which she associates with people's moral culture and enlightenment.[21] It seems plausible to relate these concepts to Kant's notion of negative and positive freedom, according to which the former is 'a condition of rational agency as such' (i.e., freedom from being determined, yet not necessarily from being affected, by sensible impulses), and the latter is 'a condition of the appropriate moral motivation (acting from duty alone)'.[22] For Reimarus and Kant, inner freedom thus constitutes the metaphysical precondition for moral agency, and outer freedom the social precondition for the full exercise of that moral agency. By implication, both hold that a human person who cannot act freely (in *both* senses) ceases to be a person in so far as she cannot be either a legal or a moral agent. The ethical risk of this, according to Reimarus, lies not only in the degradation of the person to a mere 'thing' that cannot *make use* of other things, but in the danger of *being used* 'arbitrarily by other persons'.[23] Her warning against such arbitrary instrumentalization of human beings closely resembles Kant's call for respect of persons as ends in themselves.[24] This moral imperative therefore makes the securing of freedom an end in itself. For Reimarus, and perhaps for Kant, this end can only be achieved within the civil condition.[25] The positive laws of the state therefore have a normative *raison d'être*, and their legitimacy derives from their contribution to the securing of 'external right', which consists in the compatibility of everyone's liberty with self-determined action. As Wolfgang Kersting says, for Kant 'coercion *enforces* [external] right; and right *legitimizes* coercion.'[26]

In both Reimarus and Kant, 'rightness' and 'goodness' are thus interdependent in an important way. This can be seen more clearly in their arguments for the rational nature of humans' decision to enter the civil condition, which crucially differs from Hobbes's account. Like Reimarus and Kant, Hobbes says that it is *rational* for people to enter the civil condition of right. What Hobbesian people rationalize about when making this decision is the optimization of their own self-interest. In other words, Hobbes holds that humans rationally agree that their own (long term) self-interest is best served by accepting the imposition of a law that defines and enforces justice, and they submits to this law because of that realization.[27]

Conversely, Reimarus and Kant argue that it is rational for men to submit to the civil condition – not necessarily (and not *only*) because it furthers their self-interest, but because it enables rightful external relations among people. Reimarus's *Versuch*, for example, discusses the necessity of people's entering the

---

21 Reimarus, *Versuch*, p. 504, §1; p. 513, §29.

22 H.E. Allison, 'Kant on Freedom of the Will', in P. Guyer (ed.), *The Cambridge Companion to Kant and Modern Philosophy* (Cambridge and New York, 2006), p. 381. See also Kant, *Metaphysics of Morals*, p. 42 [AA, vol. 6, 213–14].

23 Reimarus, *Versuch*, p. 504, §1.

24 Kant, *Groundwork*, p. 38 [AA, vol. 4, 429].

25 See Reimarus, *Versuch*, pp. 505–6, §6. See Kant's *Theory and Practice* in Kant, *Political Writings*, pp. 73–4 [AA, vol. 8, 289–90].

26 W. Kersting, *Kant über Recht* (Paderborn, 2004), p. 20; emphases added.

27 Hobbes, *Leviathan*, Chapter 14, pp. 79–80, 102.

civil condition in a language that is markedly free of such notions as personal gain or the optimization of some advantage.[28] Nowhere does she say that self-interest motivates acceptance of the social contract, or that it underlies the development of a notion of justice, as in Hobbes. In Reimarus's contractualism, people 'want' the securing of their outer right because this alone can secure the liberty of human beings *qua* persons.[29] Like Kant, Reimarus thus views a person's submission to the civil condition as rational because it is an expression of the moral law – or in Kantian terms, of the moral duty to respect others as ends in themselves. For Hobbes, staying in the state of nature may contradict the rationality of human self-interest, but it does not constitute a moral wrong. Hobbesians are thus morally free to remain in the state of nature – a freedom not enjoyed by Reimarusians or Kantians. Reimarus and Kant's contractualism also differs from that of Hobbes by its attachment to the Rousseauian notion of a general will, to be explored below.

Responding to Self-Interest: Legality's 'Facilitative' Potential

It is important to note, of course, that self-interest is not an alien concept in either Reimarus's or Kant's political thought. But its role is different for them and for Hobbes. While Reimarus and Kant view humans as fundamentally moral beings, both also recognize the human inclination to evil – or rather, the human inclination to act against reason, and so against the moral law or the law of nature. It is in this context that their discussions of self-interest appear. When Kant speaks of the 'dear self, which is always turning up' with its own purposes, it is from a concern for virtue.[30] Similarly, when Reimarus speaks of self-interest ('Eigennutz'), or of such closely related concepts as self-love ('Selbstliebe') and people's private will ('Privatwille'), it is from a concern for legal and moral justice.[31] Self-interest – fuelled, it seems, by contingent personal desires – is recognized as a psychological force that tends *away* from the rational principles of legal and moral justice. This is contrary to Hobbes's conception of long-term self-interest as identical with rationality. In the realm of politics, Reimarus writes, human self-love can exert a powerful 'pull' toward political imbalance and injustice:

> Subjects' self-love constantly strives towards its outer limitation through the ruling power; rulers' self-love thrives towards its outer limitation by the law. In every constitution, subjects' self-love is the ineffaceable seed of anarchy; rulers' self-love the seed of despotism.[32]

If allowed to pull too far towards either anarchy or despotism, human self-love can destroy the conditions of external right that secure justice and peace in

---

[28] For example, compare §§ 5 and 6 in Reimarus, *Versuch*, pp. 505–6.

[29] Compare §§ 5, 8, 9 in Reimarus, *Versuch*, pp. 505–7.

[30] Kant, *Groundwork*, p. 20 [AA, vol. 4, 408].

[31] See Reimarus, *Versuch*, pp. 509–13, §§ 15, 17–19, 22, 26–7.

[32] Reimarus, *Versuch*, p. 513, §27.

the civil state. Reimarus's bifocal concern with the political effects of human psychology is shared by Kant, who not only problematizes the potential misuse of power by rulers, but also citizens' potential for disobedience and revolution.[33] For Reimarus, anarchy and despotism are both illegitimate political practices, because they equally destroy the fundamental conditions of external right embodied in the three maxims of the general will. These include the protection of the outer liberty of all (as discussed above), but also everyone's submission to political representation, and protection against unequal consideration.[34] Reimarus's three maxims are akin to Kant's principles of the state as outlined in *Theory and Practice II*.[35] Interestingly, while Reimarus claims that the general will of the people is *necessarily* that these principles be made into constitutional laws of the state, she also recognizes that empirically, such unanimity of will is unlikely to be achieved. This is precisely because of people's moral imperfection and the fact that they often will not what is rational, but what fits with their contingent temperaments, talents, knowledge, inclinations, and passions.[36] Reimarus – like Kant – distinguishes empirical wills (actual, private wills) from a purely hypothetical general will, founded in the idea of reason (thereby representing the moral law).[37] Kant's contractarianism also distinguishes between the concepts of empirical and ideal man. For Kant, the fact that people in practice do not always consent to a law does not indicate that it is necessarily unjust; it might simply show that their judgement is not guided by reason. As he writes in *Theory and Practice*, rational consent is possible if and only if a certain law does not contradict the (moral) idea of law:

> [If the law is such that a whole people could not *possibly* agree to it [by the light of reason ...], it is unjust; but if it is at least *possible* that a people could [rationally] agree to it, it is our duty to consider the law as just, even if the people is at present in such a position or attitude of mind that it would probably refuse its consent if it were consulted.[38]

Reimarus and Kant's distinction between empirical man and ideal man (or between a will affected by inclination and a will determined by reason) matches Rousseau's similar distinction: the fallible 'volonté de tous' ('will of all'), and the infallible 'volonté générale' ('general will') which is aimed at the general good

---

33 See particularly the Conclusion to Kant's *Theory and Practice II*, 'On the Relationship of Theory and Practice in Political Right (against Hobbes)' in Kant, *Political Writings*, pp. 79–87 [AA, vol. 8, 297–306].

34 Reimarus, *Versuch*, p. 507, §9.

35 Kant, *Political Writings*, pp. 74–7 [AA, vol. 8, 290–95]. Note that Reimarus and Kant share a formal rather than a substantive understanding of equality, concerned with the equality of subjects as *legal* subjects: i.e., as having legal rights to protection. This is considered compatible with inequalities in people's social rank and position. See Curtis-Wendlandt, 'No right to resist?', pp. 760–63.

36 Reimarus, *Versuch*, p. 507, §11.

37 Compare Reimarus's *Versuch*, p. 512, §26.

38 Kant, *Political Writings*, p. 79 [AA, vol. 8, 297].

and therefore always 'right'.[39] Like Kant, Reimarus asserts that the general will, though hypothetical as a presumed rational agreement rather than historically actual, is nevertheless effective in legitimizing decisions of state.[40] This idea of a hypothetical general will founded in reason becomes a guiding principle in both writers' responses to morally imperfect mankind. For both, self-love and self-interest work against reason, and must be controlled in the name of justice. Ascendancy of rational politics brings legal and moral right into closer accord; Reimarus and Kant agree that this can be achieved through two facilitators of the liberty, equality, and submission principles that underlie external right: a constitutional separation of powers in the tripartite republican state, and a multi-layered system of judicial process.[41] They agree also that self-interest may be diverted to enhance political cohesion and the condition of external right. Reimarus argues that 'the connection of self-interest with the outer right' works practically to prevent injustice, and that as 'the final and most fundamental political drive', self-interest 'must be maintained and kept alive through the power and wisdom of the administrators of the highest power'.[42] The importance of this point is illustrated in her earlier rendition of Joseph Addison's stage-play *Cato*, in which Reimarus highlights the political shortcomings of a ruler whose obsession with virtue tragically blinds him to his people's inclinations and existential needs. In Reimarus's terms, Cato fails at the art of politics; he misses the tight connection between private self-interest and the general good, with consequences even for his legitimacy as leader.[43] While Kant does not lay such stress on instrumentalizing self-interest, he too admits that politics must cater to it – or rather, to mankind's natural seeking after happiness: 'Want of satisfaction with one's condition, under pressure from many anxieties and amid unsatisfied needs, could easily become a great *temptation to transgression of duty*.'[44] This suggests that Kant thought a positive, legal-political response to people's 'self-interested' needs and their striving for happiness might encourage behaviour in line with external right: in conformity with duty, even if not motivated by it.

A recent paper by Patrick Riley also discusses the relationship between legality and morality for Kant, as one that is facilitative yet indeterminate in nature. As Riley reminds us, actions in the legal and moral domains differ in their motivation: legal motives do not presuppose any *motiva moralia* or good will, the incentive being mere avoidance of punishment for transgression. But interestingly, legal

[39] See Book 2, Chapter 3, in J.-J. Rousseau, *The Social Contract*, trans. M. Cranston (Harmondsworth, 2003), p. 72.

[40] Reimarus, *Versuch*, pp. 507–8, §11.

[41] See Reimarus, *Versuch*, especially pp. 509–11, §§17–19; and see *Freiheit*, especially pp. 10–12. See also Kant's comments on republicanism, in Kant, *Metaphysics of Morals*, pp. 148–9 [AA, vol. 6, 340–41], and his *Perpetual Peace* in Kant, *Political Writings*, pp. 99–102 [AA, vol. 8, 351–3].

[42] Reimarus, *Versuch*, p. 511, §22; compare p. 506, § 6.

[43] See Curtis-Wendlandt, 'Staging Virtue'.

[44] Kant, *Groundwork*, p. 12 (emphasis in original) [AA, vol. 4, 399].

motives may *encourage* a 'good will', and so give rise to moral political motives. Riley shows how Kant links legality in two ways to morality. First, weakly: public legal justice, sanctioning some morally bad actions as illegal, at least ensures self-interested observance of certain moral ends.[45] Purely prudential legal compliance is coextensive, or outwardly identical, with what a good will would have chosen: in Kantian terms, conforming with but not moved by duty.[46] Second, Riley finds legality and morality linked more strongly for Kant. Legality may, 'by creating an environment for good will', also actually 'produce good conduct'.[47] A legal action may become not merely indiscernible from but inwardly identical to a moral action. Yet this transition remains non-deterministic: legality may or may not 'cause' morality.

Reimarus too, as we saw, recognizes the merely facilitative relationship between the legal and the moral, in discussing the political structures and conditions (i.e., republicanism and judicial process) that secure not only external right, but also an alignment of legal and moral action. At the heart of her confidence that legality can 'imitate' the rational principles of morality lies the concept of reason: an important nexus between legal and moral justice in Reimarus and Kant. For both, reason has indeterminate causal 'leverage' over the human will, just like that of legal actions over moral intentions: the will is free to follow reason, but does not do so predictably. Reimarus highlights this in *Freiheit*, warning against people taking justice into their own hands, because their judgements tend to be tainted with self-interest and bias. Parties to a conflict, she asserts, usually judge their own case by contingent criteria such as personal sentiments and desires; professionals in the judicial system, though, are supposedly impartial and disinterested, so their verdict is more likely to be grounded in an exercise of reason and to reflect the objective principles of justice.[48] Reimarus's notion of the judge shows her faith in the affinity between rationality and morality, and affirms the disputed human freedom to engage in reason. Kant presents an image of the will 'at a crossroads': 'between its a priori principle, which is formal [i.e., rational], and its a posteriori incentive, which is material [i.e., empirically given]'.[49] In essence then, the human capacity to choose reason freely is just that: a *capacity*, which may or may not guide legal or moral action. For Reimarus as for Kant, the fact that people often do not exercise their reason is an expected concomitant of their freedom; it does not diminish the regulative aptness of rationality. People's freedom to act rationally and the rarity of their actually doing so both accord, for Kant, with 'the idea of a reason determining the will by means of a priori grounds'.[50] This idea is unassailed

---

45 See P. Riley, 'Kant against Hobbes in *Theory and Practice*', *Journal of Moral Philosophy*, 4:2 (2007): p. 202.

46 Kant, *Groundwork*, p. 11 [AA, vol. 4, 398].

47 Riley, 'Kant against Hobbes in *Theory and Practice*', p. 202.

48 Reimarus, *Freiheit*, p. 10.

49 Kant, *Groundwork*, p. 13 [AA, vol. 4, 400].

50 Ibid., p. 20 [AA, vol. 4, 408].

by reason's indeterminate sway over the will,[51] which provides a psychological explanation for legal and moral action differing in practice. A will that is free to act against reason (in so far as it is affected by other inclinations and drives) must be free to make decisions that are legally right but not morally good.

What happens, though, if the focus moves from actual human conduct to legality and morality in a perfectly enlightened humanity? This question is at the core of the 'remedial controversy' in Kant scholarship, which is relevant not only to our understanding of Kant's political philosophy, but also to the relationship between legal and moral justice in Reimarus's work.

Towards Identity? The 'Remedial Reading' of Legality

The facilitative potential of legality (i.e., its capacity to motivate action that conforms to duty) has led many scholars to believe that Kant derives the need for the state primarily from humanity's morally imperfect nature. On this reading, politics and legality basically serve a remedial function, as a substitute for absent good will. The implication seems to be that morally perfected agents would no longer require a civil state to help them live 'rightfully' together, because the *raison d'être* for legality (the imperfection of morality) would have been removed. But this redundancy of legality raises a question of reverse causation: Can perfect morality always and necessarily guarantee external right? Proponents of the remedial reading affirm that it can, and insist on a fundamental causal asymmetry between the legal and the moral. While legality cannot determine morality, morality is somehow thought to entail external right. Anti-remedialists insist against this that there is indeterminacy both ways; Helga Varden has maintained that, even given perfect morality, Kant's humanity would still require a legal state in order to guarantee rightful external relations among people. His account of the civil state, she argues, is not founded on its remedial effect: legality and civil law do not primarily constitute a response to human evil.[52]

---

[51] See ibid., [AA, vol. 4, 407–8].

[52] H. Varden, 'Kant's Non-Voluntarist Conception of Political Obligations: Why Justice is Impossible in the State of Nature', *Kantian Review*, 13:2 (2008): pp. 1–45. Kersting, Ludwig, and Ripstein join Varden in giving a non-remedial reading of Kant's legal theory; see W. Kersting, *Wohlgeordnete Freiheit: Immanuel Kants Rechts- und Staatsphilosophie* (Frankfurt am Main, 1993), especially pp. 42–50; B. Ludwig, 'Commentary on Kant's Treatment of Constitutional Right (*Metaphysics of Morals II*: General Remark A; Paragraphs 51–2, Conclusion, Appendix)', in K. Ameriks and O. Hoeffe (eds), *Kant's Moral and Legal Philosophy* (New York, 2009), pp. 265–83; A. Ripstein, 'Authority and Coercion', *Philosophy and Public Affairs*, 32:1 (2004): pp. 2–35. For 'remedial' interpretations of Kant's legal theory see H. Williams, *Kant's Critique of Hobbes: Sovereignty and Cosmopolitanism* (Cardiff, 2003), especially pp. 81–6; O. O'Neill, *Bounds of Justice* (Cambridge, 2000), p. 139; and T. Pogge, 'Is Kant's Rechtslehre a "Comprehensive Liberalism"?', in M. Timmons (ed.), *Kant's Metaphysics of Morals* (New York, 2002), pp. 133–58, on 147.

Contemporary Kant studies have yielded no debate extending to the comparable legal theory of Reimarus. In fact, neither *Versuch* nor *Freiheit* presents an explicit theory of human enlightenment, making it difficult to determine what role Reimarus thought coercive legality might play once moral perfection is attained. We can, however, make inferences from the final paragraphs of *Versuch*. While most of this treatise on civil law outlines the *outer legal* conditions for a rational politics in line with the moral law or the law of nature, Reimarus leaves the reader with the thought that this also requires *inner moral* reforms: 'A higher level of political perfection depends on necessary moral and psychological conditions.'[53] Since questions of morality and conscience – which Reimarus associates with the notion of inner law and liberty – are expressly excluded from her treatise as foreign to the concerns of natural civil law, I would argue that this shift at the end of the work marks a change in her overall intent. While most of *Versuch* discusses civil law and the legal-political structures of a legitimate state, the final section takes a 'step back' so to speak, and situates legality and politics within a broader teleology of human nature. This teleology is centred on progress towards an increasingly good 'moral culture', and 'enlightenment'.[54] It is not clear whether Reimarus expected this moral development to be achieved through the forces of nature and history, or rather through individuals' realization of their inborn moral duty. What is clear from *Versuch* is that, within the parameters of her moral teleology, legality and politics serve as means to a moral end.[55] From this perspective Reimarus can claim an interdependence between moral and political progress that did not enter her discussion of positive law. While she considers moral and psychological progress necessary for attaining a 'higher level of political perfection', Reimarus also asserts that 'the higher level of political perfection always leads to a higher psychological one and enables the [higher] moral one.'[56] This interdependence, however, is tipped somewhat out of equilibrium in the following paragraph:

> Just as for the state and the *politically* lawful efficacy of its representatives, the outer law, and thus the outer freedom, is a purpose *for its own sake*, so for mankind and its ascent towards humanity ... the outer [political] freedom is *only a means to* the inner [moral] freedom, and a mere condition of moral culture. The enlightenment that does not know any other freedom but the outer one is as absurd and corruptive as the politics that aims to secure the inner freedom by means of destroying the outer one.[57]

---

[53] Reimarus, *Versuch*, p. 513, §28.

[54] Ibid., p. 513, §29.

[55] While it is not uncontroversial to adopt a teleological reading of Kant's political thought, I would argue that his functionalization of politics for the ends of enlightenment in his *Idea for a Universal History* supports such a reading. Here, political perfection in the form of a just constitution becomes the means by which nature aims to realize mankind's natural moral potential. See Kant, *Political writings*, pp. 45–6, Fifth Proposition [AA, vol. 8, 22].

[56] Reimarus, *Versuch*, p. 513, §28.

[57] Ibid., p. 513, §29 (emphasis in original).

In one sense, Reimarus is again affirming the conceptual independence of legality from the question of human moral intentionality. For politics, outer liberty and law serve their own particular imminent purposes, and need no justification from moral or other extrinsic ends. But in another sense, Reimarus functionalizes outer liberty and law within her larger 'enlightenment' teleology, the end of which is moral advancement. (Here, she can call the outer freedom 'a means' to the inner freedom: as we saw earlier, Reimarus holds that the securing of external right enables moral personhood in the first place, and so itself constitutes a moral duty.) This functionalization is for Reimarus one-directional, and it cannot be reversed. In other words, her not mentioning a vantage point from which inner moral freedom could be reduced to a mere means to outer political freedom suggests a fundamental asymmetry between the moral and legal. Is this asymmetry evidence of a remedial construction of legality in her work?

I suggest it is not. The asymmetrical functionalization of legality for moral-teleological purposes is not linked to the claim that the will can determine the world. Reimarus could still hold that individuals' 'rightful agency' is underdetermined by their moral perfection. To rephrase the 'asymmetry' Reimarus proposes in the extract above, only inner (moral) liberty is an essential condition of enlightenment; outer liberty is a vital condition for politics, *even if* this politics also pursues a moral end. There can be no politics without a legal realm that secures people's outer liberty; and there can be no enlightenment without a moral realm for the cultivation of people's inner liberty. But while legality can from a teleological standpoint be functionalized for ends other than itself, morality cannot (just as Kantian good will cannot be functionalized). Kant expresses a similar idea in Appendix I of *Perpetual Peace*, where he discusses the compatibility of politics with the concept of 'right', which is based on universal principles of reason:

> But if we consider it absolutely necessary to couple the concept of right with politics, or even to make it a limiting condition of politics, it must be conceded that the two are compatible. And I can indeed imagine a moral politician, i.e. someone who conceives of the principles of political expediency in such a way that they can co-exist with morality, but I cannot imagine a political moralist, i.e. one who fashions his morality to suit his own advantage as a statesman.[58]

For Kant – and Reimarus, I would argue – politics and legality might be functionalized for morality; but not vice versa, because morality cannot be turned to serve a contingent and extrinsic end. Legality can serve a moral end because morality encompasses legality in a certain sense. This encompassing relationship does not mean that legal justice *requires* moral motivation, since as we saw earlier the two are functionally independent (though legality may foster morality), for both Reimarus and Kant. Rather, both theorists presuppose that a morally good will, by definition, always and necessarily aims at securing outer freedom for all, and therefore requires no external incentives for this aim to arise. The observed asymmetry in the relationship between legality and morality then simply means

---

58 Kant, *Political Writings*, pp. 117–18 [AA, vol. 8, 372].

that a will directed by legal incentives often fails to be motivated by moral goodness, whereas a morally good will unfailingly desires also what is legal. In other words: while legality *underdetermines* morality, morality encompasses a wish for legality, too (in so far as civil law implements the universal principles of reason that inform the moral law).

We might be tempted to conclude from this that the moral perfection of humanity could secure external right without a civil state. Yet this inference is not supported by Kant and Reimarus, on whose account a perfectly moral community might still require coercion. As we have already seen, moral perfection remains hypothetical for both thinkers, who consider such enlightenment empirically unattainable for individuals, given their propensity for evil.[59] If Reimarus has a notion of perfect enlightenment, it must be immanent in the term 'humanity' ('Humanität'), which at the end of *Versuch* she contrasts with empirical 'mankind' ('Menschheit'). This ideal of humanity seems to inform her suggestion that a purely inner (moral) enlightenment is at least thinkable, but a purely outer (legal-political) one is not. In §29 of *Versuch* she declares only one particular species of enlightenment 'absurd and corruptive': that which is confined to the outer liberty of people. She does not say the same of an enlightenment confined to inner liberty. But if a purely inner enlightenment seems an imaginable state of being for perfectly enlightened humanity, what does this say about the need for a civil state to secure external right? Adapting a common interpretive line in Kant studies, we might take Reimarus to consider moral perfection (as Kant might be said to consider a perfectly good will) theoretically sufficient for rightful external relations that would otherwise stand in need of legal enforcement. This idea, closely linked to the 'remedial' view of legality, rests on three assumptions: (1) if mankind ever fully ascended to humanity and lived by the universal rational principles of morality, it would necessarily *want* to secure outer liberty for all; (2) this necessary 'wish' of the enlightened will is a sufficient cause for the condition of external right; and (3) it follows from (1) and (2) that perfectly moral individuals can live rightfully together, uncoerced by a legal state. Is this how Riley reads Kant's distinction between the state of moral perfection – the 'kingdom of ends', the 'corpus mysticum' – and the state of 'a mere republic, which rests on coercive laws, rather than on respect, or virtue, or good will'?[60] If so, even in republics (the best possible civil states) legality and morality diverge, and the full moral perfection of humanity is not achieved.

---

[59] Reimarus considers the striving towards moral and political perfection a process of 'eternal approximation' (Reimarus, *Versuch*, p. 512, §26). Similarly, in Kant's *Idea for a Universal History*, human beings' 'warped' nature means that they are only required to 'approximate to this idea'. Here, however, Kant does suggest that 'the species as a whole' may hope for the fulfilment of human moral destiny (Kant, *Political Writings*, pp. 46–47, and note [AA, vol. 8, 23]). See also K. Flikschuh, 'Duty, Nature, Right: Kant's Response to Mendelssohn in *Theory and Practice* III', *Journal of Moral Philosophy*, 4:2 (2007): pp. 223–41, on p. 227.

[60] Riley, 'Kant against Hobbes in *Theory and Practice*', p. 199. For 'kingdom of ends' see Kant, *Groundwork*, p. 41 [AA, vol. 4, 433]; and for 'corpus mysticum' see I. Kant,

But Reimarus and Kant may not take this view. Neither may truly deem coercive legal justice unnecessary for rightful external relations, in a morally enlightened humanity. It is one thing to dismiss coercive legality as unnecessary for idealized *intra*personal moral perfection, and another to dismiss it as unnecessary for *inter*personal rightful relationships, even given enlightenment. From the supposed conceivability of a purely inner (moral) enlightenment in *Versuch*, we are entitled to infer that Reimarus held legality unnecessary only for individual moral perfection. Ideal humanity is a *moral* notion after all; and enlightenment is an interior condition of the human will, from which causal inferences to an exterior condition of human relationships are highly problematic. Yet such an inference underlies assumption (2), above. Though Riley argues that 'public legal justice in Kant might be viewed as the partial realization of what would happen if all wills were good,' both Reimarus and Kant see the relationship between the will and the world as problematic and indeterminate.[61] Probably they would expect the outcome of public legal justice and the outcome of 'what would happen if all wills were good' to differ. We have seen Reimarus clearly state in *Versuch* that 'an action can be outwardly unjust that was believed to be just by an innocent error inside.'[62] While this concerns empirical individuals and not perfected humanity, the mere possibility of discrepancy between inner and outer right is what matters. If the morally good intentions of empirical persons cannot guarantee rightful outcomes for their actions, how could this be different for perfectly enlightened humanity? Even a perfectly good will might fail, by a residual indeterminacy, to secure rightful outcomes for its actions in the world.

Conclusion

What is wrong with the remedial reading of Reimarus and Kant's legal theory, I suggest, is not its attribution of a remedial capacity to legality *per se*. As we saw, for Reimarus and Kant legality facilitates behaviour that conforms to duty and is sometimes informed by it. One could therefore say that legality has a 'remedial effect' with regard to morality and implementation of the moral law, since its coercive power remedies the lack of moral goodness in empirical persons. Yet the remedial reading wrongly takes this effect as legality's primary aim, overlooking its most fundamental purpose: the necessary securing of external right in both empirical individuals and ideal humanity. Against the remedial reading, I have argued that Reimarus and Kant make an important distinction between the claim that a morally good will necessarily *wants* to secure external right, and the claim that the behavioural outcomes of this will are always and necessarily in line with rightful interpersonal relations. Ultimately, it seems, the gulf between the will and

---

Critique of Pure Reason, ed. and trans. P. Guyer and A.W. Wood (Cambridge, 1998), p. 679, [AA, vol. 3, 525].

61 Riley, 'Kant against Hobbes in *Theory and Practice*', p. 202.

62 Reimarus, *Versuch*, p. 504, §2; see also Kant, *Groundwork*, p. 11 [AA, vol. 4, 397–8].

the world cannot be bridged. Given the textual evidence of *Versuch* and *Freiheit*, I would therefore argue that Reimarus's notion of moral enlightenment does not dispose of the need for legal structures and institutions to secure the outer liberty of all. Ironically, legality asserts itself as an important and autonomous field for political theory and practice, and reclaims its conceptual independence from questions of moral teleology.

An open question that remains, however, is whether the observed similarities between Reimarus and Kant also apply to their views on women's capacity for moral agency, as well as on the legal-political status of women within the state. Nowhere in her works does Reimarus suggest that women are innately incapable of moral action, a view ascribed to Kant by several feminist critics of his thought.[63] Reimarus seems to hold that women *and* men, as empirical human beings, often act on their inclinations – rather than on rational principles or from a concern for duty. But she makes no suggestion that women are worse than men on this point: that they are *even less* likely to act from duty (and thus to act morally) than men. Such a view is one of the possible readings of Kant's thought on moral agency and women's nature, which Mari Mikkola puts forward in her recent – and rather refreshing – re-evaluation of the feminist critique of Kant.[64] Returning to Reimarus, if we search for any gender bias in her narratives of the moral agency of historically situated persons, it is difficult to identify a consistent philosophical standpoint on the issue (arguably, another similarity between Reimarus and Kant). As I have shown elsewhere, Reimarus's tragedy *Cato* may actually be said to skew the narrative of political virtue in favour of women. The women characters of her play exhibit a *greater* propensity for political virtue than most of the male cast, because their purely private and dependent lives necessitate a more reflective and self-conscious alignment of their own and others' self-interest and affect with the common good. In other words: Women tend to be 'better' at the art of politics, because their notion of political virtue recognizes the role of both reason and affect in the maintenance of external right.[65] Ironically, this historically mediated (rather

---

63 See, for example, S.M. Okin, 'Women and the Making of the Sentimental Family', *Philosophy and Public Affairs*, 11 (1982): pp. 65–88. For similar readings see P. Kleingeld, 'The Problematic Status of Gender-Neutral Language in the History of Philosophy: The Case of Kant', *Philosophical Forum*, 25 (1993): pp. 134–50; J.P. Rumsey, 'Re-visions of Agency in Kant's Moral Theory', in R.M. Schoot (ed.), *Feminist Interpretations of Immanuel Kant* (University Park, PA, 1997), pp. 125–44; R.M. Schott, 'Feminism and Kant: Antipathy or Sympathy?', in J. Kneller and S. Axinn (eds), *Autonomy and Community* (New York, 1998), pp. 87–100; S. Mendus, 'Kant: "An Honest but Narrow-Minded Bourgeois"?', in H.L. Williams (ed.), *Essays on Kant's Political Philsophy* (Cardiff, 1992), pp. 166–90; and V. Plumwood, 'The Politics of Reason: Towards a Feminist Logic', *Australasian Journal of Philosophy*, 71:4 (1993): pp. 436–62.

64 See M. Mikkola, 'Kant on Moral Agency and Women's Nature', *Kantian Review*, 16:1 (2011): pp. 89–111. I agree with Mikkola that, even if Kant held such a view about empirical women, it does not follow that he believed them to be innately less capable, or even *in*capable, or moral agency.

65 See Curtis-Wendlandt, 'Staging Virtue'.

than innate) gender difference seems to derive directly from women's lacking legal-political rights as active citizens. We thus unearth a double inequality in gender terms: Women potentially have a *greater* knack for political virtue, because they have *fewer* political rights.

The implications of this idea, as it is spelled out in Reimarus's *Cato*, are far from clear. Did Reimarus believe that women, if they were freed from their purely private existence and evelated to the status of active citizens, would 'lose their lead' on virtue? It is hard for us to know. While she is candid and nuanced in her discussion of the relationship between morality and legality, Reimarus's works remain notably opaque about her views on women's political rights. It is quite possible that she would have found little to object in Kant's *Metaphysics of Morals*, which insists on men and women's equal liberty as 'human beings', while defending denial of political rights to women through the famous distinction between active citizens (men) and passive citizens (women, children, servants, and others). We cannot know whether Reimarus would have shared Kant's opinion that such an inequality of political rights, anchored in different categories of citizenship, is a precondition for the formation of the state and the civil constitution.[66] Both *Versuch* and *Freiheit* remain silent on this point. Interestingly, another of Reimarus's early works, her collection of undated personal *Reflections* (written between 1755 and 1760), attempts to develop an argument *against* women's involvement in the public sphere – but these arguments break off abruptly in the text, and are never reiterated in her later works.[67]

The inconclusive textual evidence of Reimarus's view on women's rights as citizens seems no coincidence; it points us to her desire to position her political writings outside the gender paradigm, to which other women writers made such outspoken contributions. Whether this was simply to keep her guard and to bypass politically treacherous terrain, or because she truly considered the 'woman question' peripheral to her political ideas is still an open question. In either case, her work exemplifies the important fact that women's political writings in the European Enlightenment covered a much broader range of topics than 'mere' reflections on their own gendered existence in the political environment of their day.

[66] Kant, *Political Writings*, pp. 139–40 [AA, vol. 6, 314–15].

[67] See Elise Reimarus, n.d., *Reflections* Nos 23–23b in Spalding, *Elise Reimarus*, pp. 328–31.

Chapter 7
Italian Women Intellectuals and Their Cultural Networks: The Making of a European 'Life of the Mind'

Marianna D'Ezio

The Italian circulation, review, and adaptation of Mary Wollstonecraft's seminal works on the rights of men and women – particularly *A Vindication of the Rights of Woman* just after its publication in Britain and translation in France,[1] both in 1792 – reinforced the existing dialogue in Italy between languages, texts, and cultures *by* women *for* women. At its peak this dialogue constituted a collective, gendered, and European discourse. Furthermore, such cultural mediators and imitators of Wollstonecraft as Elisabetta Caminer Turra (1751–1796) and Rosa Califronia demonstrated that women also appropriated her ideas for the debate in Italy aimed at overturning conventions and at an innovative role for the woman intellectual. In particular, the presence of female salons in both Veneto (where Caminer Turra was a journalist as well as a learned *salonnière*) and Rome (where Califronia can be presumed to have frequented the famous coteries and assemblies) was decisive for the diffusion of radical ideas on women's position in society, especially those of Wollstonecraft concerning women's education.

Vindication of the Rights of Woman appeared just as the time was ripe for a more systematic assessment of women's role in society. 'The spirit of reform [was] silently pursuing its course,' noted Mary Hays in her obituary of its author.[2] Wollstonecraft had passionately demonstrated that 'women had been created for themselves', as she put it, and not 'merely to gratify the appetite of man'; the great challenge had become one of 'unsexing' the minds and souls of women – to prove that, once 'placed in [the right] station', women 'would advance, instead of retarding, the progress of those glorious principles that give substance to morality'.[3] One of the most intense invectives in *Vindication of the Rights of Woman* (and earlier in *Vindication of the Rights of Men*) is directed against a system that the author perceived as having 'pernicious effect[s] on female morals' – that

---

[1] M. Wollstonecraft, *Défense des droits des femmes, suivie de quelques considérations sur des sujets politiques et moraux* (Paris, 1792).

[2] M. Hays, 'Memoirs of Mary Wollstonecraft', in *The Annual Necrology, for 1797–8. Including, also, various Articles of neglected Biography* (London, 1800), p. 459.

[3] M. Wollstonecraft, *A Vindication of the Rights of Woman, with Strictures on Political and Moral Subjects* (1792), ed. J. Todd (Oxford, 1993), pp. 65, 107. See also M. Wollstonecraft, *A Vindication of the Rights of Men* (1791), ed. J. Todd (Oxford, 1993). All quotations from these two works will be from those editions.

is, the prevailing system of female education.[4] Dismissing Rousseau's views on education as presented in *Emile*, Wollstonecraft insisted on the need for women to be freed 'from all restraint by allowing them to participate [sic] the inherent rights of mankind'. Such participation, she argued, had to be prompted by 'individual education', the neglect of which she deplored as 'the grand source of the misery', as evidenced in women's 'conduct and manners'.[5] Wollstonecraft famously aimed at eradicating distinctions of sex; and reason and its perfectibility informed her call for women's educational opportunities.

In keeping with Talleyrand's pamphlet on national education – 'to see one half of the human race excluded by the other from all participation of government, was a political phenomenon that, according to abstract principles, it was impossible to explain', as she quotes Talleyrand in dedicating *Vindication of the Rights of Woman* to him[6] – Wollstonecraft maintained that, unless it could be demonstrated that women have no reason, governments are unjust if they deny them the natural rights of humankind. As an educator, Wollstonecraft argued that women's participation in governmental affairs had to be preceded by the exercise of their understanding. As she states in her Dedication, national education and the rights of women are therefore two sides of the same coin; and the interdependence of public and private virtues became pivotal in her political thought. Disapproving generally of private education, she argued that men and women had to be educated 'in a great degree by the opinions and manners of the society they live in'. More tellingly, she pointed to 'the social intercourse which has long subsisted between the sexes' in contemporary France, to which she attributed 'a more general diffusion of knowledge than in any part of the European world'.[7]

As for Wollstonecraft's observations on French salons and coteries as places where knowledge could be promoted and exchanged – which Steven Kale's studies of French salons confirm[8] – I suggest that the same function was performed in Italian female salons of the same period. Italian city coteries of the eighteenth century were, however, much less concerned with politics than French salons, especially in states where 'foreign' salons (that is, salons hosted by foreign residents in Italy) could be inaccessible to the Italian nobility because of a law prohibiting their association with foreign political and military representatives.[9]

---

4 Wollstonecraft, *Vindication of the Rights of Men*, p. 22.

5 Wollstonecraft, *Vindication of the Rights of Woman*, pp. 261, 71.

6 Ibid., p. 66; the quote is from C.M. de Talleyrand, *Rapport sur l'instruction publique* (Paris, 1791).

7 Ibid., pp. 86, 65.

8 S. Kale, *French Salons: High Society and Political Sociability from the Old Regime to the Revolution of 1848* (Baltimore and London, 2004) as well as S. Kale's contribution in this volume. See also D. Goodman, 'Enlightenment Salons: The Convergence of Female and Philosophic Ambitions', *Eighteenth-Century Studies*, 22:3 (1989): pp. 329–50, and D. Goodman, *The Republic of Letters: A Cultural History of the French Enlightenment* (Ithaca, NY, 1994).

9 On this point see P. Findlen et al. (eds.), *Italy's Eighteenth Century: Gender and Culture in the Age of the Grand Tour* (Stanford, 2009).

The promotion of a cross-cultural network of assemblies and conversations might nevertheless be a means by which Italian rulers could extend their power and influence. In Rome, for example, Pope Benedict XIV recognized their importance in establishing and maintaining social contacts, while at the same time enabling supervision of cultural and ideological relations between eminent foreigners and the powerful Roman nobility.[10]

It would be inaccurate, however, particularly in light of the vibrant early seventeenth-century debate on women's rights in Italy, to say that an articulate political discussions on women's rights and the education of women started in Italy only as a consequence of the circulation of such foreign works as Wollstonecraft's *Vindications* or Olympe de Gouges's *Declaration des droits de la femme et de la citoyenne*.[11] By the end of the eighteenth century the numerous female salons and coteries certainly promoted women's active participation in politics; but these had already begun to appear at the beginning of the century, and the quickening of pace occasioned by the French Revolution, together with a steadily increasing awareness of the issue of women's education, had been prepared in the decades before the 1790s. As early as 1723, a public discussion was held in Padua at the Accademia de' Ricovrati, 'intorno agli studii delle donne', debating the propriety of educating women in the liberal arts and the sciences.[12] Recognizing that women are 'half of the human species', the Paduan patrician Guglielmo Camposanpiero posited that

> since the substance of one part cannot be different from its total, in the same way one cannot admit any essential distinction between man and woman. All that one of the two can understand, the other one will also be able to understand, and wherever man's intellect can reach, a woman's intellect will also reach.[13]

---

[10] M.P. Donato, 'I salotti romani del Settecento: Il ruolo femminile tra politica e cultura', in M.L. Betri and E. Brambilla (eds), *Salotti e ruolo femminile in Italia tra fine Seicento e primo Novecento* (Venice, 2004), pp. 189, 192, 199 See also M.P. Donato, 'Cultura dell'antico e cultura dei lumi a Roma nel Settecento: La politicizzazione dello scambio culturale durante il pontificato di Pio VI', *Mélanges de l'Ecole française de Rome, Italie et Méditerranée*, 104:2 (1992): pp. 503–48. For a detailed discussion on the influence of Papal power over cultural life in eighteenth-century Rome see A. Quondam, 'L'istituzione Arcadia: Sociologia e ideologia di un'accademia', *Quaderni storici*, 23 (1973): pp. 389–438.

[11] O. de Gouges, *Declaration des droits de la femme et de la citoyenne* (1791), eds E. Gaulier and O. Fontvieille (Paris, 2007). On seventeenth-century debates see J. Broad and K. Green, *A History of Women's Political Thought in Europe, 1400–1700* (Cambridge, 2009), and the works of Moderata Fonte, Lucrezia Marinella, and Arcangela Tarabotti discussed there.

[12] The proceedings of this famous debate were published a few years later as *Discorsi accademici di varj autori viventi. Intorno agli Studj delle Donne; La maggior parte recitati nell'Accademia de' Ricovrati di Padova* (Padua, 1729). See R. Messbarger, *The Century of Women: Representation of Women in Eighteenth-Century Italian Public Discourse* (Toronto, 2002), Chapter 1. All translations from Italian into English are mine, unless otherwise noted.

[13] G. Camposanpiero, 'Che debbono ammettersi le Donne allo Studio delle Scienze, e delle belle Arti' ['That women should be allowed to study science and the fine arts'], in *Discorsi accademici*, p. 12.

Among the many interventions to the *Discorsi accademici* presented on 16 June 1723 and included in the published volume – several of which contrasted sharply with Camposanpiero's defence, and condemned any suggestion of offering education to women on the same level as men[14] – only one was written by a woman. It was attached as 'annotations' and as an 'apologia' in the second edition of the volume, and therefore arguably not intended to be delivered publicly at the Accademia on the day of the debate.[15] In response to Antonio Volpi's speech against the education of women, the 'Sienese gentlewoman' Aretafila Savini de' Rossi developed her own apology, to challenge paternalistic doubts over the social utility of culture among women. As Rebecca Messbarger accurately points out, Savini's 'speech', itself a challenge to, and an appropriation of 'an entrenched rhetorical and methodological legacy to which she has no birthright',[16] explicitly draws its arguments from the author's experience of real life as a non-academic to reinforce the legitimacy of her confutation of Volpi's assumptions.[17] One of the most incisive passages, in which Savini undermines Volpi's arguments on men's superiority over women, concerns female beauty:

> There does not exist any foundation that can persuade a woman to believe that proper studies will result in incivility of her traits, roughness of her habits, negligence in the things that are appropriate for her office, damaging not only herself, but the very body of the Republic; in housekeeping, she would be a nuisance to her husband, a burden in conversation, and finally become a misanthrope, an affected pedant, also losing the colour of her skin because of her excessive application, and thus lowering her natural beauty which is itself able to tame with a simple look, and at times with a sneer or a simpering or a sigh, that arrogant animal called man. We will leave such arts without envy to ignorant and vulgar females. We would be indeed miserable, if our major quality resided in our beauty, which soon fades, and which few of us received. But whatever this privilege could be, how would it be enhanced and polished through our studies! Undoubtedly more than through the lavish luxury of

---

14 See A. Volpi's speech 'Che non debbono ammettersi le Donne allo Studio delle Scienze, e delle belle Arti' ['That women should not be allowed to study science and the fine arts'], in *Discorsi accademici*, pp. 27–45, 66–73.

15 A.S. de' Rossi's reply was written on 20 December 1723: 'Apologia: In favore degli Studj delle Donne, contra il precedente Discorso Del Signor Gio. Antonio Volpi Scritta dalla Signora Aretafila Savini de' Rossi, Dama Senese, ad un Cavaliere' ['Apology in favour of studies for women, against the preceding speech by Signor Giorgio Antonio Volpi, written by Signora Aretafila Savini de' Rossi, Sienese Gentlewoman, to a Cavaliere'], in *Discorsi accademici*, pp. 50–65.

16 Savini first replied with a series of notes to Volpi's speech, and then with a more formal letter, the 'Apologia', employing a writing strategy that thus allowed her 'simultaneously to mock and to submit to the decorum of classic disputation, and to stand inside and outside of academic discourse', Messbarger, *The Century of Women*, p. 42.

17 In her *Breve difesa dei diritti delle donne: Scritta da Rosa Califronia contessa romana* (Assisi, 1794) Rosa Califronia adopted the same peculiar strategy. See below in this chapter.

> fashion, clothing, and special treatment, in pursuit of which things the majority of women go astray.[18]

As Messbarger notes, Savini is here deconstructing the idealization of feminine beauty as it appeared not only in Volpi's speech, but more generally in eighteenth-century writings about women.[19] At the same time, she articulates her answer in a collective voice, a powerful 'we' that aligns women of any social status on the same level, with an equal desire for formal education, which therefore must be available to all of them without class restrictions, but according 'to her particular constitution, her circumstances, and above all her talents'.[20] In order, then, to distance herself and the female sex in general from the commonplace stereotypes of femininity, Savini subscribes to the Enlightenment ethic of social utility and argues for the public good that may result from allowing women to access a better education, particularly with regard to their public function as mothers educating their children. The decades following Savini's invectives witnessed a growing participation of Italian and other European women in their cultural and political milieux, as intellectuals in their own right independently of social status. Among them were several distinguished writers: Giuseppina di Lorena, princess of Carignano – a philanthropist, translator, and proto-feminist author;[21] Cristina

---

[18] A. Savini de' Rossi, 'Apologia', pp. 52–3. Most of these texts remain unpublished today, and are only partially available through critical essays and works. A complete and annotated edition – the result of judicious archival work – would be definitely welcome. At the time of their publication, these work circulated in the form of pamphlets and limited editions, usually read in salons and exchanged among friends and relatives.

[19] Messbarger, *The Century of Women*, p. 44.

[20] Savini de' Rossi, 'Apologia', p. 54.

[21] Giuseppina di Lorena Carignano (1753–1794), wife of Vittorio Amedeo of Savoy, was a frequent guest of Piedmontese and French intellectual circles that gathered in the salons of Milan, Turin, and Paris, and was a friend of Pietro Verri, Cesare Beccaria, Rousseau, and Voltaire. In 1771 she wrote *Les Aventures d'Amélie* (1771), a political novel on a utopian female community established on an island, where the exclusively female inhabitants institute a government and a code of laws to guarantee future prosperity – laws that radically challenge any male dominion over life on the island and decree total equality between men and women, give the mother's surname to children, allow women to inherit, and provide education to all women. For more information on Giuseppina di Lorena Carignano see G. Gasperoni, *Giuseppina di Lorena principessa di Carignano* (Turin, 1938); for a selection of her writings see A. Ferraris, 'Les Nouveaux malheurs de l'amour: Appunti sugli scritti di Giuseppina di Lorena-Carignano', in M. Cerruti (ed.), *Il 'genio muliebre': Percorsi di donne intellettuali fra Settecento e Novecento in Piemonte* (Alessandria, 1990), pp. 9–22; L. Ricaldone (ed.) *Scelta di inediti di Giuseppina di Lorena-Carignano* (Turin, 1980); and L. Ricaldone, 'Un naufragio felice: L'île de Giuseppina di Lorena-Carignano', *Italies*, 2 (2000): pp. 135–43. For general information about cultural life in northern Italy during the eighteenth century see A. de Maddalena et al. (eds), *Economia, istituzioni, cultura in Lombardia nell'età di Maria Teresa* (Bologna, 1982) The manuscript of *Les Aventures d'Amélie*, originally written in French, is housed in the Royal Library of Turin, and has only been partially published in Italian translation in L. Ricaldone, 'Amelia o del desiderio: Un'utopia femminile settecentesca', *Salvo Imprevisti*, 14–15 (1978): pp. 4–10.

Roccati (1732–1797) and Diamante Medaglia Faini (1724–1770), elected as members respectively of the academy of Rovigo (1755) and the Accademia degli Unanimi of Salò (1763);[22] various aristocratic members of the Accademia dell'Arcadia in Rome; and finally the more radical personalities of Eleonora de Fonseca Pimentel (eventually arrested and put to death because of her commitment to the 1799 Neapolitan Revolution[23]) and Elisabetta Caminer Turra – journalist, translator, and writer who directed her own newspaper for twenty years.[24]

In the complex environments of these eighteenth-century Italian intellectuals, salons represented an ideal *locus* for exchanging ideas, reading books and pamphlets, discussing contemporary events with foreign guests, and promoting, supporting, and defending a political cause. In the Veneto region, for example, Italian Jacobins would regularly meet in Verona, 'in the *spezieria* of Saint Catherine, run by a Teresa Ridolfi', or in Venice, where Vincenzo Dandolo's *spezieria* – which counted Annetta Vadori, 'a woman of singular intellect', among its guests – was particularly in sympathy with the ideals of the French Revolution.[25] (Apothecary or specialist shops – *spezierie*, 'spiceries' – sometimes doubled as fashionable meeting-places.) Interest in the public good characterized many political pamphlets and manifestos appearing in Venice in the last decade of the century, and many were penned by women: the 'free citizen I. P. M.' – possibly a member of the Pisani Mocenigo family[26] – exhorted her female fellow citizens to take part:

22 See T. Plebani, 'Socialità e protagonismo femminile nel secondo Settecento', in N.M. Filippini (ed.), *Donne sulla scena pubblica: Società e politica in Veneto tra Sette e Ottocento* (Milan: FrancoAngeli, 2006), p. 41.

23 Eleonora de Fonseca Pimentel joined the Jacobean conspirators and published the republican newspaper *Il Monitore Napoletano* (1799). When the Parthenopaean Republic capitulated, she was arrested and sentenced to death and was hanged on 20 August 1799. For further information and bibliography on Pimentel see M.R. Pelizzari, 'Eleonora de Fonseca Pimentel: Morire per la rivoluzione', *Storia delle donne*, 4 (2008): pp. 103–21.

24 Caminer Turra succeded her father Domenico Caminer as chief editor of the *Giornale Enciclopedico* in 1777, and directed the newspaper until 1796, changing its name to *Nuovo Giornale Enciclopedico* (1782–1789), and then to *Nuovo Giornale Enciclopedico d'Italia* (1790–1796). See below in this essay.

25 See N.M. Filippini, 'Donne sulla scena politica: Dalle Municipalità del 1797 al Risorgimento', in N.M. Filippini (ed.), *Donne sulla scena pubblica*, p. 86. See also G. Bustico, 'Il salotto milanese di un'aspasia veneziana del periodo napoleonico', *Nuovo Archivio Veneto*, 33, fol. 1 (1917): pp. 370–78, on p. 372; and R. Fasanari, *Gli albori del Risorgimento a Verona (1785–1801)* (Verona, 1950).

26 Isabella Pisani Mocenigo had been a renowned Venetian *salonnière* during the first half of the century. Her *conversazioni*, according to Lady Mary Wortley Montagu's *Letters*, were among 'the finest she had ever attended': Lady Mary Wortley Montagu to Mr Montagu, 25 December 1739, quoted in G. Paston (ed.) *Lady Mary Wortley Montagu and her Times* (London, 1907), p. 373.

> Fellow citizens, our sex can also join into the attainment of the common weal. Let virtue in our customs and enthusiasm in our hearts be the foundation of the progress for which we all must strive.[27]

In the same year, another female 'free citizen' wrote her anonymous *Instructions* to her fellow citizens, directly drawing inspiration from the revolutionary mottos of France:

> Liberty, equality, and virtue echo all around you: let nobility, pomp, and indolence no more sit with you. Wake up, my fellow citizens![28]

With Fulvia Mattei's speech given at one of the reunions at the Sala della Pubblica Istruzione in Verona on 24 May 1797, the issue of women's education finally pairs with the recognition that women must, as the new century drew near, be allowed to contribute to a general political regeneration. Women's education is now regarded as an essential further instrument for the triumph of democracy, since

> those principles [that] are sucked with mother's milk are the only ones that remain indelible in our hearts: as a consequence, the son of an aristocratic woman will hardly be a democrat.[29]

Mattei's speech was published in Vicenza only a few years after the French translation of *Vindication of the Rights of Woman* had first appeared in Italy and after Elisabetta Caminer Turra, also in Vicenza, had received and reviewed Wollstonecraft's work in the pages of her *Nuovo Giornale Enciclopedico d'Italia*.[30]

---

27 *Pensieri della libera cittadina I.P.M. alle sue concittadine* [*Thoughts of the free citizen I.P.M. to her female fellow citizens*] (Venice, 1797), p. 4. There also exists an 'answer' to the *Pensieri*, entitled *Risposta alli pensieri della libera cittadina alle sue concitadine* [*sic*] [*Answer to the thoughts of the free citizen to her female fellow citizens*] (Venice, 1797).

28 *Istruzioni d'una libera cittadina alle sue concittadine* [*Instructions of a free female citizen to her female fellow citizens*] (Venice, 1797), p. 3. Nadia Maria Filippini has been the first historian to shed complete light on these texts, in her essay 'Donne sulla scena politica'.

29 Mattei's speech appeared in *L'Amico degli Uomini* VI on 30 May 1797, and was reprinted as *Dell'educazione che si deve dare alle donne* [*On the education that should be given to women*] (Vicenza, 1797).

30 Caminer Turra possibly received her own copy of Mary Wollstonecraft's *Vindication of the Rights of Woman* (in French) from Germaine de Staël. See R. Unfer-Lukoschik (ed.), *Elisabetta Caminer Turra (1751–1796): Una letterata veneta verso l'Europa* (Verona, 1998). She could however also read English, and since she made a first comment on the publication of Wollstonecraft's 1792 London edition of the *Vindication* in her newspaper in October 1792, and then again in August 1793 on the French translation, it is difficult to establish whether she was reviewing the original version of Wollstonecraft's book or its translation. See C.M. Sama (ed. and trans.), *Selected Writings of an Eighteenth-Century Venetian Woman of Letters* (Chicago, 2003), p. 188n102.

Besides considering Wollstonecraft herself as 'the champion of her sex',[31] Caminer Turra offered an enthusiastic response to the *Vindication*, and one that captured its polemical tone and largely contributed to its reception and dissemination in Italy. As a prominent journalist and intellectual who had also established and led literary salons in several cities in Veneto, especially in Vicenza,[32] Caminer Turra was accustomed to debating thorny questions, as she did, for example, on capital punishment and freedom of the press. Beginning her literary career as a translator of Voltaire's works, she was also well aware of the potential importance of her exemplary role as a self-taught female scholar, and of the responsibility of her position as 'educator of women', as Rita Unfer-Lukoschik characterized her.[33] Lashing out at some of her female contemporaries 'who pretend to become cultivated, to study, and who spout pretensions and unfortunately serve as fodder for the wits' laughter',[34] she encouraged women to learn 'how to sit at a writing table rather than at a toilette', and accomplish a 'desire that is rare in women, that of seeing her make herself useful to her nation by translating works that can bring her real advantages or pleasures, which is perhaps the same thing.'[35] The act of translation, Caminer Turra argued, was to be considered as an opportunity for women to enter the realm of literature and, at the same time, to offer a valuable service to their fellow citizens – besides, of course, making a living out of translating. From an ideological and critical perspective, however, translations were also ways to appropriate and share other European women writers' notions of 'femininity' – and deconstruct them with a view to challenging traditional stereotypes and carving out a new position for women in the gender hierarchy of European society.[36] The education of women,

[31] Although not without some reservations, especially when Caminer Turra pondered on the consequences of Wollstonecraft's *Vindication* and cryptically reflected: 'What will she gain? Revolutions are not so easy to or frequent in all genres'; in *Selected Writings*, p. 188. All quotations from Caminer Turra's newspapers will be taken from Sama's rich selection and translation of Turra's articles, reviews, and correspondence.

[32] In Vicenza, together with her husband Antonio Turra, at the age of twenty-nine Elisabetta also inaugurated the Stamperia Turra [Turra Publishing House] which became one of the most active publishing houses of the whole region.

[33] R. Unfer-Lukoschik, 'L'educatrice delle donne: Elisabetta Caminer Turra (1751–1796) e la "Querelle des Femmes" negli spazi veneti di fine '700', *Memorie dell'Accademia delle scienze di Torino*, 5:24 (2000): pp. 25–36.

[34] E.C. Turra, 'On Exceptional Women', *Europa Letteraria* (November 1769), in Sama, *Selected Writings*, p. 175.

[35] E.C. Turra, 'Review' [of Terenzia Ghellini's Italian translation of François Philippe Mezanguy's *Compendio dell'istoria e della morale dell'Antico Testamento con spiegazioni e riflessi*], *Giornale Enciclopedico* (January 1777), in Sama, *Selected Writings*, p. 148.

[36] In 1774, 1781, and 1782 Caminer Turra translated Jeanne-Marie Leprince de Beaumont's pedagogical *Le magasin des enfans, ou dialogues d'une sage gouvernante avec ses eleves* (1756) as *Il magazzino delle fanciulle, ovvero dialoghi tra una savia direttrice e parecchie sue allieve di grado illustre* (Vicenza, 1774); *Magasin des adolescentes, ou*

as Wollstonecraft also acknowledged, not only has an impact on the cultivation of women's minds, but more importantly is an advantage to civil society:

> What must not be neglected in the education of women, and which can go hand in hand with the management of families, and with the other functions that are prescribed to women, is a sufficient cultivation of the mind, which, if it became less rare, would bring no small number of advantages to civil society. It would shape character, and it would spare those women who in an affected manner try to pull themselves out of the ordinary embarrassment of making fools of themselves with their efforts to make it known, whether it is true or not, that they are not completely foolish. And it would prevent us from having to blush upon hearing the wonderment people express when a woman is a little less uneducated than usual.[37]

Since Caminer Turra was also claiming a clear space for women's voice in the realms of literature and literary criticism, her discussions of the education of women must be seen in relation to their impact on contemporary society.[38] Through her own example as a professional writer, Caminer Turra aimed at the full recognition of women's moral and literary merits and achievements; and in this process of improving women's minds, education was to have the principal role: it was a process that aimed at raising the female sex 'out of the void in which some would leave it', as she affirmed in reviewing *Vindication of the Rights of Woman*.[39] The encouragement, respect, and defence of a European 'female power' merges Caminer Turra's and Wollstonecraft's feminist premises in a common

Dialogues d'une sage gouvernante avec ses eleves de la premiere distinction. Pour servir de suite au magasin des enfans (1760) as *Il magazzino delle adulte, ovvero dialoghi tra una savia direttrice e parecchie sue allieve di grado illustre che serve di continuazione al Magazzino delle fanciulle* (Vicenza, 1781); and *Instructions pour les jeunes dames qui entrent dans le monde, et se marient. Leurs devoirs dans cet etat, et envers leurs enfants. Pour servir de suite au Magasin des adolescentes* (1764) as *Istruzioni per le giovani dame ch'entrano nel mondo, e si maritano, loro doveri in questo stato, e verso i loro figliuoli, per servire di continuazione e di compimento al Magazzino delle fanciulle e a quello delle adulte* (Vicenza, 1782).

37 Turra, 'On Exceptional Women', in Sama, *Selected Writings*, p. 178.

38 See for example Caminer Turra's refusal of women's anonymity in her review of an unsigned Italian translation (*Traduzioni italiane di Madamigella N.N., Italian translations by Miss Anonymous*) of Henry Manning's *Essay on the Health of Unmarried Daughters, with some Reflections on Marriage*, published in Pavia in 1794: 'Why in the world does the praiseworthy young woman "Anonymous" hide herself? Might she be of the opinion, humiliating to her sex, that in cultivating her talent she brings dishonour to women? It might not become a woman to parade herself as a professional expert, but must she blush for having played so useful a role (as translator), and for having directed her own studies toward the good of her peers?', *Nuovo Giornale Enciclopedico d'Italia* (September 1794), in Sama, *Selected Writings*, p. 190.

39 E.C. Turra, 'On Mary Wollstonecraft's *Vindication of the Rights of Woman*', *Nuovo Giornale Enciclopedico d'Italia* (August 1793), in Sama, *Selected Writings*, p. 188.

voice, and demonstrates that the 'dream of unexpected happiness'[40] (arising from improvement of women's position in the European social structure) could indeed be accomplished, notwithstanding its price:

> It is true that in Europe educated women are praised and adored, and they have a tremendous and perhaps the principal influence in the most serious of matters: but at what price? All their power depends upon youth and beauty, rather than stemming from that distributive justice which should base their power on a better education, on the development of their intellectual abilities, on the cultivation of their reason, and on the knowledge of their own purpose and their own duties. This is the source from which Madame Wollstonecraft would like female power to spring, and this is the system on which her book turns. Her book proves for the millionth time that women might deserve the honour of being considered part of the human race.[41]

Most of such literary and cultural encouragement originated in and around the female salons of the time. In the North, in the Veneto region, in Tuscany, in Naples, and particularly in Rome, aristocratic and bourgeois coteries allowed women to profess and cultivate their passion for literature and conversation, and so increasingly to dominate in public positions and international gatherings, rather than the private sphere of the home.

The relative freedom that Roman *salonnières* enjoyed, in the exchange of books, guests, manuscripts, objects, and ideas, may account for the positive response *Vindication of the Rights of Woman* had in the intellectual circles of Rome. In fact, we should consider the first major indicator of its Italian reception to be the Roman countess Rosa Califronia's *Breve Difesa dei Diritti delle Donne* [*Short Defence of the Rights of Women*] of 1794, which followed the circulation of its 1792 French translation in the salons of Maria Pizzelli Cuccovilla and Margherita Sparapani Gentili Boccapaduli.[42] Particular tribute therefore should be given to Califronia's pamphlet, which has never been studied comparatively although its similarity with *Vindication* is more than conspicuous. *Breve difesa* is in eight chapters, each of

---

[40] 'Thanks to the undefeated French nation, we are regenerated; we are free and to the purpose we confess that it seems to be a dream of unexpected happiness: but I doubt, brother citizens, that we can be happy if we do not care for educating a sex that may indeed contribute much to consolidate or destroy our liberty'; G. Ricchi, 'Dell'influenza che possono avere le donne sullo sviluppo dello spirito pubblico' ['On the influence women may have on the development of public spirit'], in *Discorsi pronunciati dal cittadino Z.R. li 16, 17, e 19 pratile nella Società patriotica* (Venice, 1797): speech included in the volume where Mattei's speech also appeared (see note 29, above; my translation).

[41] Turra, 'On Mary Wollstonecraft's *Vindication of the Rights of Woman*', in Sama, *Selected Writings*, pp. 188–9.

[42] Califronia, *Breve difesa*. The first translation of Mary Wollstonecraft's *Vindication of the Rights of Woman* has generally been acknowledged as Franca Ruggieri's *I diritti delle donne* (Rome, 1977). Califronia's text demonstrates that Wollstonecraft's *Vindication* was well known in the Papal State in the 1790s.

them marking a response to some accusation against women: the first bears the title 'The first accusation is confuted: *Women are by nature deprived of reason*'; Chapter 2 is entitled 'Defence against the second accusation: *Women have a more feeble intellect than men*', and so on. The author's intention is clearly stated in the Preface:

> With the favour of the press, the philosophical rights of men are continuously made public: yet we never see nowadays a critical work on the rights of women. Would it make any difference to say that, within mankind, the female sex is also included? Philosophers put the rights of men into practice, and the female sex is never contemplated. One need only have a quick look at the wild events of France, where with an uproar the RIGHTS OF MAN have been extolled. What perseverance for the male sex! What system has instead been established for women and for their rights?
>
> I have decided that it will be an advisable thing to produce a short defence of our sex, and I will demonstrate the irrationality of men's declamations against our sex in general; and by confessing our defects, I will defend our legitimate rights.[43]

In keeping with Wollstonecraft's assumption that 'women [are] kept in ignorance under the specious name of innocence',[44] Califronia shares the notion of a strong need to 'eliminate from the world at least half of the physical and moral distress of women, which originates from the restricted education they receive in Europe and causes women's own idleness.'[45] Both Wollstonecraft and Califronia charged that the 'domineering and tyrannical power men exert over women keeps them from becoming literati',[46] and proposed a revolution in female manners, with women claiming equal access to education to encourage enlightened intellect in opposition to gross ignorance, for the benefit of the whole society:

> If there are nations in which, more than in other nations, women are lacking intellectual abilities or culture, it is your fault, dear men, who – imposing your dominion over the family, and fearing the subtle and penetrating intellect of women more than that of numerous mean merchants – employ your wives and daughters in the vile office of being your maidservants.
>
> It is not proper, they say: it has no utility that the weaker sex applies the mind to study, although women have all possible capabilities. Women are too inconstant, and easily change from truth to error; and the fumigating fire of pride will soon inflame their excited folly. *There* is the utility of allowing women to study, they say.

---

43 Califronia, *Breve difesa*, pp. iii, vi. All translations into English are mine.

44 Wollstonecraft, *A Vindication of the Rights of Woman*, p. 84.

45 Califronia, *Breve difesa*, p. lvi.

46 Ibid., p. ciii. Wollstonecraft also obsessively writes of 'tyranny' and 'intellectual empire' throughout her *Vindication*.

> I demonstrate that the propriety of studying is not contrary to the nature of women. Study is but an exercise of the intellect, and an achievement of useful cognitions. Woman is equally capable of intellect as man.[47]

Interestingly, yet unsurprisingly, Califronia's *Short Defence* does not contemplate politics as one of the 'subjects' in which women should be engrossed: women's participation in political and ideological contemporary debates is not one of Califronia's main concerns. However, her harangues leave tentatively open the possibility of women developing their intellect toward participation in men's ideological discussions – the very basis of nineteenth-century Italian political salons. In Califronia's view, women should acquire the necessary competences to join in intellectual conversation, or remain silent:

> It is such a natural thing that women, feeling they are not without acute intellect and animated by their fervid nature, react to men and want to share with them the same drawing room to discuss every issue. They should make use of the ingenious prudence that is a characteristic of learned men, who know that intellect is no science itself, but only the means to acquire it. Women therefore should not mistake intellect for science, but only reason on those topics in which they are well versed, and observe a prudent, scrupulous silence in all the other subjects of which they have not yet acquired any knowledge.[48]

Califronia's views on women's position in intellectual circles were remarkably similar to the early Bluestockings' idea of a 'public' and recognized identity for female intellectuals – indeed a first, decisive step towards the public acknowledgement of their right to 'a life of the mind'. By nurturing a strong consciousness of a female intellectual community, they were offering a model of the educated woman – to challenge and reform stereotypes of femininity through elegant and learned conversation. Yet the *public* display of learning could at first be viewed as a dangerous exposure to hostile criticism, as well as a subversion of the traditional female roles of wife and mother. In the exclusive network of female intellectual exchange offered by a private salon, however, learned women could at least be encouraged within the boundaries of a specific, controlled social space. The ambiguous reputation of women writers such as Mary Wollstonecraft and Catherine Macaulay would be too unconventional and transgressive for the first generation of Bluestockings; they were also for countess Califronia, for whom a compromise between literary ambition and social respectability was essential.

The *femmineo potere* ['female power'] that learned women advocated, the opportunity to take part professionally as well as intellectually in European cultural life, was exactly the power of influence that Caminer Turra and the many other *salonnières* in Italy and Europe were trying to achieve. They envisaged an intellectual power that would elevate them from the private sphere of elegant

47 Ibid., pp. ciii, cv, xcviii.

48 Ibid., pp. viii–ix.

conversations to full public recognition, not confine them to what might be considered empty conversation. In turn it would offer them professional and personal emancipation in the wider panorama of European literature, matching the intellectual level to which men might aspire. Learning about each other's agency within a European public sphere was not only a necessary step towards mutual appreciation, but also a powerful way to exchange ideas and thus claim for themselves and their writings an equal share of literary authorship.

The forms of sociability, rich with literary consequences, that European women writers essayed have been exposed as more complex than those of fashionable assemblies. The international tendency of sociability and cultural mediation highlighted in this essay was toward a fuller engagement with certain influential texts of eighteenth-century European women: those that contributed to a shared awareness of issues such as women's rights and education. Eighteenth-century translations, epistolary correspondence, literary influences, and exchanges in two, three, or more languages are early examples of the potential of international sociability as a vehicle for new ideas, and as an emblem of modernity – and above all, of social and political reformation. In some cases, women in Italy took the challenge of moving beyond the salon into the political realm very seriously, and in the case of Pimentel paid a heavy price. In others the modest hidden influence of women through conversation and salon sociability remained the ideal.

Chapter 8
Women's Intellectual Agency in the History of Eighteenth- and Nineteenth-Century French Salons

Steven Kale

Introduction

Many of the principal *salonnières* of the Bourbon Restoration had strong political opinions, which they expressed clearly in their memoirs and correspondence. By political opinions, I mean simply that they critically judged public affairs and took partisan positions on the political issues of the day. This fact has been exceedingly hard to notice because nearly all traditional and contemporary representations of the role of salonnières ignore the fact that they had ideas of their own. The political ideas expressed by Restoration salonnières were consistent with conventions of polite society that emphasized harmonious relations between members of an intimate circle. They also reflected long-standing assumptions about the role of women in aristocratic society and idealized notions propagated by both men and women regarding feminine intervention in the intellectual life of the eighteenth century. My larger purpose in focusing on the Restoration is simply to rectify a gap in the now voluminous literature on salon practices in which the specificity of women's ideas has been neglected, and to answer this question: What did salonnières themselves think about the significance of the intellectual agency of women in salons?

The Liberalism of Restoration Salonnières

Aristocratic high society was at its pinnacle during the Restoration. The advent of broad civil liberties and an end to the enforced silence of the Empire favoured the re-emergence and proliferation of salons. Although the revival of *mondain* sociability benefited from peace, prosperity, and the establishment of a new royal court, the most important factor was the Charter of 1814, which created the conditions for a sustained development of parliamentary government. The Charter contributed to the vibrancy of salons because the new institutions made public opinion a force in politics, created a framework for perpetual debate, and allowed party politics to spill over into *le monde*, where the clientele of the salons participated in the same system of social networks as those involved in politics. The Restoration was also a time of bitter partisan differences between elites preoccupied with political stability. Memories of the Revolution and the emigration, intensified by the resentments cultivated during the Napoleonic era, created divisions in high society and coteries among the clientele of the salons. The Charter envisioned a political system that required notables to collaborate and coexist. Fear of another Jacobin Revolution or a return to dictatorship motivated consensus to perpetuate a monarchy governing in conjunction with a circumscribed elite, and a tactical agreement to refrain from the sort of bloody or intractable conflicts that had precluded constitutional stability in the past.[1] In such circumstances, longstanding assumptions about the civilizing power of women and the ethical virtues of polite society cast the salon as an antidote to the characteristic divisiveness of partisanship. This general image of the salon as a remedy for disunity gained political specificity under the Restoration when contrasted with the partisan bloodletting in the Chamber of Deputies – which the Duc de Richelieu, prime minister on and off until 1821, characterized as an 'annual focus of delirium and agitation'. Once the salon was made a direct counterpart to the process of parliamentary deliberation, it came to be seen as part of the political machinery: 'a sort of diplomatic forum for smoothing out factional disputes prior to votes in the Assembly or appointments to the cabinet'.[2]

The most vocal salonnières of the Restoration were political moderates who hoped for the survival of the new regime, and who blamed the 'Ultras' (the ultra-royalists) for injecting an unprecedented degree of partisan bitterness into public life. They viewed inflammatory right-wing political invective as being at odds with the sociability of the pre-Revolutionary past and insisted that conversation between political adversaries could dispel prejudices and reveal common ground. Many argued that political disputes were the product of short-sighted or egoistical judgements, bound to wither in the face of sustained contact, self-examination, and honest mutual disclosure.[3] They believed that the pacification of political conflict was their most important political task. In troubled times, wrote Blanche-Joséphine Le Bascle d'Argenteuil, Duchesse de Maillé (1787–1851), 'one must place oneself on the terrain of general interest so that the parties can be reconciled with one another.' Delphine de Girardin (1804–1855) went even further, arguing that 'those who could hold opposing forces in a state of equilibrium would contribute to national progress by preventing the final and fatal victory of either

1 See S. Fiette, *La Noblesse française des Lumières à la Belle Epoque: Psychologies d'une adaptation* (Paris, 1997), pp. 223, 245. See also S. Kale, *French Salons: High Society and Political Sociability from the Old Regime to the Revolution of 1848* (Baltimore and London, 2004), pp. 106–10.

2 E. de Waresquiel, *Le Duc de Richelieu, 1766–1822: Un sentimental en politique* (Paris, 1990), p. 275; M. Fumaroli, 'La Conversation', in P. Nora (ed.), *Les Lieux de mémoire* (3 vols, Paris: Gallimard, 1992), vol. 3, p. 734.

3 See D. de Dino, *Memoirs of the Duchesse de Dino*, 1836–1840, ed. Marie Radziwill (3 vols, New York, 1910), vol. 2, p. 18; C. de Boigne, *Mémoires de la comtesse de Boigne, née d'Osmond: Récits d'une tante*, ed. Jean-Claude Berchet (2 vols, Paris, 1986), vol. 2, p. 148.

ideological extreme, so that a sort of creative rivalry would strengthen the country by forcing the two enemies [to] perfect themselves.'[4]

The women who held such views were constitutional monarchists at the Right or Centre Right of the French political spectrum. The hallmarks of their liberalism mirrored the amicability and moderation implicit in traditional *politesse*: a respect for all opinions, a refusal to prejudge, and a distaste for orthodoxies of all kinds. As much a temperament as a set of ideas, the ideology of salonnières combined an almost reflex hatred for violent partisanship with a preference for parliamentary institutions. At the same time, it was a liberalism overtly committed to saving the Restoration, along with all the social and political arrangements that made it advantageous to the elite. Armande-Marie-Antoinette de Vignerot du Plessis de Richelieu, Marquise de Montcalm (1777–1832), sister of the Duc de Richelieu, fully identified with her brother's goal of reconciling the old nobility, the Imperial aristocracy, and the liberals as a means of stabilizing France's new constitutional monarchy. Richelieu hoped to create a durable moderate royalist majority in the electorate by demonstrating that the Charter could provide a government that was firm, efficient, and liberal, combining the best of the Old Regime with the most important gains of the Revolution. Montcalm, distressed to see political passions dividing the men she esteemed, believed she was acting as a patriot when she tried to patch things up between her brother and his political rivals. Maillé blamed the Revolution of 1830 on Charles X and the Ultras, who appalled the country with their bigotry and fanaticism. 'If I had directed the Restoration', she wrote, 'I would have wanted the government to reassure all interests, and the Court to take responsibility for calming and reassuring people's vanity.' Madame Ancelot agreed, explaining that the July Revolution would never have occurred if Charles X had embraced 'the new principles' and appointed a few liberal ministers.[5]

The ideology of conciliation was sanctioned and supported by a number of longstanding aristocratic traditions related to mondain sociability. Carolyn Lougee has argued that salons were a specific historical expression of the aristocracy's determination to regulate and control the transition from an hereditary to an open elite. They emerged as the justification of noble privileges by traditional military roles was under attack. Circumstances promoted a more modern view of nobility, based on a combination of birth, education, manners, and sociability; and the increasingly wealthy bourgeoisie, aspiring to 'live nobly', was gaining entry into an expanding service nobility. Salons appeared along with the need to provide a space for social fusion and cultural homogenisation, among the diverse

---

4 B. de Maillé, *Souvenirs des deux Restaurations: Journal inédit*, ed. Xavier de la Fournière (Paris, 1984), p. 50; D. de Girardin, *Vicomte de Launay: Lettres parisiennes* (4 vols, Paris, 1857–1868), vol. 4, pp. 11–16.

5 A. de Montcalm, *Un Salon politique sur la Restauration: Correspondance de la Marquise de Montcalm*, ed. E. de Lévy-Mirepoix (Paris, 1949), p. 25; A. de Montcalm, *Mon Journal, 1815–1818*, ed. Sébastien Charléty (Paris, 1936), p. 11; V. Ancelot, *Un Salon de Paris, 1824 à 1864* (Paris, 1866), p. 60.

elements of an aristocracy in the process of social and ideological transformation.[6] Beginning in the seventeenth century, salons had served to bring together nobles and intellectuals in an atmosphere of civility and fair play in order to educate the first and refine the second – to create a common medium of cultural exchange based on a shared notion of *honnêteté* that combined learning, good manners, and conversational skill.[7] According to Lougee, 'the salon functioned as a melting pot' by blurring social distinctions and by replacing birth as a status criterion with a 'high plateau of luxury and a uniform code of behaviour' that eliminated 'potential sources of friction [between] individuals from diverse backgrounds'.[8]

The absence, characteristic of feudal traditions of noble family life, of any strict separation between public and private spheres had placed aristocratic women at the centre of a family's public responsibilities and status concerns. The households of the noble officeholders and *grands seigneurs* who populated high society in the seventeenth and eighteenth centuries were not unlike those of ruling princes and feudal lords, where the personal and professional could not be 'sharply differentiated and specialized', where private decisions were routinely made for public purposes, and where public actions could readily be influenced by private considerations.[9] Official business, economic interests, or simply the maintenance and projection of a family's reputation routinely required aristocrats to receive a large number of people in their homes, and made the performance of the social duties associated with the salon public acts undertaken in a private domicile. Consequently, the salon was a powerful tool for linking private interests to political power and public influence.

As a 'gendered space', the salon was associated with longstanding chivalric notions of women as civilizers capable of selflessly ministering to others by virtue of their self-abnegation. Linked in the public mind to widely accepted 'feminine' characteristics, salons came to be idealized by generations of male writers, artists, intellectuals, and politicians as protected spaces for the reconciliation of differences, where neutrality was guaranteed by the salonnière's self-effacement and devotion to propriety. Anne Louise Germaine de Staël-Holstein (1766–1817), generally known as Madame de Staël, developed such common notions of sexual difference into a veritable theory of feminine political responsibility, arguing that the condition of women under French absolutism had given them a serious public responsibility to soften men's passions and encourage them to think only of the public good.[10] Similar notions formed the basis of a consensus in aristocratic

---

6 C. Lougee, *Le Paradis des Femmes: Women, Salons, and Social Stratification in Seventeenth-Century France* (Princeton, 1976), pp. 136–69.

7 See E. Goldsmith, *Exclusive Conversations: The Art of Interaction in Seventeenth-Century France* (Philadelphia, 1988), pp. 6–7, 20–25; and on the civilizing role of the seventeenth-century salon see C. Dulong, *La Vie quotidienne des femmes au Grand Siècle* (Paris, 1984), pp. 126–36.

8 Lougee, *Le Paradis des Femmes*, pp. 52, 211–13.

9 N. Elias, *Court Society*, trans. E. Jephcott (New York, 1983), p. 1.

10 G. de Staël, *Germany*, trans. O.W. Wright (2 vols, New York, 1871), vol. 1, pp. 43–4. It had been this quality of self-effacement that led the *philosophes* to eulogize the *salonnières* of the eighteenth century. See D. Goodman, 'Governing the Republic of

society – one that counted on women's civilizing role and echoed the prevailing opinion that women ought to restrain their desires in the interest of social harmony, while men were free to pursue theirs. But Madame de Staël sought to push such widely accepted ideas to their limit, contriving women's potential 'from whatever powers men have left on their plate'.[11] In effect, she used established gender norms to argue in favour of a role for elite women in public affairs. In accepting that women were agents of moral regeneration, she refused at the same time to consign them to the domestic sphere in the expectation that they would merely support men in their political work. As Madelyn Gutwirth put it, she reasoned 'that women should not be granted too frivolous or insipid a role in society, for then they would lose the power to "soften men's passions"'.[12] Salonnières worked to moderate hostility, teach civility, inspire heroism, and generally draw out the best part of human nature, not to elicit positive characteristics in individuals but to cultivate an aristocracy capable of governing.[13]

Madame de Staël used her salon as a forum for political discussion and as an instrument of political activism. She consistently denounced social arrangements in which women were denied an opportunity for learning and serious conversation. She chided the men of the Revolution for reducing women 'to the most absurd mediocrity' and criticized the male-dominated world of English high society for leaving women ignorant and mute.[14] She believed that salon conversation was supposed to be strenuous, serious, and intellectually challenging, not to make the weak-minded shine through the artifice of self-display. But she did not define the role of salonnières in terms of their personal opinions and she did not use her salon to propagate her own ideas. Political salons presided over by women effectively supported debate on constitutional issues and encouraged alliances between different factions, exploiting beliefs that associated women with wholeness and conciliation. Once the Revolution began, Staël worked to make her salon a privileged place where those exercising power would gain wisdom, and bring reason and morality to bear in crafting legislation. Her ideal salon would have combined the sociability of the eighteenth century with the highest ideals of the Enlightenment so that the most educated minds and the most rigorous philosophical considerations would inform debate among elites. It would extend those values from the private to the public sphere, drawing together talented individuals of

Letters: The Politics of Culture in the French Enlightenment', *History of European Ideas*, 13:3 (1991): pp. 183–99.

11 M. Gutwirth, *Twilight of the Goddesses: Women and Representation in the French Revolutionary Era* (New Brunswick, NJ, 1992), p. 383.

12 Ibid., p. 383.

13 G. de Staël, *De l'Influence des passions sur le bonheur des individus et des nations* (Paris, 1820), p. 10.

14 G. Fraisse, *Reason's Muse: Sexual Difference and the Birth of Democracy*, trans. Jane Marie Todd (Chicago, 1994), p. 122; S. Kale, 'Women, Salons, and Sociability as Constitutional Problems in the Works of Madame de Staël', *Historical Reflections/Réflexions Historiques*, 32:2 (2006): pp. 309–38, on pp. 328–32.

diverse backgrounds and promoting consensus on matters of common interest. Under such an arrangement, women would be respected, their views would be taken seriously, and their right to an education would be considered a social and political necessity.[15]

What made Staël unique was that she welcomed politics into the salon, at a time when most salonnières saw such politicization as a curse. Later aristocrats and writers would trace the destruction of eighteenth-century conversation and sociability to the Revolution; but Staël saw 1788 to 1791 as an enchanted epoch, when 'the French spirit showed itself in all its lustre' and elites abandoned the frivolity of society life for the intelligent discussion of public affairs.[16] Nevertheless, she presided over a salon in the way women had in previous centuries: as hostess, mediator, and facilitator on the periphery of public life. She subordinated her own goals to the larger purposes of her friends and associates. Politics was at the centre of her salon's preoccupations, but her political opinions were not.

Women's Ideas in the Representation of Salons

Our contemporary understanding of salons has been shaped by eighteenth-century perceptions, the nostalgia of nineteenth-century mondains for the salons of the Old Regime, and recent scholarship that seeks to analyse the place of salons in Enlightenment history. Each of these represents the role of salonnières in ways that mask evidence of women's intellectual autonomy and deny them independent voice. A rare exception is the literature concerning salons of the seventeenth-century *précieuses*, depicted as women-centred gatherings that encouraged novel social encounters, cultivated the new science, and affirmed a woman's right to consideration, independence, and learning.[17] A far more common template was the one that conflated the power of salonnières with the power of women at court, arguing that woman dominated government and society. The best expression of the courtly model of feminine power can be found in the works of Edmond and Jules Goncourt, who wrote that in the eighteenth century woman held within her grasp

---

15 See Fraisse, *Reason's Muse*, p. 122.

16 A. Lilti, *Le Monde des salons: Sociabilité et mondanité à Paris au XVIIIe siècle* (Paris, 2005), pp. 27–8; Kale, *French Salons*, pp. 52–3.

17 E. Harth, *Cartesian Women: Versions and Subversions of Rational Discourse in the Old Regime* (Ithaca, NY, 1992), pp. 33, 54–65, 64–5, 139; C. Dulong, 'From Conversation to Creation', in N. David and A. Farge (eds), *A History of Women in the West* (Cambridge, 1993), vol. 3, *Renaissance and Englightenment Paradoxes*, pp. 405–7. On seventeenth-century salons see F. Beasley, *Salons, History, and the Creation of Seventeenth-Century France: Mastering Memory* (Aldershot, 2006); J. DeJean, *Tender Geographies: The Politics of Female Authorship under the Late Ancien Régime* (New York, 1991); M. Maître, 'Sapho, reine de Tendre: Entre monarchie absolue et royauté littéraire', in D. Denis and A.-E. Spica (eds), *Madeleine de Scudéry: Une femme de lettres au XVIIe siècle* (Arras, 2002), pp. 179–202.

> the King and France, the will of the sovereign and the authority of public opinion – everything! She gave orders at court, she was mistress in her home. She held the revolution of alliances and political systems, peace and war, the literature, the arts and the fashions of the eighteenth century, as well as its destinies, in the folds of her gown.[18]

In this retelling of the political history of eighteenth-century France, women's power was portrayed as pervasive, but hidden from view. Woman 'lurked in the shadows', conducted secret manoeuvres, acted behind the scenes, 'granting audiences, receiving reports from her spies, and attending the Council of Ministers'.[19]

One version of this courtly representation depicted women as potent but ethereal, as sovereigns who reigned but did not rule. Often painted in the language of flattery, such women were described as queens presiding over empires, surrounded by a bevy of admiring courtiers, who exercised a secret power through coquetry, personality, or magic, but who accomplished nothing in particular. By a common variant of this account, women both reigned and ruled, but covertly: leading political coteries and factions at court, planning strategy, dictating foreign and domestic policy, taking a hand in treaty negotiations, removing ministers, arranging alliances, and getting favourite men of letters elected to the Académie française.[20] The nineteenth-century version of this tradition compared women who held political salons during the Restoration and the July Monarchy to the mythical figure of Egeria – a political metaphor suggesting that salonnières were the hidden source of ministerial decisions and parliamentary legislation. The influence attributed to such salonnières was always mysterious and occult, transmitted nocturnally, or at least far from view, and consummated in an intimacy redolent of sexual intercourse. It suggested that powerful women could have personal relationships and nefarious goals; but it did not accord them the intellectual autonomy to formulate opinions, since the courtly myth was more about conduct than the intellectual inspiration behind it.

The courtly model of feminine power does not distinguish between salonnières and the women of the court because it conflates court intrigue with the influence

---

18 J. and E. de Goncourt, *The Woman of the Eighteenth Century: Her Life, from Birth to Death, her Love and her Philosophy in the World of Salon, Shop, and Street*, trans. J. Le Clercq and R. Roeder (New York, 1927), pp. 243–51, 250, 330–31; J. and E. de Goncourt, *Histoire de la société française pendant la Révolution* (Paris, 1864), pp. 1–2.

19 J. and E. de Goncourt, *Histoire de la société française pendant la Révolution*, pp. 1–2.

20 See for example L. Abensour, *La Femme et le féminisme avant la Révolution* (Paris, 1923), p. 72, which recapitulates themes that go back to Montesquieu's *Lettres Persanes* [*Persian Letters*], in which Rica finds that no business whatsoever can be contracted in France without 'a woman through whose hands all favors ... have to pass'. When Rousseau arrived in Paris, Père Castel told him that 'One does nothing [here] without women'. C. de Montesquieu, *Persian Letters*, trans. C.J. Betts (New York, 1973), p. 92; M. Glotz and M. Marie, *Salons du XVIIIe siècle* (Paris, 1949), p. 12.

salons supposedly wielded in the literary world. It does so by replicating in descriptions of women's influence in the arts the language used to describe their covert and illegitimate political power, and by using the presence of the court, the salons, and the Republic of Letters in *le monde* as proof that women dominated everything. On the one hand, salonnières used their authority to confirm literary reputations in private before they were publicly consecrated by election to the Académie. By assuming a form of 'spiritual royalty' in presiding over the literary world and governing the Republic of Letters, women shaped public opinion. On the other hand, government during the decay of absolutism was directed by this same public opinion, which was fashioned in equal measure at court, in the salons, and by men of letters. In this imaginary world, feminine sovereignty operated through women's control of the empire of conversation – mistaken by French high society for the source of all things, entraining the idea that salons shaped public opinion and contributed to the outbreak of the Revolution. This notion rested on an eighteenth-century understanding of the salon as a tribunal of judgement in the Republic of Letters, reaffirmed in recent times by the influence of François Furet and Jürgen Habermas, who conceived of salons as discursive institutions within a new critical public sphere in which private individuals came together to reason about public affairs.[21] It was also nurtured by the connection made, especially in the nineteenth century, between eighteenth-century salons and the art of conversation: salon sociability was seen as a form of communication that circulated opinion within the sociological matrix of high society. According to this model, philosophical conversation in eighteenth-century salons spread the ideas of the *philosophes* in a manner that hastened the coming of the Revolution.[22] Salons, therefore, shaped public opinion by dominating the destiny of writers and by giving them access to the wider world of aristocratic high society; but their role in the formation of public opinion had nothing to do with the opinions of salonnières.

On this traditional account, the political influence ascribed to women operated through occult transactions and hidden encounters, divorced from the intellectual transmission of ideas. Women's ideas were always conveyed in private, rendered indistinguishable from those of the person (usually male) who carried them into the public sphere. It hardly mattered whether women were speaking for themselves or for others. A woman's personal views could be easily separated from the political or philosophical colour of her salon because her influence was construed as an element of intrigue or factional infighting rather than as part of the ideological debates swirling around the court and parliament. Her salon may have

[21] See F. Furet, *Interpreting the French Revolution*, trans. E. Foster (Cambridge, 1981); J. Habermas, *The Structural Transformation of the Public Sphere: An Inquiry into a Category of Bourgeois Society*, trans. T. Burger (Cambridge, MA, 1989). Joan DeJean has reformulated Habermas's concept in a way that takes into account the characteristics of what she calls 'the first public cultural sphere' of the seventeenth century; see J. DeJean, *Ancients against Moderns: Cultural Wars and the Making of the Fin de Siècle* (Chicago and London, 1997), pp. 36–9.

[22] Lilti, *Le Monde des salons*, pp. 43–5.

been identified with her personality and her address, but its ideological content was associated with the family of opinion to which it belonged. Salons could have their own distinctive political identity because salonnières could select guests and choose topics of conversation; but *habitués* were not expected to adhere to the opinion of the *maîtresse de maison*, and the role salons played in shaping public opinion was generally thought to rest on the way information circulated. As a result, salons were thought to represent not the political identity of the salonnière but her larger milieu, whether liberal or moderate or Ultra.[23]

The role of ideas in the history of French salons has diminished in recent years, as the historiography of the Enlightenment has shifted away from social and intellectual history towards a preoccupation with cultural practices and forms of sociability. As a result, we think more abstractly about salons, and ignore the social and political conflicts they provided an arena for, in favour of the ethical and linguistic conventions of conversation, or the mechanisms of a sociological dynamic. For Daniel Gordon, the importance of salons had very little to do with the actual content of salon conversation. He was most interested in the salon's place in an emerging eighteenth-century public sphere, where egalitarian sociability instantiated an alternative to absolutism and the corporate social order.[24] Dena Goodman, by contrast, argued that salonnières made a substantive contribution to the elaboration of the published projects of the Enlightenment, not by adding to the content of philosophical works but by using the traditions of *politesse* to bring order and harmony to the conversation of male writers. The female ambition that allowed salonnières to govern the Republic of Letters was based not on the collaborative production of texts, but on an exchange of services in which women gained an education by providing writers with a meeting place for civil conversation.[25] The burden of this argument is that the cultural influence of salonnières derived entirely from their conduct and from the consideration due to the *maîtresse de maison*, endowing her with the power to enforce rules, suppress conflict, and impose penalties for impropriety. Goodman based her case on texts that represented the authority of salonnières in metaphors of political leadership and musical virtuosity. Such authority was administrative rather than intellectual. It pertained specifically to matters of precedent, honour, and reputation, which gave salonnières the power to regulate access to *le monde* while preserving its norms and values.[26] It also engendered the idea that salonnières, far from facilitating open discussion, exercised tyrannical control over their guests.

---

23 Lilti insists on the polarization of salons in the years leading up to the Revolution of 1789, but he does not connect the subsequent reshuffling of the membership of various salons to ideological divisions or to the way individual salonnières responded to the great controversies of the day; see Lilti, *Le Monde des salons*, pp. 396–7.

24 D. Gordon, *Citizens Without Sovereignty: Equality and Sociability in French Thought, 1670–1789* (Princeton, 1994), pp. 3, 30–35, 111–12, 137, 243.

25 See D. Goodman, *The Republic of Letters: A Cultural History of the French Enlightenment* (Ithaca, NY, 1994).

26 D. Goodman, 'Governing the Republic of Letters', p. 185. See also Lilti, *Le Monde des salons*, pp. 34, 66, 114.

Sociological constructions of the role of salons naturally set aside the question of women's intellectual influence, and highlighted how salons functioned in relation to a larger social process. As already mentioned, Carolyn Lougee argued that salons emerged to handle the social transition from aristocracy to meritocracy.[27] Her work implied a model of feminine authority that required a knowledge of custom rather than an autonomy of judgment; it put salonnières in the role of social gatekeepers, endowing them with a sort of judicial licence to pass sentence on those aspiring to high society. My own book on French salons in the early nineteenth century argues that salons played a major role in structuring the political sociability of elites. That argument rested partly on the salonnière's power to invite guests, organize encounters, and direct conversation; but it also placed emphasis on extraneous or impersonal factors, such as the rise of parliamentary government, the size and composition of the post-revolutionary elite, the nature of political communications in an age of limited suffrage, upper-class fears of political factionalism, and the social geography of Paris neighbourhoods.[28] It insisted that the political influence of nineteenth-century salonnières was based not on their opinions but on the provision of services designed to promote the political and literary careers of male friends and associates. There is plenty of evidence to show that salonnières patronized artists, helped construct reputations, provided access to the court and high society, served as mediators, made connections, facilitated alliances, conveyed useful information, gave advice on comportment and presentation, and acted as executive secretaries – handling personal affairs, organizing receptions, polishing speeches, and even plotting electoral strategy.[29] Each of these services was consistent with the role traditionally played by women at court, or was a nineteenth-century extension of earlier practices relating to the preparation of aspirants to society. Stressing such practices is not historically inaccurate, but it tends to configure the world of the salon entirely around the needs of men. As a result of my focus, I concluded that 'women in politics were more often than not instruments of male ambition' and that salonnières were engaged in a common social practice, the goal of which was not to achieve for women a role in public affairs but to serve the public needs of men who had the power to determine the limits of their public participation.[30]

The notion that salons played a role in French intellectual and political life rested fundamentally on its definition as a semi-public institution, where conversation and sociability contributed to the diffusion of ideas and the organization of

27 Lougee, *Paradis des Femmes*, pp. 136–69.

28 Kale, *French Salons*, pp. 8–15.

29 See Kale, *French Salons*, pp. 27–8, 146–56; Lilti, *Le Monde des salons*, pp. 173, 177, 363–4, 371–2, 388, 404–5; A. Lilti, 'The Kingdom of *Politesse*: Salons and the Republic of Letters in Eighteenth-Century Paris', *Republics of Letters: A Journal for the Study of Knowledge, Politics and the Arts*, 1:1 (2009), online at http://rofl.stanford.edu/node/38.

30 Kale, *French Salons*, p. 149; S. Kale, 'Women, the Public Sphere, and the Persistence of Salons', *French Historical Studies*, 25:1 (2002): p. 138; see also a review of my book *French Salons* by K. Hamerton, in *The Journal of Modern History*, 79:3 (2007): p. 675.

political life. In his recent book on the world of French salons in the eighteenth century, Antoine Lilti denies the salon's status as a public institution and rejects the idea that salon sociability had anything to do with literary judgement, the formation of public opinion, or serious political reflection. According to Lilti, salons were private gatherings connected to a larger world of aristocratic *mondanité* that operated in keeping with a specific set of internal practices and conventions. Their primary function was to provide entertainment for a bored, selective, and highly elitist category of participants who regulated the composition of high society according to aristocratic social norms. In this world, salonnières conducted themselves according to the traditions of aristocratic hospitality; and their actions took place entirely within *l'espace du monde*, where they presided over 'little courts ... ruled by the ideals of politesse, witty conversation, social distinction, and *galanterie*'.[31] Lilti tries to show that salon talk consisted of word games, gossip, and political intrigue, and was concerned mainly with society itself. There was no serious political debate or philosophical discussion because all topics were filtered through 'an economy of mondain entertainment', which made everything frivolous or significant only in relation to the values of *le monde* itself. Salon conversation, therefore, was a ritual of narcissism that served only to reinforce the cohesion of the group.[32] As a consequence, the salon was not a public space in the sense meant by Habermas because it did not involve the public use of private individuals' critical reasoning. Writers, he notes, frequented salons and often read their work to an appreciative private audience; the fate of this or that minister at court may have consumed hours of salon banter and repartee, but neither activity constituted a serious intellectual enterprise because the salon was poorly suited to the exercise of critical judgement.[33]

Lilti's portrait of the salon is radically different from that offered by other scholars, and even more forceful than theirs in discounting serious consideration of the intellectual activity of salonnières. He insisted that salons were rarely sites for collective literary production in the eighteenth century. The many plays, poems, eulogies, and character portraits that were read aloud in society were neither produced in common nor meant to be anything other than forms of entertainment. The success of a salon depended on qualities that discouraged seriousness and pedantry. Salonnières, who were expected to gain consideration for their hospitality, were eulogized for their talents as hostesses but never praised for their intellectual qualities. The best known salonnières of the eighteenth century were keen to present themselves as women with no intellectual ambition, since those aspiring to publish faced violent ridicule. They usually lacked a formal education and limited themselves to forms of writing that were appropriate to mondain sociability (correspondence, prose portraits, poems, and songs for the amusement of guests).

31 Lilti, *Le Monde des salons*, pp. 69, 112; Lilti, 'Kingdom of Politesse', pp. 2, 10.

32 Lilti, *Le Monde des salons*, pp. 320–21.

33 Ibid., pp. 329, 334–8.

The question of whether the norms of polite society helped salonnières settle disputes and conciliate factions is central: both to the political identity of nineteenth-century salonnières and to Goodman's thesis on the role of salons in the Enlightenment. It is a question to which Lilti pays virtually no attention because he does not credit the sources associated with what he sees as a nineteenth- and twentieth-century historiographical myth as evidence of what actually happened in salons. Lilti allows that salonnières may have interceded to resolve conflicts between writers, but he is more determined to show that salon conversation abounded in sarcasm and mockery and that salon society was criss-crossed by factional rivalries, personal animosities, and ideological polarities.[34] In contrast to Goodman, Lilti insists that salons did not oversee the fusion of elites and the confusion of ranks but were often the scene of vicious ridicule and exclusion: they did not harmonize every dispute and soften all bitterness because they were frequently torn by jealousies and hatreds. Lilti finds that the *habitués* of eighteenth-century salons spent much of their time discussing politics, but he emphasizes that they did not do so in a detached critical spirit. As with all other topics discussed in salons, politics was treated in a rather whimsical and disorganized fashion, with the conversation moving arbitrarily from one thing to the next without much concern for veracity or importance. The aim of such conversation was not enlightenment or a deeper understanding of events but a sense of partisan solidarity. Salons were fixated not on political theory but on the traditional politics of the Old Regime, with its power struggles, rumours, coteries, and intrigues. Proximity to court gave certain salons privileged access to political news, but such news often circulated in the form of songs, jokes, and anecdotes and became just another form of entertainment rather than an occasion for serious thought. In short, Lilti's recent intervention into what has become a hotly contested field of study takes us further away from an account of salons that focuses on women's opinions than any of its predecessors.

Women's Opinion and the Invention of the Salon

The climate of opinion surrounding women's intellectual ambition in the late eighteenth and early nineteenth century did make it risky for them to assert their personal views in the public arena. During the last years of the Old Regime, salonnières who tried to use the prestige of their salons to build a reputation in the field of arts and letters were often stigmatized.[35] During the Revolutionary and Napoleonic periods, Madame de Staël was routinely denounced for her political activities. In the nineteenth century, 'Egerias' who advised politicians and corrected their speeches were ridiculed as excessively masculine or accused of harbouring a secret agenda.[36] The Comte de Ségur complained that women's political talents went unrecognized because men always received credit for actions

---

[34] Ibid., p. 175.

[35] Ibid., pp. 116–18.

[36] See M. Price, *The Perilous Crown: France Between Revolutions* (London, 2009).

taken upon their advice; but most public figures at the time were content to find women ignorant of political affairs and worthy of praise only for their opinions on matters of propriety and etiquette.[37] At the same time, many women worried that the convivial traditions of French sociability were harmed by an obsession with politics and by the divisiveness that overtook society after the outbreak of the Revolution. Partisanship, they feared, bred hostilities, separated friends, divided society, and undermined the friendly neutrality of salonnières. It harmed personal relations and made it harder to converse. Worst of all, it prevented women from defending the traditions of hospitality and *politesse*, making them complicit in the demise of sociability.[38]

In such circumstances, even the most politically engaged women of the Restoration cast their activities in terms acceptable to public opinion. Montcalm, for example, professed to view politics as a 'personal affair' because her 'most cherished interests' were attached to her brother's career, and because the issues that monopolized his attention were 'closely related to all my affections'.[39] She was annoyed at partisan judgements formed in salons about her brother's decisions without knowledge of his true motives; and she scoffed when women whose opinions were tailored according to fashion presumed to pronounce on subjects 'far beyond their reach'.[40] Montcalm thought salon women tended to pursue political ambitions that were impossible to realize. She wondered whether she herself would perhaps have been better off as a prefect's wife,

> because it is nearly the only [existence] in which one could enjoy the good one could do; one's action becomes more direct within well-defined limits, and a woman busying herself with the direction of a hospital, or with alleviating misery, can hope to make her action useful without men reproaching her for seeking importance or fame.[41]

Lilti argued that most of the attributes associated with salons, including the ability to regulate conflict, conciliate ideological differences, and forge consensus, are historiographical fictions invented by nineteenth-century writers and aristocrats to legitimize the mondain social practices of the Old Regime. As a critique of the literature this is a powerful and convincing observation; but it fails to explain why the nineteenth century had such an interest in the salon's retrospective invention, and it ignores entirely the role Restoration salonnières played in re-imagining the salon: from idyllic site of intellectual exchange and social cooperation, to engine

---

37 A. de Ségur, *Women: Their Condition and Influence in Society* (3 vols, London, 1803), vol. 1, pp. ix–x.

38 See, for example, Girardin, *Vicomte de Launay*, vol. 3, p. 311; de Dino *Memoirs*, vol. 3, p. 48; E. Herriot, *Madame Récamier*, trans. A. Hallard (2 vols, New York, 1926), vol. 2, pp. 72–3.

39 Montcalm, *Mon journal*, pp. 121, 130, 136.

40 Ibid., pp. 88, 111–13.

41 Ibid., pp. 284, 295.

of political compromise.[42] Many eighteenth-century salon *habitués* survived the Empire and contributed to a general eulogizing of the pre-revolutionary past. Fifteen years of Napoleonic dictatorship and Louis XVIII's willingness to concede constitutional government tended to obscure the old monarchy's link to absolutism, connecting it to the memory of a liberated public sphere in the last years of the Old Regime. Seen through this nostalgic lens, salons became ornaments of a golden age when the enjoyment of true civility, intelligence, and polite conversation first became possible.[43] At the same time, the sociability of the past was reconstrued as a path to political reconciliation – by a reactionary generation fearful of electoral democracy and worried about the politically and socially destructive consequences of conflict within a small ruling elite. François Villemain presented this ideal as most firmly established in a handful of salons of the Restoration,

> where politics had not set aside *politesse*, where ranks, and even opinions, were brought together by the best and truest equality, that of knowledge and noble sentiments, where men, engaged in great matters, could still find improvement, where men of science were greeted by men of leisure, and all were more or less inspired by the good taste that the influence of women has contributed to high society, and which often added less to the progress of useful truths than to the grace of the conversations.[44]

Marie Françoise Sophie Gay (1776–1852) considered the political task performed by the salonnières of the Restoration a bridge to broader national reconciliation: they would guarantee harmony in the short term among men who had persecuted and exiled one another, while providing a model of unity for the future, once the nation as a whole acquired 'the great virtues and the higher wisdom indispensable to good government and to the happiness of the governed'. In the meantime, she asked,

> Why toss on the fire the finery that embellishes us before having acquired the good solid clothing that would shelter us from all political inclemencies? Before

42 Lilti, *Le Monde des salons*, pp. 15–58. Lilti presents the myths associated with eighteenth century as a way of reopening the book on what eighteenth-century salons were actually like. He is not interested in how such myths functioned in subsequent decades.

43 See R. de Chateaubriand, *Mémoires d'outre-tombe* (6 vols, Paris, 1910), vol. 2, p. 304; F. Guizot, *Madame de Rumford (1758–1836)* (Paris, 1841), pp. 3–4, 14–15; C. de Rémusat, *Memoirs of Madame de Rémusat*, trans. C. Hoey and J. Lillie (3 vols, New York, 1880), vol. 1, p. 67; C. de Rémusat, *Mémoires de ma vie* (5 vols, Paris, 1959), vol. 1, pp. 41, 181–2; Lettre to Madame Swetchine, November 19, 1817, in G. Pailhès, *La Duchesse de Duras et Chateaubriand* (Paris, 1910), pp. 424; Duras to Chateaubriand, in A. Bardoux, *La Duchesse de Duras* (Paris, 1898), pp. 334–6. Girardin, *Vicomte de Launay*, vol. 1, pp. 128–9, vol. 2, p. 203, vol. 3, pp. 258–9, 265. A. Martin-Fugier, *La Vie élégante, ou la formation de Tout-Paris* (Paris, 1990), p. 151.

44 F. Villemain, *Souvenirs contemporaines d'histoire et de littérature* (2 vols, Paris, 1854), vol. 1, p. 453.

> arriving at this national paradise, where the martyrs of all parties rest their palm branches on the altar of *la patrie*, can we not content ourselves with the patrimony of our fathers?[45]

Lilti argued that the nineteenth-century invention of the salon drew on an earlier discourse concerning the merits of mondain civility developed by *philosophes* like Morellet, Marmontel, and Suard to justify their insertion into the world of the Old Regime aristocracy.[46] The salonnières of the Restoration did not create this language; but they appropriated it and stressed links between the affections and compatibilities of members of a select group and the reconciliation of differences of opinion. Perhaps the idealization of seventeenth- and eighteenth-century salons served early nineteenth-century polemics by helping factions within the elite define themselves and denigrate their opponents. Or it may be that Restoration salonnières consciously embraced and promoted an earlier sociable ideal, to assert a public role for aristocratic women in an era when salons were becoming associated with the harmonizing function of polite conversation. If Restoration salonnières judiciously forgot that eighteenth-century salon society ejected non-conformists and used mockery and ridicule to enforce cohesion, it was because they sought to use prevailing opinion to reinforce the salon's specific political utility. After all, salon women were nostalgic for the Restoration too. Aging, bored, and pining for their youth, a number of aristocratic women born around the turn of the century wrote their memoirs during the Second Empire, expressing unanimous regret for the passage of the Bourbon era. In the early nineteenth century, the generation of 1815 memorialized the salon society of the eighteenth century as a lost paradise of charm and wit; in the 1860s, the same generation of salonnières remembered the Restoration as a time when women possessed real power, when the persistence of tradition had given them jurisdiction over high society, and when the limited scope of political life placed them at the centre of all that was stimulating and exciting. Women in the 1860s may have been more educated, wrote the Comtesse de Bassenville (1806–1884), but they were also more sedentary, isolated, and alone, having far less access to the public sphere than in the past. According to Marie d'Agoult (1805–1876), democratic France had forgotten how aristocratic traditions gave women influence in salons; it honoured mothers and wives, but made them into 'subalterns in their own homes'.[47]

The notion that salonnières had real political power during the Restoration is mostly an illusion. They may have mediated political encounters, channelled information, interceded with friends and associates, advised men in power on matters of oratory and diplomatic etiquette, discussed ideas, and even voiced their opinions, but there was no clear connection between what they thought and

---

[45] S. Gay, *Salons célèbres* (Paris, 1882), pp. 178–9.

[46] Lilti, *Le Monde des salons*, pp. 187, 207, 190–91.

[47] A. de Bassanville, *Salons d'autrefois: Souvenirs intimes* (4 vols, Paris, 1853), vol. 1, p. 1; vol. 3, p. 187; vol. 4, pp. 129–32; M. d'Agoult, *Mémoires, souvenirs et journaux de la comtesse d'Agoult*, ed. C.F. Dupêchez (Paris, 1990), p. 278.

the power to make things happen. It may be an expression of masculinist bias to suggest that the only opinions that mattered were those with efficacy in public life, but this is what the political institutions founded in 1789 implied. Men could deny women opportunities to act upon their knowledge and convictions because they had the power to prohibit women from acting in their own behalf. As a result, salonnières routinely contributed to the success of policies in whose confection they took no part, or assisted in the accomplishment of political ends that may or may not have run counter to their own political views.[48]

And yet, Restoration salonnières certainly did have political opinions; they used their position in society to persuade others and contributed to the elaboration of ideas. In a regime that sought to unify a tiny electorate by forgetting the antagonisms of the past, the reconciliation of opposing factions was a serious political objective, one supported by moderate royalists and doctrinaire liberals from the Duc de Richelieu to François Guizot and opposed by those who wanted the Restoration to evolve in a more liberal direction. One could argue that the preference for conciliation expressed by salonnières reflected nothing more than the aristocratic values of a traditional society; or one might insist that women could have opinions only if they were freed from the expectations and obligations imposed by a mondain existence.[49] But the salons of the Restoration belonged neither to the world of courtly traditions preserved by the old monarchy nor to the world of individual citizenship fostered by democracy. After Waterloo, the return of the court and the reestablishment of aristocratic high society coincided with the advent of limited suffrage and parliamentary government. In such circumstances, aristocratic salonnières had access to power and were in a position to analyse politics and interpret events.

---

[48] See Kale, *French Salons*, pp. 152–3.

[49] See Fraisse, *Reason's Muse*, p. 124.

PART II
Women's Political Ideas in the British Isles

Chapter 9
The Right to Resist: Women's Citizenship in Catharine Trotter Cockburn's *The Revolution of Sweden*

Elizabeth M.K.A. Sund

Introduction

Catharine Trotter Cockburn (1674–1749) was well known during her lifetime as a playwright and moral philosopher. In her final play, *The Revolution of Sweden* (1706), she explores themes of duty and citizenship that reappear throughout her later philosophical works in the form of arguments defending moral obligation and disinterested benevolence. However, her traditionally structured philosophical works never directly address the political or feminist concerns that are the focal point of *The Revolution of Sweden*, so the play and her philosophical writings must be understood together to appreciate her radical conception of citizenship. According to Cockburn, citizenship requires individuals to use reason to control passions and place the public good above self-interest. This is consistent with her later philosophical view that the moral sense, when aided by reason, can allow someone to discover immutable moral laws and the will of God. Because the use of reason, which is central to Cockburn's ideal of citizenship, is open to both men and women equally, both sexes are required to show loyalty to the state in the same way. But because men and women are both citizens within her scheme, Cockburn must deal with the problem that duties to the state may sometimes conflict with duties to one's spouse. In *The Revolution of Sweden*, Cockburn supports the view that when duties are in conflict, obligations to the state take precedence over individual concerns like marriage. She supports a woman's right to resist her husband if he tries to keep her from acting in accordance with her obligations to the state. Not only are women full citizens in Cockburn's eyes (a radical view, for the early eighteenth century): married women are *citizens first* and *wives second*. In this respect she takes the theme of justified resistance further than other political thinkers of her time.

Cockburn was probably (according to a baptismal record) born in 1674, despite her early biographer Thomas Birch's assertion that she was born in 1679.[1] Her five plays were published between 1695 and 1706 while she was still

---

1 A. Kelley, *Catharine Trotter: An Early Modern Writer in the Vanguard of Feminism* (Farnham and Burlington, 2002), p. 1n1; for Birch see note 3, below.

quite young. In 1702 she published her first philosophical work, which defended Locke's epistemological arguments against innate ideas, because she believed his principles could form part of a strong foundation for moral obligation. Later in life she defended Samuel Clarke's principles of moral fitness, which argue that relationships between objects or ideas necessitate certain immutable moral rules that are part of human nature. Almost all of Cockburn's philosophical works have the form of defending the principles of her favourite thinkers. Because Cockburn used a defence format in her writing, if she is remembered by philosophers at all today it is incorrectly as a follower of Locke and Clarke, rather than as a philosopher in her own right.[2]

In her purely philosophical works, which were mainly published between 1726 and 1751 (shortly after her death), Cockburn provides a unique argument for moral obligation. She proposes a threefold theory of moral obligation that builds on Locke's epistemological principles and includes a version of fitness theory that is closely related to Clarke's. Her account of the moral sense is similar to that of Scottish Enlightenment thinker Francis Hutcheson, but she did not consider herself a defender of his views because despite her 'great esteem for that ingenious author's writings, in which are many useful truths'; she believed his version of the moral sense was really a 'blind instinct' that could not be improved through moral education.[3] Instead Cockburn argues that eternal fitness relations, the moral sense, and the will of God all play a role in moral obligation. Although most thinkers of her time believed that only one principle should be the foundation for moral obligation, Cockburn argues that all of their theories have been deficient, because they leave the foundation too weak, 'but all three together make an immovable foundation for, and obligation to moral practise; the moral sense or conscience, and the essential differences of things discovering to us what the will of our maker is.'[4] Any theory that is based on just one of these aspects, such as Clarke's fitness theory or Hutcheson's moral sense theory, are doomed to fail because the individual aspects are too weak on their own.

Oddly, Cockburn has almost nothing to say specifically about women or politics in her philosophical works, despite her obvious interest in those issues. She does not seek to avoid controversy, so it does not seem likely that she shunned discussions of politics out of politeness or fear. Locke's *Essay* was considered a dangerous work by many, and yet Cockburn took a personal risk by defending

---

2 M.B. Bolton, 'Some Aspects of the Philosophy of Catharine Trotter', *Journal of the History of Philosophy*, 31:4 (1993): pp. 565–88.

3 C. Trotter Cockburn, 'Remarks Upon the Principles and Reasonings of Dr Rutherforth's Essay on the Nature and Obligation of Virtue: In Vindication of the Contrary Principles Inforced in the Writings of the Late Dr Samuel Clarke', in *The Works of Mrs Catharine Cockburn, Theological, Moral, Dramatic, and Poetical. Several of Them Now First Printed. Revised and Published, with an Account of the Life of the Author*, ed. Thomas Birch (London, 1751), p. 18.

4 C. Trotter Cockburn, 'Letters between Mrs Cockburn, and Several of Her Friends', in *The Works of Mrs Catharine Cockburn*, p. 296.

the epistemology of 'one of the most illustrious and controversial thinkers of her society'.[5] Cockburn's play *The Revolution of Sweden* is important because it contains her keen political and feminist arguments, which would be missed if her philosophy were read in isolation from this theatrical work. The virtuous characters in the play provide concrete examples of her threefold theory of moral obligation in practice, while the plot helps the reader to understand the political consequences of her moral and epistemological arguments.

The Plot and Historical Context for *The Revolution of Sweden*

Because *The Revolution of Sweden* was written after Cockburn's move into philosophy, the plot takes a backseat to the moral themes of disinterested benevolence and the public good that continue throughout Cockburn's many philosophical publications over the course of her life. It is set during the Swedish revolt against Denmark (1521–1523); and the virtuous leader of the Revolution, Gustavus, is based on the real King Gustav I of Sweden (1496–1560). Although Gustavus is technically revolting against the Danish government, Cockburn tells the tale from the Swedish point of view, so acts against Sweden are considered treasonous within the play. In the prologue, she warns her audience not to expect a 'soft Effeminate Feast' simply because the play is written by a woman.[6] In her dedication to Lady Harriet Godolphin, a patroness of the arts, Cockburn explains that her goal is to write a play that will be both pleasurable and 'useful to our Morals, serve to correct our Vices, and animate the Mind to Virtue'.[7] *The Revolution of Sweden* is intended to incite 'disinterested and resolute Care of the Publick Good'.[8]

The Revolution of Sweden was written and performed during the reign of Queen Anne, whose rule sparked public debate about whether a married woman could rule while remaining a dutiful wife. Anne (1665–1714) ascended to the throne in 1702, and became the first married woman since Mary I to reign in her own right in England. According to Edward Gregg, Anne was devoted to her husband for her entire life, but it was 'a devotion resting securely on the fact that she was the undisputed head of their household'.[9] Carol Barash credits Anne's just military triumph over Louis XIV with inspiring women writers of the early eighteenth century, like Cockburn, to come to Anne's defence.[10] According to Barash, 'for

[5] Kelley, *Catharine Trotter*, p. 170.

[6] C. Trotter Cockburn, *The Revolution of Sweden. A Tragedy. As It Is Acted at the Queens Theatre in the Hay-Market.* (London, 1706), prologue.

[7] Ibid., prologue.

[8] Ibid., prologue.

[9] E. Gregg, 'Anne (1665–1714)', in H. Matthew, and B. Harrison (eds), *Oxford Dictionary of National Biography* (Oxford, 2004).

[10] C. Barash, '"The Native Liberty ... Of the Subject": Configurations of Gender and Authority in the Works of Mary Chudleigh, Sarah Fyge Egerton, and Mary Astell', in I. Grundy and S. Wiseman (eds), *Women, Writing, History: 1640–1740* (London, 1992), p. 56.

women writers, Anne is both a leader and a comrade in battle – against men – for the authority to write as women and in defence of women's political demands.'[11] Anne must balance her duties to the state with her duties to her husband, just as the female characters do in *The Revolution of Sweden*, by placing the public good above her self-interest. Cockburn seeks to show that these two roles in the public and private spheres are compatible, both for the women in the play and for Anne. In the verse prologue, she explains that the 'Publick Good is now that Sexes Care'; and a few lines later:

> Nor can the vainest haughtiest Man disdain
> A Woman's Precepts in Great ANNA's Reign.[12]

Now that a woman is in power, she believes, the thoughts and ideas of women writers such as herself deserve greater respect. The fact that a married woman was on the throne when Cockburn wrote *The Revolution of Sweden* provides important context for understanding why the conflicting natures of citizenship and marriage are the focus in the play.

The plot centres on two couples in the Swedish nobility, in which the wives make the difficult decision to place their duty to Sweden above their duty to their husbands when faced with accusations of the men's treason. The first couple are the happily married Arwide and Constantia, who are both virtuous and reasonable. As the play unfolds, Arwide is wrongly accused of treason because the evidence against him seems insurmountable. The Danish viceroy tricks him into signing his name to treasonous articles as part of a plot to convince Constantia to leave Arwide and marry him instead. Because of the confusion surrounding the situation and the viceroy's trickery, Arwide accidentally confirms to his wife that the articles containing his signature are not a forgery. Constantia must then weigh her duty to Sweden to turn Arwide in for treason against her duty to remain loyal to Arwide as his wife. After much internal debate she reluctantly exposes Arwide's alleged treason to Gustavus, but never consents to marry the Danish viceroy. Arwide is sentenced to death by the court, but his innocence is revealed at the last moment before the execution. Arwide praises Constantia for her reasonableness, and the couple continue their happy marriage based on mutual respect.

The second couple, Christina and Beron, are estranged because of Beron's actual treason and Christina's patriotism. Beron commits treason against Sweden by becoming the Danish viceroy's supporter. He believes his wife Christina has committed adultery, because she helped save Gustavus. Beron cannot accept that Christina helped Gustavus out of duty to her country rather than lust; and for this reason Beron wants Christina dead. When Christina is captured by Danish soldiers, her maid suggests that she disguise herself as her nephew Fredage to avoid being recognized by Beron, and so save her life. Beron is fooled by the disguise, which gives Christina the opportunity to witness his deception of Arwide

[11] Ibid., p. 56.

[12] Cockburn, *Revolution of Sweden*, prologue.

and Constantia. She is able to return to Gustavus's camp dressed as Fredage just in time to reveal Arwide's innocence but dies immediately afterwards from stab wounds inflicted by Beron. Gustavus praises Christina's patriotism and bravery, while Beron is sentenced to death for the murder of his wife.

Many characters and plot points in the play have their basis in historical fact, which is important because it shows readers and audience members that women are capable of being good citizens in reality, not just in fiction. Almost ten years before the publication of Cockburn's play, abbé de Vertot's *The History of the Revolutions in Sweden* (1697) was translated into English. It is likely to be the source of Cockburn's historical knowledge, and the inspiration for her fictitious plot lines. Many of the names in the play are real, including Arwide and Fredage, although those characters bear no resemblance to the historical bearers of those names. The female principals, Constantia and Christina, seem to be loosely based on a blend of two real women. A princess named Christina is probably the main inspiration for Constantia, despite her name. The historical Princess Christina was the widow of Prince Sterno, who died fighting against the Danes in the Swedish revolt. Vertot explains that Princess Christina passionately refused to submit when the king of Denmark demanded the surrender of her land after her husband's death. Vertot describes Princess Christina's response as expressing 'Heroical Resolution' because she sent the King of Denmark word that she 'wou'd never submit to the Destroyer of her Family and Country, nor comply with the Resolutions of an Assembly that was compos'd of Traitors and Rebels, and govern'd by the Enemies of the Nation'.[13] Vertot sees Princess Christina's bold refusal was sufficiently intimidating to convince the Danish king that he ought to invade elsewhere. But the king of Denmark later ordered her to be drowned, in part as punishment for her late husband's support of the Swedish Revolution. She was spared because Admiral Norbi, the man who was supposed to execute her, secretly hoped to marry her.[14] Gustavus had great respect for Princess Christina and was later able to help return her to a position suitable for a woman of her 'Birth and Merit'.[15] Princess Christina's steadfast patriotism and bravery are character traits found in both female characters, but some specific events in Princess Christina's life, such as being spared death because a Danish officer falls in love with her, loosely appear in Constantia's plotline.

The real Gustavus is saved from a treasonous plot by an unnamed woman: another factual element in Cockburn's story. The woman's husband had tricked Gustavus and made him a prisoner, but the traitor's wife helped Gustavus to escape. Vertot explains that the woman 'was prompted by Pity, and perhaps by a more tender Passion' to help Gustavus, and that it was only by 'the Kindness and

---

13 Abbé de Vertot, *The History of the Revolutions in Sweden Occasioned by the Change of Religion, and Alteration of the Government in That Kingdom / Written Originally in French by the Abbot Vertot ...; and Done into English by J. Mitchel ...*, trans. J. Mitchel, 2nd edn (London, 1697), vol. 1, p. 96.

14 Ibid., vol. 1, pp. 112–13.

15 Ibid., vol. 2, p. 26.

Discretion of that generous Lady' that Gustavus was able to escape his enemies undiscovered.[16] Cockburn's character Christina helped Gustavus escape in a similar manner, which is the cause of Beron's accusations of adultery against her. Both the unnamed woman and Princess Christina took their duties to the state seriously and were willing to sacrifice their private happiness for the public good. It makes sense that Cockburn was inspired by these women's heroics to explore the conflict between duties to one's spouse and obligations to the state using strong female characters.

It is likely that she chose this particular revolution as a backdrop for her play because a romanticized version of the historical Gustav embodied the civic virtues she wanted to highlight. The character Gustavus is reasonable, virtuous, and intelligent, and respects these attributes in both the men and the women who support him. He thinks only of the public good and favours benevolence over revenge. When asked why he would bother negotiating with the opposition, the idealized Gustavus explains that he would never 'destroy one Enemy Whom I cou'd make a Friend; a Victory More noble far, than the most glorious Battle'.[17]

It is also possible that Cockburn chose to set the play around Gustavus's revolution because he was an integral part of the Protestant reformation in Sweden. In 1707, one year after the publication of *The Revolution of Sweden*, Cockburn published *A Discourse Concerning a Guide in Controversies*, which marks her return to Protestantism after several years as a practising Catholic. Cockburn's Protestantism correlates with her philosophical view that immutable moral laws must be recognized through the use of reason, and that individuals must recognize these laws for themselves without blind adherence to traditional authority. The topic of religion is not as prominent in *The Revolution of Sweden* as citizenship; but the following exchange between the archbishop and Constantia while she is a prisoner in the Danish camp illustrates Cockburn's position. After Constantia's assertion that religion should not be used to justify violence, the archbishop responds:

> *Arch.* Is it for you
> To judge of your Superiors, t' instruct your Guide?
> When Women preach, 'twill be with *Luther's* Aid;
> A blessed Reformation.
> *Const.* Not to instruct, my Lord, but to awake;
> You've shut your Eyes against our present Miseries
> And future Dangers, else wou'd you not oppose
> Your Countries Liberty, or give pretext
> To *Luther's* growing Schism, which (with its fatal
> Consequences) will all be set to the Account
> of those Ambitious Church-Men, who've turn'd
> The Spiritual Pow'r, to Secular Tyrannical
> Dominion, and giv'n Libertines occasion
> In detecting the Usurp'd, to throw off

16 Ibid., vol. 1, pp. 157–8.

17 Cockburn, *Revolution of Sweden*, p. 6.

Undistinguish'd, the just Authority.
Arch. Insolent Assertions!
Such are th' Insinuations which support
Your Party – But we shall quell these impious
Reformers ...[18]

The right to revolt against unjust husbands and governments will be discussed in the next section of this chapter; but it could be argued that Cockburn would also support people's resistance to a tyrannical religious hierarchy for the same reasons. Protestantism, as opposed to the teachings of the Catholic Church at the time, requires individuals to read the Bible for themselves. In *A Discourse Concerning a Guide in Controversies*, Cockburn argues that Protestants are only obliged to submit to the infallible authority of the scriptures rather than to clergy, although church leaders make very useful guides. She argues that we owe obedience to church leaders only in areas where they have jurisdiction.

> But if they will go beyond that [jurisdiction], by commanding any thing contrary to the word or will of God, in that we must not obey them; and consequently we must have a liberty of *judging for ourselves*, whether they do so or not. Now if this is true, with relation to our natural and civil governors (as I believe everybody will allow that it is) why is not the same limitation as consistent with our obligation of obeying spiritual governors? No doubt, this liberty of judging for ourselves may be abused in all those relations: wicked children and rebels, as well as *Hereticks*, may make this a pretence for throwing off their duty; but that does not make the rule less true, or hinder those from being justified by it, who act sincerely in it.[19]

This resistance against instances of unjust authority among Catholic clergy and reliance upon one's own judgement about moral rules correlates with Cockburn's ideal of citizenship in the play. In the following two sections I will discuss Cockburn's similar views on resistance against instances of the unjust authority of governments and husbands, as well as the connection between Cockburn's political and philosophical views. I will show that the moral theory Cockburn develops later in her career supports her conception of citizenship as described in *The Revolution of Sweden*.

Citizenship and the Right to Resist Unjust Authority

Along with other social groups like servants and slaves, women were not considered citizens in the eighteenth century. Status as a citizen required the possession of certain rights and of certain duties to the state. Locke, for example,

---

[18] Ibid., p. 21.

[19] C. Trotter Cockburn, 'A Discourse Concerning a Guide in Controversies, in Two Letters. Written to One of the Church of Rome, by a Person Lately Converted from That Communion', in *The Works of Mrs Catharine Cockburn*, p. 24.

emphasizes the right to hold property in exchange for giving up certain liberties available in the state of nature.[20] Women could not make this trade through allegiance to the state the way their free male counterparts could. Hilda Smith writes extensively about conceptions of female non-citizenship in England from 1640 to 1832. It was not that thinkers ignored the problem of gender when it came to citizenship, she explains, but rather that they tended to conclude that women were free from political obligations because they were subjects of their husbands, not of political authority.[21] One such view is espoused by Margaret Cavendish, Duchess of Newcastle (1623–1673). According to Jacqueline Broad and Karen Green, within Cavendish's scheme women are not directly subject to political authority, but only indirectly because of their husbands' allegiance to it.[22] Broad and Green call the freedom women experience as a result of their lack of direct allegiance to political authority 'hollow', because women are trapped in the domestic sphere.[23] Cavendish laments women's subjection to tyranny and lack of freedom under some governments and husbands, but she does not make any feminist call to change the system.[24] Like Hobbes, she believes that it would be irrational to resist a ruler, because the basis of our allegiance to governments is self-interest. According to Cavendish, write Broad and Green, 'a severe ruler is – paradoxically – the protector of human liberties: only by voluntarily giving up their absolute liberty to a coercive power can human beings have the peace and security they desire.'[25] Cavendish goes on to argue that rebellion is worse than living under a tyrant because it tends to result in more suffering, so citizens do not have the right to resist even tyrannical rulers. She believes that living under one ruler is the best way to ensure peace for citizens.[26]

By exploring themes of women's political resistance in *The Revolution of Sweden*, Cockburn argues directly against the common view of women as non-citizens in her time. Her position on resistance to tyrannical leaders is representative of the Whig view; more radical are her assertions that women can also claim a right to resist, and that duties to the state sometimes take precedence over duties to one's husband. Whigs agreed that people had the right to resist authority, but they disagreed on the circumstances that justified resistance.[27] According to Lois

20 J. Locke, *Two Treatises of Government*, ed. P. Laslett, 2nd edn (Cambridge, 1967), Book II, §127, p. 370.

21 H.L. Smith, *All Men and Both Sexes: Gender, Politics, and the False Universal in England, 1640–1832* (University Park, PA, 2002), pp. 30–31.

22 J. Broad and K. Green, *A History of Women's Political Thought in Europe, 1400–1700* (Cambridge, 2009), pp. 219–20.

23 Ibid., p. 221.

24 Ibid., pp. 223–4.

25 Ibid., p. 213.

26 Ibid., p. 213.

27 L.G. Schwoerer, 'The Right to Resist: Whig Resistance Theory, 1688 to 1694', in N. Phillipson and Q. Skinner (eds), *Political Discourse in Early Modern Britain* (Cambridge, 1993), p. 250.

Schwoerer, Whig resistance theory formed through parliamentary debate and the publication of nearly one hundred pamphlets between 1688 and 1694, so there is no single Whig voice that encompasses every position.[28] For the purposes of this chapter I will discuss only Locke's *Two Treatises of Government* as an analogue to Cockburn's political views, because there is no single unified view espoused by the Whigs for comparison. I do not suggest that Locke's *Two Treatises* were the most representative or most popular work on resistance theory at the time.

Although Locke published *Two Treatises* anonymously, there is reason to believe that Cockburn may have been aware of his authorship when she wrote *The Revolution of Sweden*. Even though she never refers directly to his political views, it is likely she would have read them since she was a prominent defender of his epistemological principles in *An Essay Concerning Human Understanding*. Locke only acknowledged his authorship of the *Two Treatises* in his will, but it may have been common knowledge long before his death in 1704.[29] Even if Cockburn never read Locke's political works, the views on justified resistance that she expresses in *The Revolution of Sweden* are remarkably similar to Locke's. But what makes her arguments interesting is her feminist expansion of the right to resist unjust governments to include the right of a woman to resist the unjust authority of her husband. A woman's resistance comes in the form of placing her duties to the state above her duties to her husband, when the two are in conflict.

Locke discusses marriage and the family in the *Two Treatises* and argues that women sometimes have the right to separate from their husbands. He explains: 'The *Power of the Husband* being so far from that of an absolute Monarch, that the *Wife* has, in many cases, a Liberty to *separate* from him; where natural Right, or their Contract allows it.'[30] Locke's reasons stem not from any version of citizenship for women, but from his view that the purpose of marriage is procreation. As long as the children can be cared for by either the mother or father following the divorce, separation is reasonable in some cases. As Ruth Grant explains, although Locke is not a feminist, his arguments concerning women and the family are part of his broader argument in support of revolution against tyrannical governments.[31] Grant points out the important fact that although Locke did not argue directly against political inequality for women, he did not argue in support of it either.[32] Cockburn goes further than Locke by making an explicitly feminist argument: women not only *can* resist their husbands, but under certain circumstances their duties as citizens *require* that they do so in favour of the public good.

In the *Two Treatises*, Locke argues that if a ruler abuses his power citizens have the right to resist. He explains that the government's power 'is *limited to the*

---

[28] Ibid., p. 233.

[29] P. Laslett, editor's 'Introduction' in *Two Treatises of Government*, pp. 4–7.

[30] Locke, *Two Treatises of Government*, Book II, §82, p. 339.

[31] R.W. Grant, 'John Locke on Women and the Family', in *Two Treatises of Government and a Letter Concerning Toleration*, ed. I. Shapiro (New Haven, 2003), p. 286.

[32] Ibid., p. 298.

publick good of the Society', and it 'can never have a right to destroy, enslave, or designedly to impoverish the Subjects'.[33] When citizens' trust in the ruler is betrayed, they have a right to answer that betrayal with revolution. Cockburn holds a similar view in *The Revolution of Sweden*, which grounds the obligations between citizens and the government on laws of nature. When Constantia is a prisoner in the Danish camp, she argues for Sweden's right to a revolution based on natural law. The Archbishop believes the state has the right to 'punish lawless Rebels', but Constantia replies:

> Is it Rebellion for a wretched People
> Oppress'd and Ruin'd, by that Power they gave
> For their Defence, the safety of their Rights,
> To seek Redress? When Kings who are in Trust
> The Guardians of the Laws, the publick Peace and Welfare,
> Confess no Law but Arbitrary Will,
> Or know no use of Pow'r but to Oppress,
> And Injure, with Impunity, themselves
> Disown their Office, tacitly acquit
> The People, of whose due Obedience, just
> Protection, is the Natural and Essential Condition.[34]

Cockburn argues for the same reasons as Locke that we owe obedience to the state. If rulers do not protect citizens and preserve their liberties, then the citizens' duty to obey is dissolved.

Locke explains that 'the *end of Civil Society* [is] to avoid, and remedy those inconveniencies of the State of Nature'.[35] Gustavus recognizes this need for a government in order to protect the rights of the Swedish people. He makes a speech in support of the election of a new king of Sweden following the Revolution, because it is the only way to ensure peace:

> The Wast and Miseries of Civil War now ceas'd,
> All are return'd to the first State of Nature,
> When, uncontrol'd, each had the savage Liberty
> Of living without Head, or Laws, or Order,
> A Freedom worse than Slavery, the Seed
> Of everlasting Broils, where all by turns
> Oppress, and are oppress'd – 'Tis our next Care
> That an Administrator be elected,
> Under whose just Authority our Laws
> May be restor'd, and the divided Nation
> Secur'd from a Revolt ...[36]

---

33 Locke, *Two Treatises of Government*, Book II, §135, pp. 375–6.

34 Cockburn, *Revolution of Sweden*, p. 19.

35 Locke, *Two Treatises of Government*, Book II, §90, p. 344.

36 Cockburn, *Revolution of Sweden*, p. 54.

We know through the use of reason that the rule of a just arbiter is the only way to avoid the 'everlasting broils' of the state of nature. Although everyone is free and equal in the state of nature, nobody is safe or secure.[37] Unless Sweden unites under one ruler, the population will never be safe from constant violence.

Neither Locke nor Cockburn believes citizens have the right to resist the power of government without cause. Locke explains that '*Force* is to be *opposed* to nothing, but to unjust and unlawful *Force*', meaning that all normal governmental channels for compromise should be exhausted and that rebellion is only justified in the most extreme cases.[38] On the first page of the play Cockburn makes it clear that Sweden is justified in revolting against the Danes:

> By Treachery secur'd, none durst oppose
> Th' Usurper's growing Pow'r, all *Swede* submitted
> On Conditions which the Faithless King
> No sooner made than broke, regarding neither
> Treaties, Law, or Justice: But oh remember
> That bloody Massacre which solemniz'd
> His Coronation Feast! The Reverend Senate,
> And every worthy Citizen of *Stockholm*,
> Butcher'd by the inhuman King's command;
> That horrid Scene of Murders, Rapes and Rapine,
> The Prelude to unparallell'd Barbarities
> Committed daily since in every Province!
> These are the Tyrannies, *Gustavus* arm'd ye
> To avenge, and free your suffering Country[39]

The tyranny of the Danes is so extensive that the Swedes cannot be expected to submit to Danish authority. The type of power the Danes attempt to wield over the Swedish people is wholly arbitrary. Locke argues against 'Absolute Arbitrary Power' because it is not consistent with the purpose of society, which is to preserve the rights of citizens. It would be irrational to leave the state of nature to join such a society, because they would put themselves in a worse position than the state of nature by having 'disarmed themselves, and armed him, to make a prey of them when he pleases.'[40]

Once Sweden is freed, Gustavus plans to rule based on the consent of the public because 'Suppressing Tyranny's an ill pretect [pretext] For our becoming Tyrants.'[41] Under Gustavus, the Swedes will use only the force necessary to secure their independence from the tyrannical Danish government without seeking revenge. Cockburn reiterates this point several times throughout the play, which helps maintain the Swede's moral superiority over the Danes. If Gustavus planned

---

37 Locke, *Two Treatises of Government*, Book II, §123, p. 368.

38 Ibid., Book II, §204, p. 420.

39 Cockburn, *Revolution of Sweden*, pp. 1–2.

40 Locke, *Two Treatises of Government*, Book II, §137, p. 378.

41 Cockburn, *Revolution of Sweden*, p. 4.

to seek revenge beyond freeing Sweden, he would no longer be justified in his revolt against the Danes within Cockburn's system of morality.

Cockburn describes the mistreatment of Christina by her husband as analogous to Denmark's oppression of Sweden. Gustavus deems Christina's resistance to the authority of her husband justified, because of Beron's treason and his mistreatment of her. Christina calls Beron 'A Tyrant Husband' when describing his violent and vengeful nature.[42] After Christina presents herself to Beron disguised as Fredage, he informs her of his unshakeable belief that his wife is an adulteress because she gave aid to Gustavus. He describes in gruesome detail the punishment he believes would be suitable:

> *Ber.* What other motive cou'd she have
> To Sacrifice her Int'rest for *Gustavus*,
> But that he was a Youth, Handsome and Amorous,
> Form'd to her wanton Wishes?
> *Chris.* Oh Horrid!
> *Ber.* Horrid indeed, my Boy, and cou'd I find the Strumpet,
> Her Punishment shou'd be as shameful as
> Her Guilt, I'll have her strip'd, and in the open Streets
> Fix'd on a Rack, expos'd to publick view,
> Till she expire, more with the sense of Infamy,
> Than Tortures ...[43]

He refuses to believe Christina could have any reason besides lust for helping Gustavus, because she is only a woman. The punishment he suggests is barbaric and beyond the rights of a husband to enforce. Both Christina and Constantia are within their rights to resist their husbands' authority.

Cockburn's conception of citizenship is gender-inclusive because both men and women must prioritize public safety over personal concerns. For example, Constantia would rather die for her country than have Arwide turn himself in as her ransom, both because she loves him and because he is more vital to the Revolution:

> *Const.* Lament me not – We're Born to Dye,
> And when occasion's giv'n us to improve
> Th' inevitable universal Doom,
> To Virtue, and a publick Benefit,
> 'Tis a just cause of Gratitude to Heav'n.
> I'm ready Officer. – This only to my Woman,
> If thou escape the Tyrants Cruelty,
> Tell my dear Lord I bless'd his Resolution,
> But Dying beg'd him not to seek Revenge,
> Beyond what's needful to his Countries Safety.[44]

42 Ibid., p. 24.

43 Ibid., p. 31.

44 Ibid., p. 35.

Both men and women have obligations to the state as part of their citizenship. Constantia must sacrifice herself for the public good, and Arwide must resist the desire for revenge since doing so would jeopardize the Revolution. As citizens, both partners must place their personal desires below the good of society.

The Roles of Reason and the Moral Sense in Citizenship

Cockburn's characterization of citizenship in *The Revolution of Sweden* is closely related to the version of disinterested benevolence that she defends later in life. Cockburn believes that humans have an innate faculty by which they approve of actions that accord with the eternal moral laws or fitness relations. This faculty, which she calls the moral sense, must be used in conjunction with reason to discern moral obligations. When individuals act according to virtue, it is not because they will be rewarded. Cockburn believes it is because 'they find something in it fit and right, worthy of their approbation and choice, something which they cannot counteract, without standing self-condemned'.[45] People make these choices for themselves by using reason and the moral sense. This is not an unproblematic epistemic process, but individuals are morally required to make every reasonable attempt to acquire accurate information before making moral decisions. Cockburn does not delve too deeply into strategies for insuring accurate information, but she does point to the importance of education for moulding the moral sense properly – to recognize eternal moral truths.

Cockburn argues that people are capable of disinterested benevolence because the moral sense allows them to place the good of others above their own when fitness relations require it. But each must use her own reason to understand moral obligations and must be prepared to stand self-condemned if she does not act in accordance with morality:

> Whatever principle we suppose obligation to be originally founded on; a free-agent must be always the *immediate* obliger of himself: Whether he judges, that the will of a superior is to be the only rule of his actions; or that he ought to act conformably to the necessary relations, and essential differences of things, or to his consciousness of right and wrong; or that a prospect of rewards and punishments should solely influence his actions; in either case it is equally the perception and judgment of his own mind, or his *reason*, that obliges him to act accordingly; and this is so far from being an absurdity, that it is essential to *moral choice* and *free agency*.[46]

---

[45] Cockburn, 'Remarks Upon the Principles and Reasonings of Dr Rutherforth's Essay', p. 82.

[46] C. Trotter Cockburn, 'Remarks Upon Some Writers in the Controversy Concerning the Foundation of Moral Virtue and Moral Obligation; Particularly the Translator of Archbishop King's 'Origin of Evil and the Author of the Divine Legation of Moses. To Which Are Prefaced Some Cursory Thoughts on the Controversies Concerning Necessary Existence, the Reality of Infinity of Space, the Extension and Place of Spirits, and on Dr Watt's Notion of Substance', in *The Works of Mrs Catharine Cockburn*, p. 446.

When Cockburn's account of citizenship in *The Revolution of Sweden* is placed in the context of her later work on virtue, a clear picture of a gender-inclusive citizenship emerges. Constantia's inner struggle over whether or not to turn Arwide in for treason is an example of the moral sense and reason at work. The very attributes that make Constantia virtuous are what make her a good citizen, as is evident in Arwide's following description of her virtue:

> Oh! She has all that Softness which endears
> And melts the Soul to transport: But superior
> Reason holds the Reins, guides and restrains
> Her most impetuous Wishes, nor suffers 'em
> To bound her to any indirect, unequal Path,
> From her determin'd Course.[47]

Constantia's reasonableness allows her to place public safety above her own happiness because she would be incapable of living with herself if she acted for selfish reasons. Her moral sense is properly informed by reason, which restrains her passions and allows her to maintain an unbiased view of her circumstances.

In her 1702 defence of Locke's epistemological principles, Cockburn maintains that our knowledge is limited by what we can perceive through sensation and reflection, and therefore cannot be expected to reach certainty. Cockburn's epistemological position has an effect on her political views because no person can ever have perfect knowledge of a situation. Because Constantia is confronted with what seems like incontestable evidence of Arwide's treason, she makes the difficult decision to turn him in. Although she is ultimately mistaken, she makes the best use of reason possible in her circumstances by earnestly searching for the truth. She carefully weighs the information available to her with her moral duties to herself, her husband, and the state. When asked by her servant Maria whether she plans to turn Arwide in for treason, Constantia cites the priority of public safety as her main motivation:

> *Const.* I cannot tell thee, know not yet what I intend,
> Therefore I did not, cou'd not, see my Lord,
> 'Till I determin'd. Oh *Arwide*, *Arwide*,
> Oh what a Tryal hast thou set my Virtue!
> Thus to divide my Duty to my Country, and my Husband
> At what an easie Rate we keep our Virtue,
> When it has no Affection to contest with,
> But when oppos'd, how weak are our Resolves,
> Or were they firm, how difficult it is
> To judge aright, on what we shou'd resolve;
> So liable are all things to receive a Colour
> From those Passions, through which our Reason views 'em;
> I fear 'tis that, the soft Reflection of my Love,
> That wou'd perswade, I ought not to reveal
> My Husband's Guilt.

---

[47] Cockburn, *Revolution of Sweden*, p. 25.

Mar. No law, Divine or Human,
Has oblig'd a Wife to be th' accuser of her Husband.
Const. 'Tis not perhaps exacted; but cou'd I answer
To my Conscience, my Country, or the sole
Equitable judge, and Framer of the whole,
That to conceal the Treachery of one,
I suffer'd the Destruction of a Nation?
Is there a tye so Sacred to be held
In competition with the Publick Safety?
And yet – Oh! can my Heart consent t'expose
My *Arwide*, to the Mercy of an injur'd Enemy?
He comes, *Gustavus* comes, and I am still irresolute.
Oh! Thou who know'st the combat of my Thoughts,
Direct them to preserve in this sad Exigence,
Both what I owe my Husband, and my Country.[48]

Although she is wrong about the facts of the case, Constantia is not blamed for the mistake because she made the best use of her reason possible in that situation. She was misled intentionally by Beron, but she recognizes her error and changes her position as soon as the truth of the plot against Arwide is revealed by Christina. In Gustavus's view, any good citizen would have chosen to turn Arwide in given the same false yet convincing information. When Arwide is sentenced to death, he does not blame Constantia for her actions but rather praises her for her reason, virtue, and consistent search for the truth.

Arw. Thou dost not need Forgiveness – Rise my Love,
With such Appearances against me, what thou didst
Deserves the highest Honours – Come to my Heart,
To which thou'rt now more Dear than ever.
May my Country
Be Juster to thy Worth, than it has been
To thy unhappy Husband – I must leave thee.[49]

Constantia's actions are deemed justified by all the reasonable people around her, and none accuses her of wrongly prioritizing public safety over her duty to submit to her husband.

Cockburn believes nature has given us the faculty to approve and disapprove of actions; but the use of that faculty is not predetermined, meaning that individuals can make poor use of their moral sense. Constantia makes good use of her moral sense despite the false information she based her decision on; but Beron makes poor use of his, by wilfully ignoring Christina's innocence and accusing her of adultery without any evidence:

> Though our passions, our benevolent affections, our love of truth, and approbation of what appears to us right and fit, are natural, and implanted in us for good and

[48] Ibid., pp. 50–51.

[49] Ibid., p. 69.

> useful purposes; yet the *application* of any of these, is not determined by nature, but is put in our own power so that we may make either a right or a wrong use of them: It is our fault, if we suffer our passions or affections to be *our masters*: that indeed is not natural, tho' the affections themselves are so; for it is the province of reason to keep them in subjection, to regulate them, and to point out the proper application of them.[50]

Constantia uses her reason to control her passions and makes good use of her moral sense, while Beron allows his passions to override reason completely and is therefore at fault for his lack of virtue. The attributes that make Constantia a good citizen, and Beron a bad one, are not related to their gender. Christina, Arwide, and Gustavus are all described as being virtuous because they exemplify these same attributes as Constantia. Because the use of reason and the moral sense are open to both sexes, all people are capable of being good citizens if they are dedicated to reasonableness and disinterested benevolence.

Conclusion

Although it is uncertain why Cockburn chose not to write about overtly political or feminist matters again after *The Revolution of Sweden*, it is clear that these themes are strongly connected to her later work on morality and religion. Being a good citizen is one aspect of being a virtuous person, and it is open both to men and to women – provided they are willing to place the public good above their own when the two are in conflict. By subordinating self-interest and by exercising reason and the moral sense, both sexes can exemplify civic virtues. The rather radical consequence is that citizens must be prepared to question authority figures and to resist their power if those figures act against the public good. This requires that women think for themselves and be willing to question the authority of their husbands. But given that such resistance can have grim consequences (such as Christina's murder), Cockburn's standards of citizenship are set quite high. Only by regulating one's passions using reason – and accepting the consequences of choosing the moral path – can one become a truly virtuous citizen.

---

50 Cockburn, 'Remarks Upon the Principles and Reasonings of Dr Rutherforth's Essay', p. 31.

Chapter 10
Catharine Macaulay and Laetitia Barbauld: Two Eighteenth-Century 'Republicans'

Karen Green

Introduction

On 20 December 1790 Horace Walpole mentioned, in a letter to his young friend Mary Berry who was travelling in Italy, how much he admired Edmund Burke's book *Reflections on the Revolution in France*. After commending Burke's intervention as timely and effective, Walpole continued:

> His foes show how deeply they are wounded by their abusive pamphlets. Their Amazonian allies, headed by Kate Macaulay and the virago Barbauld, whom Mr Burke calls our *poissardes*, spit their rage at eighteen pence a head, and will return to Fleet Ditch, more fortunate in being forgotten than their predecessors immortalized in the *Dunciad*.[1]

For Walpole, writing at the end of 1790, it is evidently Catharine Macaulay (née Sawbridge; 1731–1791) and Anna Laetitia Barbauld (née Aiken; 1743–1825) who are the foremost Amazonian *poissardes* ('fishwives', 'market-women') raising strident voices in favour of France, republicanism, and tolerance of dissent. The younger Mary Wollstonecraft (1759–1797), who had published her *Vindication of the Rights of Men* in response to Burke in late November, contemporaneously with Catharine Macaulay's *Observations on the Reflections of the Right Hon. Edmund Burke*, is not the focus of his disdain.[2] She is at most included among the

1 W.S. Lewis (ed.), *The Yale Edition of Horace Walpole's Correspondence* (New Haven, 1944), vol. 11, pp. 169–70. Also quoted in S. Wiseman, 'Catharine Macaulay: History, Republicanism and the Public Sphere', in E. Eger et al. (eds), *Women, Writing and the Public Sphere, 1700–1830* (Cambridge, 2001), p. 181.

2 C. Macaulay, *Observations on the Reflections of the Right Hon. Edmund Burke, on the Revolution in France, in a Letter for the Right Hon. The Earl of Stanhope* (London, 1790); M. Wollstonecraft, *A Vindication of the Rights of Men, in a Letter to the Right Honourable Edmund Burke* (London, 1790). Six months later, after Macaulay's death, Wollstonecraft seems to have still not come to Walpole's notice. He repeats the fish-wife motif in another letter to Berry written in July 1791, when he reports disturbances in Birmingham that led to the arrest of some republican agitators, and Thomas Paine's non-attendance at a meeting of the Revolution Club at the Crown and Anchor on 14 July: 'Eleven of these disciples of Paine are in custody; and Mr Merry, Mrs Barbauld, and Miss Helen Williams will probably have subjects for elegies. Deborah and Jael, I believe, were invited to the Crown and Anchor, and had let their nails grow accordingly – but somehow or

Amazonian followers of Kate and the virago Barbauld. Barbauld had not in fact responded to Burke's published observations, but her *Address to the Opposers of the Corporation and Test Acts* had been written as a reply to Burke's anticipatory comments, delivered in a speech to the Commons in February 1789.[3] By the first years of the twenty-first century however, the reputations of these notorious female republicans had been almost completely swamped by Wollstonecraft's later fame, and her subsequent elevation to the status of first modern feminist.[4] This is a pity, for both Macaulay and Barbauld made significant contributions to the republican discourse of the second half of the eighteenth century. Here I offer a preliminary comparative sketch of their political views, beginning with the parallels between their lives, for Macaulay and Barbauld moved in overlapping circles and their careers followed similar trajectories. In the 1760s and 1770s their early works received considerable praise. Indeed, Walpole himself had previously seemed to be a friend of Macaulay's. They had shared a box at the theatre to see a play in which Macaulay was satirized.[5] He had arranged for her introduction to a friend in Paris, Mme du Deffand (Marie Anne de Vichy-Chamrond, marquise du Deffand; 1697–1780), and wrote in conclusion to a letter to Macaulay on 31 January 1778:

> You know the high respect I have for your Writings; & Madame du Deffand ventured an expression in my behalf that, however just [I should not have] presumed to use myself – yet why not? Tho it is taking liberties for a man to tell a lady he loves her, because it generally implies no very respectfull Intentions; yet to love Virtue implies respect; and tho respect without love may content Monarchs, it would be too mean [*illegible*] to be offerred to Mrs Macaulay by her most sincere
>
> Admirer & obedient
> Humble Sevt.
> Hor Walpole.[6]

---

other no poissonnières were there, and the two prophetesses had no opportunity that day of exercising their talents or talons'; Lewis (ed.), *Horace Walpole's Correspondence*, vol. 11, p. 320. By 1792 Wollstonecraft had come to his attention, only to be excommunicated from his library; three years later, in a letter to Hannah More, he called her Alecto and a 'hyena in petticoats'; Lewis (ed.), *Horace Walpole's Correspondence*, vol. 33, pp. 373, 97.

3 W. McCarthy, *Anna Letitia Barbauld: Voice of the Enlightenment* (Baltimore, 2008), pp. 274–8.

4 J.G.A. Pocock, 'Catharine Macaulay: Patriot Historian', in H.L. Smith (ed.), *Women Writers and the Early Modern British Political Tradition* (New York, 1998). For a rather different account of the relative importance of Macaulay and Wollstonecraft's philosophies for modern feminism see Green, 'Catharine Macaulay as Enlightenment Philosopher', in *Intellectual History Review*, 22:3 [Special Issue on Women, Philosophy and Literature in the Early Modern Period, ed. P. Anstey and J. Harris] (2012): pp. 411–26.

5 Lewis (ed.), *Horace Walpole's Correspondence*, vol. 39, p. 102. The play was William Combe's *The Devil upon Two Sticks in England: Being a Continuation of Le Diable boiteux of Lesage* (London, 1790), after Le Diable boiteux ['The limping devil'] by Alain René Le Sage (1707). In another letter Walpole had also jokingly expressed the hope that Macaulay would be elected to Parliament (ibid., vol. 32, p. 40).

6 New York Historical Society; Gilder Lehman Collection, MS GLC01799.

This letter is representative of earlier attitudes; but before long both women were reviled by former supporters, as they came to be identified with the most radical wing of British political thought. They were for a while 'celebrated', later vilified, and eventually forgotten.

Biographical Background

Neither Macaulay nor Barbauld was deliberately educated to a high degree, but each was able to take advantage of unusual circumstances to furnish herself with an excellent grounding in history, rhetoric, and political thought. Macaulay established herself as a scholarly historian, while Barbauld was revered as a poet, and wrote essays in a polished style that has withstood the test of time.

The slightly older Macaulay benefited from the rise of the new wealthy financial class but was also caught up in the teething troubles of capitalism. Her paternal grandfather, Jacob Sawbridge, had been a banker and one of the directors of the South Sea Company, which crashed in December 1720 after a spectacular and unsustainable bubble.[7] The family remained wealthy, and Catharine grew up at Olantigh – a large estate in Kent that her grandfather purchased in 1706. But Sawbridge's descendants believed that he had been unfairly made a scapegoat. When Macaulay later gave an account of the South Sea debacle, she did not deny that the public had been fleeced as a result of their own naivety and greed, and the contrivance of some of the promoters; but she defended her grandfather's innocence.[8] It has been suggested that the family's history was responsible for its being consistently averse to arbitrary power.[9] Whatever the cause, Catharine and her brother John grew up to be strong supporters of liberty and parliamentary reform. John, who was elected a London Alderman in 1769, became in the same year a founding member of the Society of the Bill of Rights, established with Horne Tooke and others to support John Wilkes, who had been denied the parliamentary seat he had won for Middlesex after publishing an article critical of the king.[10]

When Macaulay was only two years old her mother died; and along with her sister Mary she received a standard education for girls, at the hands of a governess she did not greatly admire. She had, however, access to a considerable library, and was free to read whatever interested her, history in particular. She maintained a close friendship with her brother, and through him was drawn into radical London circles.[11] By the age of twenty-six Catharine Sawbridge had grown to be a highly intelligent, fashionable, wealthy young lady – a learned conversationalist who,

---

7 In what follows I am indebted to B. Hill, *The Republican Virago: The Life and Times of Catharine Macaulay, Historian* (Oxford, 1992), pp. 4–24.

8 C. Macaulay, *History of England from the Revolution to the Present Time in a Series of Letters to a Friend* (Bath, 1778), pp. 297–308.

9 Hill, *The Republican Virago*, p. 5.

10 Ibid., pp. 55–62.

11 B.B. Schnorrenberg, 'The Brood-Hen of Faction: Mrs Macaulay and Radical Politics, 1765–75', *Albion*, 11 (1979): pp. 33–45; Hill, *The Republican Virago*, pp. 52–77.

having sought out Elizabeth Carter (the Bluestocking translator of Epictetus) at a fair, impressed her as being both agreeable and 'more learned than becomes a fine lady'.[12]

Macaulay did not marry until she was almost thirty. When she did, it was to a Scottish widower fifteen years her senior: a physician and treasurer of the Brownlow Lying-in Hospital. It is clear that he encouraged her historical writing; he corrected the first volume, tending to moderate her expression to be more suitably humble.[13] This marriage, which produced one daughter, was based on affection and free choice; but it lasted only six years, leaving Macaulay an independent widow who was often found daunting by her contemporaries.[14]

Laetitia Aiken came from a less wealthy middle-class background, which made her more acutely aware of the inconsistencies and arbitrariness of contemporary political practice. She was born into a family of Dissenters; her father John Aiken ran a boarding school at Kibworth, and later taught at a Dissenting college at Warrington. He belonged to the tradition of Rational Dissent, whose adherents had given up the Calvinist emphasis on faith and believed in a good God whose principles were discoverable by the light of reason.[15] Catharine Macaulay defended a version of this doctrine at length in her *Treatise on the Immutability of Moral Truth* (1783), and it is clear that, although she remained a member of the Church of England, her Latitudinal theological views were aligned with Rational Dissent.[16]

With one brother but no sisters, and surrounded from an early age by the boys at her father's school, Laetitia Aiken had little contact with other girls.[17] Not offered the same depth of education as the boy pupils, she nevertheless persuaded her father to teach her Latin and a little Greek.[18] She was free to read the school's fine stock of books and discussed these with her father, her brother, and others in the family. She was particularly close to her brother, feeling somewhat superior because she was two years his senior. They remained friends and in later life collaborated on literary projects. His support and high opinion of her abilities no doubt contributed to the confidence of her poetic voice.

---

12 M. Pennington (ed.), *A Series of Letters Between Mrs Elizabeth Carter and Miss Catherine Talbot, from the Year 1741 to 1770* (4 vols, London, 1809), vol. 2, pp. 260–61; quoted in Hill, *The Republican Virago*, p. 11.

13 M.B. Geiger, 'Mercy Otis Warren and Catharine Macaulay: Historians in the Transatlantic Republican Tradition', doctoral dissertation (New York University, 1986), pp. 161–4.

14 Hill, *The Republican Virago*, pp. 13–15.

15 For this biographical background I am indebted to McCarthy, *Anna Letitia Barbauld*. He relies for much of his information on the memoir written by Lucy Aiken, Anna Laetitia's niece, printed in A.L. Barbauld, *The Works of Anna Laetitia Barbauld* (2 vols, London, 1996), vol. 1, v–lxxii.

16 C. Macaulay, *A Treatise on the Immutability of Moral Truth* (London, 1783). The general similarity between Dissenters and Latitude-men is noted in McCarthy, *Anna Letitia Barbauld*, pp. 14–15.

17 McCarthy, *Anna Letitia Barbauld*, p. 23.

18 Ibid., p. 32; Barbauld, *Works*, pp. vi–ix.

Like Macaulay, Laetitia Aiken married late. Indeed, she was thirty-one when she married Rochement Barbauld: a descendant of French Huguenots, with whom she was deeply in love. The union was against her parents' advice, and she may have come to regret this show of independence. Her husband was emotionally unstable – probably what we would now call bipolar; in later life his manias caused her a great deal of trouble. Nevertheless, when he committed suicide in 1808 they had been married for thirty-two years, many of which were spent in a successful partnership running Palgrave: a boarding school for boys that helped nurture a new generation of socially active young men.

One reason for the relative neglect of both Macaulay and Barbauld is that, although both were clearly advocates of egalitarian marital relationships and critics of constraints imposed on women, neither wrote the kind of polemical feminist text that has endeared Mary Astell and Mary Wollstonecraft to contemporary feminist scholars. Both seem to have been confident of their equality with, or superiority to, the men they knew; and they experienced egalitarian relationships with their brothers and husbands. The late seventeenth century and the first half of the eighteenth furnished them with unimpeachable models – learned and respected female authors such as Elizabeth Carter (1717–1806), whose *Epictetus* both quoted.[19] Hannah More (1745–1833) captured the mood in 1774:

> But in our chaster time 'tis no offence,
> When female virtue joins with female sense;
> When moral Carter breathes the strain divine,
> And Aikin's life flows faultless as her line;
> Where all-accomplished Montagu can spread
> Fresh-gathered laurels round her Shakespeare's head;
> When wit and worth in polished Brooke unite,
> And fair Macaulay claims a Livy's right.[20]

Despite being associated here with Elizabeth Carter, neither belonged to the 'bluestocking circle', though Laetitia was approached by Elizabeth Montagu after the success of her poems in 1774.[21] The existence of this circle also testifies to the contemporary acceptance of learned women as 'ornaments' of civilized society.[22] Laetitia Barbauld's early attitude to female education was more equivocal than that

---

19 J. Aiken and A.L. Aiken [Barbauld], *Miscellaneous Pieces in Prose* (London, 1773), pp. 59–60; Macaulay, *Immutability of Moral Truth*, p. 197.

20 Quoted in Hill, *The Republican Virago*, p. 20. From R. Lonsdale, ed., *Eighteenth-Century Women Poets* (Oxford, 1989), pp. 325–6. This from a woman who would later refuse to read Wollstonecraft's *A Vindication of the Rights of Woman* because 'there is something fantastic and absurd in the very title' (Lewis [ed.], *Horace Walpole's Correspondence*, vol. 31, p. 370).

21 McCarthy, *Anna Letitia Barbauld*, p. 116.

22 Richard Samuel's painting *The Nine Living Muses of Great Britain*, an engraving of which was included in a Joseph Johnson ladies' pocket book for 1778, also captures this mood. See E. Eger and L. Peltz, *Brilliant Women: 18th-Century Bluestockings* (London, 2008), pp. 58–67.

outlined in Macaulay's 1790 *Letters on Education*, but like Macaulay she had no feeling of intellectual inferiority. Barbauld rejected Elizabeth Montagu's suggestion that she open a college for young women, fearing that such an institution would turn out *précieuses*, and apparently endorsing Rousseau's suggestions for Sophie's education in *Emile*.[23] She thought that her situation had been peculiar and was 'no rule for others'. Nevertheless, like Macaulay, she aspired to an authoritative status, which did not appear to be out of her reach. While their interest in liberty and rights was universal, their authority to speak for all humanity has not been recognized by male posterity, and their failure to speak up loudly for its female half has not endeared them to women. Yet both were significant actors in eighteenth-century radical circles, articulately voicing political opinions that are now commonplaces of democratic liberalism, but were then unusually enlightened and humanitarian.

While this is not the place to articulate a detailed account of Macaulay and Barbauld's shared connections, it is worth recording a few of the most notable. Among the tutors at Warrington was Joseph Priestley, and he and his wife Mary became lifelong friends and correspondents of Barbauld. Indeed, Priestley claims in his *Memoir* that Barbauld was induced to take up poetry after reading some of his own verses.[24] This acquaintance gave her entrée to other English radicals. When she circulated her poem 'Corsica', Priestley wrote to tell her how it had been praised by William Turner (a minister in Wakefield), who proposed transmitting it to James Boswell (through Vaughan, Macaulay, or other London sympathizers), to support fund-raising for the Corsican leader Pasquale Paoli's struggle against Genoese suzerainty.[25]

Priestley's letter indicates that he was acquainted with Macaulay, but I have not yet been able to determine how close this friendship was. She was certainly an admirer of his works, and refers to his influence on her account of the will, in her *Treatise on the Immutability of Moral Truth*.[26] She also dedicated to the Earl of Stanhope her observations on Burke's *Reflections*. Stanhope was Priestley's patron, having employed him in the position of librarian at the recommendation of the Rev. Richard Price – himself another shared link, as was Thomas Brand, the friend and beneficiary of Thomas Hollis, who after Hollis's death changed his surname to Brand Hollis.[27] Macaulay had sent Thomas Hollis a copy of the second volume of her history, and from that point onwards he anonymously provided her, at considerable expense, with Civil War pamphlets and other materials.[28] She also

---

23 Barbauld, *Works*, pp. xvii–xxiv.

24 J. Priestley, *Memoirs of Dr Joseph Priestley, to the year 1795, written by himself: With a continuation, to the time of his decease, by his son, Joseph Priestley* (London, 1904), p. 32.

25 McCarthy, *Anna Letitia Barbauld*, p. 103; A.L. Le Breton, *Memoir of Mrs Barbauld* (London, 1874), pp. 34–6.

26 Macaulay, *Immutability of Moral Truth*, p. xiv.

27 McCarthy, *Anna Letitia Barbauld*, pp. 228, 68.

28 F. Blackburne, *Memoirs of Thomas Hollis, Esq. F.R. and A.S.S.* (London, 1780), vol. 1, pp. 264, 269.

corresponded with Brand Hollis, but I have not found evidence of her dining with him, as did Barbauld.[29] Indeed, despite their having shared so many friends and acquaintances, it is not known whether these two very similarly disposed women ever actually met.

Corsica, and the Praise of Pasquale Paoli

In February 1768 James Boswell published his *Account of Corsica*, which was an immediate success. By March he was boasting to his friend William Temple: 'My Book has amazing celebrity. Lord Lyttelton, Mr Walpole, Mrs Macaulay, Mr Garrick have all written me noble letters about it.'[30] The exemplary character of Pasquale Paoli's virtues, along with the Corsicans' long struggle for independence from the Genoese, elicited published responses from both Laetitia Barbauld and Catharine Macaulay. These are indicative of the similarities in their political attitudes, as well as the differences in their style. Barbauld, at this stage still Miss Aiken, confected her poem 'Corsica' in blank verse, and it was printed as the first of her collected poems in 1773.[31] Macaulay offered Paoli advice, in the form of a letter published in 1767, on the structure of a Corsican Republic. Since this was before the appearance of Boswell's *Account*, either she had seen something of it before publication or, more probably given that she seems unaware of Boswell description of Corsica's actual government under Paoli, she wrote in anticipation of it.[32]

Boswell's introduction to the *Account* begins with praise of liberty: 'Liberty is so natural, and so dear to mankind, whether as individuals or as members of society, that it is indispensably necessary to our happiness.'[33] He goes on to assert that no more restraint should be laid by society on natural liberty than 'what the necessities of society require'.[34] Barbauld takes up this theme, marrying it with Boswell's descriptions of Corsica (the dense-wooded island whose people are noble rustics, where chestnuts are a staple food), and producing a hymn to liberty:

> And glows the flame of LIBERTY so strong
> In this lone speck of earth! this spot obscure,
> Shaggy with woods, and crusted o'er with rock,
> By slaves surrounded and by slaves oppress'd!

---

29 J. Disney, *Memoirs of Thomas Brand Hollis* (London, 1808), p. 42.

30 James Boswell to William Temple, 24 March 1768, in T. Crawford (ed.) *The Correspondence of James Boswell and William Johnson Temple: 1756–1777* (Edinburgh, 1997), p. 227.

31 A.L. Barbauld, *Poems* (London, 1773).

32 C. Macaulay, *Loose Remarks on Certain Positions to be Found in Mr Hobbes's 'Philosophical Rudiments of Government and Society', With a Short Sketch of a Democratical Form of Government, in a Letter to Signor Paoli* (London, 1767).

33 J. Boswell, *An Account of Corsica, the Journal of a Tour to that Island; and Memoirs of Pascal Paoli*, 2nd edn (London, 1768), p. 1.

34 Ibid., p. 3.

What then should BRITONS feel? – should they not catch
The warm contagion of heroic ardour,
And kindle at a fire so like their own?[35]

As we will see, it would transpire that the liberty Paoli sought for Corsica (essentially national self-determination) did not resemble the liberty for which radical Britons were agitating: a Bill of Rights, the repeal of the Test and Corporation Acts, and parliamentary reform. But in 1768 when Barbauld penned her poem, this was not apparent. She continued with her praise of liberty after passages of veneration for Corsica's 'lonely scenes of unbroken nature' that anticipate later Romanticism:

... LIBERTY,
The mountain goddess, loves to range at large
Amidst such scenes, and on the iron soil
Prints her majestic step: for these she scorns
The green enamel'd vales, the velvet lap
Of smooth savannahs, where the pillow'd head
Of luxury reposes; ...[36]

Soon after the poem was completed, Paoli was ousted from Corsica by the French and came to London seeking refuge. Barbauld was forced to provide a new ending for her poem and fell back on liberty in another sense, the freedom of the mind that is 'beyond the proud oppressor's cruel grasp'.[37]

The poem 'Corsica' is a celebration, closely following Boswell's description of Corsica and its people's struggle. In her letter to Paoli, Macaulay shows herself rather more presumptuous and original than Barbauld. Boswell was known to have brought to Corsica a letter of introduction from Jean-Jacques Rousseau, whose guest he had been before setting out.[38] Rousseau was an iconic supporter of the Corsican struggle. He himself had been invited by Paoli, ostensibly (according to reports contradicted by Boswell) to formulate a constitution and laws for the new Republic;[39] so in advising on the constitution of Corsica, Macaulay seems to present herself as a substitute for Rousseau. Alternatively, since her counsel followed principles laid out in James Harrington's *Oceana*, she might have sought to offer Paoli a digest of the best British opinion on framing a democratic constitution.[40]

Macaulay begins her letter with an epitome of Harrington's conclusions:

> Of all the various models of republics, which have been exhibited for the instruction of mankind, it is only the democratical system, rightly balanced, which can secure the virtue, liberty and happiness of society.[41]

---

35 Barbauld, *Works*, p. 2.
36 Ibid., pp. 5–6.
37 Ibid., p. 12.
38 Boswell, *Account of Corsica*, pp. 263–8.
39 Ibid., pp. 365–8.
40 Hill, *The Republican Virago*, pp. 170–71.
41 Macaulay, *Loose Remarks*, p. 29.

This 'democratical system, rightly balanced' has to be understood against the background of *Oceana*, in which Harrington gives a rather surprising definition of a *commonwealth* as the proportion of a territory that is owned by the people. He contrasts a commonwealth with an absolute monarchy and with what he calls the 'Gothic' – a feudal system, in modern terms. So according to his definitions:

> If one Man be sole Landlord of a Territory, or over-balance the People, for example three parts in four, he is Grand Signor: for so the *Turk* is call'd from his Property; and his Empire is absolute Monarchy.
>
> If the Few or a Nobility, or a Nobility with the Clergy be Landlords, or over-balance the People to the like proportion, it makes the *Gothic* balance (to be shewn at large in the second part of this Discourse) and the Empire is mix'd Monarchy, as that of *Spain*, *Poland*, and late of *Oceana*.
>
> And if the whole People be Landlords, or hold the Lands so divided among them, that no one Man, or number of Men, within the compass of the *Few* or *Aristocracy*, over-balance them, the Empire (without the interposition of Force) is a Common-wealth.[42]

For Harrington, power ultimately rests in the possession of land, this power is upheld by the sword; since an unfed soldier is useless, the ultimate power is realized in *control* of the land, by the capacity to feed one's troops.[43] Different forms of government are the result of different distributions of the ownership of land, so a popular or 'democratical' government depends on the landed (or commercial) wealth of the populace not being over-balanced by that of the aristocracy. Harrington believes, however, that the optimal structure of the government of a commonwealth is not entirely democratical. Talent and education reside in a natural aristocracy that should debate and propose laws; these should be accepted by a body representative of the people, and the laws should be executed by the magistracy. The result is a mixed form of government:

> The Common-wealth consists of *the Senate proposing, the People resolving, and the Magistracy executing*: whereby partaking of the *Aristocracy* as in the Senate, of the *Democracy* as in the People, and of *Monarchy* as in the Magistracy, it is complete.[44]

In her letter to Paoli, Macaulay accepts much of this, so her reference to a 'democratical government properly balanced' might be read as allowing some place for aristocracy; and indeed, Bridgit Hill and Christopher Hill have argued

---

42 J. Harrington, *The Oceana of James Harrington, Esq; And His Other Works; With an Account of His Life Prefix'd, by John Toland. To Which is Added Plato Redivivus or, a Dialogue Concerning Government* (Dublin, 1737), pp. 39–40.

43 Ibid., p. 41.

44 Ibid., p. 48.

that both Harrington and Macaulay should be seen as 'aristocratic republicans'.[45] But while Harrington was much impressed by Venice, and may well be thought to be proposing an aristocratic republic, Macaulay's prescription differs. Like Harrington, she accepts that a stable democratic government requires mechanisms to prevent excessive accumulation of land (she does not consider other forms of wealth). This is what 'properly balanced' amounts to. The imposition of equality results in what has been one of her most challenging and apparently anti-feminist prescriptions: equal male inheritance and 'no females inheriting or bringing any dower in marriage'.[46] In fact, her scheme is less aristocratic than Harrington's, and she is prepared to sacrifice women's wealth to democracy, perhaps convinced by arguments for the inconsistency of luxury with democracy and virtue.

Despite the clear influence of Harrington on her scheme, there is no class distinction between the Senate and the Representatives in Macaulay's version of a two-house parliament. The large Representatives contingent, 'not under two hundred and fifty', is elected by the people; and the people further elect members from that body to the Senate,[47] whose membership is maintained at 'not above fifty'. With rotation of one third of the Senate every year, incumbency in it extends to three years (after earlier service in the Representatives). The generals, admirals, and civil magistrates are to be elected from the senators by the Representatives, for one-year terms. So Macaulay envisages that the Senate will be made up of a group of the people, elected from the Representatives by the people, because of their aptitude. This is more clearly democratic than Harrington's original scheme, which assumed that the wise Senate would be selected from an aristocratic class.

Like Harrington however, Macaulay assumes that the Senate and Representatives will be men. She also, by excluding them from inheritance for the sake of equality among men, denies women any franchise based on property. While she does call for unmarried women to be provided with annuities by their male kin, that exclusion is decidedly at odds with her principles. She writes near the beginning of her letter:

> The very nature of slavish dependence and proud superiority are equally baneful to the virtues inherent in mankind: The first, by sedulous attention and mean adulation to please its master, undermines, and at last subdues the innate generous principles of the soul; and the fond delights of superiority extinguish all the virtues which ennoble human nature, such as self-denial, general benevolence, and the exalted passion of sacrificing private views to public happiness.[48]

This expresses her conviction that democracy and economic equality are necessary as means to the cultivation of virtue. But in denying women economic equality

---

45 Hill, *The Republican Virago*, p. 177; B. Hill and C. Hill, 'Catharine Macaulay and the Seventeenth Century', *The Welsh History Review*, 3:4 (1967): p. 398.

46 Macaulay, *Loose Remarks*, p. 37.

47 Ibid., p. 35.

48 Ibid., p. 30.

with men, Macaulay overlooks the fact that, according to her own principles, she is preventing women from acquiring the means to develop their virtue. In 1793 Wollstonecraft would apply this reasoning to the situation of women, arguing that female virtue is incompatible with 'slavish dependence'.[49] In 1767 it seems that Macaulay was blind to this consequence.

There is no evidence that Paoli appreciated Macaulay's political advice. In June of 1769, not long before he withdrew from Corsica to refuge in London, a subscription had been set up to support his cause, and Bridget Hill suggests that Macaulay had contributed.[50] But despite speculation in the press that the two defenders of liberty would join forces, Paoli, who was soon indebted to the king for a pension, at least once excused himself from visiting her, probably to avoid being associated with those who were seen to be the king's enemies.[51] Perhaps he was warned off by Boswell, who, having boasted of Macaulay's praise of his book, visited her in early April 1768. The visit was not a success:

> She was very complimentative to me, but formal and affected, and she whined about liberty as an old Puritan would whine about grace. In short I was rather disgusted with her.[52]

Barbauld's 'Corsica' fared a little better; in 1774 Elizabeth Montagu reported to her that she had made General Paoli very happy by presenting him with a copy of Barbauld's *Poems* in which it is the first item.[53]

The Responses to Burke

As well as both being among those praising Paoli, Macaulay and Barbauld are united in their opposition to Edmund Burke's conservative Whig politics. Macaulay's first response to Burke was published in 1770, when she took issue with his pamphlet, *Thoughts on the Cause of the Present Discontents*.[54] Burke's pamphlet lamented the fact that Parliament was fast becoming the passive instrument of the court. It was prompted by two proposed pieces of legislation, which if passed would have further undermined the independence of Parliament. One, a consequence of the controversy concerning Wilkes, would have allowed Parliament to expel any of its members at its pleasure. The other committed Parliament to paying the debts accumulated in the Civil List. In response to these proposals Burke laments:

---

[49] M. Wollstonecraft, *The Works of Mary Wollstonecraft*, ed. J. Todd and M. Butler (7 vols, London, 1989), vol. 5, pp. 86–7, 92–3, 102–6.

[50] Hill, *The Republican Virago*, p. 63. However, the list of subscribers in *The Public Advertiser*, 7 June 1769, does not demonstrate this.

[51] Ibid., pp. 64–7.

[52] F. Brady and F.A. Pottle (eds), *Boswell in Search of a Wife* (New York, 1956), p. 161.

[53] Le Breton, *Memoir of Mrs Barbauld*, p. 40.

[54] C. Macaulay, *Observations on a Pamphlet entitled 'Thoughts on the Cause of the Present Discontents'*, 4th edn (London, 1770).

> The power of discretionary disqualification by one law of Parliament, and the necessity of paying every debt of the Civil List by another law of Parliament, if suffered to pass unnoticed, must establish such a fund of rewards and terrors as will make Parliament the best appendage and support of arbitrary power that ever was invented by the wit of man.[55]

He looks back with favour to the time of Queen Anne, when the Whig party had control of Parliament, and argues that it is only through the power of parties, grounded in aristocratic influence, that Parliament can exercise an effective control over the executive.[56]

Macaulay does not disagree with Burke's account of the degeneration of Parliament into an instrument of court policy, but she roundly turns on his analysis of the origins of the problem, and the ineffectual character of his suggested remedies. She represents him as the mouthpiece of an aristocratic faction that sowed the seeds of their own fall from power, at the time of the Glorious Revolution. They settled William on the throne on terms that gave him too much independence from parliament, and led to what she deems a 'settled Corruption'.[57] According to her version of the history of the eighteenth century:

> A system of corruption began at the very period of the Revolution, and growing from its nature with increasing vigor, was the policy of every succeeding administration. To share the plunder of a credulous people, cabals were formed between the representatives and the ministers. Parliament, the great barrier of our much boasted constitution, while it preserved its forms, annihilated its spirit; and, from a controuling power over the executive parts of government, became a mere instrument of regal administration.[58]

The Whigs in fact were more destructive of liberty than the Tories. They concealed their desire for power under the rhetoric of liberty and were only reaping the consequences of their own actions, which were the result of a strong monarch freeing himself from the influence they had previously been able to exercise over a weak one.[59]

Macaulay had no doubt which reforms were needed to remedy the situation: triennial elections, in place of the septennial ones which placed parliamentarians in a position to accumulate too much power of patronage; and 'a more extended and equal power of election'.[60] Burke had considered the first possibility, but rejected it as leading to too great an expense and disruption. The second idea, a broader and more egalitarian franchise, did not even come within his horizon. In her short pamphlet Macaulay sets out the essence of her account of eighteenth-

55 E. Burke, *Thoughts on the Cause of the Present Discontents*, 4th edn (London, 1770), p. 94.

56 Ibid., p. 109.

57 Macaulay, *Observations on a Pamphlet*, p. 7.

58 Ibid., p. 13.

59 Ibid., p. 18.

60 Ibid., p. 28.

century British history, which she would publish eight years later in the *History of England from the Revolution to the Present Time in a Series of Letters to a Friend.*[61] She anticipates remedies and attitudes that would not become firmly established until the passing of the reform bills of the nineteenth century, and she shows her principles to be very different from those of the aristocratic Whigs defended by Burke.

Later, responding to Burke's *Reflections on the Revolution in France*, Macaulay takes direct aim at the fundamental difference in their understanding of the source of legitimate government. Burke begins his attack on the principles of the French Revolution by disputing the claim (made by Richard Price, in a sermon preached on the anniversary of the Glorious Revolution of 1688) that the king of Great Britain owes his crown to the choice of the people.[62] Burke argues that the intention of the *Declaration of Right*, which established William II on the throne, was to confirm the rights and liberties of the subjects of Great Britain and to settle the succession of the crown.[63] So, despite a small deviation in the line of succession, British kings continued to owe their crowns to inheritance in the royal line. He quotes an earlier *Petition of Right* to show that it is inherited custom that grounds and legitimizes the government:

> In the famous law of the 3d of Charles I called the *Petition of Right*, the parliament says to the king, 'your subjects have *inherited* this freedom,' claiming their franchises not on abstract principles 'as the rights of men,' but as the rights of Englishmen, and as a patrimony derived from their forefathers.[64]

Against this, Macaulay argues that while the Commons might have used this language as more likely to be listened to, if they had they been challenged with regard to the basis of this patrimony they must ultimately have fallen back on a basic claim to rights:

> Had the *circumstances* of Charles enabled him to *speak* and to *enforce* the sentiments of his mind, he would have undoubtedly made the following reply: You tell me upon your *own* authority, and the authority of *your lawyers*, that what you plead so strenuously for, is a patrimony derived from your fore-fathers, and grounded on the ancient law of the land. Be it so – Was not this ancient law *superseded by the authority of arms*, and the *entire* submission of the people to the Norman code established by William the Conqueror? *Magna Charta*, then, and the other charters, must either have been *extorted* from the *imbecility* of the princes who granted them, or they must have issued from the *voluntary donations of monarchs*; in either case, they only stand on *resumable* right.
>
> What the parliament could have answered to this plea, I know not, without calling in the aid of an *abstract right*.[65]

---

61 Macaulay, *History of England.*

62 E. Burke, *Reflections on the Revolution in France* (London, 2004), pp. 96–7.

63 Ibid., p. 100.

64 Ibid., p. 118.

65 Macaulay, *Observations on the Reflections*, pp. 30–31.

She argues that rights must be universal, since no other ground for asserting them is secure. She disagrees with Burke's parochial defence of right grounded in tradition and insists that whatever rights there are should extend to all people.

At the conclusion of the pamphlet she returns to this basic argument. In between, she refutes Burke point by point. To his claim that aristocrats, who control considerable wealth, are necessary as defenders of the state, she responds: 'Every citizen who possesses ever so *small* a share of property, is *equally* as tenacious of it as the most opulent member of society.'[66] Inequality, in fact, leads to envy and ultimately civil disturbance. And while she agrees that different classes have different interests she asserts:

> I know of no *rational* objection; nor can I think of any expedient to remove the well-grounded apprehensions of the different interests which compose a commonwealth, than a *fair* and *equal* representation of the *whole* people.[67]

She responds to his criticism of the French form of representative government, and praise of the British system, by pointing out that under the system then in place representation depended on votes controlled by landowners, which could in effect be bought and sold. Under the circumstances,

> the important interests of the great body of the Commons is, by our *present inadequate state of representation*, sacrificed to the ambition of *private* individuals, who, by their *command* over boroughs, may make their *market* with government at the *expence* of the public.[68]

She concludes with a lucid argument by dilemma, which returns to her fundamental difference from Burke, and her unswerving commitment to democratic principles:

> For if we say that *lawful* governments are formed on the authority of conventions, it will be asked, *who gave these conventions their authority*? If we grant that they derived their authority from the *assent of the people*, how came the people, it will be said, to exert such an authority at *one* period of society, and not at another? If we say it was *necessity* that recovered to the social man the full rights of his nature, it will be asked, *who is to be the judge* of this necessity? Why *certainly* the people.
>
> Thus, in *every* light in which we can place the argument, in every possible mode of reasoning, we shall be driven back to elect either the first or the second of these propositions, either that an individual, or some privileged persons, have an inherent and indefeasible right to make laws for the community, or that this authority rests in the unalienable and indefeasible rights of man.[69]

---

66 Ibid., pp. 40–41.

67 Ibid., p. 48.

68 Ibid., p. 51.

69 Ibid., pp. 94–5.

Macaulay does not bother to prove the absurdity of the first horn of this dilemma. She takes it that her audience will agree that there are no individuals who have an inalienable right to rule others. So she is able to conclude her work with the resounding principle that government, 'can have no *legitimate* force, but *in the will of the people*'.[70]

Just as Barbauld excelled Macaulay in rhetorical flourishes when responding to Paoli, though Macaulay had the firmer and more original arguments, so too with their responses to Burke. Barbauld's immediate reason for writing the *Address to the Opposers of the Corporation and Test Acts* was the failure of a Bill to pass through parliament, which would have removed the prohibition on members of dissenting sects from standing for office.[71] She attacks with trenchant irony those opposing equal rights for dissenters, thanking them for considering the dissenters so powerful that immediately on being given the right to stand for office, they would take over the country and destroy the established church. Only near the end of her pamphlet does she account for the inequitable treatment of dissenters as a relic of past attitudes – undone by the French Revolution, and soon to be eradicated altogether in the growing enlightenment:

> Obscure murmurs gather, and swell into a tempest; the spirit of Enquiry, like a severe and searching wind, penetrates every part of the great body politic; and whatever is unsound, whatever is infirm, shrinks at the visitation. Liberty, here with the lifted crosier in her hand, and the crucifix conspicuous on her breast; there led by philosophy, and crowned with the civic wreath, animates men to assert their long forgotten rights. With a policy, far more liberal and comprehensive than the boasted establishments of Greece and Rome, she diffuses her blessings to every class of men; and even extends a smile of hope and promise to the poor African, the victim of hard, impenetrable avarice. Man, *as* man, becomes an object of respect.[72]

Like Macaulay, Barbauld believes in the rights of humanity, which she here ties in with the abolition of slavery. Both held to principles that are now generally accepted, but neither has been properly acknowledged in the history of democratic political thought as it is now generally represented.

Conclusion

Both Macaulay and Barbauld thought themselves worthy to speak for humanity. They divested themselves almost completely of the self-deprecation characterizing earlier women writers. They did not speak from a position of humility; nor did

---

70 Ibid., p. 95.

71 For a longer discussion of the circumstances, arguments, and responses to Barbauld's essay see McCarthy, *Anna Letitia Barbauld: Voice of the Enlightenment*, pp. 275–81.

72 A.L. Barbauld, *Address to the Opposers of the Corporation and Test Acts* (London, 1790), pp. 32–3.

they apologize for the impertinency of a woman's pen, but wrote confidently about universal subjects with full awareness that, as women, they were not guaranteed equal rights. This self-assurance is quite surprising. It quickly earned them such epithets as 'Amazon' and 'virago'; it shows that almost from the middle of the seventeenth century there were women writers and scholars to serve as exemplars to younger women – to feel confident in their own contributions to culture. Macaulay and Barbauld shared an optimism about humanity's future, and about the promise that enlightenment made to women as part of humanity. This happy expectation was bitterly betrayed as the French Revolution unfolded, and though Macaulay died too early to see the dashing of her hopes, Barbauld responded to the gloomy outcome in her last poem, 'Eighteen Hundred and Eleven':

> Colossal Power with overwhelming force
> Bears down each fort of Freedom in its course;
> Prostrate she lies beneath the Despot's sway,
> And the hushed nations curse him – and obey.

Chapter 11
'The Manly Virtues': Macaulay's Influence, Wollstonecraft's Legacy

Mary Caputi

Introduction

In her *Letters on Education* (1790), Catharine Macaulay argues forcefully that an ideal education fosters 'the manly virtues' in women, and dissuades them from an indulgent interest in traditional feminine frivolity. As one who bemoans 'coquetry', Macaulay insists that such superficiality is 'as dangerous as it is dishonourable' and should be discouraged in favour of a female character that is 'grave, *manly*, noble, full of strength and majesty ...'.[1] Moreover, it is well known that Macaulay's attention to 'the manly virtues', so crucial to her idealized profile of a serious and educated woman, greatly influenced the thought of Mary Wollstonecraft, whose *A Vindication of the Rights of Woman* (1792) constitutes a founding manifesto in Western feminist theory.[2] Given the historical and intellectual weight of these two texts, it behoves those interested in feminism to unpack precisely what these authors mean by 'the manly virtues', and to ascertain if indeed they mean the same thing. This is a worthwhile undertaking, given that it offers insight into why Wollstonecraft's writings have had a more profound impact on Western feminism – as indeed on Western political thought – than have Macaulay's. Wollstonecraft exhorts women to be 'manly' for reasons differing from those of her predecessor, and these differences explain why Wollstonecraft now assumes canonical status while Macaulay remains less well known.

For both authors, the revered 'manly virtues' go hand-in-hand with the topic of female education. Macaulay and Wollstonecraft alike acknowledge the utmost

---

1 C. Macaulay, *Letters on Education* [1790] (Oxford and New York, 1994); p. 221, my emphasis.

2 For Macaulay's influence on Wollstonecraft see, in particular, B. Hill, 'The Links Between Mary Wollstonecraft and Catharine Macaulay: New Evidence', *Women's History Review*, 4:2 (1995): pp. 177–92. For more general discussions, C. Villanueva Gardner, *Rediscovering Women Philosophers: Philosophical Genre and the Boundaries of Philosophy* (Boulder, 2000); C.S. Sotiropoulos, *Early Feminists and the Education Debates: England, France, Germany, 1760–1810* (Madison and Teaneck, 2007); S. Wiseman, 'Catharine Macaulay: History, Republicanism and the Public Sphere', in E. Eger et al. (eds), *Women, Writing and the Public Sphere, 1700–1830* (Cambridge, 2001), pp. 181–99; M. Ferguson and J. Todd, *Mary Wollstonecraft* (Boston, 1984).

importance of cultivating a new sensibility in women through education, since in their view women's moral schooling and intellectual formation are, in the late eighteenth century, nothing less than 'absurd'.[3] Macaulay goes so far as to claim that women are in 'a state of abject slavery' given their underdeveloped faculties, while Wollstonecraft laments that women are in a state of 'perpetual childhood, unable to stand alone'.[4] Each of these deplorable conditions – bondage and unending youth – can nevertheless be remedied, these authors maintain, through a high-quality education that hones critical thinking skills and encourages a 'manly' intellect.

Yet a closer look at these women's thoughts on female education reveals that they understand the longed-for 'manly virtues' differently. It is my argument that Macaulay perceives these virtues as a set of qualities drawing on an important tradition within political theory – one relating to the desirability of republicanism tempered by what Catherine Villanueva Gardner has termed an 'ethicoreligious system', now informed by Christian values.[5] The topic of gender is thus enlisted in the historical emergence of a revived republican polity: therefore, to argue that women should be better educated is part and parcel of the larger project of eighteenth-century political theory.

Conversely, for Wollstonecraft a discussion of the 'manly virtues' has bearing less on the correct political order and more on woman's nature. Wollstonecraft disagrees especially with Jean-Jacques Rousseau and rejects his assertion that a woman's value is measured largely in terms of her sexual charm, her ability to please, and willing confinement to the private sphere. Wollstonecraft decries the manner in which Rousseau counterposes an eternal, essential femininity to an historically situated masculinity in a manner that highlights female allure and underscores woman's ability to evoke sensual pleasure. This highly sexualized reading of femininity does a deep disservice to women, Wollstonecraft argues, making them 'anxious to inspire love, when they ought to cherish a nobler ambition, and by their abilities and virtues exact respect'.[6] Indeed, Wollstonecraft's stance on the 'manly virtues' pits her against Rousseauian claims that woman's overpowering allure trumps all other female qualities: 'I wish to see my sex become more like moral agents.'[7] It is this defence of woman's character, framed in more generalized terms, that explains why Wollstonecraft's writing has had heightened importance in the Western tradition than the writings of Macaulay. For when Wollstonecraft exhorts women to develop the 'manly virtues', it is not in relation to political developments in England, nor to her reading of the masculinized *virtù* extending back to the Roman republic. Rather, these virtues pertain to woman's nature and potential in virtually any historical setting.

---

3 Macaulay, *Letters*, p. 207.

4 Ibid., p. 206; and M. Wollstonecraft, *A Vindication of the Rights of Woman*, ed. C.H. Poston, 2nd edn (New York and London, 1988), p. 9.

5 Gardner, *Rediscovering Women Philosophers*, p. 42.

6 Wollstonecraft, *Rights of Woman*, p. 7.

7 Ibid., p. 178.

Catharine Macaulay and the Inherent Virtues of 'an Expanded Mind'

Catharine Macaulay was an eighteenth-century historian and political pamphleteer, also known for her feminism. Her great love and knowledge of history is evidenced in her eight-volume *History of England* (1763–1783), a text that like her *Letters on Education* is informed by political philosophizing. Consistent with this historical, theoretical mindset, the topic of women's education emerges in Macaulay's writings in connection with a larger treatment of civic virtue, and the question of how human conduct relates to an ethical, rational, well-ordered public sphere. Addressed to an imagined female reader called Hortensia, her *Letters* does address what at first seems an array of unrelated issues, so that some readers consider it a scattered volume devoid of any unifying theme. In Catherine Villanueva Gardner's words, 'it appears that, due to its structure, the *Letters* does not appear to be able to contain a sustained philosophical argument.'[8] Vegetarianism, the merits and demerits of sugar, kindness to animals, the lessons garnered from antiquity: all of these contribute to her epistolary musings with Hortensia.[9] Yet amid this apparent panoply of unrelated topics a unifying theme in fact emerges, beginning in Part 3.[10] This is the question of how to educate for the moral betterment of society. Gender, for Macaulay, is enlisted in the interest of political ends: the more a superior education succeeds in promoting virtue founded 'on immutable principles', the more advanced our society will be in the ways that matter.[11] Thus, whether we are practising abstemiousness in our diet, treating our pets gently, or studying the history of Athens and Rome, all these ways of educating women to become accomplished and thoughtful creatures contribute to a well-ordered public sphere.

Indeed, the ultimate end of education for Macaulay is to instil a strong sense of civic duty in its citizens. She laments any form of education focused solely on the individual, arguing that the highest aims of physical and intellectual training are to produce refined citizens whose sense of duty and moral integrity benefit the larger collective. Her ardent commitment to republican principles therefore does not simply emanate from a love of antiquity – she greatly admired Cicero – but from her concerns for the present. For her, 'republicanism' denotes the desire to preserve public virtue and extol a commitment to the *res publica*, now under threat given that rising commercial interests instil a new appreciation for wealth and a growing, unmanly effeminacy.[12] Writing as an Old Whig, Macaulay feels that the

8 Gardner, *Rediscovering Women Philosophers*, p. 27.

9 While many claim that the *Letters*' epistolary form and far-reaching themes prevent the book from having a unified argument, Gardner disagrees. The book does adhere convincingly, she argues, around the need to improve women's education for the sake of an improved society founded on republican principles.

10 See Gardner, *Rediscovering Women Philosophers*, p. 40.

11 Macaulay, *Letters*, p. 201.

12 For a broader discussion of republicanism and its history see P. Pettit, *Republicanism: A Theory of Freedom and Government* (Oxford, 2002), and Q. Skinner, *Liberty Before Liberalism* (Cambridge, 1998).

party's former commitment to high ideals has been betrayed by newcomers who have succumbed to the materialism and love of luxury that accompanies a growing commercial class. Such interests have harmful effects on society. In *A Treatise on the Immutability of Moral Truth*, she writes that 'the essential principles of commerce tend to increase that selfishness in man, which most powerfully militates against the qualities of honesty, integrity, frugality, moderation, sobriety, and a ... regard to the interests of the community at large.'[13] At the extreme, Macaulay argues, her contemporaries have 'grown so lax in their devotions to the shrine of patriotism' that they 'are content with privations which have no foundation in the common good'.[14]

In Macaulay's eyes, the moral corrosion wrought by a growing commercialism she witnessed in her contemporaries is tantamount to an effeminate quality lacking moral rectitude. Indeed, the very concept of 'manliness' has, she feels, changed in her day to fall short of antiquity's commitment to public virtue. For the new, urban rendition of 'manliness' denotes a host of attributes unaligned with antiquity's vision. As Philip Hicks explains, 'By the eighteenth century, a "man" might be urban, refined, polite ... he might take greater interest in economic and social than in political activity; he might be content to pay others to fight his wars and govern his country.'[15] Macaulay therefore exhorts her public to embrace a 'manliness' strong enough to counter the pernicious effects of commercialism and to return the British people to a morality commensurate with antiquity's *virtù*. 'Macaulay saw the luxury of the court as the biggest threat to republican virtue,' Hicks explains.[16]

Republican institutions and practices can, Macaulay believes, counter such nefarious influence by refining a society's morals. For her, republicanism is a form of rule committed to public virtue, something that inspires civic pride in its citizens while safeguarding against such evils as excessive tenure in office, the hoarding of property, and the self-serving of politicians motivated by private greed. It is therefore not necessarily incompatible with monarchy. Clearly, Macaulay's writing is far more concerned with the erosion of public virtue and corruption of morals than it is with the elimination of monarchy, and she is as much a constitutional monarchist as she is a republican. In J.G.A. Pocock's words, Macaulay's republic is 'a community of virtue', and because such communities are now under threat, 'histories are written in order to praise the memory and hold up the example of those who have it.'[17] To be sure, 'writing history in order to preserve virtue is the best thing a woman can do.'[18] In her *Letters*, Macaulay especially praises the ancient Roman republic as a society marked by its shared

13 C. Macaulay, *A Treatise on the Immutability of Moral Truth* (London, 1783), p. 10.

14 Macaulay, *Letters*, p. 272.

15 P. Hicks, 'Macaulay's Civil War: Gender, History, and Republicanism in Georgian Britain', *Journal of British Studies*, 41:2 (2002): p. 176.

16 Ibid., p. 187.

17 J.G.A. Pocock, 'Catharine Macaulay: Patriot Historian', in H.L. Smith (ed.), *Women Writers and the Early Modern British Political Tradition* (New York, 1998), p. 247.

18 Ibid., p. 247.

devotion to the larger public cause. She admires how, in keeping with the ideals of ancient political theory, Romans understood their private lives in connection with the public arena; the pursuit of even mundane daily tasks stood on a continuum with an expansive republican duty. In the days of the republic, she writes, Romans constituted 'a nation of heroes', for their love of civic duty 'gave a lustre to these republicans which never was acquired by any people in the same state of society'.[19] Before Rome succumbed to the decadence and corruption of its later days, it was nothing less than a paragon of virtue that excelled at infusing the private sphere with a patriotic sentiment that benefited the whole. Macaulay is eager to see such commitment to the public realm revived, one that will now be informed by Christian values.

This revival, which will hopefully illuminate the present as did the 'lustre' of the past, demands a thorough rethinking of the overall purpose of education. It is only education – which in addition to book learning involves discipline, order, structure, and the careful cultivation of good habits – that will revive this ancient republican sentiment, now tempered with Christian theology. Importantly, such an education must be gender-neutral, with the same measure of intellectual seriousness and disciplinary structure accorded to women as to men. For although women were not highly visible in the late eighteenth-century's public sphere, Macaulay insists that girls must receive the same education as boys if a patriotic sentiment is to revive. If we are truly to progress toward the virtuous, equitable, Christian society that alone for Macaulay is worthwhile – 'What use are we making of our advances in knowledge?'[20] – education must be administered consistently between the two sexes in ways showing no preference for the intellectual formation or moral development of boys over girls. Educating the female sex is therefore part and parcel of a larger move away from the ills that plague society and toward a newfound republican order aligned with an overarching moral mandate to achieve Christian ends: 'I repeat my assertion, that modern times produce but few real Christians.'[21]

Macaulay is eager to defend the claim that it is education alone, not some mistaken notion of the eternal feminine, that explains why women currently do not demonstrate a more 'manly' demeanour. Unfortunately, there is 'much false speculation on the natural qualities of the female mind' put forward by those who wrongly propound the concept of 'innate ideas, and innate affections'.[22] Yet those given to such all-encompassing abstractions typically do not think through their arguments carefully, she insists, for they dare not 'bring forth a conclusion which in no respect militates with their premises'.[23] If Macaulay's cohort proved incapable of understanding the continuum that joined the lives of women to the purpose of the larger collective, it was only further proof that 'moderns' had

---

19 Macaulay, *Letters*, p. 239.

20 Ibid., p. 13.

21 Ibid., p. 137.

22 Ibid., p. 203.

23 Ibid., p. 203.

grown deplorably 'lax'.[24] As in antiquity, women *are* on a continuum with the public sphere even if from within the home. Thanks to this continuum, they should develop their 'manly' side, since the value in being 'grave ... noble, full of strength and majesty' serves the public cause.[25]

To the contemporary student of gender, Macaulay's use of the term 'manly' appears curious if not objectionable. At first blush, she appears to be endorsing an androcentric norm. Yet Macaulay's adherence to the time-honoured definitions of gendered spheres does not make her an essentialist where these categories are concerned; she does not naturalize 'masculine' and 'feminine'. On the contrary, her stance on the importance of education weighs heavily in favour of nurture over nature. In arguing that environment and socialization – more than any inherited disposition – determine who we become, she subscribes to the position that the human mind is not founded upon innate concepts. In keeping with Locke's argument promulgated in *An Essay Concerning Human Understanding* (1690) – or closer to her own time, with David Hartley's *Observations on Man, his Frame, his Duty, and his Expectations* (1749) – Macaulay maintains that the mind does not build upon an unchanging, inherited structure.[26] Instead, her writings uphold the Lockean tenet that the human mind begins from a tabula rasa, and takes shape only in response to sense perceptions. This insistence on interaction leads the analysis outward to objects of sense, and credits experience with shaping our ideas *a posteriori*. 'Let us then suppose the mind to be, as they say, a white paper ... how comes it to be furnished?' asks Locke. His answer is simple: 'To this I answer in one word, from experience.'[27]

All that enters the mind through our involvement with the outside world thus shapes the quality of our intellect: subsequently, there is no 'feminine' or 'masculine' predisposition that determines how women and men think or behave. Instead, for Macaulay as for Locke, the intellect is an impressionable thing eminently capable of change. And for Macaulay, because 'the mind receives all its intelligence through the organs of sense', it follows that with proper education, women's intellectual energies can be just as easily enlisted in the service of civilization's refinement as can men's.[28] The potential for a civically oriented woman, whose 'manliness' derives from culture and not nature, is therefore eminently before us. Even alongside the fashionable coquetry and vaunted female frivolity that Macaulay so despises, the education of women holds the potential to impact radically the society around her. For indeed, 'all those vices and

---

24 Ibid., p. 272.

25 Ibid., p. 221.

26 See J. Locke, *An Essay Concerning Human Understanding*, ed. Peter H. Nidditch (Oxford, 1975); and D. Hartley, *Observations on Man, his Frame, his Duty, and his Expectations* (1749).

27 Locke, *An Essay*, p. 189.

28 Macaulay, *Letters*, p. 295. Here Macaulay differs from Locke; for although Locke upholds the premise that there are no innate ideas, he does not conclude that there are no innate differences between the sexes.

imperfections which have been generally regarded as inseparable from the female character, do not in any manner proceed from sexual causes, but are entirely the effects of situation and education.'[29]

To ensure that a girl receives an education conducive to the 'manly virtues', Macaulay argues in favour of both sexes being taught together in the setting of the home. This insistence on gender-blind co-education at home distinguishes her as a revolutionary in terms of pedagogical practices. Yet when it comes to curricular content and the actual substance of what is studied, Macaulay's prescriptions actually identify her as a traditionalist. She is unaligned with the 'modern' focus on mathematics and the natural sciences, propounded by the 'dissenter academics' who in the eighteenth century emphasize a pedagogical utilitarianism.[30] Indeed, she is as opposed to their instrumental approach to learning as she is critical of the aristocratic focus on refinement, gallantry, and sensibility. Contrary to the utilitarians' argument that mathematics and science produce a visibly more efficient social good according to the philosophy of utilitarianism, Macaulay remains a staunch defender of traditional academic disciplines 'that proponents of utilitarian education could legitimately question', also assuming 'that women are the intellectual equals of men'.[31]

Macaulay thus advocates a curriculum that includes history, literature, religion, politics, the classics, and some scientific texts. She endorses such canonical luminaries as Plutarch, Cicero, Milton, Shakespeare, Voltaire, and Molière. Added to this is the study of foreign languages including French, Latin, and Greek. Travel too is recommended, as pedagogically useful; in this, she has 'Milton, Locke, and common sense on [her] side'.[32] And she cautions against activities that may have a corrupting influence on the mind. In her *Letters*, she decries the extent to which the ancient Romans' horrific public displays could influence society's morals: 'Their public shows, both from the expensive magnificence, and the nature of the exhibition, were adapted both to debauch their taste, and to render them callous to the feelings of humanity.'[33] In this way, reading Macaulay's prescription for a well-rounded education in the late eighteenth century one might easily be reading the guidelines for the great-books tradition today. 'What use are we making of our advances in knowledge?' she asks.[34]

That women develop a personal interest in the public sphere is sufficient proof that their educational parity with men is worthwhile; for if their thoughts, actions, and attitudes support a republican worldview, this is reason enough to educate them in the ways adumbrated by Macaulay. It is not mandatory that there

---

[29] Ibid., p. 202.

[30] For a thorough discussion of the dissenter academics see Sotiropoulos, *Early Feminists*, pp. 122–8.

[31] Ibid., p. 145.

[32] Macaulay, *Letters*, p. 141.

[33] Ibid., p. 257.

[34] Ibid., p. 13.

be an instrumentally efficient utilitarian value in women's improved education, measured in terms of some abstract greatest good for the greatest number. Moral refinement along the lines mentioned here is 'progress' enough. Yet most in her day measured progress and civilization in more materialist terms.

> When the term civilized, Hortensia, is opposed to the term savage, a refinement in morals is commonly understood; but the general sense of the word civilization, as it is used by modern authors, conveys no other idea than a refinement in the enjoyments of sense. Therefore, when I speak of any higher degree of civilization which one modern society has attained over the other, I would be understood to imply no other meaning than what is annexed to the lowest sense of this word.[35]

And so, echoing the Socratic pronouncement that justice is its own reward, Sotiropoulos writes that for Macaulay 'an expanded mind serves as its own utility'.[36]

One such expanded female mind belonged to Wollstonecraft, on whom Macaulay exerted considerable influence. We may inquire why her legacy has so overshadowed the earlier legacy of Macaulay. Why has Wollstonecraft's writing assumed canonical status in the history of Western political thought, while Macaulay's remains largely unknown to all but scholars of the eighteenth century? It is to these questions that I now turn.

Wollstonecraft's Opposition to 'Rich Soil' and 'Gorgeous Draperies'

It is well known that Macaulay's writings exercised a profound impact on the thought of Wollstonecraft. There can be little doubt that her thoughts on women's education heavily impacted Wollstonecraft's views on this subject as expressed in her groundbreaking manifesto *A Vindication of the Rights of Woman* (1792). Expanding upon her earlier ideas articulated in *A Vindication of the Rights of Men, in a letter to the Right Honorable Edmund Burke* (1790), Wollstonecraft leans heavily on Macaulay's premises, and certainly on her advocacy of a 'manly' intellect. And while many have commented on the indebtedness of one author to the other, here I wish to underscore a significant difference in their approach to 'manliness' and to the 'revolution in female manners' that Wollstonecraft desired. Specifically, it is in her interpretation of 'the manly virtues', as they weigh against Rousseau's sexual politics. For Wollstonecraft, these virtues are less about reviving a lost political tradition in modern times than they are about correcting the *ongoing*, pernicious, and self-serving opinions of men regarding women. For these opinions rely upon mistaken notions of 'an eternal feminine' as they interpret the female sex according to maternal instinct, a charged eroticism, and an innate feminine modesty, all of which wholly discounts woman's intellectual

---

35 Ibid., p. 300.

36 Sotiropoulos, *Early Feminists*, p. 145.

and moral strengths. '[E]verything reminds her of her sex,' Rousseau asserts.[37] And this statement is true, Wollstonecraft concurs, but only when women have not been properly educated.

Throughout *Rights of Woman* the author is concerned less with reviving the glories of a revered republicanism, than with refuting the view of her male contemporaries regarding women's inherent nature. It is out of this defence of women's underdeveloped intellectual and moral capacity that Wollstonecraft's understanding of the 'manly virtues' emerges. For her, these virtues look forward rather than backward, given that their goal is to aid in defining a new version of femininity: one that defies the over-sexualized, infantilizing assumptions of her day. Her aim is not to educate in political theory based on historical knowledge, as in Macaulay's writings, but to change public opinion about the true capabilities of her sex. 'I plead for my sex – not for myself,' she writes in a letter to Talleyrand, looking forward to the day when the newly revised French constitution will comprise the rights of women and when universal education will include girls.[38]

Wollstonecraft identifies the gendered convictions of Rousseau as emblematic of the popular opinion that she wishes to change. This is the position that describes women as essentially deficient in reason, incapable of paralleling the seriousness of the male sex due to the innately empathic nature of women that subsequently aligns them with the private sphere.[39] They belong in the home, concerned with children, food, clothing, the care of the body, sex – in sum, all that Simone de Beauvoir describes as the immanent realm focused on the reproduction of everyday life.[40] In his *Letter to d'Alembert*, Rousseau goes so far as to say that a woman occupied in activities outside the home lacks decency; when she 'shows herself off', she 'disgraces herself'.[41] Woman's natural leanings are divorced from abstract reasoning and conceptual uniformity, he maintains, and remain far more attuned to emotions, human interactions, detailed specificity, and aesthetic appeal. Rousseau therefore argues that woman naturally gravitates toward the private sphere; her talents lie in relating to other people individually, not in contemplating philosophical principles in the abstract. 'In the cheerful home life the mother finds her sweetest duties,' he opines in *Emile*.[42]

According to Rousseau, this pronouncement does not denigrate the female sex but merely assigns women to a different sphere of influence, which undergirds the workings of the republic. To his mind, women's natural tendency to gravitate toward interpersonal relations ('Love is the realm of women') in fact accords

---

37 J.-J. Rousseau, *Emile*, trans. Barbara Foxley (London, 1993), p. 388.

38 Wollstonecraft, *Rights of Woman*, p. 3.

39 For a discussion of the origins of Rousseau's public–private distinction see K. Green, 'Madeleine de Scudéry on Love and the Emergence of the "Private Sphere"', *History of Political Thought*, 30:2 (2009): pp. 272–85.

40 S. de Beauvoir, *The Second Sex*, trans. H.M. Parshley (New York, 1989).

41 Rousseau, *Emile*, p. 83.

42 Ibid., p. 15.

them a power over men that serves the larger purpose of the republic.[43] Karen Green has argued convincingly that Rousseau 'ascribes a very important place to them in society', given that they exert a moral influence over men, safeguarding a moral dimension of life that otherwise risks being eradicated in civil society.[44] Drawing upon a tradition articulated especially by the seventeenth-century novelist Madeleine de Scudéry, Rousseau defends the notion of a caring private realm wherein women have 'uncontested power to govern the hearts and passions of men that must be confined to what becomes the private sphere'.[45] Woman's 'sweetest duties' thus serve political ends. Yet must this sweet realm preclude the 'manly' virtues?

Denaturalizing the gendered claims of Rousseau and other eighteenth-century thinkers, Wollstonecraft insists that it is women's rearing, not their nature, that accounts for their behaviour. With proper education, women will be no less capable of reasoned conversation and considered judgement than men, even when they move within private circles that display caring relationships. Arguments regarding woman's innate inability to reason are the self-serving prejudices of men, Wollstonecraft argues, often out of step with their larger philosophical reasoning; if scrutinized more closely, these would reveal their intellectual inconsistencies:

> Men, indeed, appear to me to act in a very unphilosophical manner when they try to secure the good conduct of women by attempting to keep them always in a state of childhood. Rousseau was more consistent when he wished to stop the progress of reason in both sexes, for if men eat of the tree of knowledge, women will come in for a taste.[46]

Contrary to Rousseau's conclusions regarding the cultivation of woman's 'sweet duties' then, Wollstonecraft advocates gender-neutral education to facilitate the emergence of a new society. For her, there is no argument regarding women's innate intellect, emotions, or sexual appeal that justifies differentiating how boys and girls are educated. And with proper education women, like men, will easily prefer a life marked by temperance, seriousness, and rational pursuits rather than the frivolity that now captures their attention. As educated wives and mothers, women will rely heavily on finely honed critical-thinking skills, and let 'the practice of every duty be subordinate to the grand one of improving our minds'.[47] It is therefore imperative that both women and men be disabused of the notion that female sexuality vitiates woman's intellectual strength. As with men, women's

---

43 J.-J. Rousseau, *Politics and the Arts: Letter to d'Alembert on the Theater*, trans. A. Bloom (Ithaca, NY, 1960), p. 47.

44 K. Green, *The Woman of Reason: Feminism, Humanism, and Political Thought* (New York, 1995), p. 70.

45 J. Broad and K. Green, *A History of Women's Political Thought in Europe, 1400–1700* (Cambridge, 2009), p. 197.

46 Wollstonecraft, *Rights of Woman*, p. 20.

47 Ibid., p. 92.

sexuality can easily be interpreted as a force that coexists alongside intellect, something that need not give rise to 'contemptible infantine airs that undermine esteem even whilst they excite desire'.[48] Wollstonecraft subsequently praises modesty, discretion, and restraint in both sexes:

> In fact, it is a farce to call any being virtuous whose virtues do not result from the exercise of its own reason. This was Rousseau's opinion respecting men: I extend it to women and confidently assert that they have been drawn out of their sphere by false refinement.[49]

Wollstonecraft's energy in *Rights of Woman* typically focuses on these 'false refinements' that have done such harm in keeping women uneducated. She has many ways of describing how this chimera operates: it is a ruse, a lie, a trick played on women to keep them oppressed, convinced that their only purpose in life is to excel in seductive charms rather than be full participants in social and cultural literacy. Since their primary purpose in life is to marry a man who will support them, they are told since childhood to cultivate a slightly childish disposition, given that female helplessness is supposedly alluring to men and thus strategically useful.

> Women are told from their infancy, and taught by example of their mothers, that a little knowledge of human weakness, justly termed cunning, softness of temper, *outward* obedience, and a scrupulous attention to a puerile kind of propriety, will obtain for them the protection of man; and should they be beautiful, everything else is needless, for, at least, twenty years of their lives.[50]

She bemoans the rampancy of this mentality and roundly criticizes women falling for the pleasures of a leisured life rather than submitting to the discipline of a formal education. Importantly though, Wollstonecraft insists that this female preference for a life focused on coquetry does not reflect any essential penchant of the female mind but is wholly the by-product of women's not having been educated from a young age. Women are not 'a swarm of ephemeron triflers', but beings who are just as shaped (or unshaped) by their education as men are.[51] Given that women at present are not taken seriously as persons capable of higher intellectual and moral aims, we cannot conclude that 'the giddy whirl of pleasure' in which they are now caught up is all they can achieve.[52] As with Macaulay, false arguments about an eternal feminine nature thus come under fire as the need for a more rigorous education is defended. Indeed, Sotiropoulos argues forcefully that a central tenet of Wollstonecraft's *Rights of Woman* is the conviction that once

48 Ibid., p. 11.
49 Ibid., p. 21.
50 Ibid., p. 19.
51 Ibid., p. 19.
52 Ibid., p. 149.

women are educated properly, they will 'reject Rousseauian notions of "female virtue" as false dogma, a critical first step to transformation'.[53]

In refuting this false dogma, Wollstonecraft deliberately uses simple, straightforward language that appeals to reason rather than emotion. It is part of her understanding of the manly virtues that simple language employed in a cogent argument proves far more compelling than flowery prose intended merely to please the ear. In an effort to demonstrate that women are as capable as men of sustained and reasoned debate, she self-consciously avoids the 'turgid bombast of artificial feelings' that has too easily convinced women that they are truly man's intellectual inferior.[54] A recurrent theme in *Rights of Woman* is the insistence that women should avoid forms of communication that are too decorative or too frivolous, given that such aesthetic flourishes form part of the deceptive logic designed to convince women of their sentimentalism. To prove the point, her style is deliberately 'manly', for she seeks

> to persuade by the force of my arguments, [rather] than dazzle by the elegance of my language ... I shall try to avoid the flowery diction which ... create[s] a kind of sickly delicacy that turns away from simple unadorned truth.[55]

Wollstonecraft's efforts to disabuse her reader of woman's rationally deficient nature therefore take aim at what she perceives as *Rousseau's own* seductive speech. It is Rousseau, not woman herself, who relies on sensual pleasure in order to make an argument for women's essential inferiority to men. His claim that all women belong in the home, unschooled and at the pleasure of men, derives from a spurious logic; he cannot prove 'the eternal feminine' on which his argument depends. Therefore, women who succumb to this argument are 'like flowers which are planted in too rich a soil', where the soil metaphorically represents the engulfing, enveloping argument that women are designed to be 'alluring mistresses'.[56] This unhealthy soil of Rousseauian logic only re-inscribes women within a statically gendered universe, with few choices and little latitude for development.

This effort to unmask the misogynistic strain implicit in Rousseau's prose also prevails in Wollstonecraft's treatise *A Vindication of the Rights of Men* (1790).[57] This earlier work was addressed to Edmund Burke in response to his *Reflections on the Revolution in France* (1790).[58] An adamant defender of the French monarchy and opponent of the Revolution, Burke is famous for lamenting the lost beauty and dignity of the *ancien régime*. Refined manners, elegance and

---

53 Sotiropoulos, *Early Feminists*, p. 155.

54 Ibid., p. 10.

55 Ibid., p. 10.

56 Ibid., p. 7.

57 M. Wollstonecraft, *A Vindication of the Rights of Woman and A Vindication of the Rights of Men*, ed. J. Todd (New York and London, 2009).

58 E. Burke, *Reflections on the Revolution in France* (1790), ed. J.G.A. Pocock (Indianapolis and Cambridge, 1987).

style, attention to protocol, a willing subservience to rank and hierarchy – these and other decorous hallmarks of Louis XVI's reign are giving way, he says, to the benighted abstract reasoning of the *philosophes*. The gentility of the *ancien régime*, metonymically embodied in what Burke deems the sumptuous appearance and refined comportment of Marie Antoinette, has been displaced by those focused on social justice, an equal sharing of power, and the voice of the people. Subsequently, the supposed natural hierarchy believed to ensure order in the world – 'that generous loyalty to rank and sex, that proud submission' – will soon be eclipsed by a cold, calculating, highly rational world emphasizing rights rather than duty.[59] According to Burke, the sensibilities of *le peuple* will replace those of the aristocracy, as a coarsely hewn republicanism will displace the centuries-old worldview propounded at Versailles; the thinking of 'sophisters, economists, and calculators' has triumphed over the gracefulness and devotion to beauty that typified the Bourbon reign.[60]

In response to this conservative jeremiad, Wollstonecraft insists that Burke, like his nemesis Rousseau, conceals the falsehood of his argument in the floweriness of his language. Although his prose may be compelling by its rhetorical refinement and allure, the reasoning behind it does not stand up to scrutiny. Wollstonecraft holds that Burke's flourishes and emotional appeal mask the weakness of his argument, reflecting a larger eighteenth-century debate over sense and sensibility: feminine emotion and aesthetic appeal versus masculine reason. It is the effeminate, 'pampered sensibility' of Burke's writing that for her suggests the courtly refinement and aristocratic sensibility that she abhors.[61] Such attention to outward refinement typifies the *ancien régime* and a political position wholly out of tune with her own egalitarian aspirations. 'At the center of her analysis was an attack on the twin evils of female degeneracy and male effeminacy, both of which she associated with the gender politics of court culture,' writes Wendy Gunther-Canada.[62]

As with her critique of Rousseau, she deliberately employs a 'manly' style as she separates linguistic elegance from logical fallacy, arguing that the philosophy behind her *Rights of Men* is far more sound than Burke's reactionary stance could encompass. She accuses Burke of having concealed his logical inconsistencies in fancy adornment – 'gorgeous drapery' – which, as with Rousseau's 'too rich soil', has the effect of producing a faulty argument.[63] Yet because one's attention

---

59 Ibid., p. 66.

60 Ibid., p. 66.

61 W. Gunther-Canada, 'The Politics of Sense and Sensibility: Mary Wollstonecraft and Catharine Macaulay Graham on Edmund Burke's *Reflections on the Revolution in France*', in H.L. Smith (ed.), *Women Writers and the Early Modern British Political Tradition*, p. 132.

62 Ibid., p. 133. For an in-depth analysis of the Burke–Wollstonecraft debate concerning the meanings of the French Revolution see D. O'Neill, *The Burke-Wollstonecraft Debate: Savagery, Civilization, and Democracy* (University Park, PA, 2007).

63 Quoted in L. Gordon, *Vindication: A Life of Mary Wollstonecraft* (New York, 2005), p. 142.

is directed at the drapery rather than at the argument's content, the reader often fails to perceive its weaknesses, as with Rousseau's visually appealing but ill-tended flower. In response to Burke, she writes: 'it is only some of your pernicious opinions that I wish to hunt out of their lurking holes; and to show you to yourself stripped of the gorgeous drapery [of rhetoric].'[64] Thus, in Virginia Sapiro's words, her *Vindication of the Rights of Men* 'responded both to *what* Burke wrote and *how* he wrote it'.[65]

In divesting the arguments of Rousseau and Burke of their harmful adornments – in showing them to themselves – Wollstonecraft hopes to allow the 'manly virtues' to emerge, virtues that will correct the ingrained, mistaken notions of an essentially disorganized and disorganizing female nature intended for pleasure. In opposition to the anxieties that are either implicit or explicit in Rousseau and Burke, she evinces no anxiety that women who have developed their 'manly' side will become asexual, unappealing beings whose caring emotions have atrophied in favour of harsh, unfeeling arguments. Wollstonecraft maintains on the contrary that a better-educated and more rational woman will prove a better wife and mother, for her body and mind will be in a superior state. Looking ahead to a time when women indeed display the 'manly virtues' honed through education, she writes that 'even love would acquire more serious dignity', given the changed and more intellectually equitable relationship between the sexes.[66]

Furthering this line of argument, Gardner insists that such a cultivation of reason need not bring on a concurrent denigration of emotion, since Wollstonecraft does not see the two as locked in opposition. Green agrees that for Wollstonecraft reason and emotion are not dichotomous; rather, they can be integrated with the help of imagination to produce sounder moral judgement.[67] We must not overstate Wollstonecraft's investment in reason at the expense of feeling, for emotion too plays an important role in honing 'the manly virtues'. Wollstonecraft's writings on reason and the passions do not offer 'a clear-cut case of the former controlling or subordinating' the latter, and it is not true that 'her concept of self-governance is equated with rationality pure and simple'.[68] This refusal to see reason and passion as mutually antagonistic also dissipates other anxieties. For instance, Wollstonecraft displays no fear that this future 'manly' woman will be without sexual appeal. For although many now fear that 'woman would be unsexed by acquiring strength of body and mind', Wollstonecraft herself is 'of a very different opinion'.[69] An educated woman will display a 'dignified beauty' unlike the needy version that in her day resulted from its cultivation in 'too rich a soil'.[70] Educating women's

---

64 Quoted in Gordon, *Vindication*, p. 142.

65 Quoted in Gunther-Canada, 'The politics of sense and sensibility', p. 131.

66 Wollstonecraft, *Rights of Woman*, p. 119.

67 See K. Green, 'The Passions and the Imagination in Wollstonecraft's Theory of Moral Judgement', in *Utilitas*, 9:3 (1997): pp. 271–90.

68 Gardner, *Rediscovering Women Philosophers*, p. 93.

69 Wollstonecraft, *Rights of Woman*, p. 171.

70 Ibid., p. 171.

minds and disabusing them of 'the eternal feminine' would ultimately have a salutary effect on the sexes, as her understanding of manliness proves a boon to human relations. As wife and mother, Wollstonecraft's newly constituted woman will act as a more mature member of the republican collective; the author's solid argument spoken in simple language will indeed have outlasted the decorous allure of rich soil and elegant drapery. It is her simple speech that will prevail. She writes: 'Rousseau exerts himself to prove that all *was* right originally: a crowd of authors that all *is* now right: and I, that all will *be* right.'[71]

Conclusion

Many have commented that Catharine Macaulay's influential writings on the 'manly' qualities in women have been overshadowed by the later writings of Mary Wollstonecraft. Both authors extol 'the manly virtues', yet this term is most readily associated with Wollstonecraft's *Vindication* in its rebuke of Rousseau. I have argued that the reason Wollstonecraft has had a more profound impact on the Western canon of political theory is precisely because her writings address far-reaching, deeply embedded notions of woman's nature. Macaulay's *Letters on Education* enlists gender in the collective interest and stresses women's 'manly virtues' as serving the late eighteenth-century re-emergence of republicanism.

Wollstonecraft writes, like many authors of her time, in universalizing terms on a topic that endures throughout history. The fact that she addresses herself to long-standing human prejudices regarding woman's nature helps explain why her *Vindication* has had more impact on the canon than Macaulay's *Letters*. With her simple language, her straightforward manner of address, and her ability to demonstrate precisely what she endorses, the writings of Wollstonecraft have found a permanent place in Western political thought. Without question, changing public opinion constitutes a larger task than Macaulay's undoubtedly respectable goal of advancing the cause of republicanism.

71 Ibid., p. 15.

Chapter 12
Between Enlightenment, Feminism, and Abolitionism: Mary Wollstonecraft's Thoughts on Women and Slavery

Jeanette Ehrmann

Introduction

Modernity, freedom, and revolution are an inextricably interwoven nexus in the eighteenth century, as Hannah Arendt states in her famous book *On Revolution*. In that era, the emergence of the modern conception of freedom coincides with the genuinely new idea of revolution – as the overthrow of traditionally legitimized authority and oppression, and the establishment of a realm of freedom.[1] In sharp contrast, servitude or slavery as the ownership of persons stands as a metaphor for the condition to be overcome. According to the dominant narrative, liberation from this form of subordination manifest in absolutism and feudalism is commonly read as the beginning of political modernity, deeply anchored in Western civilization. In his impressive *The Age of Democratic Revolution*, Robert R. Palmer integrates the revolutionary upheavals in Western Europe and North America, arguing that the American Revolution and the French Revolution together herald the idea of democracy based on human equality.[2] This novel approach traces the movement of political ideas and movements across the Atlantic, giving a foundation for the concept of Atlantic history.

Palmer's account, however, like most accounts of modern revolutions, ignores the Haitian Revolution. This was the only successful liberation from slavery, which in 1804 gave rise to the first free Black republic outside of Africa. It exposed a contradiction between the proclamation of freedom and equality and the legitimation of slavery – not only in the United States of America and the European colonies, but also in the philosophy of Enlightenment. Until now, the history of political thought has been marked by oblivion both to this singular historical event and to slavery in general: the imagined antonym to liberty, but equally a social reality that determined the lives of about twelve million people of African descent, who were dehumanized, deported, and exploited in the plantation

---

1 H. Arendt, *On Revolution* (New York, 2006), pp. 3–4.

2 See R.R. Palmer, *The Age of the Democratic Revolution: A Political History of Europe and America, 1760–1800* (Princeton, 1959), vol. 1, pp. 3–4.

colonies of the New World. Cutting off these transatlantic connections between Europe, Africa, and the Americas produces an inaccurate picture of history, displacing European violence and exploitation from the collective memory. But it also leads to conceptual confusions in political thought by omitting gendered and racialized forms of domination, which are mirrored in the writings produced by white European men in the Age of Enlightenment.

In this context women's political thought of the time illuminates by highlighting, in a global scope, both the androcentric bias of their male contemporaries and racialized forms of domination. In particular, Mary Wollstonecraft's writings in the aftermath of the French Revolution are revealing. She challenges the freedom of white property-owning men – not only by claiming women's rights and the end of the suppression of women in Europe, but also by referring to colonial slavery in the plantation colonies of the Caribbean as an injustice that contradicts natural law. In what follows, my aim is to shed light on Wollstonecraft's conception of women's subordination and slavery – to counter androcentric notions of universalism, and to complicate the account of European political thought during the Enlightenment. I will therefore place Wollstonecraft's thoughts in the broader context of feminist and abolitionist discourses of her time, with a tableau of the multifaceted gender–race relations produced by the transatlantic slave trade and slavery in the Caribbean. I will conclude by reflecting on how this approach can help to re-conceptualize the historiography of political thought – especially women's political thought.

Metropolitan Discourses on Women's Subordination and the Abolition of Slavery

Since the late seventeenth century, the horrors of colonial slavery in the New World were negotiated by British women writers, such as Aphra Behn in her novel *Oroonoko*, of 1688.[3] Women's writings also clearly echoed the emerging social contract theories, which were based on the innate freedom of men and deployed the term 'slavery' for the condition diametrically opposed to this natural disposition. In 1700 Mary Astell (1666–1731) – the writer and philosopher known as the 'first English feminist' – published 'Some Reflections Upon Marriage', in which she discusses the inequality inherent in the institution of marriage and calls for female independence and autonomy through access to education.[4] By comparing women's subordination with slavery, she reveals the androcentric bias of the social contract theories: Aimed at preserving the freedom of men exclusively, they went further to construct a hidden 'marriage contract' that cemented the subordination of women in marriage through the husband's control over his wife

---

3 A. Behn, *Oroonoko: Or the Royal Slave: A True History* (London, 2003). For a comprehensive account see M. Ferguson, *Subject to Others: British Women Writers and Colonial Slavery, 1670–1834* (New York, 1992), pp. 27ff.

4 M. Astell, 'Some Reflections upon Marriage' (3rd edn, 1706), in *Astell: Political Writings*, ed. P. Springborg (Cambridge, 1996), pp. 1–80.

and the children.[5] Representing marriage as slavery, Astell portrays as plainly scandalous this contradiction between freedom and rule of law (in the state) and inequality and arbitrary power (in the family):

> If *all Men are born free*, how is it that all Women are born slaves? as they must be if the being subjected to the *inconstant, uncertain, unknown, arbitrary Will* of Men, be the *perfect Condition of Slavery*? and if the Essence of Freedom consists, as our Masters say it does, in having a *standing Rule to live by*?[6]

The reference to slavery as a metaphor for marriage can be traced to Judith Drake's 'Essay in defence of the female sex', of 1696. Here we find a first direct comparison of women's suppression through marriage with both the *concept* of slavery and the *real conditions* on the plantations in the colonies. European women are equated with 'our Negroes in our Western Plantations, ... born Slaves, ... Prisoners all their Lives'.[7] The analogy became a common trope of the time, reflected in the numbers of women politically engaged in the British abolitionist movements. On the basis of religious and philanthropic arguments, the abolitionist discourse was characterized by arousing pity for the slaves' fate. As slavery was regarded as against Christian faith, its abolition was perceived as a duty of benevolence. This line of argument can also be found in the writings of Hannah More: religious writer, poet, and one of the most influential women activists of the Society for Effecting the Abolition of the African Slave Trade. More's engagement in abolitionism was part of her overarching commitment to promote Evangelicalism, which considered slavery a moral sin.[8] Against the dehumanizing racist discourse favouring slavery, her poem 'Slavery' (1788) condemns the capture of Africans on the west coast of Africa and emphasizes the slaves' human qualities, including their sensitivity to physical pain and their entitlement to freedom.[9] In her poem 'The Sorrows of Yamba; or, the Negro Woman's Lamentation' (1795; eventually the most popular antislavery poem of the time) the situation of the female slave is central.[10] Yamba, an African woman deported to the Caribbean colony St Lucia, is depicted as the helpless victim of the white man, finding her salvation in conversion to Christianity. This staging of feelings of solidarity with male and female slaves on the grounds of philanthropy changes into a rights-based discourse precisely when a conception of freedom emerges, based on the secular idea of natural law.[11]

---

5 See C. Pateman, *The Sexual Contract* (Stanford, 2006).

6 Astell, 'Some Reflections upon Marriage', pp. 18–19; emphasis in the original. According to Patricia Springborg, this passage is a direct polemic against John Locke's description of slavery in his *Second Treatise of Government*; see Astell, 'Some Reflections upon Marriage', p. 18n20.

7 J. Drake, *An Essay in Defence of the Female Sex* (4th edn, London, 1721), pp. 19–20.

8 On Hannah More's role in the Society's entanglement with Evangelicalism see C.L. Brown, *Moral Capital: Foundations of British Abolitionism* (Chapel Hill, 2006), pp. 377–89.

9 A. Ashfield, *Romantic Women Poets: An Anthology* (Manchester, 1998), pp. 21–7.

10 Ibid., pp. 27–31.

11 See Ferguson, *Subject to Others*, p. 183.

In particular, the French Revolution was a catalyst in the shift of women's discourse on slavery. Wollstonecraft and Olympe de Gouges (1748–1793), both writing in the midst of revolutionary turmoil and at the height of empire, challenged the philosophical discourse of their male contemporaries. They critiqued the supposed universalism of the white man's emancipation by reference to the subordinate status of both women and Black people. Executed in 1793 for her perceived monarchism, and famous for her *Declaration of the Rights of Woman and the Female Citizen* of 1791, Gouges had in 1788 written an anti-slavery play published under the title 'The Slavery of the Blacks, or the Lucky Shipwreck' in 1792.[12] Similarly, Wollstonecraft in her two 'Vindications' argues from the revolutionary paradigm of natural law to claim freedom for every person regardless of gender and skin colour.[13] Wollstonecraft is therefore the first to criticize colonial slavery and women's subordination simultaneously. But there is tension between these central concepts in her political thought. In what follows, I will discuss the analogy between women's subordination in European societies and slavery on the sugar plantations of the Caribbean. First I reconstruct Wollstonecraft's thoughts on the comparable status of women and slaves in her two Vindications. Second, I contextualize Wollstonecraft's writings by illuminating the gendered and racialized inequalities in colonial Europe and the Caribbean. From this I move to a critical examination of women's political thought as conditioned by Enlightenment, feminism, and abolitionism.

On Freedom and Slavery: *A Vindication of the Rights of Men* (1790)

Mary Wollstonecraft enters the stage of modern political thought with a sharp-tongued reply to Edmund Burke's *Reflections on the Revolution in France*.[14] With reference to the innate dignity of human beings, to freedom and reason, she advocates human rights most strongly as a birthright:

> It is necessary emphatically to repeat, that there are rights which men inherit at their birth, as rational creatures, who were raised above the brute creation by their improvable faculties; and that, in receiving these, not from their forefathers but, from God, prescription can never undermine natural rights.[15]

---

[12] O. de Gouges, *L'Esclavage des nègres, ou l'heureux naufrage* (1789), ed. S. Chalaye and J. Razgonnikoff (Paris, 2006).

[13] According to Ferguson, mention of slavery in Wollstonecraft's earlier works is reserved as a metaphor for women's condition within the institution of marriage. With the rise of abolitionist discourse in English and French parliamentary debates (elevating public exposure of the colonial slavery issue), Wollstonecraft began to make reference to conditions in the plantation colonies; M. Ferguson, 'Mary Wollstonecraft and the Problematic of Slavery', in M.J. Falco (ed.), *Feminist Interpretations of Mary Wollstonecraft* (University Park, PA, 1996), pp. 126–7.

[14] E. Burke, *Reflections on the Revolution in France* (1790), ed. J.G.A. Pocock (Indianapolis and Cambridge, 1987).

[15] M. Wollstonecraft, 'A Vindication of the Rights of Men', in *The Works of Mary Wollstonecraft*, ed. J. Todd and M. Butler (7 vols, London, 1989), vol. 5, p. 14.

Arguing against Burke's conservatism, with which he defended the 'rights of an Englishman' based on tradition and property, Wollstonecraft makes clear that the source of rights rests solely on being born human. It is well known that she would later claim these rights equally for women. She makes it clear, however, that a distinction on the basis of race is not sustainable either:

> But on what principle Mr Burke could defend American independence, I cannot conceive; for the whole tenor of his plausible arguments settles slavery on an everlasting foundation. Allowing his servile reverence for antiquity, and prudent attention to self-interest, to have the force which he insists on, the slave trade ought never to be abolished; and, because our ignorant forefathers, not understanding the native dignity of man, sanctioned a traffic that outrages every suggestion of reason and religion, we are to submit to the inhuman custom, and term an atrocious insult to humanity the love of our country, and a proper submission to the laws by which our property is secured.[16]

By defining the slave trade as an insult to humanity, Wollstonecraft anticipates the many waves of abolition in United States of America, the newly established Latin American countries, and the European colonies in the course of the nineteenth century. Along with More, Gouges, and less-known writers such as Anna Laetitia Barbauld and Félicité Louise Keralio-Robert, Wollstonecraft vigorously opposes the dominant philosophical and political discourses on slavery and Blacks produced by many of her respected male counterparts.[17] Notorious for his remarks on the basic inferiority of women, no less a figure than Immanuel Kant introduced race as a *category* in relation to humans to provide a philosophical justification of racial inequality. In 'Determination of the Concept of a Human Race'[18] and 'Of the Different Races of Human Beings'[19] Kant does not merely offer scattered statements on the inferiority of Africans (whom he sees as predestined for slavery on the plantation colonies), Asians, and so-called 'mixed-bloods': he constructs the most systematic philosophical theory of race of his time. He is therefore 'one of the central figures in the birth of modern "scientific" racism'.[20]

Wollstonecraft, by contrast, uncovers the economic interests of slaveholders and traders, which are irreconcilable with morality, by providing an ideological criticism of Burke's defence of the slave trade on grounds of the legal status quo and the preservation of property:

---

[16] Ibid., p. 14.

[17] For Barbauld's opposition to slavery see W. McCarthy, *Anna Letitia Barbauld: Voice of the Enlightenment* (Baltimore, 2008), pp. 292–304. For Keralio-Robert, see Keralio-Robert et al. (eds), *Mercure National ou Journal d'état et du citoyen* (Paris, 1789–1790), vol. 1.6 (January 31, 1790), pp. 302–4.

[18] I. Kant, *Anthropology, History, and Education*, ed. G. Zöller and R.B. Louden (Cambridge, 2007), pp. 143–59.

[19] Ibid., pp. 82–97.

[20] C.W. Mills, 'Kant's Untermenschen', in A. Valls (ed.), *Race and Racism in Modern Philosophy* (Ithaca, NY, 2005), p. 173.

> You find it very difficult to separate policy from justice: in the political world they have frequently been separated with shameful dexterity. To mention a recent instance. According to the limited views of timid, or interested politicians, an abolition of the infernal slave trade would not only be unsound policy, but a flagrant infringement of the laws (which are allowed to have been infamous) that induced the planters to purchase their estates. But is it not consonant with justice, with the common principles of humanity, not to mention Christianity, to abolish this abominable mischief?[21]

This discrepancy between justice and politics is mirrored in the legislation of revolutionary France. While in 1789 the *Declaration of the Rights of Man and of the Citizen* claims rights for every man and the right of self-determination for every people, in 1791 the universal scope of these rights is suspended for the colonies by decree. As deputy Antoine Barnave explains: 'The rigorous and universal application of general principles cannot be suitable for the colonies ... the difference in places, mores, climate, and products seemed to us to require a difference in laws.'[22] This creation of a legal state of exception beyond the confines of Europe, which served to justify the maintenance of slavery in the colonies, was the stimulus for a controversial debate, not only within the *Society of the Friends of the Blacks*, but also in the journal *Mercure national*. Keralio-Robert, editor of the journal, suggested that it was only economic self-interest that prevented the assembly from abolishing slavery, concluding that from a moral point of view slavery was a violation of the principle of human freedom.[23] Slavery was eventually abolished by the assembly of the First Republic in 1794, granting every man living in the colonies full citizenship. After slavery had been restored by Napoleon Bonaparte in 1802, the effective abolition of slavery in the French colonies was not definitively codified and enforced by the Second Republic until 1848.[24]

Women and Slavery: *A Vindication of the Rights of Woman* (1792)

In her 'Vindication of the Rights of Woman', Wollstonecraft explicitly demands the constitutionalization of women's rights in revolutionary France, uniting the two previously separate themes of women's subordination and colonial slavery as analogous forms of domination by the white European man. As Moira Ferguson highlights, 'the constituency Wollstonecraft champions – white, middle-class women – is constantly characterized as slaves' in more than eighty references.[25]

---

21 M. Wollstonecraft, 'Vindication of the Rights of Men', pp. 50–51.

22 Quoted in L. Hunt, *Inventing Human Rights: A History* (New York, 2007), p. 162.

23 See Keralio-Robert et al. (eds.), *Mercure national ou journal d'état et du citoyen*, vol 1.6 (January 31, 1790), pp. 302–4.

24 See J. Champion, '30 Floréal An X: La rétablissement de l'esclavage par Bonaparte', in M. Dorigny (ed.), *Les Abolitions de l'esclavage: De L.F. Sonthonax à V. Schoelcher, 1793, 1794, 1848* (Saint-Denis and Paris, 1995), pp. 265–71.

25 Ferguson, 'Mary Wollstonecraft and the Problematic of Slavery', p. 125.

Already in the introduction, which is directed to the French deputy Charles Maurice de Talleyrand-Périgord, Wollstonecraft opens up an analogy between white women's subordination in Europe and the phenomenon of slavery. By denying women civil and political rights, she argues, they 'remain immured in their families groping in the dark'.[26] Invoking a classical Aristotelian dichotomy, she depicts white women as captives in the darkness of the *oikos* – the apolitical space (literally 'household') reserved for them and for slaves – as opposed to the *polis*. Only a few lines later, Wollstonecraft writes of European women: 'They may be convenient slaves, but slavery will have its constant effect, degrading the master and the abject dependent.'[27] Tyranny, in this context, is notably reserved for the relations between the genders within Europe. In closing the introduction, Wollstonecraft reasserts that she demands 'justice for one half of the human race',[28] meaning not Black people who are enslaved, but the women of Europe.

Only in a footnote does she mention slavery as a more general social phenomenon: 'Supposing that women are voluntary slaves – slavery of any kind is unfavourable to human happiness and improvement.'[29] The most telling passage in the second Vindication is a direct comparison between European women and the slaves on the sugar plantations, embedded in a discussion of women's difficulties to realize their disposition toward virtue and reason:

> Rousseau, and a numerous list of male writers, insist that [a woman] should all her life be subjected to a severe restraint, that of propriety. Why subject her to propriety – blind propriety, if she be capable of acting from a nobler spring, if she be an heir of immortality? Is sugar always to be produced by vital blood? Is one half of the human species, like the poor African slaves, to be subject to prejudices that brutalize them, when principles would be a surer guard, only to sweeten the cup of man? Is not this to indirectly deny woman reason? for a gift is a mockery, if it be unfit for use.[30]

While Ferguson interprets this striking reference to slavery on the sugar plantations as a 'subtle approach to the sexual abuse of black women' in the plantation colonies,[31] I would rather suggest reading this passage as a comparison of the economic exploitation of slaves for the purpose of sugar production with the exclusion of European women from the realm of virtue and reason, degrading them to an object of sexual exploitation sweetening the 'cup of man'. This reading is made plausible by the immediately following statement that women 'are made slaves to their persons' by making themselves dependent on the reason of

---

26 M. Wollstonecraft, 'A Vindication of the Rights of Woman', in *The Works of Mary Wollstonecraft*, ed. J. Todd and M. Butler (7 vols, London: Pickering & Chatto, 1989), vol. 5, p. 67.

27 Ibid., p. 68.

28 Ibid., p. 69.

29 Ibid., p. 168.

30 Ibid., p. 215.

31 Ferguson, 'Mary Wollstonecraft and the Problematic of Slavery', p. 140.

their husband.[32] Therefore, it can be argued that the reference to sugar serves to underline the condition of white women as being both voluntary slaves, reluctant to free themselves, and dehumanized as a mere property of man. As a political consequence, Wollstonecraft suggests that to resist the gendered norms that prevent women from developing their natural capacities of reason and subject them to their male counterparts, there needs to be a 'revolution in female manners – time to restore to [women] their lost dignity – and make them, as part of the human species, labour by reforming themselves to reform the world'.[33]

With reference to the second Vindication, Ferguson appraises Wollstonecraft's invocation of colonial slavery for the sake of the enhancement of women's rights positively, calling her a 'political pioneer, fundamentally altering the definition of rights and paving the way for a much wider cultural dialogue'.[34] However, by equating the positions of European women and male slaves, her writings completely obscure the situation of the female slave. Without devaluing Wollstonecraft's powerful engagement for women's rights and her critique of the false universalism of Enlightenment thought, I will offer – through the lens of more than 200 years of historical distance – an alternative reading of the second Vindication by complicating the relation of women's subjugation in Europe and slavery on the plantation colonies. To establish my argument, I will first sketch a picture of the complex web of gendered and racialized relations of power within the Caribbean plantation societies before discussing the pitfalls of a direct comparison between women's subordination within Europe and slavery in the colonies.

Intersections of Gender and Race; or the Sexual and the Racial Contract

Between 1740 and 1860 plantation slavery – especially for the production of sugar and coffee – was the most important source of profit for the European economy. France's most lucrative colony, Saint-Domingue ('the Pearl of the Antilles', later to become Haiti), had a slave population of 90 per cent. Alongside Enlightenment philosophy's invocation of the freedom and equality of all humans, the enslavement of Africans and indigenous people in the Americas was a constitutive facet of European modernity. In fact, 'slavery in the Caribbean was one of the first and most brutal appearances of modernity':[35] a laboratory for the industrialization, rationalization, and exploitation of human labour. Within the planter societies, this reality was not seen as a contradiction to the emergent European idea of natural freedom. According to historian Michael Zeuske, the creole white elites of the Americas believed that slavery, technical progress, and modernity were 'naturally'

32 Wollstonecraft, 'Vindication of the Rights of Woman', p. 215.

33 Ibid., p. 114.

34 Ferguson, 'Mary Wollstonecraft and the Problematic of Slavery', p. 145.

35 S. Fischer, *Modernity Disavowed: Haiti and the Cultures of Slavery in the Age of Revolution* (Durham, 2004), p. 12.

interlinked, whereas free labour was seen as an experimental exception limited to the west of Europe.[36]

Gender played a fundamental role in slave-holding societies. It is important to acknowledge that slavery did not build on pre-existing notions of femininity and masculinity. Rather, the social, economic, and juridical order of the plantation regime *produced* a specific gender regime, with mutually constituted gendered and racialized identities that contrasted sharply with gender relations in Europe.

While there was clearly a gendered division of labour between white women and men, with women being expected to do no or little work outside, there was no gendered division of labour on the plantations. Working conditions were equally demanding for slave women and men, except that women's circumstances brought no relief. Despite the use of women in hard field work, even during the ninth month of pregnancy, and thus their 'equality' with their male counterparts, women had little access to more prestigious jobs, which presupposed special skills such as sugar refining, carpentry, and masonry. Only a few women and men became 'house slaves'; and even if this work was not as physically hard as field work, it brought vulnerability to the arbitrariness of master and mistress and exposed women to sexual violence by the slaveholder.[37]

This racialized gender regime was also enforced juridically. In 1685, King Louis XIV decreed the *Code noir*, which comprised sixty articles policing different aspects of slavery in the colonies, including working conditions, forms of punishment, the exercise of religion, and marital law. It was in force until the French abolition of slavery in 1848.[38] Articles VIII to XIII regulated concubinage, marriage, and the status of children born to enslaved women. Most importantly, the *Code noir* stipulated that status as a slave was passed on by the mother, establishing maternal succession in the colonies. Article XII ensured the biological reproduction of slavery: 'The children born of marriages between slaves will be slaves and will belong to the master of the female slaves, and not to those of their husbands, if the husband and the wife have different masters.'[39] In most of the plantation societies, paternity suits were explicitly prohibited, in order to protect slaveholders from claims to hereditary titles made by children they had with female slaves. This stands in sharp contrast to the European custom of paternal law, and demonstrates that regimes of gender and reproduction at that time were not unchangeable and static. Rather, they could be easily adjusted to the prevailing economic needs of the planters and the French motherland, whose prosperity was heavily dependent on the transatlantic sugar and coffee trade.

---

[36] M. Zeuske, 'Handlanger der Globalisierung: Sklaverei, "schwarze" Karibik und Globalgeschichte', *iz3w*, 278/279 (2004): pp. 34–7.

[37] See R.E. Reddock, 'Women and Slavery in the Caribbean: A Feminist Perspective', *Latin American Perspectives*, 12:1 (1985): pp. 63–80.

[38] For the entire text and a comprehensive comment see L. Sala-Molins, *Le Code noir ou le Calvaire de Canaan* (Paris, 2006); English translation in L. Dubois and J.D. Garrigus (eds), *Slave Revolution in the Caribbean, 1789–1804: A Brief History with Documents* (New York, 2006), pp. 49–54.

[39] Dubois and Garrigus, *Slave Revolution in the Caribbean*, p. 51.

The *Code noir* had also established whipping as a common punishment, and female slaves were as severely punished as male slaves. In 'The Black Jacobins', his seminal work on the Haitian Revolution, C.L.R. James illustrates vividly the cruel methods of physical punishment imposed on women, even during pregnancy.[40] Particularly, specific forms of torture were performed on female slaves who were accused of the control of fertility through herbal birth control or abortion, which was carried out both according to traditional African knowledge as well as mechanically. Furthermore, infanticide was a common incident among the slave populations. Instead of picturing the female slaves as helpless victims, these phenomena can be read as acts of gendered resistance – as 'gynaecological resistance' – against the reproduction of the slaveholding society.[41]

The institution of marriage differed significantly among the enslaved. The constant possibility of partners and children being sold to other plantations, or even their death by work or punishment, impeded the formation of families among the slaves. Furthermore, female slaves distanced themselves from the idea of marriage as it meant the additional work of caring for husband and children. Last, the marriage of slaves was framed by the encompassing colonial order, which subjected both women and men to the arbitrary power of the white planters. This includes social inequalities between slave women and free women in the colonies.

Wollstonecraft's writings, in contrast, convey the impression that there was no linkage between slave women and women of the colonial empires of Europe. Female slaves disappear in her general comments on African slaves; but also, by labelling both women and African slaves as 'one half of the human species', Wollstonecraft juxtaposes the power relations between European men and European women on the one side, and European men and African slaves on the other. Attributing domination, exploitation, and violence ('tyranny') solely to white masculinity, she cuts through any kind of relation between European women and slavery. The delineation of European women as subordinate conceals them as beneficiaries of European colonialism and slavery – and as accomplices in perpetuating it. Although this holds true for white upper-class women in general, the fact becomes most obvious in complex gender, class, and race hierarchies in the Caribbean colonies. White women in the colonies were woven into a complicated texture of power, exploitation, and suppression. Subordinated because of their gender, and suffering from discrimination and subjugation within a patriarchal order, they were themselves agents in a system of race and class hierarchies, and benefited from colonialism and slavery as it allowed them privileged social status.

All these socio-economic and legal circumstances render any direct comparison between European women and enslaved women in the Caribbean impossible. The conflation of slavery and European women's subordination to men is revealing: to speak universally in the name of all women and all slaves is to obscure completely

---

40 C.L.R. James, *The Black Jacobins: Toussaint L'Ouverture and the San Domingo Revolution* (London, 2001), p. 10.

41 See K.E. Wood, 'Gender and Slavery', in R.L. Paquette and M.M. Smith (eds), *The Oxford Handbook of Slavery in the Americas* (Oxford, 2010), p. 521.

the specific situation of enslaved women. European women had to suffer from legal subordination and objectification by being reduced to their beauty (although the latter holds true only for a certain class of women); in contrast, the enslaved woman's objectification was a complete commodification in the service of profit. And while European women were, according to Wollstonecraft, immured within the family, this was not the case for enslaved women; they were completely deprived of their freedom in the true sense of the word and merely lived a 'bare life'.[42] The crucial difference here is that European women were oppressed through the ascription of certain essential features to their social gender. This – according to the androcentric model – disqualified them from the realm of freedom, but it was nevertheless a locus of normative negotiations, as can be seen in the writings of Astell, Wollstonecraft, and Gouges. Denied *human* subjectivity, enslaved women on the plantations necessarily also lacked *gendered* subjectivity entirely. They were reduced to their bodily functions and their anatomy, which secured the labour supply on the fields.[43] As a consequence, based on the particular description of European women as 'of all creatures the most miserable',[44] Wollstonecraft's thoughts on women's liberation cannot simply be transferred to the lived reality of enslaved women and men in the colonies, who had a radically different social position underwritten by a 'racial contract'.[45] The vision of emancipation presented by Wollstonecraft is therefore a partial one and does not hold for all of those excluded from the humanity of the white man.

The representation of slaves by European women can therefore be read as a displacement of white women's fears about their own assumed status of powerlessness and inferiority. As Ferguson has observed, the emancipatory discourses in favour of the abolition of slavery were characterized by projections of patriarchally prescribed notions of femininity: the innocent victim, the grieving mother, or the loyal servant.[46] Conversely, the 'colonized Other' served as a blueprint for white women's subordination in the patriarchal societies of Europe. Instead of reading the abolitionist writings as a pure solidary manifesto against European colonial domination and the exploitation and dehumanization of the colonized, we can see them also as a mirror of the social and political status of white women themselves and as an entry point to the sphere of the political.[47] Though not necessarily consciously, the abolitionist discourse implied the appropriation of the colonized, lifting upper-class women onto the political stage to speak on their own behalf. In the process, slaves were objectified, victimized, and marginalized by distorted and homogenizing representations. They were also

---

42 See G. Agamben, *Homo sacer: Sovereign Power and Bare Life* (Stanford, 1998).

43 See S. Broeck, 'Enslavement as Regime of Western Modernity: Re-reading Gender Studies Epistemology through Black Feminist Critique', *Gender Forum: An Internet Journal for Gender Studies*, 22 (2008): p. 2.

44 M. Wollstonecraft, 'Vindication of the Rights of Woman', p. 114.

45 C.W. Mills, *The Racial Contract* (Ithaca, NY, 1999), pp. 10–11.

46 See Ferguson, *Subject to Others*, p. 4.

47 See Fischer, *Modernity Disavowed*, pp. 16–17.

rendered subaltern, since speaking in the name of the slaves, even as it allowed white women political participation, silenced the Other and deprived her of her own political agency.[48] Political agency is intimately intertwined with the privilege of textual representation and voice, which can also produce hegemonic silences and marginalizations.

Women's Political Thought between Enlightenment and Empire: Some Lessons from the Post-Colony

How can we assess Mary Wollstonecraft's political thought against the background of European colonialism? Wollstonecraft was no doubt a pioneer, attacking the particularism of Enlightenment thought not only through a feminist lens, but also by denouncing the slave trade and slavery as contradicting the proclaimed moral universalism. She thereby extended Enlightenment thought beyond the borders of Europe as well as beyond the borders of masculinity, opening to scrutiny more than one species of exclusion from humanity. The juxtapositions presented above do not convict Wollstonecraft of overlooking the intersections of gender and race – a concept that emerged only in the early 1990s.[49] Following Gayatri Spivak's postcolonial approach to Western philosophy, the perspective should not be narrowed by either accusing or excusing Wollstonecraft for her writings. Instead, it is more productive to reflect on which insights can be drawn from her theoretical interventions into the hegemonic discourse of Enlightenment for critical theory today.[50]

For feminist political theory today, it is necessary to acknowledge that besides the 'sexual contract', social contract theory also implied a 'racial contract', which materialized itself in 'European expansionism and the establishment of white/nonwhite relations of domination'.[51] It is still in place at present, in modified form: both between the global South and North and within countries of the North. The renegotiation of emancipatory concepts – to be valid across differences of race, gender, and class – requires a careful analysis of interdependent power relations. This includes that norms and utopias constructed in certain historical circumstances be critically assessed by recourse to social theory, including their potential abuse in asymmetrical relations of power and domination. If political theory is understood as a critical reflection of power and domination and as a search for emancipatory alternatives, an intersectional approach to the working of different forms of power mediated through gender, race, and class can also shed light on modern forms of oppression.

---

[48] See G.C. Spivak, 'Can the Subaltern Speak?' in C. Nelson and L. Grossberg (eds), *Marxism and the Interpretation of Culture* (Urbana, 1988), pp. 271–313.

[49] See K.W. Crenshaw, 'Mapping the Margins: Intersectionality, Identity Politics, and Violence against Women of Color', *Stanford Law Review*, 43:6 (1991): pp. 1241–99.

[50] See C.G. Spivak, *A Critique of Postcolonial Reason: Toward a History of the Vanishing Present* (Cambridge, 1999).

[51] C. Pateman and C.W. Mills, *Contract and Domination* (Cambridge, 2007).

A major lesson to be learned from critical race theory and postcolonial theory is that political theory (and its history) can hardly be neutral. It is precisely these asymmetries of power and domination that produce a *politics* of the history of political thought and ideological accounts of the political. Consequently, relations of domination must be taken into consideration as having an impact on the underlying epistemology. In this vein, Charles W. Mills criticizes mainstream political theory for mystifying the racist history of Europe by excluding the philosophical justifications of racism, colonialism, and slavery.[52] Instead, he suggests supplementing the standard narrative of political theory with the politics of the anti-colonial, anti-slavery, anti-imperialist, and anti-segregationalist struggles that were led by excluded others. Similarly, the writing of women's political thought in Europe should not solely reconstruct Enlightenment thought with regard to the category of gender, but also consider intersections with other forms of domination – to counter the narrative of the white male bourgeois disguising himself as the universal norm, and Europe as the 'silent referent'.[53] A promising approach would be the analysis of female slave narratives to unfold their normative premises and ideas of emancipation, and their juxtaposition with European women's emancipatory writing. This could provide a multifaceted picture of women's political thoughts in the plural and raise awareness for the relation of political agency, power, and speech.

[52] Mills, 'Kant's Untermenschen', pp. 169–93.

[53] D. Chakrabarty, *Provincializing Europe: Postcolonial Thought and Historical Difference* (Princeton, 2008).

Chapter 13
'Doing an Acceptable Service to my Country': Political Thought in Charlotte Brooke's *Reliques of Irish Poetry*

Lesa Ní Mhunghaile

The *Reliques of Irish Poetry* (1789) by Charlotte Brooke (1740–1793) was a groundbreaking work for a number of reasons.[1] Apart from the fact that it was undertaken by a woman in a world dominated by male scholarship, it was the first substantial anthology of Irish poetry translated into English, incorporating extensive scholarly apparatus and a commentary to each of the poems. Its seventeen verse translations – poems from the mythological cycles, up to more recent folksongs – were laid out in chronological order, with the Irish-language originals printed at the end of the book in the distinctive Irish character. The inclusion of folksongs provides an early example from Ireland of the awakened interest in popular culture by the upper classes that had been taking place throughout Europe from the middle of the century.[2] Drawing on Irish-language manuscript sources, Brooke sought to present authentic Gaelic texts, together with English translations, to an English-speaking public; her *Reliques* was therefore the first major point of intersection between oral tradition, the manuscript tradition, and print culture in Ireland.[3] It was informed by important contemporary antiquarian and historical debates on issues such as Celticism, Orientalism, Gothicism, primitivism, the progress of civilization, and the nature of oral tradition. It also engaged, albeit implicitly, with the controversy sparked by James Macpherson's so-called translations from Scottish Gaelic in *Fragments of Ancient Poetry* (1760), *Fingal* (1761/2), *Temora* (1763), through the inclusion of a number of

---

1 C. Brooke, *Reliques of Irish Poetry* (Dublin, 1789). For a new edition and comprehensive treatment of the work see L. Ní Mhunghaile, *Charlotte Brooke's Reliques of Irish Poetry* (Dublin, 2009).

2 For a discussion see P. Burke, *Popular Culture in Early Modern Europe*, rev. edn (Aldershot, 1994).

3 L. Ní Mhunghaile, 'The Intersection between Oral Tradition, Manuscript, and Print Cultures in C. Brooke, *Reliques of Irish Poetry* (1789)', in A. Carpenter and M. Cabal (eds), *Oral and Print Cultures in Ireland 1600–1900* (Dublin, 2010), pp. 14–31.

genuine Irish Ossianic lays. *Reliques* can therefore be read as an important Irish contribution to that controversy.[4]

The work also marked an important milestone in the appropriation of Gaelic culture by the Protestant Anglo-Irish Ascendancy – an elite group, to which Brooke belonged, whose ancestors were sixteenth- and seventeenth-century English settlers. They had once claimed distinction as 'the English in Ireland'; but by the beginning of the eighteenth century, the group had begun to redefine themselves. They increasingly identified more with their country of birth, and looked more favourably on the native Gael whom they no longer viewed as a credible threat to their elite status.[5] Many began not only to consider themselves Irish but also to regard Gaelic culture as their own, and this new-found interest in Gaelic antiquities was reflected in such pursuits as the collection and copying of ancient Irish-language manuscripts. Their closer affinity with Ireland and its native culture proved to be problematic, however, as Gaelic culture had been denigrated for centuries by English commentators. The Anglo-Irish community came to realize that the term 'barbarous Irish', once reserved for the native Gael, now applied to them also, and it became imperative for them to vindicate their adopted culture.[6] The *Reliques* was an attempt by Brooke to mediate the Gaelic world to members of this class, as well as to English readers, by portraying its culture in a sympathetic manner and making a case for its value.

Reliques provided a suitable vehicle for Brooke to assert both her Anglo-Irish identity and her credentials as a serious scholar; and it should also be considered in the context of women's increasing interest in political and social affairs. Commenting on writing by Irish women during this period, Siobhán Kilfeather has observed that the dominant theme is 'the tension between feeling included and feeling excluded by society. Sometimes that tension is dramatized as part of the female condition, sometimes it is about being Irish, sometimes it is both.'[7] While female authors were still a rarity, a precedent had been set earlier in the century by the publication of Sarah Butler's *Irish Tales; or Instructive Histories for the Happy Conduct of Life* (1716), the earliest example of Anglophone fiction featuring an

---

4 For a discussion of the Irish reaction to the controversy generated by Macpherson's publications see C. O'Halloran, *Golden Ages and Barbarous Nations* (Cork, 2004); M. Mac Craith, '"We Know all these Poems": The Irish Response to Ossian', in H. Gaskill (ed.), *The Reception of Ossian in Europe* (London, 2004), pp. 91–108.

5 For a discussion of Anglo-Irish identity see C. Kidd, *British Identities before Nationalism: Ethnicity and Nationhood in the Atlantic World, 1600–1800* (Cambridge, 1999), pp. 146–81; L. Ní Mhunghaile, 'Anglo-Irish Antiquarianism and the Transformation of Irish Identity, 1750–1800', in D.A. Valone and J.M. Bradbury (eds), *Anglo-Irish Identities, 1571–1845* (Lewisburg, PA, 2008), pp. 181–98.

6 For a discussion see J. Leerssen, *Mere Irish and Fíor-Ghael* (Cork, 1996), pp. 254–376.

7 S. Kilfeather, 'The Profession of Letters, 1700–1810', in A. Bourke et al., *Field Day Anthology of Irish Writing: Irish Women's Writing and Traditions* vol. 5 (Cork, 2002), p. 774.

episode from early Irish history: Gaelic Irish resistance to Viking invasions.[8] Butler's work displays Jacobite sympathies that are alien to Brooke's outlook; but the preface to *Reliques* is prefigured in Butler's defence of early Gaelic culture and sources, and in its refutation of alleged native Irish barbarity:

> Some (upon what Grounds I know not) would needs have their manner and way of making Love, which I have brought as near as I could to our modern Phrase, to be too Passionate and Elegant for the *Irish*, and contrary to the Humours, they alledge, of so Rude and Illiterate a People; when all the while they do not consider, that altho' they may seem so now, in the Circumstances they lie under, (having born the heavy Yoke of Bondage for so many Years, and have been Cow'd down in their Spirits) yet that once *Ireland* was esteem'd one of the Principal Nations in Europe for Piety and Learning.[9]

Brooke's defence of Gaelic culture was also foreshadowed in a plea by Lady Lucan (Margaret Bingham) for compassion on the part of the English administration in their dealings with Ireland, in *Verses on the Present State of Ireland* (1768):

> The writer of the following verses, owes many obligations to the country, which is the subject of them; she has a long time lamented the unhappy situation of the people of Ireland, both as to trade and religion; and as a relief to her feelings, she wrote these lines. There now seems to be something in agitation with regard to Ireland, and she thinks that at this crisis, her hints may be of some use, and may raise compassion in the breast of power: to contribute her mite therefore to so important an end, she lets them go into the world with all their imperfections: hoping that her intentions will apologize for her verses. She, however, is aware of its being objected, that the subject she has undertaken, was not suited to a female pen: and her performance perhaps proves it; but she is willing to suffer every critical censure, provided any benefit accrues to the cause she endeavours to plead.[10]

Lucan's main grievances were against English legislation restricting Irish trade – and the Penal Laws, a series of acts introduced progressively from the 1690s that curtailed the rights of Catholics to property, education, the bearing of arms, and the practice of their religion.[11] She believed that the laws were detrimental to family structures, the maintenance of which was imperative for the State's existence.[12]

---

8 S. Butler, *Irish Tales: Or, Instructive Histories for the Happy Conduct of Life*, in I. Campbell Ross et al. (eds), *Early Irish Fiction, c. 1680–1820* (Dublin, 2010). See also Kilfeather, 'Profession of Letters', pp. 782–7. Nothing is known of Butler, and questions have been raised as to whether she ever existed.

9 Butler, *Irish Tales*, p. 39.

10 M. Bingham, *Verses on the Present State of Ireland* (Dublin, 1768), pp. iii–iv; see Kilfeather, 'Profession of Letters', pp. 806–8.

11 T.P. Power and K. Whelan (eds), *Endurance and Emergence: Catholics in Ireland in the Eighteenth Century* (Dublin, 1990); T. Bartlett, *The Fall and Rise of the Irish Nation: The Catholic Question, 1690–1830* (Dublin, 1992), pp. 17–29.

12 Kilfeather, 'Profession of Letters', p. 806.

Her comments are of particular interest because unlike Butler and Brooke she was English-born and had moved to Ireland on her marriage to Charles Bingham in 1760. Furthermore, the work was extensively annotated, indicating Lucan's concern to explicate Ireland to the English. This strategy was later successfully adopted by Brooke and by other women authors such as Maria Edgeworth.[13]

The preface to *Reliques*, in which Brooke presented her aims and theories on the art of translating, begins with a claim of unworthiness for the task in hand and a denial of both knowledge and authority. These were typical devices employed by eighteenth-century women authors moving into an area previously occupied by men, as a means of deflecting criticism for undertaking a 'male' role:[14]

> In a preface to a translation of Irish poetry, the reader will naturally expect to see the subject elucidated and enlarged upon, with the pen of learning and antiquity. I lament that the limited circle of my knowledge does not include the power of answering to so just an explanation.[15]

Brooke introduced herself as 'an unnecessary foil' to the names of the scholars Charles O'Conor, Sylvester O'Halloran, and Charles Vallancey, members of the Royal Irish Academy who had assisted her research.[16] By linking her name to those antiquarians, she proclaimed her political allegiance from the outset, signalling her adherence to the supporters of the Milesian/Phoenician theory of origin, as opposed to the Gothic theory. These were highly contentious paradigms of the ethnic origin of the ancient Gael that proved divisive within the world of late eighteenth-century Irish antiquarianism. On the one hand, the Milesian origin myth portrayed a highly civilized and literate Gaelic past that had gone into decline in the aftermath of the English invasion; on the other hand, the Gothic theory was promoted by those Protestants who wished to argue in favour of the civilizing influence of the English.[17] Later in the preface Brooke again invoked the stereotypical image of a weak subservient female, bowing to the superior genius of her father, the novelist, dramatist, and political pamphleteer Henry Brooke (1703–1783). She wonders in these terms, concerning the British muse and the Irish muse:

> Will they not rather depute some favoured pen, to chide me back to the shade whence I have allured, and where, perhaps, I ought to have remained, in respect to the memory, and superior genius of a Father – it avails not to say how dear! – But my feeble efforts presume not to emulate, – and they cannot injure his fame.[18]

---

[13] Ibid., p. 806.

[14] See J.N. Radner and S.S. Lanser, 'Strategies of Coding in Women's Cultures', in J. Newlon Radner (ed.), *Feminist Messages: Coding in Women's Folk Culture* (Urbana and Chicago, 1993), p. 22.

[15] Brooke, *Reliques*, p. 3.

[16] Ibid., p. 3.

[17] For a detailed discussion of these theories see O'Halloran, *Golden Ages and Barbarous Nations*.

[18] Brooke, *Reliques*, p. viii.

This was clearly a ploy, however, aimed at disarming her potential critics, because although she professed herself to be inadequate to the task, during the course of the work she proved herself to be very capable and demonstrated that she was able to speak with authority on the subject of Gaelic poetry. So much so, in fact, that eventually she is confident enough to contradict some of the opinions expressed by her friend Joseph Cooper Walker in his *Historical Memoirs of the Irish Bards*, published three years previously.[19] The image of Brooke progresses, therefore, from that of a weak female who plays down her competency to someone who can speak with authority on her subject, direct the reader on how to read the poems correctly, and make important observations on the political situation in the country, albeit often in an implicit manner.

Her primary aim was to offer examples of Gaelic poetry, both originals and translations, and defend Gaelic culture against accusations of barbarity: 'With a view to throw some light on the antiquities of this country, to vindicate, in part, its history, and prove its claim to scientific as well as to military fame'.[20] In doing so, her hope was to awaken 'a just and useful curiosity, on the subject of our poetical compositions'.[21] She, like many native scribes and scholars, realized that the literary tradition was in danger of extinction; she endeavoured, therefore, to provide what she believed to be 'a service' to her country: 'I trust I am doing an acceptable service to my country, while I endeavour to rescue from oblivion a few of the invaluable reliques of her ancient genius.'[22] She hoped that by doing so she could demonstrate to her countrymen 'the lustre reflected on them by ancestors so very different from what modern prejudice has been studious to represent them'.[23] Brooke wished to counter the arguments of modern writers whom she termed 'anti-Hibernian', who represent 'our early ancestors' as 'barbarians, descended from barbarians, and ever continuing the same' by pointing to the Phoenician origin of the Gael, by vindicating Gaelic civility and by asserting the value of Irish antiquities.[24] *Reliques* was an attempt, therefore, to restore some honour to the Irish, both native and non-native:

> The productions of our Irish Bards exhibit a glow of cultivated genius, – a spirit of elevated heroism, – sentiments of pure honour, – instances of disinterested patriotism, – and manners of a degree of refinement, totally astonishing, at a period when the rest of Europe was nearly sunk in barbarism: And is not all this very honorable to our countrymen?[25]

[19] J.C. Walker, *Historical Memoirs of the Irish Bards* (Dublin, 1786); L. Davis, 'Birth of the Nation: Gender and Writing in the Work of Henry and Charlotte Brooke', *Eighteenth-Century Life*, 18:1 (Feb., 1994): p. 37.

[20] Brooke, *Reliques*, p. v.

[21] Ibid., p. v.

[22] Ibid., p. vii.

[23] Ibid., p. vii.

[24] Ibid., p. 27.

[25] Ibid., p. vii.

The work may also be seen as rejecting a certain emphasis on the inevitability of civil degeneracy – resulting from intermarriage between the Old-English (Anglo-Norman families that had settled in Ireland before the English Reformation) and the native Irish – by the English commentators Edmund Spenser (*A View of the Present State of Ireland*, 1596) and Sir John Davies (*A Discovery of the true Causes why Ireland was never entirely subdued*, 1612). It was, therefore, an endorsement of the contrary view expounded by Catholic Counter-Reformation historians such as Geoffrey Keating in the seventeenth century.[26] Brooke, like Keating, assured her readers that there was no shame in the fact that Gaelic and English blood had mixed in the veins of the Anglo-Irish and argued instead that it was enriching: 'Let them tell her, that the portion of her blood which flows in our veins is rather ennobled than disgraced by the mingling tides that descend from our heroic ancestors.'[27] The Catholic scholar Sylvester O'Halloran had made a similar comment in the preface to *An Introduction to the Study of the History and Antiquities of Ireland* seventeen years earlier:

> For, though unhappily for this antient kingdom, *unnatural* distinctions have but too long been kept up by artful and designing enemies, to the almost entire ruin of the whole; yet are we in fact, but *one* people, and as unmixt a race as any in Europe. There is not at this day a Milesian, or descendant of Strongbow, whose bloods are not so intimately blended, that it would be impossible to determine which should preponderate.[28]

Brooke clearly viewed her role as that of mediator between Ireland and England, and aspired to bringing about mutual respect and understanding between the Irish, the Anglo-Irish, and 'our noble neighbour Britain'. She believed that her publication of *Reliques* would assist these efforts: 'Were we better acquainted, we should be better friends. The British muse is not yet informed that she has an elder sister in this isle; let us then introduce them to each other!'[29] Having thereby implied the seniority and superiority of Irish culture, Brooke continues ambiguously: 'Together let them walk abroad from their bowers, sweet ambassadresses of cordial union between two countries that seem formed by nature to be joined by every bond of interest, and of amity.'[30] Although she called for a union between both countries, she clearly did not view the union as equal, since the British muse was younger. Her employment of the familial trope here is significant. During the eighteenth century some Anglo-Irish considered their relationship with England to be one of equality, likening both countries to 'sister' or indeed 'brother' kingdoms,

---

26 Ibid., p. viii. For a discussion of Keating's history of Ireland, Foras Feasa ar Éirinn, see B. Cunningham, *The World of Geoffrey Keating: History, Myth and Religion in Seventeenth-Century Ireland* (Dublin, 2000).

27 Brooke, *Reliques*, p. viii.

28 S. O'Halloran, *An Introduction to the Study of the History and Antiquities of Ireland* (Dublin, 1772), p. i.

29 Brooke, *Reliques*, p. vii.

30 Ibid., pp. vii–viii.

as for example William Molyneux in his pamphlet *The Case of Ireland's being bound* (1698, reprinted in 1720). Some English commentators, for their part, viewed the relationship as equal, though they employed a child-parent paradigm instead in their depiction of it, with Ireland being the child colony and England the mother country. Thomas Bartlett has noted that while they conceded 'elder sister' or 'elder brother' status to England, the Anglo-Irish could 'rarely be brought to admit the validity of the mother-child metaphor' as the notion of Ireland being the child-colony bore the implication that it would eventually grow up and seek independence.[31] It also implied that the Anglo-Irish were colonists, a label they did not wish to carry as they considered Ireland their home.[32] In the aftermath of the 1801 Act of Union between Britain and Ireland, which brought legislative union, the familial trope also formed an important element in the writing on Ireland by women such as Lady Morgan (Sydney Owenson) and Maria Edgeworth, who depicted the relationship between the two countries as a marital union in their respective works: *The Wild Irish Girl* (1808) and *The Absentee* (1812).[33]

Political commentary also forms an important element in the detailed textual notes to the translations in the main body of the work. What is particularly striking, however, is the fact that in a number of cases the English renditions are completely at odds with their Gaelic equivalents and contain ideas that are not present in the original poems. In fact, in some instances Brooke included complete verses of her own invention. An examination of this extraneous material points to a very definite political agenda for its inclusion in the volume as it can be read in terms of commentary on the contemporary political situation. In her translation to the poem 'Ode to Gaul, the son of Morni' ('Rosg Ghoill') for example, the emphasis placed on the maritime theme is striking.[34] In the original Gaelic, the poem belongs with the mythological tales known as the Fionn Cycle, which recount the exploits of the third century warrior Fionn mac Cumhail and his band of warriors known as the Fianna. Goll mac Morna, the leader of the Connacht branch of the Fianna, was a rival of Fionn; and the poem is an exhortation to combat spoken to him at the battle of Ventry.[35] The maritime theme does not feature in the original Gaelic, however,

---

[31] T. Bartlett, '"A People Made Rather for Copies than Originals": The Anglo-Irish, 1760–1800', *International History Review*, 12:1 (1990): pp. 11–25; T. Bartlett, 'Ireland, Empire, and Union, 1690–1801', in K. Kenny (ed.), *Ireland and the British Empire* (Oxford, 2004), pp. 61–89.

[32] Bartlett, *Fall and Rise of the Irish Nation*, pp. 36–7.

[33] J.A. Miller, 'Acts of Union: Family Violence and National Courtship in Maria Edgeworth's *The Absentee* and Sydney Owenson's *The Wild Irish Girl*', in K. Kirkpatrick (ed.), *Border Crossing: Irish Women Writers and National Identities* (Tuscaloosa and London, 2000), pp. 13–37.

[34] For a more detailed discussion see also Ní Mhunghaile, *Brooke's Reliques*, pp. 73–82.

[35] For the Fionn Cycle in Gaelic mythology see D. Ó Hogáin, *Myth, Legend, and Romance: An Encyclopedia of the Irish Folk Tradition* (New York, 1991), pp. 203–8, 213–23, 246–7.

and the only reference to such matters is where Goll is compared to a strong ocean wave and said to be stronger than a wave. Brooke took liberties with the translation and expanded this theme a number of times. Therefore, lines such as 'Champion of the navy's pride' and 'Mighty ruler of the tide! / Rider of the stormy wave / Hostile nations to enslave!' are Brooke's own invention. Her motive for manipulating the original becomes evident when these lines are read in conjunction with stanza 6, for which there is also no corresponding Gaelic stanza, and when account is taken of her inclusion in a footnote of Sylvester O'Halloran's assertion in *Introduction to the Study of the History and Antiquities of Ireland* that the ancient Irish had kept a considerable naval force with which 'they poured troops into Britain and Gaul, which countries they long kept under contribution':[36]

> Did all the hosts of all the earth unite,
> From pole to pole, from wave to wave,
> Exulting in their might:
> His is that monarch of soul
> To fit him for the wide controul,
> The empire of the brave![37]

The references to 'empire' and 'controul', when placed in the context of the reference in the preface to Ireland and England as 'sisters', and by implication sister kingdoms, suggests that this poem should be read in terms of contemporary discussions regarding Ireland's relationship with Britain. Through the medium of this poem, Brooke both rehearsed the Protestant ruling elite's claim to equal status with Britain and contributed to the contemporary discourse of Ireland's place within the British Empire. By emphasizing the naval power of the ancient Irish, Brooke asserted Ireland's right to play a full role within the Empire. To further support her claim, she drew attention to ancient Irish knowledge of maritime matters; and she added that there were between forty and fifty words in the Irish language for the English word 'ship'.[38] She employed the ode for her translation, mirroring poets in Britain who used this form when contributing to the civic discourse of the nation.[39] The genre therefore provided Brooke with an appropriate forum in which to contribute to this discourse. Poems such as Edward Young's 'Ocean: An Ode, Occasioned by His Majesty's Royal Encouragement of the Sea Service' (1728) and 'Imperium Pelagi: A Naval Lyric' (1730), celebrated contemporary Britain's imperial power and commercial might and asserted its imperial ambitions.[40]

---

36 Brooke, *Reliques*, p. 165; O'Halloran, *Introduction to the Study of the History and Antiquities of Ireland*, p. 125.

37 Brooke, *Reliques*, pp. 167–8.

38 Ibid., p. 166n.

39 S. Kaul, *Poems of Nation, Anthems of Empire: English Verse in the Long Eighteenth Century* (Charlottesville and London, 2000), p. 5.

40 M.M. Koehler, 'The Ode', in C. Gerrard (ed.), *A Companion to Eighteenth-Century Poetry* (Oxford, 2006), p. 400.

Brooke's English rendition of *Rosg Ghoill*, with its discussion of imperial power in the line 'Hostile nations to enslave!', may be read as complementary to odes such as James Thomson's jingoistic 'Rule, Britannia!' (1740), with its vehement declaration that 'Britons never will be slaves'.[41]

A further concern in the paratextual remarks on the translation is a repetition of Brooke's claims regarding the civility and learning of the ancient Irish – a recurring theme throughout the work. The barbarity associated with the ancient Irish is brought to the fore again in a note challenging their negative stereotyping, and making obvious reference to the English traveller and author Fynes Moryson's *Itinerary of Ireland* (1617):

> The ideas which these passages convey, are rather inconsistent with the disgusting ones that must be conceived of the early Irish, by those who give credit to the accounts of writers who tell us, *they wore shirts dyed in saffron, for the convenience of hiding the dirt*, and further add, that *they never pulled them off until fairly worn out*.[42]

She refuted these assertions, and argued further that the Irish were 'so *remarkably cleanly*, as never to rest from fatigue, or sit down to meat, after exercise, until they had first refreshed and cleansed themselves by ablutions'. There is a distinct patriotic tone to Brooke's translation of this poem, which serves further to illustrate her comment later in the work that 'the heroic poetry of our countrymen was designed for the noblest purposes; – love indeed was still its object, – but it was the sublime love of country that those compositions inspired.'[43] In this instance, the faithfulness of the target text to its source text took second place to Brooke's attempts to instil national pride in her readers, to refute negative stereotypes of the Irish, and to assert Ireland's right to equal status with Britain within the British Empire.[44]

The patriotic theme is taken a step further at the end of the volume, where Brooke included a long poem of her own composition entitled 'Mäon: An Irish Tale'.[45] It is presented within the framework of the dream vision genre in which the fourth-century bard Craiftne appears to the poetess in a dream and relates the love story of Mäon and Moriat. Dream vision poems known as *aislingí*, in which Ireland was personified as a beautiful woman who appeared to the male poet in a dream, were popular in eighteenth-century Gaelic poetry composed in Munster. They were employed effectively as a vehicle for political propaganda in support of

---

[41] For a discussion of the emergence of a British identity and its links to an expanding overseas empire see L. Colley, *Britons: Forging the Nation, 1707–1837* (New Haven, 1992).

[42] Brooke, *Reliques*, p. 171n.

[43] Ibid., p. 171n.

[44] For an assessment of patriotism in eighteenth-century Ireland see S. Small, 'The Twisted Roots of Irish Patriotism: Anglo-Irish Political Thought in the Late-Eighteenth Century', in Éire-Ireland, 35:3–4 (2000–2001): pp. 187–216.

[45] See also Ní Mhunghaile, *Brooke's Reliques*, pp. 156–63.

the Jacobite cause.[46] It is particularly striking that Brooke should employ this genre since this was the first instance in the *Reliques* where she indicated familiarity with it. Her framework constituted a complete inversion of the Gaelic *aisling*, however, as it was a male muse in the guise of Craiftne who appeared to the female poet.

The poem deals with a number of the themes that are central to the *Reliques*, such as her argument in favour of the antiquity of Gaelic learning and the respect in which the ancient Gael held the bard, and thus learning. Furthermore, her comment in the preface on the relationship between the Irish and British muses, where she had presented both countries as sisters, is echoed in the following lines: 'But, to the eye of Britain's Muse, / Present a sister's charms.'[47] The poem is based on the prose tale that tells the love story of Mäon and Moriat, related in Geoffrey Keating's *Foras Feasa ar Éirinn* (Compendium of wisdom about Ireland). This was a major seventeenth-century historical work that circulated in manuscript form, in the Irish language and also in English and Latin translation. Brooke made some alterations to Keating's version of the story. The young Mäon was forced into exile after his father, the king, was usurped by his own brother. He first fled to Kerry in the south-west of the country where he met the young woman Moriat, whose father provided him with refuge; but he later left Ireland for France, where he joined the king's army. While there he became betrothed to the king's daughter, princess Aide. Moriat sent the harper Craiftne to France to sing a song she had composed, reminding Mäon of his duty to avenge his father's and grandfather's deaths. He eventually returned to Ireland and, with the help of the French army, regained possession of the throne and married Moriat.

The poem's central theme concerns the role of the patriot and the expression of patriotic sentiment by women through the act of writing. Charlotte may have been inspired to give prominence to this theme by the way Joseph Cooper Walker began his account of the story in his *Historical Memoirs of the Irish Bards*, with the statement that 'a great revolution was occasioned in Ireland by the united powers of female poesy and music'.[48] In effect, he attributed the ability to influence the nation's destiny to women. Brooke seized the opportunity offered by Walker's statement to explore the theme, arguing that through Moriat's intervention – the writing of a song – the rightful king was restored to the throne. She also used this poem to examine her own role as a patriot, arguing that patriotic expression was not exclusively a male activity: 'And patriot fire, a female breast, / May sure unquestion'd warm.'[49] Expanding this argument further, she suggested that women could legitimately engage in an activity that had hitherto been considered

---

[46] The dream vision genre had been firmly established in Irish literature since the eighth century, when the sovereignty of Ireland was portrayed as a beautiful woman married to the rightful king. See S. Ó Tuama, *Repossessions: Selected Essays on the Irish Literary Heritage* (Cork, 1995), p. 107.

[47] Brooke's *Reliques*, p. 327.

[48] Walker, *Historical Memoirs*, p. 33.

[49] Brooke, *Reliques*, p. 327.

exclusively in the male domain, namely literary endeavour: 'For oft the Muse, a gentle guest, / Dwells in a female form.'[50] Aware that such a comment would draw criticism, she emphasized that the poetess should not allow herself to become discouraged by the critics:

Let not the frown of critic wrath,
Or smile of critic scorn,
Affright thee from the splendid path,
Fame and the Muse adorn.[51]

Significantly, we see a stronger voice emerge here than in the preface. Her voice in this poem is decidedly assertive and self-confident; she appears assured of her right to participate in the male-dominated literary world, where she could contribute in her own right to the discourse of patriotism. This is in stark contrast to her modest claims in the preface that she played only a supporting role to the patriotic endeavours of Charles O'Conor, Sylvester O'Halloran, and Charles Vallancey. This theme is revisited in 'Mäon' where the poetess asks of the bard Craiftne what contribution she could make to the glory of her country: 'What favours can her hand bestow, / That were not theirs before?'[52] It is clear from Craiftne's reply that the very act of collecting Gaelic reliques or 'pride of ancient days' was a patriotic act; and that by compiling the *Reliques*, Brooke had moved from her supporting role to becoming one of those 'champions':

Bear them the pride of ancient days;
Truth, science, virtue, fame;
The lover's faith, the poet's praise,
The patriotic flame![53]

Furthermore, the poetess was reminded that it was her duty to make the literary heritage of Ireland known to her neighbouring isle or 'sister Muse', and thereby obtain its esteem:

No more thy glorious task refuse,
Nor shrink from fancy'd harms,
But, to the eye of Britain's Muse,
Present a sister's charms.[54]

The following stanza could be read as a metaphor for the relationship between Ireland and Britain, as it brings to mind Brooke's call in the preface for conciliation and mutual respect between the two countries:

---

50 Ibid., p. 327.
51 Ibid., p. 326.
52 Ibid., p. 329.
53 Ibid., p. 329.
54 Ibid., p. 327.

'Rivals no more, we then shall meet;
'In air's bright chariots move;
'And joyful join in union sweet,
'And everlasting love.[55]

When placed in the context of the impending 1801 Act of Union between Ireland and Britain, the reference to 'union sweet' becomes even more significant; it appears to be an argument in favour of some sort of union between both countries as being the only viable solution. The poem ends with further commentary on the nature of patriotism, and the honour that is bestowed upon the patriot by 'grateful nations':

Conceive the Patriot's glowing breast
Whom grateful nations crown!
With virtue, love and empire blest,
And honor's clear renown.[56]

It is also significant that the restoration of the rightful king, in this case Mäon, was the outcome of Brooke's poem, whereas in Gaelic Jacobite poetry it remained only an aspiration, supporting the claims of the Stuarts to the English throne. This theme, which emphasized lineage as a determining factor in the legitimacy of a ruler, was commonly found in European chivalrous romances where status was believed to be 'ascribed rather than achieved' and where 'personal qualities [were] inherited rather than learned'.[57] Emphasis on descent and the validation of lineage were also key concerns of Irish bardic poetry due to the aristocratic nature of Gaelic society. The story of Mäon fits neatly into this framework: he was the rightful king by virtue of his blood, and he eventually triumphed over adversity as a result of his own bravery and military skill. Brooke's reason for including this tale in her collection could be interpreted in two ways. First, when read in the context of the contemporary situation in Ireland, which saw parliamentary debates on the question of landownership during the 1780s and 1790s, it might be viewed as potentially subversive because its central theme could be used in support of the cause of the dispossessed, some of whom were of a higher social rank than many of the newcomers who had taken possession of their land. Second, it might have been a warning by Brooke to members of her elite class, pointing out the potential consequences if they failed to heed her call for conciliation between the two communities in Ireland.

It is noteworthy that women are arguably the strongest characters in Brooke's poem. The French Princess, Aide, demonstrates strength of character in her release of Mäon from his betrothal to her; and as Leith Davis has argued, Moriat is the

55 Ibid., p. 365.

56 Ibid., p. 369.

57 N. Ó Ciosáin, *Print and Popular Culture in Ireland, 1750–1850* (Basingstoke, 1997), p. 170.

true patriot in the poem because as a direct result of the song she composed, Mäon succeeded in regaining the kingdom that was rightfully his.[58] Furthermore, Moriat was willing to sacrifice her love for Mäon in order to ensure French military assistance, something she perceived to be her duty:

> 'For me, on duty I rely
>   'My firm support to prove,
> 'And Erin shall the room supply
>   'Of Mäon and of Love.[59]

This echoes the theme of personal desire and public duty: a popular literary convention in fiction of that time, and found in Sarah Butler's *Irish Tales*.[60] Clearly then, the image of women presented in 'Mäon' is completely at odds with how Brooke portrayed herself in the preface as someone who had a 'limited circle [of] knowledge': a 'feeble' hand, in the shadow of her father. As the author of 'Mäon', she stepped out from that shadow and presented herself as strong, confident, and highly capable.

Charlotte Brooke's *Reliques* was a testament to the enthusiasm for Gaelic antiquities that prevailed among a core group of Irish Protestant antiquarians for a brief period during the 1780s – one that witnessed the finding of common ground between Protestant and Catholic scholars in their efforts to vindicate and explicate Gaelic culture. She herself was exceptional in that she was a female antiquary in a predominantly male domain. The *Reliques* succeeded in portraying Gaelic Ireland's literary heritage in a sympathetic light, and left a lasting legacy: one that would inspire other scholars to seek out Gaelic material for translation and ultimately result in its preservation. Crucially, her own composition, 'Mäon', dealt with ideas of status and the legitimacy of a ruler, issues that had ramifications in eighteenth-century Ireland. Furthermore, it introduced a stronger, more confident author than was apparent in the preface, one who was willing to tackle the thorny issue of the right of women to play their part in the public sphere and insist on her own right to be considered a patriot alongside her fellow antiquarians Charles O'Conor, Joseph Cooper Walker, and Charles Vallancey. Nevertheless, commenting on the political implications of antiquarian investigations such as Brooke's, Gregory Schirmer makes the significant point that:

> Probably unthinkable to Charlotte Brooke, the revitalization and authentication of Ireland's Gaelic culture leads directly to the marginalization of Brooke's class, and ultimately to a separatist politics and the reversal of the political and cultural hierarchies that governed eighteenth-century Irish life.[61]

---

[58] L. Davis, *Music, Postcolonialism, and Gender: The Construction of Irish National Identity, 1724–1874* (Notre Dame, 2006), p. 89.

[59] Brooke, *Reliques*, p. 362.

[60] Butler, *Irish Tales*, p. 23.

[61] G.A. Schirmer, *Out of What Began: A History of Irish Poetry in English* (Ithaca, NY, 1998), pp. 65–6.

Indeed, it may be said that in the aftermath of the 1798 Rebellion the study of Irish antiquities became suspect and was avoided by many Protestant antiquarians who did not wish to risk being equated with those sympathetic to the goals of the United Irishmen, who had sought to establish an independent Irish republic. It is ironic that those Anglo-Irish antiquarians who had led the way in the late eighteenth century into investigations pertaining to the Gaelic literary heritage played a significant role in the ultimate reversal of fortune of their class. *Reliques* was a landmark publication; and undoubtedly Charlotte Brooke succeeded in her aim of 'doing an acceptable service to her country'.

Bibliography

Abensour, L., *La Femme et le féminisme avant la Révolution* (Paris: Leroux, 1923).

Abray, J., 'Feminism in the French Revolution', *The American Historical Review*, 80:1 (1975): 43–62.

Aelders, E.P. de, 'Discours de réception prononcé à la société fraternelle par Etta Palm, née d'Aelders le 12 juin 1791, et justification sur la dénonciation de Louise Robert', in d'Aelders, *Appel aux françoises*, pp. 31–36.

Aelders E.P. de, *Réflexions sur diverses questions politiques* [Dutch language], in Papiers d'Elisa Lubina Johanna, baronne d'Aelders, épouse de Chrétien Ferdinand Louis Palin [*sic*] (French National Archives [Archives Nationales]: AN T 364).

Aelders, E.P. de, *Réflexions sur l'ouvrage intitulé Aux Bataves sur le stadhoudérat, par le comte de Mirabeau* (Paris, 1788).

Aelders, E.P. de, *Appel aux françoises sur la régénération des mœurs, et la nécessité de l'influence des femmes dans un gouvernement libre* (Paris: Imprimerie du Cercle Social, 1791).

Agamben, G., *Homo sacer: Sovereign Power and Bare Life* (Stanford: Stanford University Press, 1998).

Agoult, M. de, *Mémoires, souvenirs et journaux de la comtesse d'Agoult*, ed. C.F. Dupêchez (Paris: Mercure de France, 1990).

Aiken, J., and A.L. Aiken [Barbauld], *Miscellaneous Pieces in Prose* (London: J. Johnson, 1773).

Allison, H.E., 'Kant on Freedom of the Will', in P. Guyer (ed.), *The Cambridge Companion to Kant and Modern Philosophy* (Cambridge and New York: Cambridge University Press, 2006), pp. 381–415.

Ancelot, V., *Un Salon de Paris, 1824 à 1864* (Paris: E. Dentu, 1866).

Angeto, M. *Les Champions des femmes* (Quebec, 1977).

Applewhite, B., and Levy, D.G., *Women and Politics in the Age of the Democratic Revolution* (Ann Arbor: University of Michigan Press, 1993).

Arboit, G. ' "Souvent femme varie": Une espionne hollandaise à Paris', *Notes historiques*, 12 (March 2008), at http://www.cf2r.org/fr/notes-historiques/souvent-femme-varie-une-espionne-hollandaise-paris.php.

Archives parlementaires de 1787 à 1860 (Paris: Librairie administrative de Paul Dupont).

Arendt, H., *On Revolution* (New York: Penguin, 2006).

Artaize, F. de, *Réflexions d'un jeune homme* (Paris: Royez, 1786).

Artaize, F. de, *Lettre à Mme Gacon-Dufour* (Paris: 'chez tous les marchands de nouveauté', 1788).

Ashfield, A., *Romantic Women Poets: An Anthology* (Manchester: Manchester University Press, 1998).

Astell, M., *Political Writings*, ed. P. Springborg (Cambridge: Cambridge University Press, 1996).

Astell, M., 'Some Reflections upon Marriage' (3rd edn, 1706), in *Astell: Political Writings*, ed. P. Springborg (Cambridge: Cambridge University Press, 1996), pp. 7–80.

Aubert, F., *Sylvain Maréchal: Passion et faillite d'un égalitaire* (Pisa: Goliardica, 1975).

Barash, C., '"The Native Liberty ... Of the Subject": Configurations of Gender and Authority in the Works of Mary Chudleigh, Sarah Fyge Egerton, and Mary Astell', in I. Grundy and S. Wiseman (eds), *Women, Writing, History: 1640–1740* (London: B.T. Batsford, 1992), pp. 55–69.

Barbauld, A.L., *Poems* (London: J. Johnson, 1773).

Barbauld, A.L., *Address to the Opposers of the Corporation and Test Acts* (London: J. Johnson, 1790).

Barbauld, A.L. *The Works of Anna Laetitia Barbauld* (2 vols, London: Routledge/ Thoemmes, 1996).

Bardoux, A., *La Duchesse de Duras* (Paris: Calmann-Lévy, 1898).

Bartlett, T., '"A People Made Rather for Copies than Originals": The Anglo-Irish, 1760–1800', *International History Review*, 12:1 (1990): 11–25.

Bartlett, T., *The Fall and Rise of the Irish Nation: The Catholic Question, 1690–1830* (Dublin: Gill and Macmillan, 1992).

Bartlett, T., 'Ireland, Empire, and Union, 1690–1801', in K. Kenny (ed.), *Ireland and the British Empire* (Oxford: Oxford University Press, 2004), pp. 61–89.

Bassanville, A. de, *Salons d'autrefois: Souvenirs intimes* (4 vols, Paris, 1853).

Beasley, F.E. *Salons, History, and the Creation of Seventeenth-Century France: Mastering Memory* (Farnham and Burlington, VT: Ashgate, 2006).

Beaumont, J.-M.L. de, *Il magazzino delle fanciulle, ovvero dialoghi tra una savia direttrice e parecchie sue allieve di grado illustre* (4 vols, Vicenza: Francesco Vendramini Mosca, 1774).

Beaumont, J.-M.L. de, *Il magazzino delle adulte, ovvero dialoghi tra una savia direttrice e parecchie sue allieve di grado illustre che serve di continuazione al Magazzino delle fanciulle* (4 vols, Vicenza: Francesco Vendramini Mosca, 1781).

Beaumont, J.-M.L. de, *Istruzioni per le giovani dame ch'entrano nel mondo, e si maritano, loro doveri in questo stato, e verso i loro figliuoli, per servire di continuazione e di compimento al Magazzino delle fanciulle e a quello delle adulte* (4 vols, Vicenza: Francesco Vendramini Mosca, 1782).

Beauvoir, S. de, *The Second Sex*, trans. H.M. Parshley (New York: Vintage, 1989).

Beckstrand, L., *Deviant Women of the French Revolution and the Rise of Feminism* (Cranbury, NJ: Associated University Press, 2009).

Behn, A., *Oroonoko: Or the Royal Slave: A True History* (1688; London: Penguin, 2003).

Belot, O., *Réflexions d'une provinciale sur le discours de Monsieur Rousseau, citoyen de Genève, touchant l'origine de l'inégalité des conditions parmi les hommes* (London, 1756).

Belot, O., *Observations sur la noblesse et le tiers-état* ('Amsterdam' [Rouen]: Arkstée and Merkus, 1758).

Belot, O., *Mélanges de littérature angloise, traduits par Madame B**** (2 parts in 1 vol., La Haye [Paris: Prault], 1759).

Belot, O., *Histoire de Rasselas, prince d'Abyssinie, par M. Jhonnson* [*sic*] *et traduite de l'anglois par Mme B**** (Amsterdam [Paris: Prault], 1760).

Belot, O., *Histoire de la maison de Tudor sur le trône d'Angleterre. Traduite de l'anglois* (2 vols, 'Amsterdam' [Paris: Desaint and Saillant], 1763).

Belot, O., *Ophélie, roman traduit de l'anglois par M. B**** (2 vols, 'Amsterdam': 1763).

Belot, O., *Histoire de la maison de Plantagenet sur le trône d'Angleterre depuis l'invasion de Jules César jusqu'à l'avènement de Henri VI, par M. Hume. Traduite de l'anglois par madame B***** (2 vols, 'Amsterdam', 1765).

Berlanstein, L.R., 'Women and Power in Eighteenth-Century France: Actresses at the Comédie Française', in C. Adams, J.B. Censer, and L.J. Graham (eds), *Visions and Revisions of Eighteenth-Century France* (University Park, PA: Pennsylvania State University Press, 1997).

Bibliothèque Nationale de Paris, LN-27–8120.

Bingham, M. [Lady Lucan], *Verses on the Present State of Ireland* (Dublin: Wogan, Bean and Pike, 1768).

Blackburne, F., *Memoirs of Thomas Hollis, Esq. F.R. and A.S.S.* (London, 1780).

Blanc, O., *Les Libertines: Plaisir et liberté au temps des Lumières* (Paris: Perrin, 1997).

Bloch, J., 'The Eighteenth Century: Women Writing, Women Learning', in Sonya Stephens (ed.) *A History of Women's Writing in France* (Cambridge: Cambridge University Press, 2000), pp. 84–101.

Bluche, F., *Les Magistrats du parlement de Paris au XVIIIe siècle (1715–1771)* (Besançon: Imprimerie Jacques et Demontrand, 1960).

Blum, C., *Rousseau and the Republic of Virtue: The Language of Politics in the French Revolution* (Ithaca, NY: Cornell University Press, 1986).

Boigne, C. de, *Mémoires de la comtesse de Boigne, née d'Osmond: Récits d'une tante*, ed. Jean-Claude Berchet (2 vols, Paris, 1986).

Bordeaux, P., *La Médaille d'honneur offerte par la Municipalité de Creil à Madame Palm Dalder, en février 1791* (Beauvais: Imprimerie départementale de l'Oise, 1908).

Boswell, J., *An Account of Corsica, the Journal of a Tour to that Island; and Memoirs of Pascal Paoli*, 2nd edn (London: Edward and Charles Dilly, 1768).

Boswell, J., to W. Temple, 24 March 1768, in T. Crawford (ed.) *The Correspondence of James Boswell and William Johnson Temple: 1756–1777* (Edinburgh: Edinburgh University Press, 1997).

Boudon, J.-O., *Napoléon et les cultes: Les religions en Europe à l'aube du XIXe siècle, 1800–1815* (Paris: Fayard, 2002).

Brady, F., and Pottle, F.A. (eds), *Boswell in Search of a Wife* (New York: McGraw-Hill, 1956).

Brancourt, J.-P., 'Un théoricien de la société au XVIIIe siècle: Le chevalier d'Arcq', *Revue historique*, 250 (1973): 337–62.

Brandt Bolton, M., 'Some Aspects of the Philosophy of Catharine Trotter', *Journal of the History of Philosophy*, 31:4 (1993): 565–88.

Brennan, T., and C. Pateman, ' "Mere Auxiliaries to the Commonwealth": Women and the Origins of Liberalism', *Political Studies*, 27:2 (1979): 183–200.

Broad, J., *Women Philosophers of the Seventeenth Century* (Cambridge: Cambridge University Press, 2002).

Broad, J., and K. Green, *A History of Women's Political Thought in Europe, 1400–1700* (Cambridge: Cambridge University Press, 2009).

Broeck, S., 'Enslavement as Regime of Western Modernity: Re-reading Gender Studies Epistemology through Black Feminist Critique', *Gender Forum: An Internet Journal for Gender Studies*, 22 (2008): 1–4.

Brooke, C., *Reliques of Irish Poetry* (Dublin: George Bonham, 1789).

Brown, A., and U. Kölving, 'A la recherche des livres d'Emilie Du Châtelet', in U. Kölving and O. Courcelle (eds), *Emilie Du Châtelet: Eclairages et documents nouveaux* (Ferney-Voltaire: Centre International d'Etude du XVIIIe Siècle, 2008), pp. 111–120.

Brown, C.L., *Moral Capital: Foundations of British Abolitionism* (Chapel Hill: University of North Carolina Press, 2006).

Buchez, P.-J.-B., and P.C. Roux, *Histoire Parlementaire de la Révolution française* (Paris: Paulin, 1834).

Buell Hale, Sarah, *Woman's Record: Or, Sketches of all Distinguished Women, from the Creation to A.D. 1868* (New York: Harper, 1874).

Burke, E., *Thoughts on the Cause of the Present Discontents*, 4th edn (London: J. Dodsley, 1770).

Burke, E., *Reflections on the Revolution in France* (1790), ed. J.G.A. Pocock (Indianapolis and Cambridge: Hackett Publishing Company, 1987).

Burke, E., *Reflections on the Revolution in France* (London: Penguin, 2004).

Burke, P., *Popular Culture in Early Modern Europe*, rev. edn (Farnham and Burlington, VT: Ashgate, 1994).

Burton, J.K., *Napoleon and the Woman Question: Discourses of the Other Sex in French Education, Medicine, and Medical Law, 1799–1815* (Lubbock, TX: Texas Tech University Press, 2007).

Bustico, G., 'Il salotto milanese di un'aspasia veneziana del periodo napoleonico', *Nuovo Archivio Veneto*, 33, fol. 1 (1917): 370–78.

Butler, S., *Irish Tales: Or, Instructive Histories for the Happy Conduct of Life*, in I. Campbell Ross, A. Douglas, and A. Markey (eds), *Early Irish Fiction, c. 1680–1820* (Dublin: Four Courts Press, 2010).

Cahier du Tiers-Etat de la Ville de Paris, *Archives Parlementaires de 1787–1860*, 1st series, 5 (Paris: Paul Dupont, 1879).

Califronia, R., *Breve difesa dei diritti delle donne: Scritta da Rosa Califronia contessa romana* (Assisi: Ottavio Sgariglia, 1794).

Caminer Turra, E., 'On Exceptional Women', *Europa Letteraria* (November 1769), in C.M. Sama (ed. and trans.), *Selected Writings of an Eighteenth-Century Venetian Woman of Letters* (Chicago: University of Chicago Press, 2003), pp. 167–84.

Caminer Turra, E., 'On Mary Wollstonecraft's *Vindication of the Rights of Woman*', *Nuovo Giornale Enciclopedico d'Italia* (August 1793), in C.M. Sama (ed. and trans.), *Selected Writings of an Eighteenth-Century Venetian Woman of Letters* (Chicago: University of Chicago Press, 2003), pp. 188–9.

Caminer Turra, E., Review of Terenzia Ghellini's Italian translation of François Philippe Mezanguy's *Compendio dell'istoria e della morale dell'Antico Testamento con spiegazioni e riflessi*], *Giornale Enciclopedico* (January 1777), in C.M. Sama (ed. and trans.), *Selected Writings of an Eighteenth-Century Venetian Woman of Letters* (Chicago: University of Chicago Press, 2003), pp. 146–50.

Caminer Turra, E., Review of *Traduzioni italiane di Madamigella N.N.*, *Italian translations by Miss Anonymous* [anonymous translation of Henry Manning, *Essay on the Health of Unmarried Daughters, with some Reflections on Marriage*] (Pavia, 1794) in C.M. Sama (ed. and trans.), *Selected Writings of an Eighteenth-Century Venetian Woman of Letters* (Chicago: University of Chicago Press, 2003), p. 190.

Camposanpiero, G., 'Che debbono ammettersi le Donne allo Studio delle Scienze, e delle belle Arti' ['That women should be allowed to study science and the fine arts'], in *Discorsi accademici di varj autori viventi. Intorno agli Studj delle Donne; La maggior parte recitati nell'Accademia de'Ricovrati di Padova* (Padua: Stamperia del Seminario presso Giovanni Manfrè, 1729).

Carroll, B.A. and H.L. Smith (eds), *Women's Political and Social Thought: An Anthology* (Indiana: Indiana University Press, 2000).

Castel, L.-B., *L'Homme moral opposé à l'homme physique de M. R***: Lettres philosophiques où l'on réfute le déisme du jour* (Toulouse, 1756).

Cavendish, M., *Sociable Letters*, ed. J. Fitzmaurice (Peterborough, Ontario: Broadview, 2004).

Chakrabarty, D., *Provincializing Europe: Postcolonial Thought and Historical Difference* (Princeton: Princeton University Press, 2008).

Champion, J., '30 Floréal An X: La rétablissement de l'esclavage par Bonaparte', in M. Dorigny (ed.), *Les Abolitions de l'esclavage: De L.F. Sonthonax à V. Schoelcher, 1793, 1794, 1848* (Saint-Denis and Paris: Presses Universitaires de Vincennes; UNESCO, 1995), pp. 265–71.

Chateaubriand, R. de, *Mémoires d'outre-tombe* (6 vols, Paris, 1910).

Cheney, P.B., *Revolutionary Commerce: Globalization and the French Monarchy* (Cambridge, MA: Harvard University Press, 2010).

Chénier, M.-J., *Les Nouveaux saints* (Paris, 1801).

Clément-Hémery, A. [anonymously], *Les Femmes vengées de la sottise d'un philosophe du jour, ou réponse au projet de loi de M. S – M – portant défense d'apprendre à lire aux femmes, par Madame –* (Paris, 1801). Modern edition in G. Fraisse (ed.), *Opinions de femmes de la ville au lendemain de la Révolution française* (Paris: Côté-femmes, 1989), pp. 81–128.

Colley, L., *Britons: Forging the Nation, 1707–1837* (New Haven: Yale University Press, 1992).

Combe, W., *The Devil upon Two Sticks in England: Being a Continuation of Le Diable boiteux of Lesage* (London, 1790).

Condorcet, J.-A.-N. de Caritat marquis de, 'Sur l'admission des femmes au droit de cité' ['On giving women the right of citizenship'], *Journal de la société de 1789*, 5 (3 July 1790): 1–13.

Condorcet, J.-A.-N. de Caritat, marquis de, 'Letters from a Freeman of New Haven to a Citizen of Virginia on the Futility of Dividing the Legislative Power among Several Bodies (1787)', in Iain McLean and Fiona Hewitt (eds.) *Condorcet: Foundations of Social Choice and Political Theory* (Aldershot: Edward Elgar, 1994), pp. 292–3.

Coyer, G.-F., *La Noblesse commerçante* (Paris, 1756).

Crenshaw, K.W., 'Mapping the Margins: Intersectionality, Identity Politics, and Violence against Women of Color', *Stanford Law Review*, 43:6 (1991): 1241–99.

Cunningham, B., *The World of Geoffrey Keating: History, Myth and Religion in Seventeenth-Century Ireland* (Dublin: Four Courts Press, 2000).

Curtis-Wendlandt, L., 'No Right to Resist? Elise Reimarus's *Freedom* as a Kantian Response to the Problem of Violent Revolt', *Hypatia*, 27:4 (2012): 755–73.

Curtis-Wendlandt, L., 'Staging Virtue: Women, Death, and Liberty in Elise Reimarus's *Cato*', *Journal of the History of Ideas*, 74:1 (2013): 69–92.

Dahl, K.A., 'At the Center of the Movement towards Enlightenment: Louise Keralio Robert and the French Revolution', PhD thesis (University of Minnesota, 1996).

Darnton, R., *The Literary Underground of the Old Regime* (Cambridge, MA: Harvard University Press, 1982).

Darnton, R., *George Washington's False Teeth: An Unconventional Guide to the Eighteenth Century* (Cambridge, MA: Harvard University Press, 2003).

Davis, L., 'Birth of the Nation: Gender and Writing in the Work of Henry and Charlotte Brooke', *Eighteenth-Century Life*, 18:1 (February 1994): 27–47.

Davis, L., *Music, Postcolonialism, and Gender: The Construction of Irish National Identity, 1724–1874* (Notre Dame: University of Notre Dame Press, 2006).

DeJean, J., *Tender Geographies: The Politics of Female Authorship under the Late Ancien Régime* (New York: Columbia University Press, 1991).

DeJean, J., *Ancients against Moderns: Cultural Wars and the Making of the Fin de Siècle* (Chicago and London: University of Chicago Press, 1997).

Desmahis, J., 'Femme, morale', in Diderot and d'Alembert (eds), *Encyclopédie* (Paris: Briasson, 1750–1765), vol. 6.

Dhavernas, M.-J., 'Préface' to H.C. Agrippa de Nettesheim, *Discours abrégé sur la noblesse et l'excellence du sexe féminin, de sa prééminence sur l'autre sexe et du sacrement du mariage*, 1537 (Paris: Côté-femmes, 1990).

Diderot, D., *Sur les Femmes*, in A. Billy (ed.), *Œuvres* (Paris: NRF Gallimard, Bibliothèque de la Pléiade, 1951).

Diderot, D., *Supplément au Voyage de Bougainville* (1770–1773), ed. Herbert Dieckmann (Genève: Droz, 1955).

Diderot, D., (1771) *Paradoxe sur le comédien* (Paris: A. Colin, 1992).

Dino, D. de, *Memoirs of the Duchesse de Dino*, 1836–1840, ed. M. Radziwill (3 vols, New York: Charles Scribner's Sons, 1910).

Discorsi accademici di varj autori viventi. Intorno agli Studj delle Donne; La maggior parte recitati nell'Accademia de' Ricovrati di Padova (Padua: Stamperia del Seminario presso Giovanni Manfrè, 1729).

Disney, J., *Memoirs of Thomas Brand Hollis* (London: T. Gillet, 1808).

Donato, M.P., 'Cultura dell'antico e cultura dei lumi a Roma nel Settecento: La politicizzazione dello scambio culturale durante il pontificato di Pio VI', *Mélanges de l'Ecole française de Rome, Italie et Méditerranée*, 104:2 (1992): 503–48.

Donato, M.P., 'I salotti romani del Settecento: Il ruolo femminile tra politica e cultura', in M.L. Betri and E. Brambilla (eds), *Salotti e ruolo femminile in Italia tra fine Seicento e primo Novecento* (Venice: Marsilio, 2004).

Dorigny, M., and Zins, M. (eds), *Les Traites négrières coloniales: Histoire d'un crime* (Paris: Cercle d'art, 2009).

Doyle, W., *Aristocracy and its Enemies in the Age of Revolution* (Oxford: Oxford University Press, 2009).

Drake, J., *An Essay in Defence of the Female Sex* (4th edn, London, 1721).

Du Châtelet, E., *Institutions de physique* (Paris: Prault fils, 1740).

Du Châtelet, E., *Lettres de la marquise du Châtelet*, ed. T. Besterman (Geneva: Institut et Musée de Voltaire, 1958).

Du Châtelet, E., *Discours sur le bonheur*, in *Selected Philosophical and Scientific Writings*, ed. J.P. Zinsser, trans. I. Bour and J.P. Zinsser (Chicago: University of Chicago Press, 2009).

Du Châtelet, E., *Examens de la Bible*, ed. Bertram E. Schwarzbach (Paris: Honoré Champion, 2009).

Du Châtelet, E., 'Translator's Preface' to Bernard [de] Mandeville, *The Fable of the Bees*, in *Selected Philosophical and Scientific Writings*, ed. J.P. Zinsser, trans. I. Bour and J.P. Zinsser (Chicago: University of Chicago Press, 2009).

Dubois, L., and J.D. Garrigus (eds), *Slave Revolution in the Caribbean, 1789–1804: A Brief History with Documents* (New York: Bedford/St. Martins, 2006).

Dulong, C., *La Vie quotidienne des femmes au Grand Siècle* (Paris: Hachette, 1984).

Dulong, C. 'From Conversation to Creation', in N. David and A. Farge (eds), *A History of Women in the West*, vol. 3, *Renaissance and Englightenment Paradoxes* (Cambridge: Harvard University Press, 1993), pp. 395–419.

Eger, E., and L., Peltz, *Brilliant Women: 18th-Century Bluestockings* (London: National Portrait Gallery, 2008).

Elias, N., *Court Society*, trans. E. Jephcott (New York: Urizen Books, 1983).

Fasanari, R., *Gli albori del Risorgimento a Verona (1785–1801)* (Verona: Vita Veronese, 1950).

Fauré, C., *Enciclopedia histórica y política de las mujeres: Europa y América* (Madrid: Akal, 2010).

Féletz, C.-M. [anonymously], Review of *Mémoires, anecdotes secrètes, galantes, historiques et inédites, sur mesdames de la Vallière, de Montespan, de Fontanges, de Maintenon, et autres illustres personnages du siècle de Louis XIV*; par Mad. Gacon-Dufour', *Journal de l'Empire* (31 January 1807): 3–4.

Ferguson, M., *Subject to Others: British Women Writers and Colonial Slavery, 1670–1834* (New York: Routledge, 1992).
Ferguson, M., 'Mary Wollstonecraft and the Problematic of Slavery', in M.J. Falco (ed.), *Feminist Interpretations of Mary Wollstonecraft* (University Park, PA: Pennsylvania State University Press, 1996), pp. 125–50.
Ferguson, M., and Todd, J., *Mary Wollstonecraft* (Boston: Twayne, 1984).
Ferraris, A., 'Les Nouveaux malheurs de l'amour: Appunti sugli scritti di Giuseppina di Lorena-Carignano', in M. Cerruti (ed.), *Il 'genio muliebre': Percorsi di donne intellettuali fra Settecento e Novecento in Piemonte* (Alessandria: Dell'Orso, 1990), pp. 9–22.
Fiette, S., *La Noblesse française des Lumières à la Belle Epoque: Psychologies d'une adaptation* (Paris: Perrin, 1997).
Filippini, N.M., 'Donne sulla scena politica: Dalle Municipalità del 1797 al Risorgimento', in N.M. Filippini (ed.), *Donne sulla scena pubblica: Società e politica in Veneto tra Sette e Ottocento* (Milan: FrancoAngeli, 2006), pp. 81–137.
Findlen, P., W.W. Roworth, and C.M. Sama (eds), *Italy's Eighteenth Century: Gender and Culture in the Age of the Grand Tour* (Stanford: Stanford University Press, 2009).
Fischer, S., *Modernity Disavowed: Haiti and the Cultures of Slavery in the Age of Revolution* (Durham: Duke University Press, 2004).
Flikschuh, K., 'Duty, Nature, Right: Kant's Response to Mendelssohn in *Theory and Practice* III', *Journal of Moral Philosophy*, 4:2 (2007): 223–41.
Fonte, M., *Il Merito delle donne*, ed. A. Chemello (Venice: Eidos, 1988).
Fonte, M., *The Worth of Women*, ed. and trans. V., Cox (Chicago: University of Chicago Press, 1997).
Fontenay, E., *Diderot ou le matérialisme enchanté* (Paris: Grasset, 1981).
Fraisse, G. (ed.), *Opinions de femmes de la ville au lendemain de la Révolution française* (Paris: Côté-femmes, 1989).
Fraisse, G., *Reason's Muse: Sexual Difference and the Birth of Democracy*, trans. J.M. Todd (Chicago: University of Chicago Press, 1994).
Fraisse, G., *Muse de la Raison: Démocratie et exclusion des femmes en France* (Paris: Gallimard, 1995).
Fumaroli, M., 'La Conversation', in P. Nora (ed.), *Les Lieux de mémoire* (3 vols, Paris: Gallimard, 1992).
Furbank, P.N., *Diderot: A Critical Biography* (London: Secker and Warburg, 1992).
Furet, F., *Interpreting the French Revolution*, trans. E. Foster (Cambridge: Cambridge University Press, 1981).
Gacon-Dufour, M.-A.J., *L'Homme errant fixé par la raison, ou Lettres de Célidor et du marquis de Tobers, par le Comte d'Ay ... et Madame Filh. D'Hu...* (Paris, 1787).
Gacon-Dufour, M.-A.J., [anonymously], *Contre le projet de loi de S***M***, Portant défense d'apprendre à lire aux femmes, Par une femme qui ne se pique pas d'être femme de lettres* (Paris, 1801).

Gacon-Dufour, M.-A.J., *La Femme grenadier* (Paris, 1801).

Gacon-Dufour, M.-A.J., *Recueil pratique d'économie rurale et domestique* (Paris, 1804).

Gacon-Dufour, M.-A.J., *Manuel de la ménagère, à la ville et à la campagne, et de la femme de basse-cour* (Paris, 1805).

Gacon-Dufour, M.-A.J., *Correspondance inédite de Mme de Châteauroux avec le duc de Richelieu, le maréchal de Belle-Isle, MM. Duverney, de Chavigni, Mme de Flavacourt et autres, précédée d'une notice historique* (2 vols, Paris: L. Collin, 1806).

Gacon-Dufour, M.-A.J., *Mémoires, anecdotes secrètes, galantes, historiques et inédites, sur mesdames de la Vallière, de Montespan, de Fontanges, de Maintenon, et autres illustres personnages du siècle de Louis XIV* (2 vols, Paris: Léopold Collin, 1807).

Gacon-Dufour, M.-A.J., [anonymously], 'Notice sur Sylvain Maréchal', in S. Maréchal, *De la Vertu, suivi du Livre de tous les âges* (Paris, 1807), pp. 1–71.

Gacon-Dufour, M.-A.J., *Réponse à M. A. ..., l'un des Rédacteurs du 'Journal de l'Empire'... L'Abbé Félès Dorimon* (Paris, 1807).

Gacon-Dufour, M.-A.J., *Correspondance de plusieurs personnages illustres de la cour de Louis XV, depuis le années 1745 jusques et y compris 1774* (2 vols, Paris: L. Collin, 1808).

Gacon-Dufour, M.-A.J., [anonymously], *Mémoire pour le sexe féminin contre le sexe masculin* (London [Paris], n.d.); modern edition in G. Fraisse (ed.), *Opinions de femmes de la ville au lendemain de la Révolution française* (Paris: Côté-femmes, 1989), pp. 20–46.

Garaud, M., and R. Szramkiewicz, *La Révolution française et la famille* (Paris: Presses Universitaires de France, 1978).

Gardener, E.J., 'The Philosophes and Women: Sensationalism and Sentiment', in E. Jacobs, W.H. Barber, J.H. Block, F.W. Leakey, and E. Le Breton (eds), *Women and Society in Eighteenth-Century France* (London: Athlone Press, 1979), pp. 19–27.

Gardner, C.V., *Rediscovering Women Philosophers: Philosophical Genre and the Boundaries of Philosophy* (Boulder, CO and Oxford, UK: Westview Press, 2000).

Gasperoni, G., *Giuseppina di Lorena principessa di Carignano* (Turin: Paravia, 1938).

Gay, S. *Salons célèbres* (Paris: Calmann-Lévy, 1882).

Geffroy, A., 'Louise de Keralio-Robert: Pionnière du républicanisme sexiste', *Annales historiques de la Révolution française*, 344 (2006): 107–24.

Geiger, M.B., 'Mercy Otis Warren and Catharine Macaulay: Historians in the Transatlantic Republican Tradition', doctoral dissertation (New York University, 1986).

Genlis, S.-F., *Étude du cœur humain, suivie des cinq premières semaines d'un journal écrit sur les Pyrénées*, (Paris: Cellot, 1805).

Ginzburg, C., *Clues, Myths, and the Historical Method*, trans. J. and A.C. Tedeschi (Baltimore: Johns Hopkins, 1989).

Girardin, D. de, *Vicomte de Launay: Lettres parisiennes* (4 vols, Paris: Michel Lévy Frères, 1857–1868).

Girou Swiderski, M.-L., 'Une chambre à soi: Le thème du logement dans la correspondance de Mme Belot', in S. Woodward (ed.), *Altered Narratives: Female Eighteenth-Century French Authors Reinterpreted* (London, Ontario: Mestengo, 1997), pp. 15–31.

Glotz, M., and M. Marie, *Salons du XVIIIe siècle* (Paris: Nouvelles éditions latines, 1949).

Goldsmith, E., *Exclusive Conversations: The Art of Interaction in Seventeenth-Century France* (Philadelphia: University of Pennsylvania Press, 1988).

Goncourt, E. de, *La duchesse de Châteauroux et ses sœurs, Nouvelle édition, revue et augmentée de lettres et documents inédits, tirés de la Bibliothèque nationale, de la Bibliothèque de Rouen, des Archives nationales et des collections particulières* (Paris, 1906).

Goncourt, J., and E. de, *The Woman of the Eighteenth Century: Her Life, from Birth to Death, Her Love and Her Philosophy in the World of Salon, Shop, and Street*, trans. Jacques Le Clercq and Ralph Roeder (New York: Minton, Balch, 1927).

Goncourt, J., and E. de, *Histoire de la société française pendant la Révolution* (Paris: Flammarion, 1864; reprint, Geneva: Slakine, 1971).

Goodman, D., 'Enlightenment Salons: The Convergence of Female and Philosophic Ambitions', *Eighteenth-Century Studies*, 22:3 (1989): 329–50.

Goodman, D., 'Governing the Republic of Letters: The Politics of Culture in the French Enlightenment', *History of European Ideas*, 13:3 (1991): 183–99.

Goodman, D., *The Republic of Letters: A Cultural History of the French Enlightenment* (Ithaca, NY: Cornell University Press, 1994).

Gordon, D., 'Philosophy, Sociology, and Gender in the Enlightenment', in 'Forum: The Public Sphere in the Eighteenth Century', *French Historical Studies*, 17:4 (1992): 882–911.

Gordon, D., *Citizens Without Sovereignty: Equality and Sociability in French Thought, 1670–1789* (Princeton: Princeton University Press, 1994).

Gordon, F., and Furbank, P.N. (eds), *Marie Madeleine Jodin, 1741–1790: Actress, Philosophe, and Feminist* (Farnham and Burlington, VT: Ashgate, 2001).

Gordon, L., *Vindication: A Life of Mary Wollstonecraft* (New York, NY: Harper Collins, 2005).

Gottman, F., 'Du Châtelet, Voltaire, and the Transformation of Mandeville's Fable', *History of European Ideas*, 38:2 (2012): 218–32.

Gouges, O. de, *Ecrits politiques* (Paris: Côté-femmes, 1993).

Gouges, O. de, *L'Esclavage des nègres, ou l'heureux naufrage* (1789), ed. S. Chalaye and J. Razgonnikoff (Paris: L'Harmattan, 2006).

Gouges, O. de, *Declaration des droits de la femme et de la citoyenne* (1791), eds E. Gaulier and O. Fontvieille (Paris: Mille et une nuits, 2007).

Gournay, M. de, 'Adieu de l'âme du Roy de France et de Navarre Henry le Grand, à la Royne, avec la Defence des Peres Jesuistes', in *Œuvres Complètes*, ed. Jean-Claude Arnould et al. (Paris: Champion, 2002), vol. 1, pp. 653–82.

Grant, R.W., 'John Locke on Women and the Family', in *Two Treatises of Government and a Letter Concerning Toleration*, ed. I. Shapiro (New Haven: Yale University Press, 2003).

Green, K., *The Woman of Reason: Feminism, Humanism, and Political Thought* (New York: Continuum, 1995).

Green, K. ,'The Passions and the Imagination in Wollstonecraft's Theory of Moral Judgement', *Utilitas*, 9:3 (1997): 271–90.

Green, K., 'On Translating Christine de Pizan as a Philosopher', in K. Green and C.J. Mews (eds), *Healing the Body Politic: The Political Thought of Christine de Pizan* (Turnhout: Brepols, 2005), pp. 109–28.

Green, K., '*Phronesis* Feminized: Prudence from Christine de Pizan to Elizabeth I', in J. Broad and K. Green (eds), *Virtue, Liberty, and Toleration: Political Ideas of European Women 1400–1800* (Dordrecht: Springer, 2007), pp. 23–38.

Green, K., 'Madeleine de Scudéry on Love and the Emergence of the "Private Sphere"', *History of Political Thought*, 30:2 (2009): 272–85.

Green, K., 'Catharine Macaulay as Enlightenment Philosopher', in *Intellectual History Review*, 22:3 [Special Issue on Women, Philosophy and Literature in the Early Modern Period, ed. Peter Anstey and Jocelyn Harris] (2012): 411–26.

Grimm, F.M. von, and D. Diderot, [letter of 1763] *Correspondance littéraire, philosophique et critique par Grimm, Diderot, Raynal, Meister, etc.*, ed. Maurice Tourneur (16 vols, Paris, 1877–1882).

Guizot, F., *Madame de Rumford (1758–1836)* (Paris: Crapelet, 1841).

Gunther-Canada, W., 'The politics of Sense and Sensibility: Mary Wollstonecraft and Catharine Macaulay Graham on Edmund Burke's *Reflections on the Revolution in France*', in H.L. Smith (ed.), *Women Writers and the Early Modern British Political Tradition* (Cambridge: Cambridge University Press, 1998), pp. 126–47.

Gutwirth, M., *Twilight of the Goddesses: Women and Representation in the French Revolutionary Era* (New Brunswick, NJ: Rutgers University Press, 1992).

Habermas, J., *The Structural Transformation of the Public Sphere: An Inquiry into a Category of Bourgeois Society*, trans. T. Burger (Cambridge, MA: MIT Press, 1989).

Hamerton, K., Review of S.D. Kale, *French Salons: High Society and Political Sociability from the Old Regime to the Revolution of 1848*, in *The Journal of Modern History* 79:3 (2007): 674–6.

Hardenberg, H., *Etta Palm: Een Hollandse Parisienne, 1743–1799* (Assen, 1962).

Harrington, J., *The Oceana of James Harrington, Esq; And His Other Works; With an Account of His Life Prefix'd, by John Toland. To Which is Added Plato Redivivus or, a Dialogue Concerning Government* (Dublin: J. Smith and W. Bruce, 1737).

Harth, E., *Cartesian Women: Versions and Subversions of Rational Discourse in the Old Regime* (Ithaca, NY: Cornell University Press, 1992).

Hartley, D., *Observations on Man, his Frame, his Duty, and his Expectations* (1749), [Facsim. reproduction with an introduction by T.L. Huguelet] (The British Library, 2010).

Havens, G.R., 'Eighteenth-Century Critics of Rousseau's Second *Discourse*', in J. Macary (ed.), *Essays on the Age of Enlightenment: In Honor of Ira O. Wade* (Geneva: Droz, 1977), pp. 143–54.

Hays, M., 'Memoirs of Mary Wollstonecraft', in *The Annual Necrology, for 1797–8. Including, also, various Articles of neglected Biography* (London: Printed for R. Phillips, 1800), pp. 232–3.

Herriot, E., *Madame Récamier*, trans. A. Hallard (2 vols, New York: Boni and Liveright, 1926).

Hesse, C., 'Reading Signatures: Female Authorship and Revolutionary Law in France, 1750–1850', *Eighteenth-Century Studies*, 22:3 (Spring 1989): 469–487.

Hesse, C., *The Other Enlightenment: How French Women Became Modern* (Princeton: Princeton University Press, 2001).

Hicks, P., 'Macaulay's Civil War: Gender, History, and Republicanism in Georgian Britain', *Journal of British Studies*, 41:2 (April 2002): 170–98.

Hill, B., *The Republican Virago: The Life and Times of Catharine Macaulay, Historian* (Oxford: Clarendon Press, 1992).

Hill, B., 'The Links Between Mary Wollstonecraft and Catharine Macaulay: New Evidence', *Women's History Review*, 4:2 (1995): 177–92.

Hill, B., and C. Hill, 'Catharine Macaulay and the Seventeenth Century', *The Welsh History Review*, 3:4 (1967): 381–402.

Hirschmann, N., and J. Wright (eds), *Feminist Interpretations of Thomas Hobbes* (University Park, PA: Pennsylvania University Press, 2012).

Hobbes, T., *Leviathan: Or the Matter, Forme, and Power of a Common-Wealth Ecclesiasticall and Civill*, ed. I. Shapiro (New Haven and London: Yale University Press, 2010).

Hofmeester, N., *Etta Palm: Feministe van Hollandse bodem* (Amsterdam: Witte Leile, 1978).

Holbach, P.H. baron de, *Système Social ou Principes Naturels de la Morale et de la Politique avec un examen de l'Influence du Gouvernement sur le mœurs* (Paris, London, 1773).

Homiak, M.L., 'Feminism and Aristotle's Rational Ideal', in *A Mind of One's Own*, ed. L.M. Antony and C.E. Witt (Boulder, San Francisco, and Oxford: Westview Press, 1993), pp. 1–17.

Hunt, L., *The Family Romance of the French Revolution* (Berkeley and Los Angeles: University of California Press, 1992).

Hunt, L., *Inventing Human Rights: A History* (New York: W.W. Norton, 2007).

Huntington Library, San Marino, California; Elizabeth Robinson Montagu Collection.

Israel, J.I., *Radical Enlightenment: Philosophy and the Making of Modernity 1650–1750* (New York: Oxford University Press, 2001).

Israel, J.I., *Enlightenment Contested: Philosophy, Modernity, and the Emancipation of Man 1670–1752* (Oxford: Oxford University Press, 2006).

Israel, J.I., *A Revolution of the Mind* (Princeton: Princeton University Press, 2010).

Israel, J.I., *Democratic Enlightenment: Philosophy, Revolution, and Human Rights 1750–1790* (Oxford: Oxford University Press, 2011).

Istruzioni d'una libera cittadina alle sue concittadine [*Instructions of a free female citizen to her female fellow citizens*] (Venice: Andrea Martini, 1797).

James, C.L.R., *The Black Jacobins: Toussaint L'Ouverture and the San Domingo Revolution* (London: Penguin, 2001).

Jimack, P.D., 'The Paradox of Sophie and Julie: Contemporary Response to Rousseau's Ideal Wife and Ideal Mother', in E. Jacobs, W.H. Barber, J.H. Block, F.W. Leakey, and E. Le Breton (eds), *Women and Society in Eighteenth-Century France* (London: Athlone Press, 1979), pp. 152–65.

Jodin, M.M., *Vues législatives pour les femmes* (Angers: Mame, 1790).

Jodin, M.M., 'Legislative Views for Women', in F. Gordon and P.N. Furbank (eds), *Marie Madeleine Jodin 1741–1790: Actress, Philosophe, and Feminist* (Farnham and Burlington, VT: Ashgate, 2001), pp. 282–330.

Kale, S., 'Women, the Public Sphere, and the Persistence of Salons', *French Historical Studies*, 25:1 (2002): 115–48.

Kale, S., *French Salons: High Society and Political Sociability from the Old Regime to the Revolution of 1848* (Baltimore and London: Johns Hopkins University Press, 2004).

Kale, S., 'Women, Salons, and Sociability as Constitutional Problems in the Works of Madame de Staël', *Historical Reflections/Réflexions Historiques*, 32:2 (2006): 309–38.

Kant, I., *Gesammelte Schriften*, edited by the Königlich-Preussische Akademie der Wissenschaften zu Berlin (Berlin, 1902–), vols 3, 4, 6, and 8.

Kant, I., *The Metaphysics of Morals* (Cambridge and New York: Cambridge University Press, 1991).

Kant, I., *Political Writings*, ed. H.S. Reiss (Cambridge: Cambridge University Press, 1991).

Kant, I., *Critique of Pure Reason*, ed. and trans. P. Guyer and A.W. Wood (Cambridge: Cambridge University Press, 1998).

Kant, I., *Groundwork of the Metaphysics of Morals*, ed. and trans. M.J. Gregor (Cambridge: Cambridge University Press, 1998).

Kant, I., *Anthropology, History, and Education*, ed. G. Zöller and R.B. Louden (Cambridge: Cambridge University Press, 2007).

Kaul, S., *Poems of Nation, Anthems of Empire: English Verse in the Long Eighteenth Century* (Charlottesville and London: University Press of Virginia, 2000).

Kelley, A., *Catharine Trotter: An Early Modern Writer in the Vanguard of Feminism* (Farnham and Burlington, VT: Ashgate, 2002).

Keralio-Robert, L.-F., *Adelaide, ou mémoires de la Marquise de M***, écrits par elle-même* (Paris, 1783).

Keralio-Robert, L.-F., *Histoire d'Elizabeth reine d'Angleterre* (5 vols, Paris: Lagrange, 1786–1788).

Keralio-Robert, L.-F., *Collection des meilleurs ouvrages François composés par des femmes, dédiée aux femmes françoises* (14 vols, Paris: Lagrange, 1786–1789).

Keralio-Robert, L.-F. [and various] (eds), *Mercure national ou Journal d'état et du citoyen* (Paris: L. Poitier de Lille, 1789–1790).

Keralio-Robert, L.-F., L. Guynement de Keralio, and F. Robert, (eds), *Mercure national et révolutions de l'Europe, journal démocratique* (Paris: Lefort, 1790).

Keralio-Robert, L.-F., F. Robert, and P.-H.-M. Lebrun, *Mercure national et étranger ou journal politique de l'Europe* (Liège, 1791).

Kersting, W., *Wohlgeordnete Freiheit: Immanuel Kants Rechts- und Staatsphilosophie* (Frankfurt am Main: Suhrkamp, 1993).

Kersting, W., *Kant über Recht* (Paderborn: Mentis, 2004).

Kidd, C., *British Identities before Nationalism: Ethnicity and Nationhood in the Atlantic World, 1600–1800* (Cambridge: Cambridge University Press, 1999).

Kilfeather, S., 'The Profession of Letters, 1700–1810', in A. Bourke et al., *Field Day Anthology of Irish Writing: Irish Women's Writing and Traditions* vol. 5 (Cork: Cork University Press, 2002).

Kleingeld, P. 'The Problematic Status of Gender-Neutral Language in the History of Philosophy: The Case of Kant', *Philosophical Forum*, 25 (1993): 134–50.

Koehler, M.M., 'The Ode', in C. Gerrard (ed.), *A Companion to Eighteenth-Century Poetry* (Oxford: Oxford University Press, 2006).

Koppius, W.J., *Etta Palm (Barones Aelders): Nederland's eerste féministe tijdens de Fransche revolutie te Parijs* (Zeist: Ploegsma, 1929).

Lalande, J., *Notice sur Sylvain Maréchal, avec des supplémens pour le Dictionnaire des athées* ([Paris, 1805]).

Landes, J.B., *Women and the Public Sphere in the Age of the French Revolution* (Ithaca, NY: Cornell University Press, 1988).

Laslett, P. 'Introduction', in John Locke *Two Treatises of Government* (Cambridge: Cambridge University Press, 1997).

Le Breton, A.L., *Memoir of Mrs Barbauld* (London: George Bell and Sons, 1874).

Leerssen, J., *Mere Irish and Fíor-Ghael* (Cork: Cork University Press, 1996).

Lettres de Mme de Meinières à Mme de Lénoncourt (1770–1774), in E.C. Goldsmith and C.H. Winn (eds), *Lettres de femmes: Textes inédits et oubliés du XVIe au XVIIIe siècle* (Paris: Champion, 2005), pp. 379–420.

Lévy-Bruhl, H., 'La noblesse de France et le commerce à la fin de l'ancien régime', *Revue de l'histoire moderne*, 8:8 (1933): 209–35.

Lewis, W.S. (ed.), *The Yale Edition of Horace Walpole's Correspondence* (New Haven: Yale University Press, 1944).

Lilti, A., *Le Monde des salons: Sociabilité et mondanité à Paris au XVIIIe siècle* (Paris: Fayard, 2005).

Lilti, A., 'The Kingdom of *Politesse*: Salons and the Republic of Letters in Eighteenth-Century Paris', *Republics of Letters: A Journal for the Study of Knowledge, Politics and the Arts*, 1:1 (2009), at http://rofl.stanford.edu/node/38.

Lloyd, G. (ed.), *Feminism and History of Philosophy* (Oxford: Oxford University Press, 2002).

Locke, J., *Two Treatises of Government*, ed. P. Laslett 2nd edn (Cambridge: Cambridge University Press, 1967).

Locke, J., *An Essay Concerning Human Understanding*, ed. P.H. Nidditch (Oxford: Clarendon Press, 1975).

Lonsdale, R. (ed.), *Eighteenth-Century Women Poets* (Oxford: Oxford University Press, 1989).

Looser, D., *British Women Writers and the Writing of History* (Baltimore: Johns Hopkins University Press, 2000).

Lorena-Carignano, G. di, *Les Aventures d'Amélie* (Royal Library of Turin, *Varia* 176, Box 1, Envelope 12, 1771).

Lougee, C., *Le Paradis des Femmes: Women, Salons, and Social Stratification in Seventeenth-Century France* (Princeton: Princeton University Press, 1976).

Ludwig, B., 'Commentary on Kant's Treatment of Constitutional Right (*Metaphysics of Morals II*: General Remark A; Paragraphs 51–2, Conclusion, Appendix)', in K. Ameriks and O. Hoeffe (eds), *Kant's Moral and Legal Philosophy* (New York: Cambridge University Press, 2009), pp. 265–83.

Mac Craith, M., '"We Know all these Poems": The Irish Response to Ossian', in H. Gaskill (ed.), *The Reception of Ossian in Europe* (London: Thoemmes Continuum, 2004), pp. 91–108.

Macaulay, C., *The history of England from the accession of James 1. To that of the Brunswick line* (8 vols, London: vols 1–4, printed for the author and sold by J. Nourse, J. Dodsley, and W. Johnston; vols 5–8 Charles Dilly, 1763–1783).

Macaulay, C., *Loose Remarks on Certain Positions to be Found in Mr Hobbes's 'Philosophical Rudiments of Government and Society'. With a Short Sketch of a Democratical Form of Government, in a Letter to Signor Paoli* (London: T. Davies, in Russell-Street, Covent Garden; Robinson and Roberts, in Pater-Noster Row; and T. Cadell, in the Strand, 1767).

Macaulay, C., *Observations on a Pamphlet entitled 'Thoughts on the Cause of the Present Discontents'*, 4th edn (London: Printed for Edward and Charles Dilly, 1770).

Macaulay, C., *History of England from the Revolution to the Present Time in a Series of Letters to a Friend* (Bath: R. Cruttwell, 1778).

Macaulay, C., *A Treatise on the Immutability of Moral Truth* (London: A. Hamilton, 1783).

Macaulay, C., *Observations on the Reflections of the Right Hon. Edmund Burke, on the Revolution in France, in a Letter for the Right Hon. The Earl of Stanhope* (London, 1790).

Macaulay, C., *Letters on Education* [1790] (Oxford and New York: Woodstock Books, 1994).

MacIntyre, A., *After Virtue* (London: Duckworth, 1981).

Maddalena, A., E. Rotelli de, and G. Barbarisi (eds), *Economia, istituzioni, cultura in Lombardia nell'età di Maria Teresa* (Bologna: Il Mulino, 1982).

Maillé, B. de, *Souvenirs des deux Restaurations: Journal inédit*, ed. Xavier de la Fournière (Paris: Perrin, 1984).

Maître, M., 'Sapho, reine de Tendre: Entre monarchie absolue et royauté littéraire', in D. Denis and A.-E. Spica (eds), *Madeleine de Scudéry: Une femme de lettres au XVIIe siècle* (Arras: Artois Presses Université, 2002), pp. 179–202.

Mandeville, B. [de], 'Préface de l'autheur' to *The Fable of the Bees*, trans. E. Du Châtelet, in I.O. Wade, *Studies on Voltaire, with Some Unpublished Papers of Mme Du Châtelet* (Princeton: Princeton University Press, 1947).

Mannucci, E.J., 'Opposizioni al Concordato: L'ultima fiammata dei lumi?', in A. De Francesco (ed.), *Da Brumaio ai Cento giorni: Cultura di governo e dissenso politico nell'Europa di Bonaparte* (Milano: Guerini e Associati, 2007), pp. 157–76.

Mannucci, E.J., 'Conformité et hétérodoxie chez Sylvain Maréchal', in M. Biard (ed.), *Les politiques de la Terreur, 1793–1794* (Rennes: Presses Universitaires de Rennes/Société des études robespierristes, 2008), pp. 379–89.

Mannucci, E.J., 'Sylvain Maréchal, le donne, una donna', in S. Levati and M. Meriggi (eds), *Con la ragione e col cuore: Studi dedicati a Carlo Capra* (Milano: Franco Angeli, 2008), pp. 405–24.

Mannucci, E.J., *Finalmente il popolo pensa: Sylvain Maréchal nell'immagine della Rivoluzione francese* (Naples: Guida, 2012).

Maréchal, S., *Correctif à la gloire de Bonaparte: Ou lettre à ce général* (Venice, 1798).

Martin, J.-C., *La Révolte brisée: Femmes dans la Révolution française et l'Empire* (Paris: Armand Colin, 2008).

Martin-Fugier, A., *La Vie élégante, ou la formation de Tout-Paris* (Paris: Fayard, 1990).

Mason, J.H., 'The *Lettre à d'Alembert* and its Place in Rousseau's Thought', in M. Hobson, J.T.A. Leigh, and R. Wokler (eds), *Rousseau and the Eighteenth Century: Essays in Memory of R.A. Leigh* (Oxford: Voltaire Foundation, 1992), pp. 547–72.

Mathorez, J.M.H., *Les Etrangers en France sous l'ancien régime: Histoire de la formation de la population française* (Paris: Champion, 1919).

Mattei, F., *Dell'educazione che si deve dare alle donne* [*On the education that should be given to women*], in *L'Amico degli Uomini* (Vicenza: Bartolomeo Paroni, 1797).

Matthew, H., and B. Harrison (eds), *Oxford Dictionary of National Biography* (Oxford: Oxford University Press, 2004).

Maugras, G. *Les Comédiens hors la loi* (Paris: Calman Lévy, 1887).

Maza, S., 'Luxury, Morality, and Social Change: Why there was no Middle-Class Consciousness in Pre-Revolutionary France', in G. Kates (ed.), *The French Revolution: Recent Debates and New Controversies*, 2nd ed. (London: Routledge, 2008), pp. 113–30.

Mazel, G., 'Louise Kéralio et Pierre-François Robert, précurseurs de l'idée républicaine', *Bulletin de la Société de l'Histoire de Paris et de l'Ile-de-France* 116 (1989): 163–237.

McCarthy, W., *Anna Letitia Barbauld: Voice of the Enlightenment* (Baltimore: Johns Hopkins University Press, 2008).

McManners, J., *Abbés and Actresses: The Church and the Theatrical Profession in Eighteenth-Century France* (Oxford: Oxford University Press, 1986).

Mémoires secrets pour servir à l'histoire de la République des Lettres en France depuis 1762 jusqu'à nos jours [anonymous, attributed to Louis Petit de Bachaumont] (London, 1783–1789).

Mendus, S., 'Kant: "An Honest but Narrow-Minded Bourgeois"?', in H.L. Williams (ed.), *Essays on Kant's Political Philsophy* (Cardiff: University of Wales Press, 1992), pp. 166–90.

Messbarger, R., *The Century of Women: Representation of Women in Eighteenth-Century Italian Public Discourse* (Toronto: University of Toronto Press, 2002).

Michelet, J., *Histoire de la Révolution française*, vol. 2 (Paris: A. Lacroix, 1869).

Michelle, C., 'Etta Lubina Johanna Derista Aelders', in K.M. Wilson (ed.), *An Encyclopedia of Continental Women Writers* (New York: Garland, 1991).

Miller, J.A., 'Acts of Union: Family Violence and National Courtship in Maria Edgeworth's *The Absentee* and Sydney Owenson's *The Wild Irish Girl*', in K. Kirkpatrick (ed.), *Border Crossing: Irish Women Writers and National Identities* (Tuscaloosa and London: University of Alabama Press, 2000), pp. 13–37.

Mills, C.W., *The Racial Contract* (Ithaca, NY: Cornell University Press, 1999).

Mills, C.W., 'Kant's Untermenschen', in A. Valls (ed.), *Race and Racism in Modern Philosophy* (Ithaca, NY: Cornell University Press, 2005), pp. 169–93.

Mirabeau, H.-G. de Riquetti comte de, *Aux Bataves sur le Stathoudérat* (Amsterdam, 1788).

Mittman, B.G., 'Women and the Theater Arts', in *French Women and the Age of Enlightenment*, ed. Samia I. Spencer (Bloomington: Indiana University Press, 1984), pp. 155–69.

Moffat, M.M., *Rousseau et la querelle du théâtre au XVIIIe siècle* (Paris: Broccard, 1930).

Montcalm, A. de, *Mon Journal, 1815–1818*, ed. Sébastien Charléty (Paris: Grasset, 1936).

Montcalm, A. de, *Un Salon politique sur la Restauration: Correspondance de la Marquise de Montcalm*, ed. E. de Lévy-Mirepoix (Paris: Editions du Grand Siècle, 1949).

Montesquieu, C.L. baron de, *Persian Letters*, trans. C.J. Betts (New York: Penguin, 1973).

Montesquieu, C.L. baron de, *The Spirit of the Laws*, trans. A.M. Cohler, B.C. Miller, and H.S. Stone (Cambridge: Cambridge University Press, 1989).

New York Historical Society; Gilder Lehman Collection, MS GLC01799.

Ní Mhunghaile, L., 'Anglo-Irish Antiquarianism and the Transformation of Irish Identity, 1750–1800', in D.A. Valone and J.M. Bradbury (eds), *Anglo-Irish Identities, 1571–1845* (Lewisburg, PA: Bucknell University Press, 2008), pp. 181–98.

Ní Mhunghaile, L. (ed.), *Charlotte Brooke's Reliques of Irish Poetry* (Dublin: Irish Manuscripts Commission, 2009).

Ní Mhunghaile, L., 'The Intersection between Oral Tradition, Manuscript, and Print Cultures in Charlotte Brooke's *Reliques of Irish Poetry* (1789)', in A. Carpenter and M. Cabal (eds), *Oral and Print Cultures in Ireland 1600–1900* (Dublin: Four Courts Press, 2010), pp. 14–31.

Ó Ciosáin, N., *Print and Popular Culture in Ireland, 1750–1850* (Basingstoke: Palgrave, 1997).

Ó Hogáin, D., *Myth, Legend, and Romance: An Encyclopedia of the Irish Folk Tradition* (New York: Prentice-Hall, 1991).

Ó Tuama, S., *Repossessions: Selected Essays on the Irish Literary Heritage* (Cork: Cork University Press, 1995).

O'Halloran, C., *Golden Ages and Barbarous Nations* (Cork: Cork University Press, 2004).

O'Halloran, S., *An Introduction to the Study of the History and Antiquities of Ireland* (Dublin: Thomas Ewing, 1772).

O'Neill, D., *The Burke-Wollstonecraft Debate: Savagery, Civilization, and Democracy* (University Park, PA: Pennsylvania State University Press, 2007).

O'Neill, E., 'Disappearing Ink: Early Modern Women Philosophers and their Fate in History', in *Philosophy in a Feminist Voice: Critiques and Reconstructions*, ed. J.A. Kourany (Princeton: Princeton University Press, 1998), pp. 17–62.

O'Neill, E., 'Women Philosophers and the History of Philosophy', *Australian Journal of French Studies*, 40:3 (2003): 257–74.

O'Neill, E., 'Early Modern Women Philosophers and the History of Philosophy', *Hypatia*, 20:3 (2005): 185–97.

O'Neill, E., 'Justifying the Inclusion of Women in Our Histories of Philosophy', in *The Blackwell Guide to Feminist Philosophy*, ed. Linda Alcoff and Eva Kittay (Oxford: Blackwell, 2007), pp. 17–42.

O'Neill, O., *Bounds of Justice* (Cambridge: Cambridge University Press, 2000).

Offen, K., 'Women's Memory, Women's History, Women's Political Action: The French Revolution in Retrospect, 1789–1889–1989', *Journal of Women's History*, 1:3 (1990): 211–30.

Offen, K., 'Republishing French Feminist Texts', *History of European Ideas*, 17:2–3 (1993): 319–23.

Okin, S.M., *Women in Western Political Thought* (Princeton: Princeton University Press, 1979).

Okin, S.M., 'Women and the Making of the Sentimental Family', *Philosophy and Public Affairs*, 11 (1982): 65–88.

Pailhès, G., *La Duchesse de Duras et Chateaubriand* (Paris: Perrin, 1910).

Palmer, R.R., *The Age of the Democratic Revolution: A Political History of Europe and America, 1760–1800* (Princeton: Princeton University Press, 1959).

Paston, G., (ed.), *Lady Mary Wortley Montagu and her Times* (London: Putnam, 1907).

Pateman, C., *The Sexual Contract* (Cambridge: Polity, 1988).

Pateman, C., *The Disorder of Women* (Cambridge: Polity, 1989).

Pateman, C., '"God Hath Ordained to Man a Helper": Hobbes, Patriarchy and Conjugal Right', in C. Pateman and M.L. Shanley (eds), *Feminist Interpretations and Political Theory* (University Park, PA: Pennsylvania State University Press, 1991), pp. 53–73.

Pateman, C., and C.W. Mills, *Contract and Domination* (Cambridge: Polity Press, 2007).

Pateman, C., and M.L. Shanley (eds), *Feminist Interpretations of Political Theory* (University Park, PA: Pennsylvania State University Press, 1991).

Pelizzari, M.R., 'Eleonora de Fonseca Pimentel: Morire per la rivoluzione', *Storia delle donne*, 4 (2008): 103–21.

Pennington, M., (ed.), *A Series of Letters Between Mrs Elizabeth Carter and Miss Catherine Talbot, from the Year 1741 to 1770* (4 vols, London: F.C. and J. Rivington, 1809).

Pensieri della libera cittadina I.P.M. alle sue concittadine [*Thoughts of the free citizen I.P.M. to her female fellow citizens*] (Venice: Printed by citizen Giovanni, 1797).

Pettit, P., *Republicanism: A Theory of Freedom and Government* (Oxford: Oxford University Press, 2002).

Peyrard, F. (ed.), *De l'Excellence et de la supériorité de la femme: Ouvrage traduit du latin d'Agrippa, avec les commentaires de Roétig* (Paris: Louis, 1801).

Pizan, C., de, *The Treasure of the City of Ladies*, trans. S. Lawson (Harmondsworth: Penguin, 1985).

Pizan, C., de, *Le Livre des trois vertus*, ed. C. Cannon Willard and E. Hicks (Paris: Champion, 1989).

Pizan, C., de, *The Book of the Body Politic*, trans. K.L. Forhan, *Cambridge Texts in the History of Political Thought* (Cambridge: Cambridge University Press, 1994).

Pizan, C., de, *The Book of Peace*, trans. K. Green, C.J. Mews, and J. Pinder (University Park, PA: Pennsylvania State University Press, 2008).

Plebani, T., 'Socialità e protagonismo femminile nel secondo Settecento', in N.M. Filippini (ed.), *Donne sulla scena pubblica: Società e politica in Veneto tra Sette e Ottocento* (Milan: FrancoAngeli, 2006), pp. 25–80.

Plumwood, V., 'The Politics of Reason: Towards a Feminist Logic', *Australasian Journal of Philosophy*, 71:4 (1993): 436–62.

Pocock, J.G.A., 'Catharine Macaulay: Patriot Historian', in H.L. Smith (ed.), *Women Writers and the Early Modern British Political Tradition* (New York, NY: Cambridge University Press, 1998), pp. 243–58.

Pogge, T., 'Is Kant's Rechtslehre a "Comprehensive Liberalism"?', in M. Timmons (ed.), *Kant's Metaphysics of Morals* (New York: Oxford University Press, 2002), pp. 133–58.

Poulain de la Barre, F. *De l'Egalité des deux sexes: Discours physique et moral où l'on voit l'importance de se défaire des préjugez* (Paris, 1673).

Power, T.P., and K. Whelan (eds), *Endurance and Emergence: Catholics in Ireland in the Eighteenth Century* (Dublin: Irish Academic Press, 1990).

Price, M., *The Perilous Crown: France Between Revolutions* (London: Macmillan, 2009).

Priestley, J., and J. Priestley [his son], *Memoirs of Dr Joseph Priestley, to the year 1795, written by himself: With a continuation, to the time of his decease, by his son, Joseph Priestley* (London: H.R. Allenson, 1904).

Proctor, C.E., *Women, Equality, and the French Revolution* (New York: Greenwood, 1990).

Quondam, A., 'L'istituzione Arcadia: Sociologia e ideologia di un'accademia', *Quaderni storici*, 23 (1973): 389–438.

Radner, J.N., and S.S. Lanser, 'Strategies of Coding in Women's Cultures', in J. Newlon Radner (ed.), *Feminist Messages: Coding in Women's Folk Culture* (Urbana and Chicago: University of Illinois Press, 1993), pp. 1–29.

Raynal, G.-T., *Histoire philosophique et politique des établissemens et du commerce des Européens dans les deux Indes* (Geneva: Jean-Leonard Pellet, 1780).

Reddock, R.E., 'Women and Slavery in the Caribbean: A Feminist Perspective', *Latin American Perspectives*, 12:1 (1985): 63–80.

Reimarus, E. [anonymously], *Freiheit* (Hamburg: Meyn, 1791).

Reimarus, E., *Reflections* [undated], in A.M.G. Spalding, *Elise Reimarus (1735–1805): The Muse of Hamburg: A Woman of the German Enlightenment* (Würzburg: Königshausen & Neumann, 2005), pp. 328–31.

Réimpression de l'Ancien Moniteur (Paris: H. Plon, 1858).

Rémusat, C. de, *Mémoires de ma vie* (5 vols, Paris: Plon, 1959).

Rémusat, C. de, *Memoirs of Madame de Rémusat*, trans. C. Hoey and J. Lillie (3 vols, New York, 1880).

Ricaldone, J., 'Amelia o del desiderio: Un'utopia femminile settecentesca' [partial translation of Giuseppina di Lorena-Carignano, *Les Aventures d'Amélie*], *Salvo Imprevisti*, 14–15 (1978): 4–10.

Ricaldone, L. (ed.), *Scelta di inediti di Giuseppina di Lorena-Carignano* (Turin: Centro Studi Piemontesi, 1980).

Ricaldone, L., 'Un naufragio felice: L'île de Giuseppina di Lorena-Carignano', *Italies*, 2 (2000): 135–43.

Ricchi, G. [Zorzi], 'Dell'influenza che possono avere le donne sullo sviluppo dello spirito pubblico' ['On the influence women may have on the development of public spirit'], in *Discorsi pronunciati dal cittadino Z.R. li 16, 17, e 19 pratile nella Società patriotica* (Venice, 1797).

Richelieu, L.F.A. Du Plessis duc de, *Mémoires* (8 vols, Paris, 1793).

Riley, P., 'Kant against Hobbes in *Theory and Practice*', *Journal of Moral Philosophy*, 4:2 (2007): 194–206.

Ripstein, A., 'Authority and Coercion', *Philosophy and Public Affairs*, 32:1 (2004): 2–35.

Risposta alli pensieri della libera cittadina alle sue concitadine [*sic*] [*Answer to the thoughts of the free citizen to her female fellow citizens*] (Venice: Printed by citizens brothers Casali, 1797).

Rogister, J., *Louis XV and the Parlement de Paris (1737–1755)* (Cambridge: Cambridge University Press, 1995).

Rosenblatt, H., *Rousseau and Geneva: From the First Discourse to the Social Contract, 1749–1762* (Cambridge: Cambridge University Press, 1997).

Rossi, A.S. de', 'Apologia: In favore degli Studj delle Donne, contra il precedente Discorso Del Signor Gio. Antonio Volpi Scritta dalla Signora Aretafila Savini de' Rossi, Dama Senese, ad un Cavaliere' ['Apology in favour of studies for women, against the preceding speech by Signor Giorgio Antonio Volpi, written by Signora Aretafila Savini de' Rossi, Sienese Gentlewoman, to a Cavaliere'], in *Discorsi accademici di varj autori viventi. Intorno agli Studj delle Donne; La maggior parte recitati nell'Accademia de' Ricovrati di Padova* (Padua: Stamperia del Seminario presso Giovanni Manfrè, 1723), pp. 50–65.

Rousseau, J.-J., (1757), *Lettre à Mr. D'Alembert sur les spectacles*, ed. M. Fuch (Geneva: Droz, 1948).

Rousseau, J.-J., *Politics and the Arts: Letter to d'Alembert on the Theater*, trans. A. Bloom (Ithaca, NY: Cornell University Press, 1960).

Rousseau, J.-J., *Œuvres complètes*, ed. B. Gagnebin and M. Raymond (5 vols, Paris, 1959–1995).

Rousseau, J.-J., *Emile, or On Education*, trans. A. Bloom (New York: Basic Books, 1979).

Rousseau, J.-J., *Collected Writings of Rousseau*, ed. and trans. A. Bloom, C. Butterworth, C. Kelly (Lebanon, NH: University Press of New England, 1990).

Rousseau, J.-J., *Emile*, trans. Barbara Foxley (Vermont and London: Everyman, 1993).

Rousseau, J.-J., *The Social Contract*, trans. Maurice Cranston (Harmondsworth: Penguin, 2003).

Rousseau, J.-J., *On the Inequality among Mankind* (Minneapolis: Filiquarian, 2007).

Roussel, P., *Système physique et moral de la femme* (Paris, 1775).

Ruggieri, F., *I diritti delle donne* [translation of Mary Wollstonecraft, *Vindication of the Rights of Woman*] (Rome: Riuniti, 1977).

Rumsey, J.P., 'Re-visions of Agency in Kant's Moral Theory', in R.M. Schoot (ed.), *Feminist Interpretations of Immanuel Kant* (University Park, PA: Pennsylvania State University Press, 1997), pp. 125–44.

Sala-Molins, L., *Le Code noir ou le Calvaire de Canaan* (Paris: Quadrige/Presses Universitaires de France, 2006); English translation in *Slave Revolution in the Caribbean, 1789–1804: A Brief History with Documents* (New York: Bedford/St. Martins, 2006), pp. 49–54.

Sama, C.M. (ed. and trans.), *Selected Writings of an Eighteenth-Century Venetian Woman of Letters* (Chicago: University of Chicago Press, 2003).

Schama, S., *Patriots and Liberators: Revolution in the Netherlands, 1780–1813* (New York: Vintage, 2005).

Schirmer, G.A., *Out of What Began: A History of Irish Poetry in English* (Ithaca, NY: Cornell University Press, 1998).

Schnorrenberg, B.B., 'The Brood-Hen of Faction: Mrs Macaulay and Radical Politics, 1765–75', *Albion*, 11 (1979): 33–45.

Schott, R.M., 'Feminism and Kant: Antipathy or Sympathy?', in J. Kneller and S. Axinn (eds), *Autonomy and Community* (New York: SUNY, 1998), pp. 87–100.

Schwoerer, L.G., 'The Right to Resist: Whig Resistance Theory, 1688 to 1694', in N. Phillipson and Q. Skinner (eds), *Political Discourse in Early Modern Britain* (Cambridge: Cambridge University Press, 1993), pp. 232–52.

Scott, J.W. 'A Woman who has only Paradoxes to Offer', in *Rebel Daughters*, ed. Sara E. Melzer and Leslie W. Rabine (Oxford: Oxford University Press, 1992), pp. 102–20.

Ségur, A. de, *Women: Their Condition and Influence in Society* (3 vols, London, 1803).

Serna, P., 'The Noble', in M. Vovelle (ed.) *Enlightenment Portraits*, trans. L.G. Cochrane (Chicago: Chicago University Press, 1997), pp. 30–79.

Sieveking, H., 'Elise Reimarus (1735–1805) in den Geistigen Kämpfen ihrer Zeit', *Zeitschrift des Vereins für Hamburgische Geschichte*, 39 (1940): 86–138.

Skinner, Q., *Liberty Before Liberalism* (Cambridge: Cambridge University Press, 1998).

Skinner, Q., *Hobbes and Republican Liberty* (Cambridge: Cambridge University Press, 2008).

Small, S., 'The Twisted Roots of Irish Patriotism: Anglo-Irish Political Thought in the Late-Eighteenth Century', in *Éire-Ireland*, 35:3–4 (2000–2001): 187–216.

Smart, A.K., *Citoyennes: Women and the Ideal of Citizenship in Eighteenth-Century France* (Newark: University of Delaware Press, 2011).

Smith, H.L. (ed.), *Women Writers and the Early Modern British Political Tradition* (Cambridge: Cambridge University Press, 1998).

Smith, H.L., *All Men and Both Sexes: Gender, Politics, and the False Universal in England, 1640–1832* (University Park, PA: Pennsylvania State University Press, 2002).

Smith, H.L., 'Margaret Cavendish and the False Universal', in J. Broad and K. Green (eds), *Virtue, Liberty, and Toleration: Political Ideas of European Women, 1400–1800* (Dordrecht: Springer, 2007), pp. 95–110.

Smith, H.L., 'Women Intellectuals and Intellectual History: Their Paradigmatic Separation', *Women's History Review*, 16:3 (2007): 353–68.

Smith, H.L., 'Women's History as Intellectual History: A Perspective on the *Journal of Women's History*', *Journal of Women's History*, 20:1 (2008): 26–32.

Smith, H.L., Suzuki, Mihoko, and Wiseman, Susan (eds), *Women's Political Writings, 1610–1725* (4 vols, London: Pickering & Chatto, 2007).

Smith, J.M., *Nobility Reimagined: The Patriotic Nation in Eighteenth-Century France* (Ithaca, NY: Cornell University Press, 2005).

Soboul, A.. (ed.), *Les Femmes dans la Révolution française* [1789–1794] (reprint Paris: Editions d'Histoire Sociale, 1982).

Sotiropoulos, C.S., *Early Feminists and the Education Debates: England, France, Germany, 1760–1810* (Madison and Teaneck: Fairleigh Dickinson University Press, 2007).

Spalding, A.M.G., *Elise Reimarus (1735–1805): The Muse of Hamburg; a Woman of the German Enlightenment* (Würzburg: Königshausen & Neumann, 2005).

Spivak, G.C., 'Can the Subaltern Speak?' in C. Nelson and L. Grossberg (eds), *Marxism and the Interpretation of Culture* (Urbana: University of Illinois Press, 1988), pp. 271–313.

Spivak, C.G., *A Critique of Postcolonial Reason: Toward a History of the Vanishing Present* (Cambridge: Harvard University Press, 1999).

Staël, G. de, *De l'Influence des passions sur le bonheur des individus et des nations* (Paris: Treuttel & Würtz, 1820).

Staël, G. de, *Germany*, trans. O.W. Wright (2 vols, New York: Hurd & Houghton, 1871).

State Historical Museum, Moscow; G.V. Orlov Collection.

Sturmann, S., 'The Deconstruction of Gender: Seventeenth-Century Feminism and Modern Equality', in S. Knott and B. Taylor (eds). *Women, Gender and Enlightenment* (Basingstoke: Palgrave, 2005), pp. 371–88.

Sutcliffe, F.E., 'The Abbé Coyer and the Chevalier d'Arcq', *Bulletin of the John Rylands University Library of Manchester*, 65:1 (1982): 235–45.

Swann, J., *Politics and the Parlement of Paris under Louis XV, 1754–1774* (Cambridge: Cambridge University Press, 1995).

Talleyrand-Périgord, C.M. de, *Rapport sur l'instruction publique* (Paris: Imprimeries de Baudouin et du Pont, 1791).

Tarin, R., *Diderot et la Révolution française: Controverses et polémiques autour d'un philosophe* (Paris: Honoré Champion, 2001).

Thomas, A.L., D. Diderot, and L. de La Live d'Epinay, *Qu'est-ce qu'une femme?* ed. ['un débat prefacé par'] E. Badinter (Paris: POL, 1989).

Tomaselli, S., 'The Enlightenment Debate on Women', *History Workshop Journal*, 20:1 (1985): 101–24.

Trotter Cockburn, C., *A Defence of the Essay of Human Understanding Written by Mr Locke. Wherein its Principles with reference to Morality, Reveal'd Religion, and the Immortality of the Soul, are Consider'd and Justify'd: In Answer to Some Remarks on that Essay* (London: [Printed for Will Turner John Nutt], 1702).

Trotter Cockburn, C., *Revolution of Sweden. A Tragedy. As It Is Acted at the Queens Theatre in the Hay-Market.* (London: Printed for James Knapton and George Strahan, 1706).

Trotter Cockburn, C., *The Works of Mrs Catharine Cockburn, Theological, Moral, Dramatic, and Poetical. Several of Them Now First Printed. Revised and Published, with an Account of the Life of the Author*, ed. Thomas Birch (London: Printed for J. and P. Knapton, 1751).

Trousson, R., *Jean-Jacques Rousseau jugé par ses contemporains* (Paris: Champion, 2000).

Tuetey, A., *Répertoire générale des sources manuscrits de l'histoire de Paris pendant la Révolution française* (Paris, 1842–1918).

Unfer-Lukoschik, R. (ed.), *Elisabetta Caminer Turra (1751–1796): Una letterata veneta verso l'Europa* (Verona: Essedue, 1998).

Unfer-Lukoschik, R., 'L'educatrice delle donne: Elisabetta Caminer Turra (1751–1796) e la "Querelle des Femmes" negli spazi veneti di fine '700', *Memorie dell'Accademia delle scienze di Torino*, 5:24 (2000): 25–36.
Varden, H., 'Kant's Non-Voluntarist Conception of Political Obligations: Why Justice is Impossible in the State of Nature', *Kantian Review*, 13:2 (2008): 1–45.
Vega, J., 'Feminist Republicanism: Etta Palm-Aelders on Justice, Virtue and Men', *History of European Ideas*, 10:3 (1989): 333–51.
Vega, J., 'Luxury, Necessity, or the Morality of Men: The Republican Discourse of Etta Palm-Aelders', in M.F. Brive (ed.), *Les Femmes et la Révolution française* (Toulouse: Presses Universitaires du Mirail, 1989), vol. 1, pp. 363–70.
Vega, J., 'Etta Palm, une Hollandaise à Paris', in W. Frijhoff, R. Dekker (ed.), *Le Voyage révolutionnaire* (Hilversum: Verloren, 1991), pp. 49–57.
Vega, J., 'Geschiedenis als fictie: Het geromantiseerde leven van Etta Palm', *Historica*, 22:3 (1999): 22–4.
Vernière, P., 'Marie Madeleine Jodin, amie de Diderot et témoin des Lumières', *Studies on Voltaire*, 58 (1967): 1765–75.
Vertot, Abbé de, *The History of the Revolutions in Sweden Occasioned by the Change of Religion, and Alteration of the Government in That Kingdom / Written Originally in French by the Abbot Vertot ...; and Done into English by J. Mitchel ...*, trans. J. Mitchel, 2nd edn (London: Printed for A.S. and T.C. and sold by R. Parker, 1697).
Villanueva Gardner, C., *Rediscovering Women Philosophers: Philosophical Genre and the Boundaries of Philosophy* (Boulder: Westview, 2000).
Villemain, F., *Souvenirs contemporaines d'histoire et de littérature* (2 vols, Paris: Didier, 1854).
Villiers, M. Baron de, *Histoire des clubs de femmes et des légions d'amazones* (Paris: Plon-Nourrit, 1910).
Voet, R., *Feminism and Citizenship* (Thousand Oaks: Sage, 1998).
Volpi, A., 'Che non debbono ammettersi le Donne allo Studio delle Scienze, e delle belle Arti' ['That women should not be allowed to study science and the fine arts'], in *Discorsi accademici di varj autori viventi. Intorno agli Studj delle Donne; La maggior parte recitati nell'Accademia de' Ricovrati di Padova* (Padua: Stamperia del Seminario presso Giovanni Manfrè, 1729).
Voltaire, *Correspondence and Related Documents*, ed. T. Besterman (52 vols, Oxford: Voltaire Foundation, 1968–1977).
Vovelle, M., 'Une troisième voie pour la lecture de la *Conspiration des égaux*?', *Annales historiques de la Révolution française*, 312:1 (1998): 217–27.
Wade, I.O., *Studies on Voltaire, with some Unpublished Papers of Mme Du Châtelet* (Princeton: Princeton University Press, 1947).
Walker, J.C., *Historical Memoirs of the Irish Bards* (Dublin: Luke White, 1786).
Waresquiel, E. de, *Le Duc de Richelieu, 1766–1822: Un sentimental en politique* (Paris: Perrin, 1990).
Weiss, P.A., *Canon Fodder* (University Park, PA: Pennsylvania State University Press, 2009).

Williams, H., *Kant's Critique of Hobbes: Sovereignty and Cosmopolitanism* (Cardiff: University of Wales Press, 2003).

Wiseman, S., 'Catharine Macaulay: History, Republicanism and the Public Sphere', in E. Eger, C. Grant, C.O. Gallchoir, and P. Warburton (eds), *Women, Writing and the Public Sphere, 1700–1830* (Cambridge: Cambridge University Press, 2001), pp. 181–99.

Wokler, R., *Rousseau* (Oxford: Oxford University Press, 1995).

Wollstonecraft, M., *A Vindication of the Rights of Men, in a Letter to the Right Honourable Edmund Burke* (London: Joseph Johnson, 1790).

Wollstonecraft, M., *Défense des droits des femmes, suivie de quelques considérations sur des sujets politiques et moraux* (Paris: Buisson, 1792).

Wollstonecraft, M., *A Vindication of the Rights of Woman*, ed. C.H. Poston, 2nd edn (New York and London: W.W. Norton, 1988).

Wollstonecraft, M., *The Works of Mary Wollstonecraft*, ed. J. Todd and M. Butler (7 vols, London: Pickering & Chatto, 1989).

Wollstonecraft, M., *A Vindication of the Rights of Men* (1791), ed. J. Todd (Oxford: Oxford University Press, 1993).

Wollstonecraft, M., *A Vindication of the Rights of Woman, with Strictures on Political and Moral Subjects* (1792), ed. J. Todd (Oxford: Oxford University Press, 1993).

Wollstonecraft, M., *Wollstonecraft: A Vindication of the Rights of Men and a Vindication of the Rights of Woman and Hints*, ed. Sylvana Tomaselli (Cambridge: Cambridge University Press, 1995).

Wollstonecraft, M., *A Vindication of the Rights of Woman and A Vindication of the Rights of Men*, ed. J. Todd (New York and London: Oxford University Press, 2009).

Wood, K.E., 'Gender and Slavery', in R.L. Paquette and M.M. Smith (eds), *The Oxford Handbook of Slavery in the Americas* (Oxford: Oxford University Press, 2010), pp. 513–34.

Wright, J., 'Going against the Grain: Hobbes's Case for Original Maternal Domination', *Journal of Women's History*, 14:1 (2002): 123–48.

Zeuske, M., 'Handlanger der Globalisierung: Sklaverei, "schwarze" Karibik und Globalgeschichte', *iz3w*, 278/279 (2004): 34–7.

Zinsser, J.P., 'Entrepreneur of the "Republic of Letters": Emilie de Breteuil, marquise Du Châtelet, and Bernard Mandeville's *Fable of the Bees*', *French Historical Studies*, 25:4 (2002): 595–624.

Zinsser, J.P., *Emilie Du Châtelet: Daring Genius of the Enlightenment* (New York: Penguin, 2006).

Index

abolition of slavery 12, 72, 171, 190, 191, 193–4, 197, 199
absolutism 189
abuse (sexual, economic) 195, 197, 200
academies 17, 18, 35, 112, 114, 206
  Académie française 8, 21, 84, 86, 129–30
  Academy of Dijon 35
  Academy of Rovigo 114
  Accademia de' Ricovrati 111
  Accademia degli Unanimi of Salò 114
  Accademia dell'Arcadia 114
  Royal Irish Academy 206
Act of Union 209, 214
actors and actresses 8, 49, 54–61
Adam 23
Addison, Joseph 92, 99
Admiral Norbi 145
Aelders, Etta Palm de 3, 8, 9, 63, 64–77
Africa and Africans 171, 189–91, 193, 195, 196, 198
agency 91, 93, 96, 103, 106, 200–201
Agrippa of Nettesheim 86–7
Amazons 69, 157, 158, 172
American Revolution 189
Americas 189, 190, 193, 196
anarchy 97
Ancelot, Madame 125
Angers 56, 57
Anglo-Irish 13, 204, 208, 209, 216
Anglo-Norman 208
Anne of Hannover 65
anti-feminism 9, 87, 166
anti-Irish writers 207
apothecary shops, *see spezierie*
arbitrary power 39, 45–6, 49, 54, 57, 61–2, 69–70, 91, 150–51, 159, 168, 191, 197–8
Arendt, Hannah 18
aristocracy 6, 8, 11, 12, 21, 31, 40–41, 43, 48, 64, 65, 114, 115, 118, 123, 125–7, 132–3, 137, 138, 165, 166, 167–9, 179, 185, 214
Aristotle 3, 5, 6, 12, 195
arts and artists 34–5, 40, 85, 111–12, 126, 129–30, 132, 134, 143
Arwide (*Revolution of Sweden*) 144, 145, 152–6
Asians 193
Assembly of Representatives 61, 71, 74, 77, 102, 165
Astell, Mary 2, 161, 190–91, 199
atheism 9, 50, 51, 85–7
Athens 175
Aulnoy, Madame de 5

Barbauld, Anna Laetitia 3, 12, 157–67, 171–2, 193
Barbauld, Rochement 161
bards 207, 211–14
Barnave, Antoine 194
Barre, Chevalier de la 50
Barre, Poulain de la 59
Basire, Claude 65
Bassenville, Comtesse de 137
Batave, Le 74
Batavian Republic 65–7
Bayle, Pierre 22
Beauvoir, Simone de 181
Behn, Aphra 190
belletrists 44
Belot, Charles-Edme 34
Belot, Octavie 2, 7, 8, 33–48
Benedict XIV, Pope 111
Beron (*Revolution of Sweden*) 144–6, 152, 155–6
Berry, Mary 157
Bible 7, 19–24, 28, 31, 147; *see also* scriptures
bienveillance 28
Birch, Thomas 141
birth and hereditary distinctions 30–31, 40, 42, 112, 125–6, 145, 192, 197; *see also* aristocracy; childbirth
Blacks 13, 72, 189, 192–5, 198

Bluestockings 8, 10, 46, 120, 160, 161
Boccapaduli, Margherita Sparapani Gentili 118
Bonaparte, Napoleon 9, 79, 80, 82–9, 124, 134, 136, 194
bondage, *see* slavery
Bonnet, Charles 35
Bonneville, Nicolas de 66, 67
Bordeaux 50, 54, 56, 57
Bossuet, Jacques Bénigne 85
Boswell, James 162–4, 167
Bourbon era 137, 185
Bourbon Restoration 11, 123–5, 129, 135–6
Bourges 45
Breteuil, Baron de 17–18
Breteuil, Louis Auguste de 65
Bretonne, Rétif de la 53
Breve Difesa dei Diritti delle Donne 10, 118
Brissot, Jacques Pierre 72
Britain, and British Isles 6, 10, 11, 13, 46, 109, 164, 169, 208–14
Brooke, Charlotte 3, 13, 161, 203–16
Brownlow Lying-in Hospital 160
Brussels 18, 21, 65
Buffon, Comte de 34
Burgundy 34, 36
Burke, Edmund 3, 12, 157–8, 162, 167–71, 180, 184–6, 192–3
Butler, Sarah 204–5, 206, 215

Califronia, Countess Rosa 10, 109, 118–20
Calmet, Dom 23
Calonne, Charles Alexandre de 65
Calvinism 83, 160
Caminer Turra, Elisabetta 3, 109, 114, 115, 116, 117, 120
Camposanpiero, Guglielmo 111, 112
Caribbean, slavery and race relations 12, 190, 191, 192, 196, 198
Carignano, Giuseppina di Lorena, Princess of 113
Carra, Jean Louis 72
Carter, Elizabeth 160, 161
Castel, Louis-Bertrand 35
catechism 35
Cato 99, 106, 107
Cavendish, Margaret 13, 148
Celticism 203
censorship 9, 17, 20, 80, 84, 88
Cercle social 9, 66–7, 69
Chabot, François 65
Chagnaie, Rose Pressac de la 71
Chaillot 46, 47, 48
Chamber of Deputies 124
Champagne 18
Champs de Mars 67
chastity 28, 59n41
Châteauroux, Marie Anne de Mailly, duchesse de 80–82
Chénier, Marie-Joseph 88
childbirth 69, 71, 198
Christianity and values 25, 83, 85, 174, 177, 191
Christina (*Revolution of Sweden*) 144, 145, 146, 152, 155, 156
Christine de Pizan 5
church and clergy 7, 17, 19, 20–21, 29, 31, 35, 71, 81, 160, 165, 171; *see also* Protestantism
  Catholic Church and Catholicism 23, 25–6, 49, 52, 83, 84–8, 89, 146–7, 205, 208, 215
    conversion to and from 52, 146
    hierarchy 81
  women's exclusion from 71
Cicero 175, 179
citizenship 60–62, 64, 69, 71–6, 138, 141, 144, 146–9, 156, 194
  women's passive citizenship 3, 5, 8–10, 13, 49, 51–2, 62, 73, 107, 152–4, 156
civil disobedience 98
civility 11, 37, 112, 124–7, 136–7, 161, 178, 180, 206–7, 211
Civray 71
Clarke, Samuel 142
class 33–4, 39, 43, 48, 89–90, 113, 132, 159, 160, 165–6, 170–71, 175–6, 198–201, 214–16
Clément-Hémery, Albertine 88
clergy, *see* church and clergy
clubs 9, 66–8, 71, 74, 156n2
Code civil 83
Code noir 197–8
coercion 94–6, 102, 104–5
colonies and colonialism 189–97, 200–201
commerce and commercial values 8, 21n10, 30–31, 40–43, 175–6, 210
commons 169, 170

Commons, House of 158
commonwealth 13, 165, 170
communist group 82
Concordat 83, 86
Condorcet, J.-A.-N. de Caritat Marquis de 53, 76
conscience 30–31, 93–4, 102, 142, 155
Constantia (*Revolution of Sweden*) 144–6, 150, 152–6
Constantinople 29
constitutions 4, 12, 65, 97, 98, 107, 113, 164, 168, 181, 194
Consulate, the 79
controversies 9, 17, 41–2, 63, 85, 101, 142, 146–7, 167, 203–4
convents 47, 48, 49, 52, 80
coquetry 129, 173, 178, 183
Cordeliers 68
Corporation and Test Acts 158, 164, 171
Corsica 12, 83, 162, 163, 164, 167
cosmopolitanism 73
cosmos 20, 24
Counter-Reformation 208
Coyer, Abbé Gabriel-François 40, 41, 42, 43, 81
Craiftne 211, 212, 213
Creil 66, 75
Cuccovilla, Maria Pizzelli 118

Dacier, Anne 5
Dandalo, Vincenzo 114
Danes and Denmark 143, 145, 151, 152
Daniel 131
David 23
Davies, John 208
De la Vertu 85
Deffand, Marie Anne de Vichy-Chamrond, Marquise du 46, 158
Deists 85
democracy 10–11, 12, 43, 48, 50, 74, 89, 115, 136–8, 162, 164–6, 170–71, 189
Descartes, René 19, 24, 26
despotism 12, 39, 48, 53, 61–2, 70, 80, 83, 97–8, 172
Devaux, François-Antoine ('Panpan') 46
Dictionnaire des atheés 85
Diderot, Denis 3, 8, 49, 50, 51, 52, 53, 54, 55, 56, 57, 58, 61, 62, 70
Discorsi accademici 112
Discours sur le Bonheur 18, 22

Dissenters 160, 171, 179
divorce 51, 58, 60, 67, 70, 83, 149
domestic role of women 7, 9, 36, 53, 59, 127, 148
Dorimon, Abbé, *see* Féletz, Charles-Marie de
Dresden 56, 57
Du Châtelet, Gabrielle Emilie le Tonnelier de Breteuil, Marquise 3, 7, 17–33, 65
Dunciad 157
duty 11, 60, 73–4, 79, 91, 94n12, 94–106, 141, 144, 147–55, 175, 177, 182–3, 185, 191, 215
  legal 91, 191
  moral 94

East Indies 64
economy 7, 19–22, 80–81, 89–90, 126, 165–6
  slave economy 193–8
Edgeworth, Maria 206, 209
education 190
  women's 6, 9, 12, 18, 33, 67, 71, 73, 75, 82, 87–9, 109–13, 115–21, 128, 131, 160–62, 173–5, 177–87, 190
Egeria 129, 134
Eigennutz 97
emancipation 199–200
Emile 53, 60, 110, 162, 181
Emperor, status of 83
Empire, French 79, 83, 86, 136, 137, 192
empiricism 11, 142–3, 154
Enclos, Ninon de l' 85
Encyclopédie and the *enyclopédistes* 9, 51, 71, 73, 89
England and the English 10, 12, 13, 18, 19, 44–6, 61, 127, 143, 148, 162, 169, 174–5, 190, 193, 203–5, 206, 208–12, 214
English Civil War 6, 12, 162
English Revolution (1688) 12, 168–9
enlightenment and the Enlightenment 1, 8, 12, 20, 49, 50, 51, 53–4, 57, 62, 64, 70, 73, 77, 84, 85, 87–92, 96, 101–7, 113, 127, 128, 131, 134, 142, 171, 172, 189–90, 192, 196, 200, 201
  Moderate Enlightenment 50–53
  Radical Enlightenment 8, 23n16, 49–50, 53–4, 57, 62, 85, 87
Epictetus 160, 161

epistemology 11, 24, 142–3, 149, 154, 201
equality and inequality 7–8, 12, 34–5, 38–40, 42, 46–8, 49, 73, 98n35, 99, 106–7, 136, 166, 170, 189–92
  racial 189–201
  sexual 58, 49–60, 66, 68, 70–71, 75, 86n22, 106–7, 113n21, 115, 149, 161, 191
Essay Concerning Human Understanding 21, 31, 38, 149, 178
Estates General 76
Europe and Europeans 6, 10, 12, 13, 18, 54, 91, 109–10, 116–21, 189–201, 203, 205, 207–8
Evangelicalism 191
Eve 23
evil (human) 91, 97, 101
exploitation 189–90, 195–7

Fable of the Bees 7, 18, 19
Faini, Diamante Medaglia 114
faith 24, 160
false universal 3, 13, 196
fanaticism 81, 85, 88, 125
Fauchet, Claude 66–7
Féletz, Charles-Marie de 86
feminism 1, 3, 4–10, 12, 49, 52, 63, 66, 68, 80, 86n22, 87, 90, 92, 106, 113, 117, 141, 143, 148, 149, 156, 158n4, 161, 166, 173, 175, 189–92, 200
Femme abbé 82
Femme grenadier 82
Fénelon, François [de la Mothe-] 85
Ferrand, Elisabeth 33
Feucher, Chevalier de 79
feudalism 21, 76, 89, 126, 165, 189
Fianna 209
Fingal 203
Flanders 18, 21, 34
flattery 29, 30, 129
Fontainebleau 21, 81
Foras Feasa ar Éirinn 212
Fragments of Ancient Poetry 203
franchise 50, 76, 166, 168–9
Franklin, Benjamin 34
Fredage (*Revolution of Sweden*) 144–5, 152
free will 19, 19n6, 25–7, 38, 60, 93–6, 100–101
freedom 93–6, 100, 102–3, 106, 189–91, 194, 196, 199
  of the press 116; *see also* censorship
  political and civil 96, 103, 123
  religious 81, 83, 171, 205–6
Freiheit 93, 95, 100, 102, 106, 107
French Revolutions 9, 12, 33, 49–51, 62, 63–90, 111, 124–5, 157, 169, 172; *see also Reflections on the Revolution in France*; revolutions and revolutionary sentiment
Fréron, Elie 37
frugality 12, 176
Furet, François 130

Gacon-Dufour, Marie-Armande 3, 9, 79, 80–90
Gaelic 13, 203–16
galanterie 133
Galatea 54
Gardner, Catherine Villanueva 174, 175, 186
Gaul 209–10
Gay, Marie Françoise Sophie 136
gender 76, 92, 106–7, 109, 126–7, 148, 174–5, 178, 185, 190, 195–9
  bias 2, 88
  critique of gender roles 50, 60–62, 76, 177, 179, 181–2, 196
  stereotypes 13, 197
general will 94, 97–9
Genesis, Book of 23, 25
Geneva 34, 36, 37, 40, 49–52, 54–5, 58–9
Genlis, Madame de 84, 88
Genoa 162–3
geometry 20, 26
Germany and Germans 6, 9, 91–3
Girardin, Delphine de 11, 124
glory 18, 30, 47, 75, 213
God and theology 20, 23–8, 35, 53, 86, 141, 142, 147, 160, 192
Godolphin, Harriet 143
Golden Rule 28–9
Goll, *see* mac Mona, Goll
Goncourt, Edmond 128
Goncourt, Jules 128
Gospels 24, 35
Gothicism 84, 165, 206, 203
Gouges, Olympe de 13, 33, 64, 69, 77, 111, 192–3, 199

Gournay, Marie le Jars de 5
Graffigny, Madame de 92
Greece 171
Greek language 160, 179
Grimm, Friedrich 44
Groningen 64
Grovestins, Douwe van Sirtina 65
guardianship 60
Guizot, François 138
Gustav I, King of Sweden 143, 146
Gustavus 143–6, 150–52, 155, 156
Guyomar, Pierre 75

Habermas, Jürgen 130, 133
Hague, The 65, 67
Haiti 189, 196, 198
Haitian Revolution 198
Hamburg 92
happiness (eudemonia) 18, 21–2, 26, 28–31, 36, 70, 94, 99, 118, 136, 154, 163–4, 166, 195
Harrington, James 3, 164, 165–6
Hartley, David 178
Hays, Mary 109
Helvétius, Claude Adrien 31, 34, 50, 54, 61
heretics 23, 31, 147
Histoire des deux Indes 51
Hobbes, Thomas 3, 6, 7, 11, 35, 46, 91, 95–7, 148
honour 8, 12, 22, 29, 30, 51, 58, 60, 81, 117n38, 118, 131, 173, 207, 214
'Hortensia' 175, 180
housekeeping 9, 80, 89–90, 112; *see also* domestic role of women
Huber, Marie 33
Huguenots 18, 161
human nature 97, 99, 101
Humanität ('humanity'), *see* Menschheit
Hume, David 34, 44, 45
Hutcheson, Francis 142
Hypatia 85–6, 88

'Imperium Pelagi: A Naval Lyric' 210
indeterminism 91, 99, 101, 105; *see also* free will
innateness and innate ideas 28, 142, 177, 178
  freedom 190, 192
  modesty 180–81
  moral dispositions 7, 30, 153
  principles 166
  sexual difference 58, 106–7, 180–82
intention 91, 93–6, 99, 103
Ireland and Irish literature 13, 203–16
Irish history in anglophone fiction 204
Iroquois woman 36
Islam 83
Italy and Italians 5, 6, 10, 65, 109, 110–16, 118, 120–21, 157
Jacobi, Heinrich 92
Jacobins 65, 114, 124, 198
Jacobite 205, 212, 214
Jaucourt, Marquis de 71
Jesuits 35, 80
Jews 83
Jodin, Marie 3, 8, 13, 33, 49, 50–64, 77
Johnson, Samuel 44, 45
Jonah 24
Joshua 23–4
judiciary and legislature 13, 21, 47, 58, 60, 89, 99, 100, 209
  women's 8, 51, 58–61, 77

Kant, Immanuel 3, 9, 10, 91–107, 193
Keating, Geoffrey 208, 212
Kent 159
Keralio-Robert, Louise-Félicité 3, 9, 33, 63, 64, 68, 69, 71–7, 193, 194
Kerry 212
Kibworth 160

Lafayette, Madame de 5
Laland, Jérôme 9, 85
Lassay, Marquis de 41
Latin 86, 160, 179, 212
law and laws 6, 8, 12, 19, 20, 22–9, 31, 34–6, 40–46, 51, 55, 57–61, 66, 70–76, 83, 89, 91, 93–8, 101–5, 110, 141, 146, 150–53, 155, 164, 165, 168–70, 190–94, 197, 205; *see also* judiciary and legislature
  civil 93–5, 97, 98, 102, 106, 191
  law of nature, natural law, Naturrecht 24, 35, 93–5, 97, 102, 150, 170, 190–91
  moral 94–5, 98, 102, 105
Lebrun-Tondu, Pierre Marie Henri 67
legal positivism 91, 95
legislature 13, 47, 58, 60, 61, 89, 209

Leibniz, Gottfried Wilhelm von 7, 19, 24–6
Lénoncourt, Marquise de 46
Leszczyńska, Marie 21
letters 92
lettre de cachet 49, 56
Leviathan 95
liberalism 123, 125, 162, 171
libertines 49, 58, 73–5, 146
Lilti, Antoine 10, 133, 134, 135, 137
Locke, John 3, 6, 7, 11, 12, 22, 25, 28, 31, 35, 38, 50, 73, 142, 147–51, 154, 178, 179
London 159, 162, 164, 167
Lucan, Lady (Margaret Bingham) 205, 206
Lyttelton, Lord 163

Maanem, Cornelius 67
mac Cumhail, Fionn 209
mac Morna, Goll 209–10
Macaulay, Catharine 3, 11, 12, 61, 120, 157–81, 183, 187
Magistracy 76, 165–6
Magna Charta 169
Mailly, Marie Anne de 80
Maintenon, Madame de 80
Mandeville, Bernard 3, 7, 18, 19, 21–2, 27–31
'Mäon: An Irish Tale' 211–15
Marat, Jean-Paul 65
Maréchal, Sylvain 9, 82, 85–8
Maria (*Revolution of Sweden*) 154–5
Marie-Antoinette 77, 185
Marmontel, Jean-François 137
marriage (institution of) 3–5, 11, 18, 21, 46, 58, 60, 70–71, 75–6, 79, 83, 141, 143–5, 149, 166, 183, 190–92, 197–8, 208, 212
  and slavery 3, 5, 12, 189–201
  based on love 38, 70, 181–2, 186
marriages (of particular women) 11, 18, 19, 21, 34, 45, 64, 68, 73, 79, 92, 160, 161, 206
Marxism and sociology 1
Masons 85
massacres 47, 80, 151
materialism 50, 52–4, 85, 88, 175–6, 180
maternity, *see* motherhood; childbirth
mathematics 19–20, 30, 179
Mattei, Fulvia 115
Maupertuis, Pierre-Louis Moreau de 20, 25
mediation 2, 10–11, 13, 92, 109, 121, 128, 132, 137, 204, 208
Medici, Catherine de' 80
Meinières, Jean-Baptiste-François Durey de 45, 46, 47
Mendelssohn, Moses 92
Menschheit ('mankind') versus Humanität ('humanity') 104
Mercure de France 40, 43, 84
Mercure National 72–3, 194
Messina 65
Metaphysics of Morals 94, 107
metaphysics 7, 19, 20, 22, 25, 26, 27, 38, 96
Milesian/Phoenician theory (of Irish origins) 206–8
Milton, John 179
Mirabeau, Count 65–6
Moderate Enlightenment, *see* enlightenment and the Enlightenment
modernity and moderns 177, 189, 196
modesty 6, 10, 36, 44–5, 52, 55, 59, 75, 180, 183
Molière 179
Molyneux, William 209
monarchy 9, 12, 22–3, 35, 43, 48, 50, 77, 80–83, 124–5, 136–8, 165, 176, 185–6
Montagu, Elizabeth 8, 46, 47, 161, 162, 167
Montcalm, Armande-Marie-Antoinette de Vignerot du Plessis de Richelieu, Marquise de 125, 135
Montesquieu, Charles-Louis de Secondat, Baron de La Brède et de 3, 12, 40
Montfort-l'Amaury, Convent of 80
More, Hannah 13, 161, 191
Morellet, André 137
Morgan, Lady 209
Moriat 211–12, 214–15
Morni 209
Moryson, Fynes 211
motherhood 73, 88, 133, 115, 120, 137, 149, 181–3, 186–7, 197; *see also* childbirth
  maternal ethos 60
  maternal succession 197; *see also* birth and hereditary distinctions
Munnik, Jan 64–5

Munster 211
murder 23, 145, 151, 156
Muses 206, 208, 212–13
Muslims 83

Naples 19, 114, 118
Napoleon, *see* Bonaparte
National Assembly 63, 67, 70, 76, 77
Naturrecht 93; *see also* law and laws
Neapolitan Revolution 114
'Neuf Sœurs' 85
Neufchâteau, Nicolas-Louis François de 89
new intellectual history 1
Newton, Isaac 7, 19, 26
Nieuwenhuys, Jacob Aelders van 64
Norman code 169
Normandy 18
novels (women's use of) 2, 5–6, 9, 33, 79–80, 190
Nuovo Giornale Enciclopedico d'Italia 115

objectification 199
'Ocean: An Ode' 210
Oceana 164–5
Olantigh 159
oligarchy 12, 50, 165
On Revolution 189
Ophelia 44
Oprechte nationale courant 68
ordination of women 76
Orientalism 203
origin of society, *see* social contract
Oroonoko 190
Ossian 204

Padua 111
Palgrave (boarding school) 161
pamphlets 12, 17, 20, 33, 41n27, 66, 76–7, 113n18, 114, 149, 157, 162–3
Panpan, *see* Devaux, François-Antoine
pantheism 92
Paoli, Pasquale 162–7, 171
Paradoxe sur le comédien 54–6
Paris 18, 29, 34, 36, 45, 46, 47, 65, 71, 79, 132
Paris-Duverney, Joseph 81, 82
parlement of Paris 45–6, 130
parliamentary process and government 6, 11, 79, 123, 124, 125, 132, 138, 149, 158, 159, 164, 166, 167–9, 171, 214
passions 29, 30, 37, 98, 126, 127, 141, 154–6, 182, 186
patriarchy 17, 198–9
patriotism 67, 72, 82
Patriots, Dutch 65–7
patronage 19, 21, 168
peace 97
'Pearl of the Antilles', *see* Haiti
Penal Laws 205
perfectibility 24–6, 36–8, 58, 73, 101–5, 110
personhood 95, 103
Peyrard, François 86–7
philanthropy 191
philosophes 7, 31, 50–51, 54, 58, 61–2, 84, 88, 126n10, 130, 137, 185
Phocion 75
physiocracy 79, 89
Pimentel, Eleonora de Fonseca 114, 121
Pisani Mocenigo family 114
Place des Grèves 17
Plato 22
Plutarch 179
Poland 50, 165
political philosophy 91–2
Poniatowski, Stanislas 57
Pope, Alexander 22
popes 86, 111
pornography 57, 75
positivism and non-positivism 91, 94–5
post-colonialism 200
Price, Richard 162, 169
priesthood 25–6
Priestley, Joseph 162
Principia 7
Prior, Matthew 44
private sphere 195
private will (Privatwille) 94, 97–9
progress 12, 13, 35, 53, 102, 109, 115, 124, 182, 196, 203
property 193, 196
Protestantism 21, 49, 52, 64, 80, 81, 85, 146–7, 204, 206, 210, 215–16
Prussia 47
Pygmalion 54

race 90, 192–3, 195–7, 200
Radical Enlightenment, *see* enlightenment and the Enlightenment
Rasselas 44–5
rebellion 6, 25, 49, 82, 98, 148, 150–51, 216

Reflections on the Revolution in France 157, 169, 184
reform (social and political) 8, 51, 53, 57, 62, 65–6, 77, 81–2, 109, 120–21, 147, 159, 164, 168–9
Reformation 146, 208
reforming prostitutes 8, 56, 58
Reimarus, Elise 2, 9, 10, 90–107
Reimarus, Hermann Samuel 92
religion and religious thought 2, 9, 19, 25, 50–52, 76, 79, 80–87, 146–7, 156, 174, 179, 191, 193, 197, 205
religious authority and persecution 9, 49, 57, 80, 147, 193
Reliques of Irish Poetry 13, 203–16
republic of letters 17, 130–31
republic of virtue (Rousseau) 62
republics and republicanism 4, 7–9, 12, 36, 41, 45, 47, 49–50, 52, 54–5, 59–74, 77, 82–3, 85, 86, 88, 91, 99–100, 104, 157–68, 174–87, 189, 194, 216
Revolution of Sweden 11, 141–56
revolutions and revolutionary sentiment 17, 33, 51, 53, 62, 98, 114–15, 119, 124, 127–38, 157, 168–72, 179, 180, 189–98, 212; *see also* American Revolution; English Revolution; French Revolution; Haitian Revolution; Neapolitan Revolution
Richelieu, Louis François Armand du Plessis, duc de 19, 21, 81, 124, 125, 138
Ridolfi, Teresa 114
rights 12, 18, 36, 50, 52, 54, 57, 60, 64, 68, 83, 91, 93–8, 104–7, 110, 111, 151–3, 155, 162, 171–2
  civil right 93, 96
  divine right 23, 50
  women's 5, 10, 13, 18, 57, 61, 63–4, 69, 73–7, 107, 111, 119–21, 147, 181, 190, 192–6
Riqueti, Honoré-Gabriel, *see* Mirabeau
Roccati, Cristina 114
Romans (ancient) 66, 171, 176–7, 179
Romanticism 2, 89, 164, 214
Rome (modern) 109, 111, 114, 118, 177
'Rosg Ghoill' 209, 211
Rousseau, Charles-Louis 66
Rousseau, Jean-Jacques 3, 7–10, 31, 33–40, 42–62, 70, 79, 97–8, 110, 162, 164, 174, 180–87, 195
Rue Villedo 65

Saint Hérem, Armand Marc Montmorin 65
St Lucia (Caribbean colony) 191
Saint-Denis 83
Saint-Domingue, *see* Haiti
Sainte-Foix, Philippe-Auguste de, the chevalier d'Arcq 41–3
Sainte-Marie, Convent of 47
St-Pathus, Jules-Michel Dufour de 79
Sala della Pubblica Istruzione 115
salons, salonists, and *salonnières*, 5, 10, 11, 54, 65, 109–21, 123–38
Salpêtrière 49, 62
Satan 25
Saul 23
Savini de' Rossi, Aretafila 112–13
Sawbridge, Jacob 159
Saxon 57
Schulenburg, Werner XXV von der, Count 57
sciences 20, 24, 26, 34–5, 40, 86, 111, 120, 128, 179, 213
  women excluded from 18
scriptures 23, 28, 35, 147; *see also* Bible
Scudéry, Madeleine de 5, 6, 11, 182
Ségur, Comte de 134
Seine court 79
Selbstliebe 97
Shakespeare, William 161, 179
Sièyes, Abbé 73
slavery 12–13, 45, 66, 69, 147, 150, 163, 166–7, 174, 205; *see also* abolition of slavery; marriage; Caribbean, slavery and race relations; transatlantic slave trade
social contract 6, 7, 12, 91, 93, 96–8, 190, 200; *see also* state of nature
'Socratic sect' 85
Solomon 23
Spain 165
Spenser, Edmund 208
spezierie (spiceries or apothecary shops) 114
Spiegel, Laurens Pieter van de 65, 66, 67
Spinozism 50, 51, 53

Stadtholder 65, 66, 68
Staël-Holstein, Anne Louise Germaine de ('Madame de Staël') 3, 11, 88, 126, 127, 128, 134
Stanhope, Earl of 162
state of nature 6, 35–8, 40, 46, 73, 97, 101, 148, 150–51; *see also* social contract
Stockholm 151
Stoics 31n52
Stret Marsh 64
Strongbow 208
Suard, Jean-Baptiste-Antoine 137
subordination (and suppression) 189–92, 195–9
  biological basis for women's 52–3
Supplément au Voyage de Bougainville 51
Sweden and Swedes, *see Revolution of Sweden*
Sylvester 206, 208, 210, 213

Talleyrand-Périgord, Charles Maurice de 110, 181, 195
teleology 92, 102–3, 106
Temora 203
Tetradymus 85
theatre and plays 54–9, 92, 99, 106, 143, 158; *see also* actors and actresses
Thiriot, Nicolas-Claude 41
Thomas, Antoine-Léonard 52, 71
toleration 86
Tooke, John Horne 159
Tories 168
transatlantic slave trade 12, 189–90
Trotter Cockburn, Catharine 3, 11, 141–56
Turner, William 162
Tuscany 118

Ultras 124, 125, 131
universalism 12, 13, 190, 192, 196, 200

Vadori, Annetta 114
Vallancey, Charles 206, 213, 215
Vaughan, Samuel 162
Vendée rebellion 82
Venice and Veneto 5, 50, 109, 114–16, 118, 166
Ventry, battle of 209
Verona 114, 115
Versailles 18, 21, 185
Versuch einer Erläuterung und Vereinfachung der Begriffe vom natürlichen Staatsrecht 93, 95–6, 102–7
Vertot, Abbé de 145
vice, 7, 22, 28–31, 39, 60, 75, 84, 143
Vicenza 115–16
Viking invasions 205
Villemain, François 136
Vindication of the Rights of Men 109, 111, 157, 180, 184, 186, 192
Vindication of the Rights of Woman 10, 13, 88, 109–11, 115–18, 173, 180, 187, 192–6
vindication 115, 116, 117, 118, 157, 173, 180, 184, 186, 187, 192, 194, 195, 196
violence 190, 197
virtue 5–13, 19, 28–9, 40, 42–3, 51–3, 56, 59–62, 66, 70, 75, 84–6, 97, 99, 104, 106–7, 110, 115, 124, 136, 143, 146, 152–6, 158, 161, 163, 164, 166–7, 173–87, 195, 213–14
Volpi, Antonio 112–3
Voltaire 7, 19, 21–2, 34–5, 37, 40–41, 50, 81, 88–9, 92, 116, 179
Vues législatives 8, 49, 50, 51, 52, 54, 57–9, 61

Walker, Joseph Cooper 207, 212, 215
Walpole, Horace 157, 158, 163
Warrington 160, 162
Warsaw 54, 56, 57
Waterloo 138
Wilkes, John 159, 167
will, *see* general will; private will; intention
William II of England 168–9
William IV (Stadtholder) 65
William V (Stadtholder) 65
William the Conqueror 169
Woerden 67
Wolff, Christian 24
Wollstonecraft, Mary 2–3, 10, 12–13, 61, 109–20, 157–8, 161, 167, 173–4, 180–200

Yamba ('The Sorrows of Yamba') 191